SERIOUS
FUN

SERIOUS FUN

David R. Veerman

 VICTOR BOOKS

A DIVISION OF SCRIPTURE PRESS PUBLICATIONS INC.
USA CANADA ENGLAND

This book contains material previously published under the titles *Serious Fun* and *More Serious Fun* by David Veerman.

Designer: Grace K. Chan Mallette
ISBN: 1-56476-318-8

Produced for Victor Books by the Livingstone Corporation. David Veerman, Michael Kendrick, and Brenda Todd, project staff.

1 2 3 4 5 6 7 8 9 10 Printing/Year 00 99 98 97 96 95

Printed in the United States of America.

To my sister and three brothers,
Barb, Phil, Ralph, and Paul,
who made growing up FUN (seriously)!

TABLE OF CONTENTS

WELCOME TO SERIOUS FUN

I chose the name *Serious Fun* because it captures the essence of quality youth ministry. Our programs should be fun; that is, kids should enjoy themselves and feel accepted, affirmed, and loved. But these programs should also be serious; that is, kids should learn about themselves and how God and His Word relate to their lives.

These two goals, "serious" and "fun," can coexist. We tend to reserve exciting, high-energy activities for fun times while saving heavy-duty content for somber and serious meetings. This book will help you combine the two—to make fun educational and to make learning fun.

Also, as you know, no two groups of students are alike. In fact, each group has its own personality. So, I organized *Serious Fun* to help you design the right meetings for your particular students and group, giving you the opportunity to pick and choose which activities will work best for you. The chapters highlight twenty-seven topics important to young people today. To design *your* meeting, begin by choosing a topic. Then choose the rest of the ingredients for the meeting from the categories in that chapter: *crowdbreakers* (games to get kids mixing and to bring the group together), *discussion starters* (games and activities to get kids talking), *discussions and wrap-ups* (questions and short talks to get kids thinking), and *Bible studies* (Scripture references and questions to help kids understand and apply God's Word).

Instead of flipping through a dozen books of meetings and games, find everything you need in this one volume! Thanks for spending your hard-earned cash on this book. I pray that you will find it to be a valuable resource in your ministry. God bless you as you work in the most exciting mission field in the world—today's young people.

David Veerman

PRESSURE AND STRESS

CROWD-BREAKERS

Babel ■ Divide into teams and give each team a bag of balloons. Have each team choose a girl competitor who should stand behind a table, facing her team. The teams should also chose a runner, a person who will bring the balloons from the team to the table.

Explain that this is a contest to see which team can form the tallest tower of balloons within two minutes. The balloons should be stacked on the table, and the only person who is allowed to hold the tower in place is the competitor (stacker) behind the table. At your signal, kids can begin to blow up their balloons. The runners should take the balloons, one at a time, to the table and help the competitor stack them. The stacker may use any strategy that she devises to keep the balloons in the tower. After two minutes, declare the winner and return the balloons to the teams. Then repeat with two new, boy stackers.

Balloons ■ Divide into teams and give each person a balloon. At your signal, each team should send one person to the front of the room to blow up his or her balloon until it pops. After he or she returns, the next person leaves, and so on. The first team finished wins. You can use this activity to illustrate the pressures and stress we often feel.

Bloopers ■ Get a bloopers audio or video tape and play some of the most humorous and clean ones. Use this to show how everyone makes mistakes.

Building Blocks ■ Divide into teams of 8–15 members each, arrange them in single file lines, and give every person a piece of construction paper. Place a table in front of the lines. A representative from each team should stand behind the table, on which you have placed scissors and tape for each team. Their task is to build towers using blocks made from construction paper.

Here's how it works: at the signal, the first person from each team runs to the table, makes a block with his/her paper and the tape, gives it to the builder, and returns to the team. The next person may leave and continue the process only after the preceding one returns and only if the blocks are stacked. (If the stack falls, they have to wait.) Have a time limit of four to seven minutes for the whole game, depending on the amount of people on each team. The highest stack wins. This game illustrates the frustration we often feel when we have to do seemingly impossible tasks in very little time.

Hypnotist ■ This skit should be thought through before the meeting although it does not have to be rehearsed nor all the characters chosen ahead of time.

Announce that you have a special guest—the "Great Marvello," hypnotist extraordinaire. This should be a staff person or a student who likes to ham it up. His or her costume should include a black cape and a pendant on a golden chain.

Marvello should call for volunteers whom he will "hypnotize." At least two of these "volunteers" should be set up, one of whom should act as a belligerent skeptic. Marvello seats the three or four volunteers in front of the group and proceeds to hypnotize them, starting with the skeptic who loudly proclaims that he can never be hypnotized. Marvello swings the pendant in front of his eyes, and in the middle of a loud "You can never hypnotize me!" speech, the skeptic suddenly drops his head, asleep. Marvello then proceeds to hypnotize the others.

Marvello tells all the subjects that it is very cold in the room, in fact, it is so cold that they are freezing (he or she gives them time to react). Then Marvello says it is warming up . . . warmer . . . even warmer . . . hot . . . it is really hot (at each stage, he or she gives the subjects time to react). Then it is back to normal. Next, Marvello has each subject act like a different farm animal (for example, chicken, duck, dog, pig, and so forth). After returning everyone to normal, Marvello explains that when he or she says the number "5," person #1 will fall in love with person #2's right shoe, person #2 will want person #3's hat, person #3 will crave person #4's jacket, and person #4 will want to take person #1's left arm. Then Marvello says "5" and they react. After a few minutes, he or she brings everyone back to their seats and has them relax, draining all the stress out of their bodies . . . totally relaxed . . . every muscle, every fiber . . . (he or she allows them time to react). Then Marvello "awakes" the subjects and sends them back to their seats.

Imagine ■ Explain that you are going to help everyone relax and get rid of the stress in their lives. Then have them close their eyes and use their imaginations as they listen to you and put themselves into the situations that you describe. Slowly describe two or three relaxing and peaceful situations. Here's an example:

You're at a cabin on a lake. It's a beautiful summer morning with the sun filtering through the tall pines and reflecting on the glassy surface of the water. No one else is awake—the only sound you can hear is the breeze rustling leaves and an occasional splash from a fish or a duck. Slowly you walk to the edge of the lake, remove your shoes and socks, and wade, strolling first to the right and then to the left, taking in the peaceful beauty of the morning. You pull up the lounge chair and sit, leaning back with your eyes closed and your head against the plastic webbing.

Other situations could include walking at night after the first heavy snowfall of the year; lying in bed, exhausted after a day of hard physical labor, a hot shower, and good meal; standing on top of a mountain and taking in the view above and below; and so on.

I've Got a Secret ■ On the old time television show "I've Got a Secret," a person would say something like: "My name is _____, and I've got a secret." As he or she was taking a seat next to the host of the show, the secret would be revealed to the television audience. The host would say something like: *Our guest's secret is something she has done.* Then the celebrity panel would try to guess the secret through a series of yes/no questions, with the panelists asking their questions in order. When a question received a positive response, the questioner could ask another question. The goal was to see who could guess the secret before exceeding the allotted number of "no" answers.

Before the meeting, choose four or five contestants and have them think of "secrets," something that they are doing or have done that very few people know about. These should be very unusual and specific secrets. (For example: "I collect thimbles," "I am allergic to radishes," "I took five years of clarinet lessons," or "My dream is to live in Switzerland.") During the meeting, act like the TV host and bring the contestants to the front one at a time. Number the people in the audience and have them ask questions in numerical order. Give the person who guesses the secret a prize, or give the contestant a prize if no one can guess his or her secret.

Later, discuss how people often have hidden secrets that become tremendous burdens to carry and that cause them considerable stress.

Neanderthal Blenders ■ Have everyone wash their hands while you place two bags of fruit and two glasses on a long table. Divide the group into two teams and line them up at one side of the room.

Explain that this is a contest to see which team can squeeze the most juice into their glass from the fruit in their team's bag. When you give the signal, the first person from each team should run to the table, stand behind it facing his or her team, pull a piece of fruit out of the bag, and squeeze the fruit so that the juice goes into the glass. After about 30 seconds, signal them to stop and run back to their teams. Then the next team members should run to the table, choose a new piece of fruit, squeeze it, and so forth. After all the fruit has been squeezed, the team with the most juice in the glass wins. Then bring out small paper cups and have the losing team drink the juice from both teams as their penalty. Some fruits to try: orange, peach, grapes, plum, grapefruit, kiwi fruit, tangerine, cherries, watermelon, and mango.

One-Up-Man-Ship ■ Seat the group in circles of 7–8 kids each and designate the first person for each circle. Explain that this is a contest of "one-up-man-ship" where each person tries to outdo the previous one in telling stories. The first person begins by saying something like: *What a bad day I had today—my alarm didn't go off.* The next person, going clockwise around the circle, then could say: *You think you had it bad . . .* and then repeats what the first person said and adds something else (for example, *my shoelace broke*). This process continues around the circle until someone can't think of anything to add or can't remember the previous sequence.

Here are other opening lines to use with your group:

• My car broke down on the way to the concert . . .

• I got fixed up with a blind date . . .

• When I got to class, the teacher announced a pop quiz . . .

Perfection ■ Use the children's game Perfection made by Lakeside Games. It's a race against time with a built-in timer. You set the timer, push down the spring-loaded board, and then put 25 pieces (of various shapes) into their correct places on the board before the time runs out and the board pops up. It's exciting with the tension mounting as the clock ticks down. Play with individuals or couples.

Pies ■ Do this as a relay or with representatives from each team. With individuals, have an old-fashioned pie-eating contest where each person has a chocolate pudding pie to eat. The first person finished wins. As a relay, have a pie for each team and give every person a plastic fork with a couple of tines missing. At the signal, the first person runs to the front and eats as much as possible for about 10 seconds (when you blow a whistle) after which he or she runs back and the next person leaves and so on until one of the pies is completely eaten. Be sure to blow the whistle every 10 or 12 seconds or so. This game illustrates performing under the pressure of time.

Pressure ■ Choose 4–5 participants (team representatives) or ask for volunteers to compete in a game of coordination and pressure. Items needed for this game are: the Shape-O toy by Tupperware (a hollow, plastic ball with a variety of shapes cut into it; each cut-out has a piece which matches the shape), a stool, a cup of water, and a ticking kitchen timer.

Here's how the contest works. The first person sits on the stool and opens the Shape-O toy, dumping all the plastic pieces on his or her lap. At your signal, this person should slowly and carefully put all of the pieces through the correct openings while you keep the time. Let's assume that it takes a minute or so. Now the next person must sit on the stool and repeat the process—at least five seconds faster.

Set the timer and place it in front of the person, explaining that you will be holding a cup of water over his or her head which you will pour if he or she

doesn't finish before the timer sounds. If he or she is successful, continue the contest with the next volunteer having to complete the puzzle five seconds faster. Continue until you pour the water.

Obviously, as the required time is lowered, the pressure mounts as does the anxiety of the participants. If you do this with teams, continue to rotate through the representatives. With volunteers, do it as a challenge, asking for the next courageous person to step forward to beat the time of the previous person. It would also be good to have a prize for the person who can do it the fastest without getting wet.

Toe the Line ■ This is a relay. Using masking tape, mark out parallel lines on the floor, one for each team. These lines should be at least eight feet long.

Divide into two teams and line them up in columns at the beginning of their lines. Explain that this is a race. Each person has to walk down the line and back, placing one foot directly in front of the other and always having their *toes* on the line. Also, each person must have his or her feet in a position that no one on the team has used thus far (for example, heel to toe front wards, heel to toe backwards, heels pointing outward, legs crossed, tiptoe, etc.). After someone has finished, he or she should go to the back of the line and sit down. The first team to have everyone go down the line and back *correctly* wins. If someone repeats a position or his or her toes go off the line, send that person back to begin again.

There's a lot of pressure these days to "toe the line."

DISCUSSION STARTERS

Better and Better ■ Seat everyone in a circle (or circles if you have a large group). Give everyone a pen or pencil and a hard surface on which to write. Explain that you will be distributing papers with the beginning of a situation or story at the top. When someone gets one of the pieces of paper, he or she should add one phrase or sentence to the situation to improve it. Then the person should pass the paper to the right and wait for the next paper. Here are some possible beginnings to the stories:

• John's car . . .

• On Celeste's research paper . . .

• Travis started at defensive end in the big game . . .

• "There's a sale at the mall!" exclaimed Megan . . .

• Peter's relationship with Heather . . .

• The baseball team . . .

After they've added at least five phrases or sentences, collect the papers and read them aloud. Use this as an introduction to a discussion about striving for excellence, not perfection, and not settling for mediocrity.

Case Studies ■ Read these, and after each one ask, "What would you do?"

• Janie is a high school sophomore. Her classes this year are the toughest she has ever had, with two or three hours of homework every night. Because of her home situation, Janie has had to take a part-time job right after school, and so she doesn't get home until 7 P.M. She would also like to be active in Campus Life which meets on Tuesday evenings. Janie doesn't know how to fit it all in.

• Bill is a good basketball player. The coach expects a lot from his players, requiring them to work out year round for the next season. Bill knows that if he doesn't do what the coach wants, he may not make the team. Next month, however, his family is taking a trip to the coast to see his grandparents. Bill wants to go, but he knows that the coach won't approve. His parents say the decision is up to him.

• Traci is a member of half-a-dozen clubs at school, including the student council where she is an officer. In addition, she is president of her church youth group. As often happens, most of the kids in each group expect their leaders to do 90 percent of the work. Traci feels overwhelmed with responsibilities, and her grades have begun to slip.

Setting the Standard ■ Distribute copies of the following worksheet and pencils.

EXCELLENCE

Who sets the standard for excellence in each of these areas? Write one name in each space provided.

music _____

religion _____

drama _____

science _____

comedy _____

basketball _____

football _____

physical fitness_____

fashion_ _____

politics _____

business _____

education _____

dating _____

service _____

Collect the questionnaires and read the answers aloud, one category at a time. Then discuss why they chose the people they did, how excellence fits into the discussion, and how these people aren't perfect. Also discuss how they often feel pressured to measure up to an impossible standard, and the difference between perfectionism and excellence.

The Shaping ■ To illustrate how our trials and pressures can shape us into what God wants us to become, have a potato carving contest. Distribute potatoes and knives to everyone. Note: use regular dinner knives, not sharp ones, so that no one will get hurt.

Have everyone carve faces out of the potatoes. Be sure to put newspapers down to catch the potato scraps. After a few minutes, have everyone display their creations. Use this as an object lesson to show how God, the perfect sculpturer, uses experiences, problems, and pressures to cut away what is not needed and to conform us into the image of Christ (Romans 8:29).

DISCUSSIONS AND WRAP-UPS

Contents under Pressure ■ Read Ephesians 6:10-18 aloud. Explain that this famous passage about spiritual armor relates to how we deal with the pressures we face in the world. In order to meet and defeat any stress, we must:

1. *Tune In* (verses 10-13). This means realizing that every battle we fight is a spiritual battle because God loves us and is concerned for our well being. Therefore, we must be spiritually aware and sensitive, recognizing that God wants to be involved in our lives. The first step is to develop a spiritual awareness.

2. *Put On* (verses 14-16). This means utilizing the resources that God gives us (the "armor"). Instead of relying only on our abilities to perform or to deal with stress, we should use all the resources that God has given to us: faith, God's Word, other Christians, and so forth. We don't have to fight this battle alone.

3. *Turn Over* (verse 18). This means immersing everything we do in prayer. Turning an area over to God doesn't mean that we can sit back and do nothing. On the contrary, God expects us to use our

abilities and gifts and to do our best, striving for excellence. It does mean, however, that we can perform with a relaxed confidence, knowing that God is with us and that He will still be with us after the event, test, or performance, regardless of how we did.

Honestly Now ■ Challenge students to be honest with God about what they are feeling, including the secrets they hide from everyone else. God knows what they are going through, what they are thinking and feeling, and what they've experienced, and He wants to help. Urge them to seek help from an experienced counselor for serious situations.

Pass out paper and pencils and have them write their feelings, secrets, and so on in the form of a prayer to God. Assure them that *no one* else will see their papers, but you want them to write them anyway. Then have everyone spend time in silent prayer, talking to God about what they wrote.

Pressurized ■ Comment on how well the various competitors did in your stress and pressure related crowd-breakers. Then ask:

• What causes kids to feel squeezed? What kinds of pressures do young people face today?

• At what times do you feel stress and pressure?

• How does extreme pressure to do well affect your performance? In music? In athletics? On tests?

• Who tends to put you under pressure? Why? How do you respond to those people?

• When do you put yourself under the greatest pressure to perform? Why?

Secrets ■ Explain that most people have secrets that they hide from everyone. Then ask what general kinds of secrets people might have. Possible positive answers could include: desires and dreams for the future; talents; experiences; and feelings about a special person. Negative answers could include: something they did that no one knows about; hateful feelings; suicidal thoughts and guilt. Discuss how our secrets can put us under pressure and what we can do to relieve that stress.

BIBLE STUDIES

Excellent Verses ■ On index cards, print the words to the verses listed below, putting a word or two on each card, and mix up the cards. Distribute the cards throughout the group. Then give the signal and see how fast they can put the verses in order. Afterwards, discuss each verse and how it relates to the idea of striving for excellence and using pressure to our

advantage.

• Proverbs 12:24 (TLB)—"Work hard and become a leader; be lazy and never succeed."

• 2 Corinthians 13:11—"Aim for perfection . . . live in peace. And the God of love and peace will be with you."

• Philippians 3:14—"I press on toward the goal to win the prize for which God has called me heavenward in Christ Jesus."

• Colossians 3:23—"Whatever you do, work at it with all your heart, as working for the Lord, not for men."

Known ■ Read and discuss these passages together: After each one, ask how that passage might help someone with a terrible secret. These verses speak of how God knows us thoroughly and yet still loves us. And that no matter what happens, where we are, or what we are going through, we can never loose His love.

• Psalm 7:9—*(God knows our minds and hearts. He will bring an end to evil and secure the righteous.)*

• Romans 8:38-39—*(Nothing can separate us from the love of God.)*

• Ephesians 3:14-19—*(The Lord will strengthen with His Spirit and fill you with His love.)*

Stress Release ■ Have individuals turn to the following passages and read them aloud, one at a time. Discuss what each passage teaches about how we can respond to the stress that comes from high performance expectations.

• Proverbs 3:5-6—*(Lean on the Lord's understanding–not your own.)*

• Matthew 6:28-34—*(Do not worry about tomorrow. The Lord will take care of you. Seek God's Kingdom and you will be blessed.)*

• Philippians 4:6-7—*(Pray about what worries you and God will give you peace in your mind and heart.)*

• 1 Peter 5:7—*(Give all your worries to God because He cares for you.)*

SELF-IMAGE

CROWD-BREAKERS

Beauty and the Beast ■ Do this as a skit with one team disguising a boy as a gross, ugly, despicable beast and the other team making up a girl as a gorgeous, ravishing, sparkling beauty. Then have them lip-sync the theme song from *Beauty and the Beast* to each other. Later you may want to discuss how, in the film, the way Belle (Beauty) treats Beast affects him. Explain that how we treat others can have a powerful effect on them as well, perhaps even turning beasts into princes.

Candid Camera ■ Put together two shows with the slides you have taken all year of your group. One show should feature guys only and should be called "The Men of _____ High" (or whatever school your group represents) using "Macho Man" or another appropriate song for background music. Then show "The Women . . ." with slides only of girls and use the song "Girls Just Want to Have Fun" or another appropriate background song.

Celebrity Look-Alike ■ Bring a large assortment of wigs, makeup, clothes, and hats and stage a celebrity look-alike contest. Give suggestions for possible celebrities, but allow them to choose the ones they want to copy. Here are some possibilities: Bill or Hillary Clinton, Elvis, Bill Cosby, Don King, Madonna, Groucho Marx, Little Orphan Annie, David Letterman, Stevie Wonder, Andre Aggassi, Michael Jordan, and so on.

One at a time, have these "clones" parade and perform. See who can guess the identity and award a prize to the best look-alike. If you want to go all out

with this, have group members come to the meeting dressed and made up.

Echo ■ This is an old skit that will still work. Ahead of time, plant an accomplice in another room. During the meeting, announce that earlier you discovered that the room has a terrific echo when everyone is totally silent. Quiet them down and then begin calling out a series of words, one at a time, waiting for the echo. Of course the echo (your accomplice) returns every time. Use "hello," "good-bye," "help," then switch to foods: "hot dog," "hamburger," "baloney." Each time the echo should return, except after "baloney"—then there should be only silence. Repeat "baloney," again with no echo. Pause, and then explain that you are going to try another subject. Choose a person in the audience who can take a joke, and then call out, "_____ is a great guy!" The echo calls back . . . "baloney!"

Good Points ■ Give each group member a piece of 8 1/2"x 11" paper. Have them write their names at the tops of their papers. Next, using masking tape, stick each person's paper on his or her back, and make sure that everyone has a pencil. At your signal, everyone is to mill around the room and write a "good point" about each person without telling that person what was written. They should not repeat anything that has already been written on the paper. After a few minutes, collect the papers and read them aloud. See if they can guess the identity of the person being described. After each one, reveal the correct person and give him or her the paper.

Improve and Pass On ■ Seat everyone in a circle (for a large group, break into circles of 10-15) and explain that you will be giving them a drawing on a piece of poster board and a pen, both of which they are to pass around the circle. Each person must make some change in the picture to improve it (and explain the change to the group) before he or she can pass it on. After the first drawing goes around the circle, you will give them another one and so on. The drawings should be very basic and could include a car, a person, a house, an unnamed invention, etc. With more than one group, you may want to have each one display and explain their finished masterpieces to everyone.

Labels ■ You will need at least 26 kids to play this game. Distribute large self-adhesive labels and have each person write a letter of the alphabet on it before putting it on his or her back. Explain that you will be calling out various words. Each time they should try to get together with the correct letters to form the word. The first group to form the word wins a point for each person in the group. Each person should keep track of his or her points. At the end, the person with the most points wins. Be sure to use a variety of words drawing from the entire alphabet. Also, vary the length of the words.

Looks Aren't Everything ■ Obtain six Pepsi bottles. Fill five of them with other brown liquids (for example: tea, Dr. Pepper, Coke, root beer, prune juice cheap cola, chocolate water, etc.). Bring the bottles out during the meeting and have a taste test to see who can identify the real Pepsi. You can repeat this test with other products (Fritos, McDonald's french fries, etc.).

Mister Potatohead ■ This old toy still can be found in most toy stores. The idea is to use a real potato and turn it into a "head" by using the accessories supplied in the toy package. Supplement these accessories with a few of your own (for example: party hats, makeup, shaving cream, jewelry). Divide into teams and give each one a packet of accessories, a potato, and the task of creating their own Mr. Potatoheads. They also should give the potato person a name and a life history. Award a prize to the winner (the most creative one)—certificates for stuffed potatoes or french fries would be appropriate.

My Ideal ■ This relay involves teams. Set up a blind for each team—an area behind a sheet or in a separate room where each person will go to perform his or her part of the relay. Behind each blind, place a piece of poster board and a fiber-tip marker (or crayons). Explain that at your signal, the first person from each team will run to the designated area and begin to

draw a picture of the "ideal" person. Team members will not be able to see what has been drawn until their turn. Each person will have 10 seconds to draw after which you will blow a whistle. At each whistle, the person will return to his team and the next "artist" will leave and draw. After everyone has had a chance to draw, bring out the pictures, display them, and choose a winner. Repeat if you have time.

Passages ■ Divide into five teams of small groups and assign a "life passage" to each group. Explain that in a few minutes, a group spokesperson will go to another room and describe, on a tape recorder, a person at that specific stage of life. The groups will record in chronological order and will not be able to hear what the previous groups have said. At the end, they will have told the life story of a high school student. Assign the following life passages and then give them a few minutes to brainstorm the person's history. Encourage students to use their creative imaginations.

(Note: Be sure to supervise the taping.)

Life passages:

1. Birth–2 years old
2. 3–5 years old
3. 6–9 years old
4. 10–13 years old
5. 14–18 years old

When everyone has finished, rewind the tape and play back the composite biography.

Person Poem ■ Have everyone find a partner. Give each pair scratch paper and a pen. Explain that they are to write a simple poem about their partner. This poem should describe the person without referring to any of his or her looks. It may be humorous or serious. Suggest that they begin by listing all the personal characteristics of the person. Next, collect the poems, mix them up, and read them aloud, giving the audience the chance to guess the identity of the person poetically pictured. Then identify the person and continue with the next poem.

Photocopy ■ Before the meeting, use a photocopy machine to make copies of a number of kids' faces. (They should close their eyes tightly and press their noses to the glass.) Display the pictures to the group and see who can guess the most correct identities.

Place the Face ■ Buy two to five (depending on the size of your group) posters of well-known personalities. Cut out the faces, and glue each one to a piece of cardboard. Then cut the faces into puzzles pieces.

Divide into teams and give each team a puzzle piece from one of the puzzles. Mix together all the other puzzle pieces on a table in front of the room. Explain that the teams should put their puzzles together by sending one person at a time from their team to the table to retrieve a puzzle piece. The contest is to see which team can (1) guess their celebrity first, and (2) put their puzzle together the quickest.

Use this game as a springboard for discussing the "puzzle pieces" needed to form a good picture of one's self.

Real Beauty ■ Hold a beauty contest like the Miss America pageant, but featuring unusual parts of the body. Have each team choose a representative who must parade before the panel of judges who hold up their scores (like Olympic ice skating or diving). Determine a winner for each category. Here are some possibilities:

• most beautiful wrists (either sex)

• most shapely knees (guys)

• prettiest elbow (girls)

• loveliest ear lobe (guys)

• nicest toenails (girls)

Secrets ■ During the week before the meeting, distribute cards to group members and have them write a unique fact about themselves that no one in the group would know about. These facts should not be embarrassing, but things that they would not mind others learning. Make sure they put their names on the cards, and collect the cards before the meeting. Then, write a matching quiz using the information recorded on the cards. The quiz could look like this:

_____	Mary Finer	a. loves to fish
_____	Alvin Bodette	b. lived in Scotland
_____	Mick Teasley	c. middle name is "Precious"
_____	Anna Barney	d. has eaten possum

List at least 10 kids. To make it more difficult, add a couple of fictitious qualities and one fictitious name. After everyone has finished, give the correct answers.

Skin Deep ■ Somewhere near you there will be a store or restaurant with a game where you have to scratch off the gray material to find special information or win a prize. Even if the game is out of date, get a number of cards and use them for your own game of lottery, bingo, scavenger hunt, etc. (What are people really like underneath? How do we scratch the surface?)

The Eyes Have It ■ This will take a little work and advance preparation. Choose 5–10 young people and take close-up pictures of just their eyes and noses. Then cut out each picture above the eyebrows and below the eyes, about halfway down the nose. Mount the pictures on a piece of poster board and number them. The object is to guess the identity of each person. For laughs, throw in a phony one with a fake nose and glasses or one from a magazine. Award a nice prize to the person correctly identifying the most pictures.

This contest points out the uniqueness of each person. In our groups we seem so much alike, but God has created us with special looks and features.

The Way We Were ■ From their parents, secretly obtain baby pictures of various group members. Movies or video tapes of earlier years would be even better. Number the pictures, give everyone a piece of paper for the answers, and pass the pictures around the room. Have students guess the identities of the children. Save the movies for the end.

True Identity ■ This will take advance preparation. Buy posters of famous people (where the face is fairly large). Mount these posters on cardboard (pasting it on a side of a cardboard box will work), and then cut them into puzzle pieces. During the meeting, divide into teams and give each person in each team one piece of the team's puzzle. At the front of the room, hang pieces of poster board, and have tape dispensers available. At the starting signal, the first person from each team runs to the front and tapes his or her piece to the board. After the first person returns, the next person tapes up his or her piece and so on. Players that follow may rearrange the preceding players' pieces. The first team to guess the identity of their person wins. If this goes too quickly, redistribute the pieces and see which team can finish its entire puzzle first.

What I Like ■ Distribute papers and pens. Have each person list three things that he or she likes about him/herself that are unique. Next, they should hand the paper to another person. Select certain kids to read the papers they are holding. See who can identify the person being described.

What's in a Name? ■ Use a book that features names and their meanings and prepare a matching quiz. On one side list some names and on the other side, the meanings (out of order, of course). Have the students guess what each name means. Next, pass out pens and pieces of paper and have each person choose a first name of a person in the room and write down what he or she thinks is the meaning of that name (or should be). Collect the papers and read aloud the best ones (non-offensive and non-boring). Compare them with the real meanings if they're listed in the name book.

DISCUSSION STARTERS

Ad-sumptions ■ Tape three or four youth-oriented advertisements (video or audio). See which team can be first to recognize the ads, and then have everyone list all the qualities or benefits being claimed by the advertisers. Next, they should list what the ads imply or assume about their listeners or watchers. Discuss whether there is an actual connection between the claims for each product and the performance of the product (for example, "Will the toothpaste guarantee you a date?"). Also, discuss how these ads affect our self-concepts.

Assignment ■ Give everyone a blank card and have them list their seven best qualities that do not relate to outward appearance. Each day during the week as a part of their quiet times, they should read 1 Samuel 16:7 and thank God for one of these qualities. Obviously, they should choose a different quality each day.

Designers ■ Explain that you have noticed a number of little animals and other characters on clothes. What are some of these? (alligator, polo player, fox, crawfish, lion, dragon, etc.) Discuss briefly where these originated. Expand the discussion to include other designer clothes. Next, pass out paper and pencils and ask them to create their own designer emblems. The symbols can reflect their personalities or anything they wish. (For example, someone who loves to swim might choose a fish.) Display the emblems and have them explained. Then ask:

• When do you feel pressured to wear certain clothes?

• How serious is this whole business of wearing certain clothes to be accepted?

Feeling Good ■ Pass out half sheets of paper with the following sentences that each person must complete.

"I really enjoyed _____ ."

"My mother thinks I'm _____ ."

"I felt really successful when _____ ."

"My brother/sister thinks I'm _____ ."

"I felt really good about myself when _____ ."

"My favorite teacher is ____ because _____ ."

"My best friend is ____ because _____ ."

After they've had a chance to finish the sentences, ask for volunteers to read some of the answers aloud. Then ask:

• What do you think is the point to all these sentences? (What do they have in common?)

• What's the connection between these "sentences" and your self-concept?

• What role can we play in giving others a good self-image?

Gonna Climb a Mountain ■ Have an artist friend draw a mountain with a number of people in the process of climbing it. (A rough sketch will work also.) One climber should be at the top, planting a flag, another should be at the foot of the mountain. Others should be at a variety of positions and situations (on a ledge, helping someone up, planting a foothold, hanging by a rope, etc.). Hold up the picture for the group to see or pass it around (or make enough photocopies so that everyone has one). Ask them to look at it carefully and each choose a figure that best represents him or her. Next, go around the circle or get into small groups and have each person explain his choice and the reasons for it.

ID Card ■ Give each person a 3"x 5" card, a pen, and the assignment to create a new "ID" for him/herself without using a picture of his/her face. The ID may include physical descriptions, but it should also include other important facts about his or her identity. After a few minutes, collect the cards, read them aloud, and have group members try to guess whose they are. Then discuss how we get our identities (self-concepts), how others see us, and how we see ourselves.

Ideal Man/Woman ■ Have everyone find a partner. Then distribute old magazines, tape and scissors and give them five minutes to put together their ideal man or woman using pictures from a magazine. Have the creations displayed and explained. Then ask:

• Where do we get these ideas of the characteristics for the ideal man or woman?

• Are they valid? Why or why not?

• Where should we get our standards? What should some of these standards be?

I Give You ■ Use teams from earlier games or arrange the group in circles of 8–10 and have them number off. Make sure that each team or group has an adult to supervise and act as judge. Explain that at your signal, person #1 should turn to #2 and say, "I give you _____." The blank should be a positive statement about the person, something to enhance his or her self-esteem, such as "good looks," "a great smile," "an insightful mind," etc. Then person #2 should turn to #3 and say, "I give you *(repeat what #1 said)* and _____." This should continue all around the circle. For example, person #7 would have to repeat the six previous statements and then add a new one. If a person makes a mistake, the group has to start over. Either see which group can go the farthest in two minutes, or which group can make it around the circle twice the quickest.

In Common ■ Divide into groups of five to seven and give each group a piece of paper and a pen. Their assignment is to list as many things as possible that they have in common. Allow two minutes and then see which group has the longest list. Next, send them back into the groups to discuss the most unique characteristics that they have as individuals and as a group. After about five minutes, bring everyone back together and discuss their findings.

Inflated Self ■ Give everyone a balloon. Explain that during the meeting, every time they use any of these pronouns—I, me, mine, my—they have to blow one breath into the balloon. Near the end of the meeting, when many of the balloons have been inflated quite a bit, discuss how we seem to focus a lot of attention and energy on ourselves and what this implies about our self-concepts.

In Focus ■ At an earlier meeting, take color slides (close-ups) of various group members. Bring the slides to this meeting, but before projecting them, explain that this will be a contest to see who can identify the most people. That sounds easy enough, but begin each slide grossly out of focus. Then slowly bring it into focus until someone guesses the correct identity of the person pictured. With a small group, use some kids more than once, otherwise the later identities will be guessed by the process of elimination. Use this as a discussion starter for how we look at ourselves. Sometimes we're so close to the situation that our perspective is blurred . . . we're out of focus.

I Wish ■ Give everyone a piece of paper and a pen or pencil. Tell them to write a wish list for themselves on one side of the sheet. In other words, if they had the power, what would they change about themselves? This list should not include material items, such as

money, possessions, or circumstances, such as family or geography. It may include physical and mental characteristics, abilities, talents, gifts, personality, habits, and so forth.

After a few minutes, have everyone turn their papers over and list those items written on the other side that *they can change* (for example, weight, habits, abilities). Explain that they should accept those areas that they can't change, understanding that God wants them that way. But they should work on changing those areas that need adjustment. Then help them design a plan for change in *one* of those changeable areas.

Name Memory ■ Break into small groups and have each group come up with a positive adjective that will tell something about the character of each person in the group. The adjective should begin with the same letter as the person's first name (for example: "Magnificent Mary," "Bold Bill," "Effervescent Ellen," "Friendly Fred," "Dynamite Debi," etc.). This may be difficult, so prepare a list of possible adjectives from which they can choose or that will trigger their imaginations.

On Broadway ■ Explain that you will put on a Broadway play and that each person in the group will have an important part. These parts include producer, director, lead actors, extras, supporting actors, stagehands, makeup artist, sound effects person, lighting technician, etc. Before the meeting, list these characters on a sheet of paper and after each one include a brief description (for example: "Producer Georgio Megabucks lives in New York and loves the theater. As a young boy he used to sell apples on Broadway to help his mother pay the rent. After amassing a fortune with a unique combination of luck at the racetrack, successful pizza parlors, and dubious underworld connections, he decided to get into the business. He is now known as 'Broadway's Mr. Big.' ") Distribute copies of the characters and their descriptions and have each person write his or her name after the part that he or she would fit best. Then discuss why they chose the particular characters they did.

Real Men/Women ■ Use paper doll cutouts and hang them on the wall with a piece of poster board under each one. Then ask for phrases for each cutout (man and woman) that finish these beginnings, "Real men . . ." and "Real women . . ." in the style of the book *Real Men Don't Eat Quiche*. Then discuss how we get our ideas of "real" men and women.

Response ■ After prayer, conclude your meeting by

having everyone mill around the room saying to three different people, "I love you because you're you, and I really appreciate _____ about you."

Self Ads ■ Collect a number of "self" ads from newspapers and magazines and display them around the room or pass them around to everyone. These ads should emphasize self-concept or self-centeredness, and they could include *Self* magazine, hair coloring, vitamins, fast food, entertainment, restaurants, athletic equipment, and so on. They should say something like: "You deserve . . . ," "I'm worth it," "You're the best," "Be all that you can be," and other similar phrases.

Discuss which advertisements emphasize a healthy self-concept and which ones center around an unhealthy view of self, and what makes the difference. Note: often a person with a very poor self-concept will be attracted to those products that promise to make him or her better than he or she is.

Self Questionnaire ■ Distribute these brief questionnaires and have everyone fill them out privately and anonymously. Afterwards, either collect the questionnaires and analyze the types of answers (don't get specific) or have everyone look at their own papers as you explain how the answers reveal how they see themselves, their self-concepts. Also, ask if their friends would be able to guess what they wrote on their papers, and why or why not.

JUST ABOUT ME

(finish the sentences)

1. I'm really good at _____

_____ .

2. When I'm daydreaming about success, I'm _____

_____

3. If I could have any job in the world, I'd be_____

_____ .

4. The one thing I wish others knew about me is ___

_____ .

Song Search ■ Divide into groups of three and give everyone hymnal. Explain that you will give them a song title, a line in a song, or a theme. They should find the song and then stand to their feet and sing the first verse and chorus together. The first group to do this wins that round.

Choose songs that speak of God's love for us and affirm our self-image (for example: "What a Friend We Have in Jesus," "Jesus Loves Me," "The Love of God," "I Will Change Your Name,"). Begin by giving song titles. Then move to asking for phrases that could be hidden in a chorus, third verse, etc. End by asking for songs that center around specific themes (for example: Thanksgiving, forgiveness of sin, creation). Use these songs as discussion starters and as segues to your teaching. Close the meeting by singing some of the songs together.

Take Me to Your Leader ■ Using yourself as the guinea pig, choose a consulting team of four or five kids to improve you. Tell them to design a comprehensive, self-improvement plan for you in the areas of health, finances, appearance, social life, and spiritual life. With each one they should describe the goal and what you should do to get there. Discuss how they chose those goals and why they feel they are important.

This Is Me ■ Have everyone look through their pockets and purses to find a symbol of how they see themselves—their self-image. It could be a picture, a grade report, a letter, keys . . . almost anything. Then number off and pair all the even numbers with odd numbers. Tell them to exchange symbols with their partners, explaining what their symbols mean (explain that all the symbols will be returned to their owners later). Then pair everyone up again (with new partners) and have them exchange symbols again. They can use the symbols they just received or new ones but must explain how they represent them. After two more exchanges, have everyone return the symbols to their owners. Then discuss the experience, noting the similarities of symbols and asking why certain people chose special or unique ones.

Twins ■ Interview a set of identical twins in the meeting. If you can't find a set of twins, summarize the benefits and drawbacks of being an identical twin. Benefits could include: notoriety, security, companionship, understanding between them, help in decision-making. Drawbacks could include: lack of personal identity, confusion with the other person (names mixed-up, etc.), lack of personal freedom. Then ask group members:

1. Would you like to be a twin? Why or why not?

2. How do you think you'd feel having another person just like you?

3. Why is it important to be an individual and have your own identity?

4. What hinders you from being an individual?

Worth While ■ Explain that you are going to play a version of "The Price Is Right." You will give them an item, and they should guess how much it costs in their local grocery store. Use easy items such as laundry detergent, ketchup, a newspaper, ground beef, frozen orange juice, and other common products. After determining who came the closest with his or her guesses, ask the group how the price for each item is determined (for example: the law of supply and demand). Then ask what determines the "worth" of each item to them (possible answers: how much they need it, how much they like it). Ask how the value and worth of something could increase or decrease in other countries (for example: food in Somalia, medicine in Bosnia, etc.).

Next, pass around a mirror and have each person look into it, one at a time. Afterwards, ask what they saw and how they would value that particular item. In other words, what gives them worth? On what do they base their self-esteem? Explain that each person is a rare and valuable commodity, created by a master designer, one of a kind, and that the world needs him or her.

DISCUSSIONS & WRAP-UPS

Bad Image ■ Use this talk as a basis for discussion.

How many people do you know who have a bad or negative image of themselves? Maybe you're one of them. A poor self-image will cause all sorts of behavior: conformity, trying to be accepted, nonconformity, trying to be noticed, sarcasm and put-downs of others, trying to "put-up" themselves, sexual exploits, trying to find love, and even crime and other extreme actions. We receive ideas about ourselves (our identity) from other people. The process began with our parents. They named us, shaped our personalities, and told us what was good or bad about us. Our neighborhood friends and classmates joined the process. Mix in teachers, Scout leaders, coaches, ministers, Campus Life directors, and assorted others, miscellaneous experiences, and society in general, and our self-concepts are formed. Just as people have helped form our identities, we can be a part of the process with others. In other words, what we say to them and how we treat them is very important. We wield great power. As Christians, we must use this power wisely and in obedience to God.

Balloon ■ Blow up a balloon and hold it up in front of the group. Explain that the balloon illustrates how we often feel about ourselves. When we're inflated, we feel good. But often our self-esteem can feel like it's slipping away, "like the air seeping out of a balloon." Then we feel empty, deflated. Say that when they are feeling bad about themselves, they should:

1. Evaluate why they feel badly about themselves

2. Put themselves in places where they know people will love them

3. Take God's Word and read all the verses that tell them they are loved.

Some of these verses are: Jeremiah 29:11; Psalm 139, John 3:16, 1 John 3:16; and 4:9-10.

Do Tell ■ Ask the following questions of the whole group.

1. What do hands tell you about a person?

2. What do eyes tell you about a person?

3. What do feet tell you about a person?

4. What does a mouth tell you about a person?

Individuals . . . for Christ ■ Wrap up your discussion and talk about the following points.

1. Our identities are "who we are," or, at least, who we think we are. We get these ideas from other people, especially those who are important to us (parents, neighbors, other relatives—and in high school, teachers and friends). We see ourselves as beautiful or plain, intelligent or dumb, athletic or uncoordinated, depending on how we are accepted and affirmed and based on our accomplishments.

2. Sometimes identity and self-worth become blurred when we conform to a group and act like someone other than who we really are. Identical twins often struggle with their individuality, but so do the rest of us. We must realize that each person is a unique and special person with talents, gifts, and abilities.

3. Our true identities must begin with an understanding of how God sees us. What makes us important to Him runs contrary to what society says we need in order to be noticed. He created us and loves us for who we are and who we can become through His power—not for what we own or how we look. And He wants to make us like Christ.

4. As we understand who we are, we become free to live for Christ as unique and loved individuals.

It's a Wrap ■ Pull together all the elements of the meeting and make the following points:

1. All of us have an ideal person we would like to be and to which we compare ourselves. The ideal may be given to us by society in general, our friends, our families, or a combination. In any case, we see ourselves as successful or as failures depending on how we compare to the ideal.

2. Each person has a self-concept, a view of him/herself containing positive and negative feelings.

3. Our self-images affect how we look at life and God and how we act and relate to others.

4. When we see ourselves as others see us, we receive only a partial view. When we see ourselves as we see us, we receive only a partial view. When we see ourselves as God sees us, we receive a full view.

5. God created us, loves us, and wants the very best for us. He wants us to become all that He had in mind when He made us.

6. Begin today to see yourself as God sees you. Accept His love, and follow His direction.

Names, Names ■ Ask:

1. When you name your children, what will you consider in choosing their names? Why?

2. How much does a person's name affect the way that person develops? What examples can you give of a person's name directly relating to his or her career?

3. What about nicknames? How do they affect us?

4. Do any of you have names which you dislike, perhaps because of their connotations (for example: Ethel = gas; John = bathroom; etc.) or usual use in society (for example: Ralph, Fred)?

Wrap up the discussion with this outline:

1. Names set us apart from others and are a way to get more personal than using just a number or a pronoun. They get us "beneath the surface."

2. Names offer access to personality; they give permission to be personal.

3. Our names are precious to us; we listen for them, look for them in the newspapers, etc. Our names get our attention.

4. Names express our identity. They are common enough to lump us with our culture and distinctive enough to set us apart.

5. To be on a "first name basis" implies unusual friendship.

6. God uses names and titles to describe Himself to us, showing that He is personal and that He wants to know us. The names of God give us glimpses into His character and personality.

7. Jesus is the most personal name of God. He is the God/man and is the most perfect expression of the Father. We can look at Jesus and see what God is like (John 14:9).

8. God wants us to call Him "Father." Think of the personal implications—we can be God's very own children.

Object Lesson ■ Bring out a mirror that has been

hit in the middle so that the cracks run to all the sides (the larger the mirror the better). Explain that looking in this mirror gives a distorted picture. It would be difficult to get ready for school in the morning using a mirror like this. But that's similar to what happens when we look at others for our self-image—we get distorted pictures.

Then bring out a good mirror, with no cracks. Explain that this is a much truer picture of our physical appearance. In contrast to the cracked mirror, this one will help us. That's similar to what it means to look at God's Word for an accurate picture of ourselves. We shouldn't settle for the world's cracked mirror.

Prayer ■ Close the meeting with prayer in small groups. Have each person pray for the individual on his or her left, asking God to reaffirm His love in his or her life.

BIBLE STUDIES

Better and Better ■ Explain the value of having a goal to strive for. Discuss how being just like Christ can be both motivating and frustrating. Then discuss Romans 8:29 (God's ultimate for us is to conform us into the image of Christ—to be like Him) and Philippians 2:12-13 (God is working *in* us, changing our desires—"helping us want to obey Him"—and giving us the power—"helping us do what He wants"). Read Philippians 3:12 aloud, showing Paul as an example of someone who knew that he wasn't perfect but who worked hard to become all that God wanted. Paul wrote: *I don't mean to say I am perfect. I haven't learned all I should even yet, but I keep working toward that day when I will finally be all that Christ saved me for and wants me to be* (TLB).

Bible Search ■ Divide into three groups and give each group a passage to study, answering the question, "What does this say about my responsibility to improve myself?"

1. 2 Peter 1:3-11 (especially verses 5 and 9). The key phrase is, "If anyone does not have them, he is nearsighted and blind." Also see 1 Corinthians 14:1.

2. 2 Timothy 2:15; Romans 12:2.

3. Hebrews 5:11-14: The key phrase is, "Let us leave the elementary teachings about Christ and go on to maturity."

4. Matthew 25:14-30. This is the parable of the talents. Have the groups report their findings. The point is that we have a responsibility to "add to faith," "grow,"

"mature," "seek greater gifts," "invest wisely," and so on.

Conformed ■ Ask if conformity is wrong or right and why. Then read Romans 12:1-2 and ask: What does "conformed" mean in this context? How are we "conformed to the world"? How does this relate to your identity? Read Romans 8:29 and say: *Here's the word "conformed" again. What does it mean in this context? Put the two "conformeds" together; how does it work? How does being "conformed to the image of Christ" affect your identity? When does God want you to express your individuality?*

From Creation On ■ Break into groups. Give each group a passage of Scripture, and have them answer the listed questions. After a while, bring the whole group back together and have them report their findings. Possible answers are suggested in parentheses.

Genesis 1:24-31

1. What does this passage tell us about human beings? How are we distinct from other animals? (A special creation, made in the image of God, given dominion over all the earth.)

2. What do you think God's image is? What are examples of His image in members of the group? (spiritual nature, personality, rationality, and other internal qualities.)

3. What does this passage teach us about our identities? (God created us; we are important to Him; inner qualities are most important.)

Romans 5:6-11

1. Where do you and I fit into this passage? (We are the "sinners" and "enemies.") Is that a fair assessment of us? Why or why not?

2. Why did Christ die for us in light of the fact that it makes no sense at all according to the world's standards? (He loves us and wants to save us.)

3. How should this truth affect our self-concepts? (We are valuable in God's sight. He wants to rescue us and to give us new life; we should feel great about that!)

Romans 8:31-39

1. What does this passage promise us? (We can never be lost to God's love.) What about when we condemn ourselves? (No one will ever be able to condemn us.)

2. Paraphrase verses 35, 38, and 39 using your high school situations.

3. What image does God have of each of us? How should this change our self-images?

Matthew 8:1-3

1. Describe leprosy. What kind of response would a leper receive at your school? (Some might compare a leper to today's AIDS patients.) How would you feel if you found out you had a disease like that?

2. How did Jesus react to this outcast and gross looking person? (Jesus accepted him, had compassion for him, touched him, healed him.)

3. When do you feel like a leper? How would you be able to feel Jesus' touch? How should this passage affect your self-concept?

4. How can Christians "touch lepers"?

God's Self-image ■ Read Jeremiah 9:24 aloud and discuss God's self-concept. Ask:

• How does God feel about Himself?

• How can God's self-concept affect ours?

• How does God feel about us? (see Psalm 139)

• How should this affect how we feel about ourselves?

Jesus ■ This Bible study begins with a brief talk about Jesus and then proceeds to a discussion of a couple of passages.

Think of the image problem that Jesus must have had when He entered history: born in a barn in a small city, grew up with the whispers of being illegitimate, had a common name (about as common as the name "John" today), had a common face (Judas had to point Jesus out by kissing Him), was introduced to the world by a group of shepherds, had no riches that could make Him desirable to get to know or follow (Matthew 8:20), had a strange advance man (John the Baptist–Luke 3:7), hung around with a motley crew of 12 men, and was executed on a cross (the equivalent of the electric chair today). Jesus is fully capable of identifying with your feelings of being a nobody (if you have them) based on what others may be saying about you. He made Himself available to kings and poor people. In one way, because His earthly background was so unintimidating, Jesus gives us the freedom to be who we were created to be.

Read and discuss Psalm 139:13-16 and 1 Corinthians 12:22, 24.

Jesus Says ■ Pass out copies of the following list. In each blank group members should put a "P" if this is a "Project" on which they're working, a "Q" if they don't know what Jesus meant, and a "C" if this is a "Challenge" that they haven't yet started.

Jesus told me to be . . .

___ a sheep (John 10:1-6)

___ salt (Matthew 5:13)

___ light (Matthew 5:14-16)

___ a branch (John 15:1-10)

___ a servant (John 13:12-17)

___ a disciple-maker (Matthew 28:16-20)

___ a builder (Matthew 7:24-27)

___ good soil (Matthew 13:1-23)

___ a fisherman (Matthew 4:18-20)

___ childlike (Matthew 18:1-5)

3

KNOWING GOD

CROWD-BREAKERS

Art and Art? ■ Obtain some pictures of modern art from an inexpensive magazine (don't spend a lot of money). Cut out the pictures and mount them on cardboard. Display the pictures one at a time, asking group members for their impressions and how much they think the pictures are worth. Then reveal the title, artist, and cost. Mix in a few of your own creations (or those drawn by young children), thrown together with finger paint, fiber-tip markers, and crayons. This activity illustrates differences in perspectives—one person's junk is another person's treasure.

Creation ■ Before the meeting, clip pictures from various magazines of animal and human body parts. Make at least two sets so that two teams will be able to compete with everyone involved. Each set should contain the parts of a complete human figure. Number the backs of the pictures.

Divide into teams and give each team a packet of parts. Make sure that every person gets a numbered body part. Explain that together you will be creating creatures, by chance. You will draw out a number from a bag (prepared ahead of time), and the people from each team with that number will then come to the front and tape their body part to the team's poster board. The game will proceed until all the parts are used or the creatures are complete. This illustrates the difference between creation and chance.

Eyewitness News ■ Distribute paper and pencils. Explain that they will observe a scene that they should watch very carefully. Then present the following

scene: two guys walk across the front of the room, toward each other. They greet each other and begin to talk. During the brief discussion they get into an argument that quickly escalates. Eventually one person punches the other who retaliates by hitting back. After a couple of wild swings, one of them pulls a toy gun and shoots the other.

Stop the scene, have the actors leave the room, and ask the group to write down the answers to the following questions.

1. Who spoke first?
2. What were the colors of their shirts?
3. Why were they arguing?
4. Who started the argument?
5. Who hit whom first?
6. Who shot whom and why?

Compare the answers. This should demonstrate how often we see only part of the story given as eyewitnesses. (God sees the whole picture.)

Feets of Strength ■ Choose four kids to compete in a series of tests of strength. Have the four do all of the tests, one test at a time, or divide into teams and use four different competitors for each test. Here are the four tests for the competitors who should be seated in front of the rest of the group, sans shoes and socks.

1. Give each person an inflated and tied balloon that he or she should place between his or her feet. The first person to pop the balloon using only the pressure of the feet (no puncturing allowed), wins.

2. Place a paper towel on the floor between the feet of

each competitor. The idea is to see which person can tear the towel the *best* (two equal parts). This is a test for quality, not speed.

3. Give each competitor a thick rubber band that he or she should place around both of his or her big toes. The first person to snap the rubber band by pulling his or her feet apart, wins.

4. Place a paper cup, right-side-up, on the floor between each competitor's feet. Give them 15 seconds to turn the cup over and crush it thoroughly, using only their feet *while seated*.

Grab Bag ■ Bring a number of bags, each with an unusual item inside. Pass the bags around the room one at a time. No one should look inside, but each person may reach in with a hand and feel the item. Then have group members guess what is in each bag. Possible items could include: a shell, a plate with a picture on it, doll clothes, an unusual kitchen utensil, a car tool, coffee grounds, etc. After everyone has had a chance to guess, reveal the item. This illustrates our limited perspective; we only see part of the picture.

Hearts and Flowers ■ Choose volunteers to compete in a contest of skill and dexterity. Blindfold them and give each one a piece of red construction paper. Explain that because the theme of the meeting is God's love, when you give the signal, each person should tear a heart out of the construction paper. After a few seconds, remove the blindfolds and display the hearts. Give a prize to the person who has torn the best heart. Ask for a new set of volunteers but have them tear out a bouquet of flowers.

I am Abraham ■ Set this up like the old TV quiz program and use students with real secrets, little known Bible characters, fictitious characters, or theological concepts. Have the emcee introduce three individuals, all of whom claim to be Mr. _____. For example, they might say, one at a time, "I am the Holy Bible." Next the audience should question them. In the case of a real person with a real secret (for example, "I used to live in England"), the actual person must answer the questions truthfully, while the others may say anything they wish. In the case of a fictitious character or a biblical concept, the participants would have to rehearse beforehand to get a general direction for their answers.

After questioning, the audience should vote for their choice of the genuine article. After the votes have been cast, the emcee should state, "Will the real _____ please stand up."

This activity will help you emphasize that God is truth.

I'm Behind You All the Way ■ Arrange everyone in a single file column, winding around the room. Have them stand very close to each other. Explain that you will be leading them in "follow the leader." Each person must do exactly what the person in front of him or her does while staying as close as possible to that person. Then walk slowly around the room; begin with actions that are easy for everyone to follow (for example, raise and lower your right arm, raise and lower your left arm, hop on one foot for three steps, etc.). Then add actions that will be more difficult for everyone to do (for example, make a 360 degree turn, crouch down and do a duck walk for three steps, walk backward for a few steps, tap the person behind you on the head, etc.). End by sitting on the floor and doing the "wave."

In God We Trust ■ Make sure that each person has a U.S. coin in his or her hand and line everyone up against one wall. Tell them to take a good look at their coins and to find the phrase "In God We Trust." Explain that when you give the signal, they should flip their coins (demonstrate). Each time the coin lands with that motto up, that person may take two small steps forward (heel touching toe). Whenever it lands with the other side up, however, he or she must take one small step backward (if he or she is away from the wall). Kids may only flip their coins when you give the signal. The first person to reach the other wall (or a line on the floor) wins.

Use this exercise to discuss what the motto means, why it was put on the coins, if Americans really trust God (and why or why not), and why we can trust Him.

Instant Replay ■ This is a skit. It can feature a staged fight, a football play, a pickpocket in action, or another simple event. An announcer should say, "Watch the following scene very carefully." The scene is then enacted; it is short and seems normal. For example, if doing the pickpocket scene, two people walk toward each other, and lightly bump into each other, whereupon the pickpocket takes the wallet from the pocket. The announcer then explains how hidden cameras have recorded this event and that he will now replay the scene to show what really happened. In the "slow motion" version, many antics are added. In the replay of the pickpocket, for example, the victim is knocked to the ground, sat on, and everything he owns is stolen. The pickpocket leaves, and the victim continues on his way, oblivious to the attack. This is a humorous illustration of a limited perspective.

Lasting ■ Bring a pile of advertising sections of

magazines and newspapers. Divide into small groups and give each group some of the ads. Tell everyone to look for advertisements that tout the *lasting value* of a product. They should look for anything that speaks of staying power, endurance, long-lastingness, dependability, faithfulness, trustworthiness, and so forth. Have each group share what they found with the whole group. Then discuss how most things in our world are *not* dependable or lasting (for example, they break right after the warranty expires) and how this contrasts with God whose nature and love are constant and truly last forever.

Loose Change ■ Have kids stand to their feet if they have the item or information you ask for (seat them between items). Allow about five seconds for kids to stand each time. Award 100 points to everyone who has each item that you call. At the end, the person with the most total points wins the game. All of these items involve "change."

• 76 cents in change

• name someone in your school who has had a dramatic physical change

• name someone in the church who moved recently

• something you used to believe in that you don't any more

• a sign of growing up

• the name of a public figure who people used to trust but who turned out to be crooked

• name three technological changes of the last five years

• one change you'd like to see in your school

• something in the world that you'd like to see changed

• something in the world that you never want to change

Use this to begin discussion on how God never changes—He is the same yesterday, today, and forever —and what that means to us, today.

Love Cards ■ As kids enter the room, give each one a card from a stack that you have prepared for the meeting. Each card should have a letter of the alphabet (written large) on one side and a number (written small) on the other. Use as many letters of the alphabet as you wish, but be sure to have all the letters that you will need to form the words you choose. Also, be sure to have two sets of the letters, but number the cards consecutively.

When everyone has arrived and has a card, have them look for the number on their cards. Explain that the odd numbers are on one team and the even numbers on the other. The teams should sit on opposite sides of the room. Next, explain that they will be using their letters to form words. You will call out a word that they must form as quickly as possible by holding their cards in front of them and standing in the correct order (cards may not be handed to anyone else). The first team to form the word wins that round.

Here are some possible words. Add others, but make sure they center on "love": accept, friend, hug, thanks, respect, smile, gift, time, dear, together, listen, forever, touch, love. This can help introduce the theme of God's love.

Maze ■ Choose a number of couples and take them out of the room. Build a maze of furniture and people. One at a time, bring the couples in with one person blindfolded. The other person's task is to guide his or her partner through the maze with verbal instructions only. See who can go the farthest in the maze in two minutes with as few bumps as possible. This illustrates the fact that when our sight is limited, we need outside guidance.

Optical Illusion ■ Show a few standard optical illusions, such as the one featured regularly on the back cover of *Mad Magazine*. Next, display some such as these found in *Games You Can't Lose*:

• "Find your way through the maze from A to B."

A   B

• "Which line is longer, A or B?"

A ←——→

B >——<

• "Stare at this spot for 15 seconds."
"What do you see?" ●

After a few laughs, ask about illusions they've experienced. For example: "water" on a hot highway; mountain peaks right behind each other and a long valley between them; thinking your car is moving backward when the one next to you is edging forward; etc. This illustrates how our senses can deceive us.

Reach and Preach ■ Before the meeting, prepare a couple dozen slips of paper to use in a grab bag. Each slip should have written on it a specific instruction about an event in a person's life and whether it should be the truth or a lie. Here are some possibilities: describe the first boy/girl you had a crush on (the truth); make up a story about an unusual pet you had (a lie); explain the meaning of your middle name, why you received it, etc. (a lie); tell everyone about your most exciting vacation (the truth); make up a story about a distant relative who is royalty in a little known country; tell a true story about the fish that got away; etc.

Using teams, have members come to the front one at a time, draw out a slip of paper, and tell the story; the opposing team must decide whether or not the person told the truth or a lie. Award 1,000 points per correct identification. Keep the game moving quickly and give everyone a chance to participate. Use this activity to make the point that while people may lie, God always tells the truth.

Truth or False ■ Write a true-false quiz containing little known facts, trivia, and silly information. Be sure to include a few humorous statements. Distribute the quizzes and tell students to mark each statement either true or false. Give the correct answers and award a prize. Some possible nonsense statements could include: "You feel more like you do right now than you have all day," "It's a good thing that you are shorter than you are," "Is it not true that a true answer to this question would be false?" "Mrs. Valerie (Val) N. Tine began the holiday in February that bears her name." This activity relates to the fact that God is truth.

What's Wrong with This Picture? ■ This activity may be repeated as often as you wish if you have time and it's going well; however, each scene must be planned carefully before the meeting. Be sure to bring the necessary props. Distribute paper and pencils and explain that you will be showing typical scenes in their lives. In each scene, however, something will be wrong. They are to observe the scene and write down the mistakes they see. (Note: These scenes should be set up with kids. There should be no movement or sound, and you should set the scene verbally just before the audience writes.)

Possible scenes and mistakes:

• Kids in a class with teacher. (Guy is writing with pen upside down.)

• Guy and girl in a restaurant on a date. (Guy has shirt on inside out and girl is picking up the check.)

• Friends are talking in the hall. (Notorious "non-studier" has books under his arm; guy is carrying a purse; girl is wearing a football shoe.)

Use your imagination and add other strange elements to the scenes. After each scene, while the performers are still in front, ask for group observations. Compare what was actually in the scene with what they wrote. This activity illustrates how we don't see everything.

Wheel of Fortune ■ Choose 10 volunteers to come and stand in front of the group. Next, bring out a "spinner" that you have prepared. This should resemble the spinner for a Twister game but with 5–10 penalties and prizes. Most of the spots should be penalties. Explain that each person will get one spin of the arrow. If it stops at a penalty spot, they will have to draw from the penalty bag. If it stops at a prize spot, they should draw from the prize bag. Possible prizes could include dinner at a good restaurant, a gift certificate, a subscription to *Campus Life* magazine, a date with someone in the group, and so on. Possible penalties could include receiving a pie in the face, being a participant in the next game, singing a "serious" solo, running outside and yelling "Hello, world!" or running the gauntlet. The point is that this game depends totally on chance. You may even want to choose the participants by chance.

DISCUSSION STARTERS

Boxes ■ Break into small groups. The size of each group is not important, and they may be groups of friends. Give each group a box (bring plenty of shapes and sizes). Also, make available a supply of scissors, crayons, fiber-tip pens, tape, paper, and old magazines. Explain that each group may trade boxes with another group if they both want to trade. Each group's task is to create a picture of God using their boxes as symbols.

After everyone has finished, display the transformed boxes one at a time and let each group explain its box. Then ask:

• Why do you think I used boxes for this little exercise?

• What problem did you have with using a box to represent God?

• In his book, *Your God Is Too Small*, J.B. Phillips said that often we put "God in a box." That is, we limit Him, who He really is, to our own ideas, prejudices— in our images. When have you done that with God?

• What is God really like? How do you know?

Cross Purposes ■ Divide the group into four teams and line each team with their backs against a wall. Assign a color to each team. Explain that the idea is to see who can get to the opposite wall without touching anyone else. They have to take one step at a time and follow the instructions that you will read aloud. Then bring out two envelopes. One envelope should contain slips of paper with the colors of the teams, and the other envelope should contain slips of paper with the following words written on them: yes, no, maybe, and wait. Explain that you will draw a color from one envelope and then a word from the other envelope. The color will determine which team should move, and the word will tell them how to move. "Yes" means that they should move one step forward. "No" means that they should move one step backward. "Maybe" means that they should move one step to the left, and "wait" means that they should move one step to the right. Explain that they should make each move unless it would mean bumping into someone else. In that case, they should stay where they are.

Move this along quickly, pulling the slips out, reading them, and then placing them back in the respective envelopes.

Afterward, explain how this game illustrates Christians' prayers. It also illustrates how complicated it is for God to do everything for everybody. Sometimes we want to go a certain direction, but God wants us to go a different way. And often our moves can "bump into" and hinder others if we're not careful. In other words, sometimes what we want is cross purposes with God. Then explain that what we really should be praying is *cross* purposes, doing God's will in our lives.

Evidence ■ Before the meeting, prepare six exhibits and set them around the room. Each one should be covered. Exhibits should include:

1. a magnifying glass over a butterfly's wing

2. a model of a part of human anatomy (for example, the brain)

3. a spectacular view (slide viewer or color poster)

4. a picture of the sky at night with millions of stars

5. a picture of love (for example, a family embrace, tears flowing, etc.)

6. a cross

Tell the group to visit the exhibits in order, single file, looking at them one person at a time and moving on relatively quickly. Each person should lift the covering, take a good look, and answer the questions on his or her sheet. Here is a sample answer sheet.

THE EVIDENCE

Exhibit #1

    a. What do you see?

    b. What is your main impression?

    c. What does this exhibit tell you about God?

Exhibit #2

    a. How is this different from exhibit #1?

    b. What is your main impression?

    c. What does this exhibit tell you about God?

Exhibit #3

    a. How do you feel when you see this?

    b. What does this exhibit tell you about God?

Exhibit #4

    a. How do you feel when you view this?

    b. What does this exhibit tell you about God?

Exhibit #5

    a. What human emotions do you see here?

    b. What does 1 John 4:7 tell you?

    c. What does this exhibit tell us about God?

Exhibit #6

    a. What does this mean to you?

    b. Why is it important?

    c. What does this exhibit tell us about God?

When everyone is finished, discuss a few important answers, and then ask: *Why was this activity called "Evidence"?* (These are all visible evidences of God's work.) Read Romans 1:18-20 and John 14:9. Ask: *How do these verses relate?* (God has revealed Himself both through Christ and in creation.)

Evidence 2 ■ Have a scavenger hunt, dividing into teams and sending them outside to look for the following items:

Find something in nature that gives evidence of . . .

  1. God's power

  2. God's design

  3. God's perfection

  4. God's love

  5. God's beauty

  6. God's wisdom

  7. God's immensity

  8. God's creativity

  9. God's care

10. God's faithfulness

After you determine the winning team, discuss the experience. Ask:

• Which categories were easiest to find?

• Which were the most difficult?

• How else can we see God in nature?

Then read aloud Romans 1:18-23 and discuss the passage.

Goodness Gracious ■ Tell the group that you are going to give them a good opportunity to excel and that you'll have a good prize for the winners. Then have everyone get into groups of two or three. Each group's task is to remember as many products and/or ads that emphasize goodness. ("Mmm, mmm, good," "Real goodness in every bite," "A good deal," etc.) Read the results and award a prize to the group with the most answers. Then use this to discuss how we use the word "good" in our society, what the real meaning is, and how only God is truly "good."

Hidden Treasures ■ Have group members pair off, and give them the following sheet and the assignment to work together to complete it.

HIDDEN TREASURE

1. Name an unusual talent that someone in this room has that very few people know about.

2. Write down a secret that only one or both of you know.

3. List an object in the room that brings back a good memory for one or both of you.

4. Record a humorous experience that one of you has had with a person in the room.

5. Write down an unusual object that one of you is carrying or an unusual piece of clothing that one of you is wearing which no one can see.

6. Name a person in the room who has special significance to one of you and explain why.

7. Look around the room and write down the thing that has the greatest value for both of you.

8. Each write down one thing that you really appreciate about another person in the room that you have never told him or her.

9. Find an unusual or unique detail of this room that most people usually overlook or totally miss.

10. Write down a couple of groups in the room who have unusual characteristics in common (such as four girls wearing red, six people who moved here from Louisiana, etc.).

After group members have completed their surveys, have them report their answers. Most of these answers will be humorous; a few may be serious. In either case, during the answering and afterward ask:

• Why are these things hidden? To whom do we reveal the private side of our lives? Why?

• Think of a fact about yourself that no one else knows. How would you feel if it were revealed right now? Why? Why do we hide these things?

• Do you think God knows everything about you? Why? How does that make you feel? Why?

Memory Lane ■ Give everyone a piece of scratch paper and a pencil and then ask them to answer the following questions (or questions similar to these).

1. What is the first thing I said to begin this meeting?

2. What is the color of the hat I was wearing as the meeting began?

3. What was the song that was playing when you walked into the room?

4. What was the topic of our last meeting?

5. What was the first game we played in the meeting last week?

6. What are the names of (sponsor's) children?

7. How many chairs are on the platform in the church sanctuary?

8. What is the color of the hardware on the outside of the door to the entrance to this building?

9. What is my middle name?

10. What was the first game we played in this meeting?

Note: Be prepared. That is, wear a hat at the beginning of the meeting, have a song playing as kids arrive, know the answers to the other questions, and so on. Give the correct answers and award a prize to the winner. Then say something like: *This game relates to knowledge–our knowledge of the past. The fact is that God not only knows everything about us now, but He also has a perfect memory. He knew you before you were born and watched every moment of your life. How should this make you feel?* Discuss briefly.

Pass the Globe ■ Purchase or borrow a plastic, inflatable globe. Have everyone sit in a circle and pass the globe from person to person. It may go around the circle or be thrown across. Whenever you blow a whistle, the person holding the globe must either tell the group one fact about a country that one of his or her hands is touching or explain one evidence of God's control in the world. Note: to avoid this becoming too rowdy, explain that anyone who carelessly throws or drops the globe will be the next one to answer.

This game contrasts our "sovereignty" with God's and opens up the subject of God's control in the world.

Prayer ■ Break into groups of four or five and spend a few minutes praying together. The prayers should center around who God is: His holiness, love, goodness, and truth. When everyone has just about finished, close by singing softly and worshipfully together, "Holy, Holy, Holy" or another similar song.

Qualities ■ Have everyone list the qualities of a good friend. The list would include: faithful, loyal, honest, patient, open, communicative, available, helpful, considerate, accepting, and so forth. Discuss how these qualities are reflected in God's relationship with us. Then discuss how they are or are not reflected in our relationship with Him.

Synonym Scramble ■ Divide into four groups and have them sit in clusters on the floor. Give each group a piece of paper and a pencil or pen. Then give each group one of the following words: trust, good, submit, and providence. Explain that they have two minutes to write as many synonyms or related words as they can think of for their word. After the time is up, have each group read their words aloud. Compare what they have written to what is in a thesaurus. Then discuss how these words relate to their fears, God's providence, and their trust in Him.

What Did They Mean? ■ Have three students memorize the following script and perform it for the group. Or perform it as reader's theater if there's not much time for rehearsal.

MRS. SMITH: My goodness, it's Pastor Jones. Why hello, Pastor, it's so good of you to come by.

PASTOR JONES: Good day, Mrs. Smith. How are you?

MRS. SMITH: Good, good.

PASTOR JONES: That's good. And how is Tommy?

MRS. SMITH: Real good. By the way, I thought Sunday's sermon was very good!

PASTOR JONES: Well, good—I'm glad you liked it.

MRS. SMITH: I'm glad there was a good crowd, but I get so mad at the way those teenagers act—I could give them a good piece of my mind!

PASTOR JONES: Oh, they're really good kids at heart.

TOMMY: (entering the room loudly) Mommy, you said if I cleaned up real good I could go to the carnival with Billy.

MRS. SMITH: Good grief, Tommy! Well, OK, but be good!

TOMMY: Oh, goody!

PASTOR JONES: Well, it's been good to see you again. Have a good day.

MRS. SMITH: You too . . . good-bye.

Discuss the skit using these questions:

• What did "good" mean to Pastor Jones? Mrs. Smith? Tommy?

• When does the word "good" lose its meaning? How does this affect the way we think about God's goodness?

World Records ■ Obtain a copy of *The Guinness Book of World Records* and choose a number of records

relating to size. Hold a brief quiz to see who can come closest in guessing the correct weight, height, length, size, etc. Afterward, comment briefly on how people seem obsessed with who is the "greatest." Point out that this record book is evidence that people want to be recognized for something, no matter how silly or irrelevant. Say something like: *Our ideas of greatness, however, pale when compared to the greatness of God. Sometimes we even confuse the two uses of the word. We say, "God is great, God is good, and we thank Him for our food," but do we really understand what we mean by "great"?*

What do you think of the statement, "All of God is everywhere, all the time"? Is it true? How does it make you feel? Why?

Read Jeremiah 23:23-24 and say: *The fact is, we cannot hide from God. This will be very threatening to those who want to escape Him and His judgment, but it is very comforting for those who feel lonely or forgotten.*

DISCUSSIONS AND WRAP-UPS

Chance and Choice ■ Set up this discussion by first playing games of chance (such as flipping a coin) and choice (such as tic-tac-toe). Then point out the differences between the two types of games and ask:

• What "chance" games have you entered recently? (Bingo, sweepstakes, raffles, etc.) What were your chances of winning the big prize?

• Some people believe the world came together by chance. How do you feel about that? Do you think it's possible? Why or why not? What would be the odds?

• How does this view of the world differ from one based on a strong belief in God? (Those who believe in God believe that He created the world by design.)

• What difference does belief in God make in the world? (It can mean that we see purpose instead of chaos.)

• How does our choice fit into all this? (We can choose whether or not to believe that God created the world, and act according to our beliefs.)

Depth ■ Challenge students to change their perspective, taking their eyes off the minutiae of their lives and looking at the power of God. Explain that to understand and experience the depth of God's love, they should remember DEPTH:

D — Desire/Depend (want to be close to God)

E — Experience (allow God to be involved in their

lives)

P — Practice (trust God when they don't feel as though He loves them)

T — Time (give the relationship with God time to develop)

H — Hope (know that God will provide ways for you to discover His love)

Holiness ■ Read two definitions of "holiness," one from a dictionary and one from a Bible dictionary. Explain how holiness is the most basic and necessary of God's attributes. If God is not holy, He is not God. God must be holy to be sovereign and to be able to help us in our sinful condition. He must be holy to have perfect justice, love, mercy, grace, power, knowledge, and righteousness. Then ask what it means when the Bible says that we must be holy because God is holy (Leviticus 19:2). Next, have everyone turn to Jeremiah 9:23-24 and read it aloud. Explain that true "holiness" is "cosmic," not "cosmetic." It can't be put on or acted. But the "holier" we truly become, the more we will be able to reflect God's other attributes. In other words, we will be able to act in love and to be truthful. Jeremiah 9:23-24 states, "Let not the wise man boast of his wisdom or the strong man boast of his strength or the rich man boast of his riches, but let him who boasts boast about this: that he understands and knows Me, that I am the Lord, who exercises kindness, justice and righteousness on earth, for in these I delight" (Jeremiah 9:24).

Justice is *knowing right*; righteousness is *doing right*; kindness is doing it the *right way*. And the key to all of this is "that he understands Me and knows Me." In other words, to live as God wants us to live, we should get to know Him better and better. (See 2 Peter 1:3.)

Love ■ Ask:

• What are signs of true love?

• How do you know that you're in love?

• How will you know that "this is the one"?

• In what ways is human love different from God's love?

• In what ways is it similar?

Next, hand out sheets of paper and have everyone finish the following sentences:

• I know my friend likes me because . . .

• I know my parents love me because . . .

• I know that God loves me because . . .

Names ■ Use this outline as material for a discussion and wrap-up.

1. Names set us apart from others and are a way to get more personal than using just a number or a pronoun. They get us beneath the surface.

2. Names offer access to a personality. That is, they provide permission to be personal.

3. Your name is precious to you. (You listen for it, look for it in the newspaper, etc.) When used, your name gets your attention. (Those who remember names well are usually popular.)

4. Names express your identity. They are common enough to lump you with your culture and distinctive enough to set you apart.

5. To be on a "first name basis" implies unusual friendship.

6. God uses names and titles to describe and identify Himself to us. This means that He is personal and that He wants to relate to us personally. Each specific name of God gives us a glimpse into His character and personality.

7. Jesus is the most personal name of God. As the God/man, Jesus is the perfect expression of the Father. As we look at Jesus, we can see what God is like (John 14:9).

8. God wants us to call Him "Father." This has tremendous personal implications.

Perspective Illustrations ■

1. Jesus was tempted on a mountain top. He was offered all the kingdoms of the world—all He could see as He looked *down*. This was a temptation of perspective. When we look *down* from a mountain, we can feel powerful and in control, especially if all that we see were offered to us. But Jesus also looked *up* and remembered who He was and who His Father was. The change in perspective made all the difference.

2. There is a championship basketball game. It's in the last two seconds, the score is tied, and the star player on one team is about to shoot an uncontested three-foot basket that will win the game. Everyone knows that the team will win and that this player will be the hero, carried off the floor on the shoulders of his teammates. However, unknown to the screaming fans or to the players, a jet pilot has just ejected from his plane, and the plane is heading toward the arena where it will crash. The final two seconds of that game will not even be played. This illustrates how our limited perspective can prevent us from seeing the truth and mislead us about our futures.

3. Discuss the differences in perspective among a baby, a small child, a teenager, an adult, and a

grandparent concerning the relative size of buildings and people and the meaning of time.

Sketch ■ Lead the following discussion.

• We're all familiar with how a police sketch works. (Police take all the descriptive characteristics of a person and put together a "composite" picture.) From what we know about God through His names, what kind of "police sketch" or composite picture do we get of Him? (He is holy, all-powerful, loving, just, etc.)

• Why do you think various names of God are used in the Bible? (They give us a more complete, understandable picture of God.)

• Which name of God means the most to you and why? (Be prepared to share from your personal life.)

• How does Christ display these characteristics? (See Colossians 2:9.)

Summary ■ This summary can lead into a group discussion.

Whenever we discuss or even think about any one of God's attributes, we come to a paradox or mystery. Because we are finite and God is infinite, we cannot fully understand Him. All we can do is describe God in human language, in our terms. We talk about God seeing us, but He does not have eyes. We say that God hears our prayers, but He does not have physical ears. God has a plan for our futures, but to Him, everything is now. These are "anthropomorphisms," describing God in the form of a human being or in human terms. This doesn't seem right, but it's unavoidable–and it's important that we understand what we are doing. God is not a "big man upstairs"; God has revealed Himself through nature (general revelation), through the Bible (special revelation), and through His Son, Jesus (perfect revelation). In reality, if we want to know what God is like, we can look at Jesus–He is God "in focus." By the way, it is also supposed to be the case that if people want to know what Jesus is like, they can look at Christians (the "body of Christ" on earth). How do we measure up? Can people see Jesus in us (and, therefore, God's truth, goodness, and love)?

BIBLE STUDIES

All Things for Good ■ Read Romans 8:28-29 aloud. Then ask:

• What does "all things" mean? (Everything, both good and bad.)

• What does "work together" mean? How about "for good"? (God uses events in harmony for the ultimate good of the believer.)

• What conditions are attached to this promise? (You must love God and be willing to submit to His will for your life.)

• When has this verse helped you? (Be ready to give an example from your own life.)

Blind Man ■ Read the story of the blind man in John 9. Then ask:

• How did the disciples "see" the blind man? (as a sinner or the victim of sin) The neighbors? (as a beggar) The Pharisees? (as a challenge to their authority–a disciple of Christ) Jesus? (as a man who needed healing, and as an opportunity to show God at work)

• How do you think the blind man felt as a beggar? (alone, outcast, needy) When Jesus put mud on his eyes? (hopeful, doubtful, etc.) When he was healed? (grateful, amazed) When he was questioned? (defensive, protective of Jesus)

• What does the blind man's reply in verse 25 reveal? (He is presenting the facts truthfully, though he isn't sure what to make of them.)

• In what ways are we blind? How can Jesus heal our sight? (We can be blind to what God is doing in our lives, or blind to what He wants us to do. When He saves us, Jesus shows us the reality of our sins, then forgives us for those sins.)

Getting Close ■ Explain that becoming close to God begins with an attitude of humility (see James 4:10). This means recognizing that God is in charge, not us, and being willing to do whatever he says. With this attitude, then, there are three steps to take to move close:

1. *Submit to God* (James 4:7) This means giving Him control over every aspect of our lives.

2. *Resist the devil* (James 4:7) This means saying no to what Satan wants, actively rejecting him.

3. *Turn away from our sins or "repent"* (James 4:8) This means admitting our sins, asking for forgiveness, and determining to change our ways.

4. *Take our relationship with God seriously* (James 4:9) This means not taking God for granted and submitting to His Lordship daily.

God As a Friend ■ Give kids the following verses to read aloud: Genesis 5:21-24; 6:9; Exodus 33:11; John 15:13-15; Acts 13:23; Romans 5:10; James 2:23. Ask what all the people mentioned in these verses have in common (close friendship with God). Discuss why it would be good to have such a relationship.

God As Our Coach ■ Look up the following

passages together. After each one, ask how this characteristic of God fits into the concept of Him as a coach. Possible answers are in parentheses for your reference.

1. 1 Corinthians 1:25 (He is strong and wise.)
2. Romans 8:31-33 (He gives His all to us, so we can win the race.)
3. Matthew 6:28-33 (He gives us what we need, and rewards us.)
4. Mark 10:44-45 (He serves the members of His "team.")
5. 1 John 4:8 (He loves us, as a coach should care about team members.)

God's Friends ■ Discuss Romans 5:1-11, probing what it really means to have peace with God and to be reconciled with Him. Be sure to emphasize what changes they should make in their lives in light of this passage.

God's Names ■ Hand out the following true/false quiz about the names or "nicknames" of God in the Bible. After allowing time for group members to write T or F by each name, have them look up the answers using the references listed. Answers are given in parentheses.

GOD'S NAMES

The Bible uses these names or nicknames for God: T (true) or F (false)

___ "Daddy" (T—"Abba" means Daddy) Romans 8:14-15
___ "Father" (T) Matthew 6:9
___ "roaring lion" (F) 1 Peter 5:8
___ "Jehovah" (T—KJV) Exodus 6:2-3
___ "consuming fire" (T) Hebrews 12:29
___ "love" (T) 1 John 4:8
___ "Father of lights" or "Creator of light" (T) James 1:17
___ "Holy One" (T) Psalm 16:10
___ "I AM" (T) Exodus 3:14
___ "Ruler of the kingdom of the air" (F) Ephesians 2:2
___ "Lord of lords" (T) Revelation 17:14
___ "King of kings" (T) 1 Timothy 6:15
___ "Most high" (T) Numbers 24:16
___ "Prince of this world" (F) John 14:30
___ "angel" (F) 2 Peter 2:4
___ "man" (F) Numbers 23:19

God's Perspective ■ Use these thoughts and verses as the basis for a Bible study.

The ability to see life from a "God's-eye" point of view can be life-changing. So often we wallow in self-pity and even despair because we cannot imagine an escape from our problems. At times we feel so insignificant and alone, wondering how we can possibly fit into God's plan. But God's perspective is total, complete, deep. He sees:

1. Our hidden and blind selves. God knows us intimately–our fears, shortcomings, talents, and abilities (Psalm 139). He wants the very best for us and is weaving our experiences toward that end (Romans 8:28-29).

2. Our place in His plan. God wants to use us and to guide us into His way (Proverbs 3:5-6; Psalm 37:23-24).

3. Our past, present, and future. God forgives and forgets and will turn even our mistakes and struggles into good (1 John 1:9). He knows the direction of history and the reality of His ultimate triumph (Revelation 19:1-10). He is the eternal now.

4. The Truth. God sees through Satan's lies, and He shows us what is right (2 Timothy 3:16; John 8:44-47).

5. Our true worth. God created us in His image and pronounced us "good" (Genesis 1:26-31). He gives us high privilege and responsibility (Psalm 8:4-8). To understand and feel the reality of God's perspective frees us to live unafraid, forgiven, and fulfilled.

Job ■ Summarize Job's story. Then ask:
• How do you think Job felt about God's "plan for his life"? (He was no doubt confused, frustrated, and bitter. See chapter 10.)
• What kinds of friends did Job have? (They were "miserable comforters," trying to make Job accept the blame for his troubles.)
• (Read highlights of God's answer in chapters 38–41) What is the main point that God is making to Job? (God is all-knowing and all-powerful. It is not for man to question Him.)
• When have you felt like Job? How does God's answer to Job help you?

Love Lines ■ Hold an old fashioned Bible drill where each verse focuses on God's love. Verses to use could include: John 3:16; Matthew 10:29-31; Jeremiah 31:3; Romans 8:35-39; Proverbs 8:17; Luke 15:3-7; Ephesians 3:17-19; Hosea 14:4; Hebrews 12:5-6; 1 John 4:9; and others. Afterwards, read and discuss each passage.

Peter ■ Read the incident of Peter's walk on the water in Matthew 14:22-33. Then ask about Peter's faith. Why was he able to walk, and why did he sink?

Use an illustration from your own life, or the life of someone you know. Talk about the importance of keeping our eyes on Christ when we go through deep waters.

Power and Truth ■ Have someone read aloud selected verses from Job 38, and have someone else read aloud John 1:1-14. Then ask:

• What do these verses tell us about God's power?

• How should human beings respond to this truth?

Psalm 139 ■ Have everyone turn to Psalm 139 and either read it together aloud or have it read by selected students. Afterward, say something like: *This chapter sums up what we have been discovering about God during this meeting. God is all-powerful. He created everything and can do anything. He is everywhere; it is impossible to hide or to be lost from God. He is all-knowing; He knows everything about us, past, present, and future.*

All these attributes of God will be bad news to those who have disobeyed Him, rebelled against Him, or are running away from Him. They know that there is no place to hide and that God's judgment is certain. But to those who know and love God, these attributes are good news. They know that God wants to use His power to help them; He will be with them in every circumstance; and He accepts and loves them as they are. Where do you stand? Are these truths good or bad news?

Thomas ■ Read aloud the confrontation of Thomas by Jesus in John 20:24-29. Ask why Thomas doubted and what changed his doubting to belief. (His perspective changed when he saw and felt the nail holes in Jesus' hands.) What does verse 29 mean to us?

What's the Difference? ■ Hand out sheets with the following verses on them. The students should look up the verses and write what difference these truths should make in the world and in their lives. The answers for column two are in parentheses.

Verses	Difference in the World	Difference in My Life
1. Genesis 1:1	(Purpose for world)	_____
2. Genesis 1:26-31	(Value of human life)	_____
3. Job 38:4-11	(Purpose in world)	_____
4. Psalm 19:1-6	(Design in nature)	_____
5. Matthew 5:1-11	(Morality)	_____
6. John 1:1-5	(Jesus—God in the flesh)	_____
7. Romans 8:28	(Purpose)	_____
8. Romans 8:38-39	(God's infinite love)	_____
9. Philippians 1:21	(Reason to live)	_____
10. Philippians 2:5-11	(Incarnation)	_____
11. Hebrews 2:5-8	(Value of life)	_____

Have group members report what they wrote in both columns. Ask how their lives measure up. Challenge them to be committed to demonstrating to others their deep belief in God. For instance, do they value life? Do they love others? Do they have a purpose and meaning in their lives? Do they see God in His creation?

4
FAMILY

CROWD-BREAKERS

All Torn Up ■ Divide into teams and give each team a stack of newspaper advertising inserts or catalogs and a roll of cellophane tape. On the wall in front of each team, tape a piece of white poster board. Explain that when you call out a word, they should tear out the letters for that word and hand to their team's leader who should tape them to the team's poster board. The first team to tape the letters on the board wins that round. Here are some words to call out: patience, listen, friendship, pray, responsibility, loyalty, lessons, together. This game can illustrate how many families are torn up (just like the papers); but out of the mess can come lessons to be learned.

Baby-sitters Qualifying Exam ■ Divide the group into teams of about 12 members each and have them line up in parallel columns. (This will be a relay.) Have each team number off. Explain that the even-numbered people will be the "baby-sitters" and the odd-numbered ones will be the "babies." Before-hand, prepare bags of the necessary props, one bag per team, and cards of instructions. Prepare duplicate sets of instructions for the teams. They should know that it doesn't matter in what order they perform the tasks except that #6 must be last. At your signal, the first two contestants from each team should run to the front, choose their instruction cards, find their props, and complete their tasks as quickly as possible. The first team to complete all the assigned tasks wins.

Tasks	Props
1. Put diaper on baby.	(Baby lies on floor) sheet and safety pins
2. Feed baby his/her bottle.	(Baby sits on sitter's lap.) baby bottle filled with liquid
3. Burp baby.	(Baby leans across sitter's shoulder and is patted on the back until he/she burps.)
4. Feed baby food.	baby food and plastic spoon
5. Help baby draw a picture of a house and family.	(Must use five colors. Sitter hands paper and crayons as asked.)
6. Sitter carries baby to bed	(at designated spot in the room.)

Blocks ■ Choose teams and have each team choose a representative to compete in a spelling contest using children's alphabet blocks. Bring the contestants to the front of the room and give each one a pile of blocks (preferably on a spot on a long table so that the audience can see). Call out a word. The first person to spell the word with the blocks (so that it can be read by the audience) wins that round. Continue through eight or nine rounds using different contestants for each round. Possible words to spell could include: pabulum, diaper, mother, father, playing, burp, talking, games, family, laughs, broken, spank, tantrum.

Children's Songs ■ Play "Name That Tune" or "Draw the Song" using children's songs. ("Draw the Song" is like "Pictionary" with each contestant drawing a picture to represent the song title.) Possible songs could include: "The Farmer in the Dell,"

"London Bridge Is Falling Down," "Old King Cole," "Three Blind Mice," "Row, Row, Row Your Boat," "A Tisket, A Tasket," "Frere Jacques," "Mary Had a Little Lamb," and others.

Clean-up Challenge ■ This game involves two teams. Have each team choose two participants and then send one of these two to the front of the room. Mark off a section of the room as the "bedroom" and assign team A's representative to be the "kid" and team B's to be the "parent." Then give the "kid" a box of belongings and explain that he or she has one minute to mess up the room as thoroughly as possible with the contents of the box. (The box should contain clothing, books, school papers, tissue paper, hair care products, stuffed animals, and other typical adolescent items.) After the minute, it's the "parent's" turn to pick up the "room" as quickly as possible. The clothes must be folded, the papers put back in the notebook, etc., and everything must be packed neatly back into the box. Time him or her. Announce the "parent's" time. Then repeat the process with the next two representatives, only this time team A's person must be the "parent" and team B's the "kid." Have as many rounds as needed. The lowest total time wins.

Commuter Special ■ For this game you will need:
• two pairs of very large trousers
• two Big Wheel bikes
• two sets of empty boxes (five to seven boxes per set in a variety of sizes)

This is a competitive relay, so divide into teams. This can be done by the first letters of their fathers' first names (A to L on one team; M to Z on the other). But make sure that teams are of equal size. You will probably need a lot of room—a gymnasium, basement, or outdoors will be fine. If you don't have the space, alter the Big Wheel segment.

Line up the teams. At your signal, the first person on each team must put on the pants and ride the Big Wheel to the "office" on a designated route that should include at least one turn. Here he or she must put all the boxes in one vertical stack and then return via the Big Wheel to the next person on the team who must repeat the procedure, and so on until the entire team has "commuted to the office and back." (Between people, have an assistant knock down the boxes.) The first team to finish wins.

Creative Construction ■ Pass out sheets of construction paper and give everyone the assignment of tearing out the likeness of a nursery rhyme or children's story character (using only their fingers, of course). Possible pictures could include: three pigs,

big bad wolf, Little Miss Muffet, Humpty Dumpty on the wall, cow jumping over the moon, etc. Allow three or four minutes and then have them display and explain their creations.

Dandy Daddy ■ Props needed: balloons, eyebrow pencil, assorted wigs, hats, ties, and other "father-type" garb.

Divide your crowd into small groups of two to four in each and give each group a card with a specific characteristic written on it. Their task is to think about and record the ideal description for their particular characteristic (for a father). Characteristics could include:
• hair (color, amount on top, length, style)
• facial hair
• body build (height, weight, muscles, etc.)
• hobbies
• occupation (type of work, salary, and hours)
• personality (outgoing? serious or funny? friendly?)
• talents (musical? athletic? artistic? handy?)
• style of disciplining the children
• love and affection
• spirituality

Collect the cards and choose a boy to be the model (preferably someone outgoing, with a quick wit) or you could be the model. Next, read the characteristics, one card at a time, and dress the person accordingly. (Use a wig if necessary or style the hair; add facial hair with an eyebrow pencil; add muscles with balloons, give him a golf club or something similar to represent his hobby; have him talk about his occupation, tell a joke if he's supposed to have a good sense of humor, and sing if he's musical, etc.)

Next, set up a couple of scenes with other students acting as the children. These could demonstrate his love, spirituality, discipline, etc. Ask: Which of these ideal characteristics does your father possess? Do you know any perfect dads? Why do we expect our fathers to be perfect? How would your earthly father affect your thinking about your heavenly Father?

Diaper Race ■ Bring a few dolls dressed in diapers and other clothes. Choose a number of boys to compete in a diaper changing contest, explaining that the first person to change the diaper and re-dress the "baby" wins. Provide "diapers" (square pieces of cloth) and pins. Note: If you're short of dolls, use one doll and race against the clock.

Family Picture ■ Well before your meeting, tell youth group members to bring pictures of their parents that they don't mind cutting up. In these pictures, the faces should be clear. Ahead of time, set up a part of the meeting room (or a separate room if you are meeting in a home) as the photographer's studio. Bring an old style suit, dress, and other clothes for the costumes and a doll wrapped in a blanket and another one in a stroller. Set up an instant camera on a tripod. In another part of the room or house, set up a table with scissors and glue. The idea is for young people to switch places with their parents in their family pictures. The boy or girl (or both if they are brother and sister) should dress in the clothes and strike a serious pose holding the little "bundles." Next, they should take the picture to the table and glue their parents' faces in place of the dolls' heads. This will take a lot of preparation, but it will be worth it. Later, display the pictures on a church bulletin board.

Family Tree ■ Hand out the following quiz or read it aloud.

Who is:

1. your mother's brother?	(uncle)
2. your sister's son?	(nephew)
3. your brother's brother?	(brother or self)
4. your father's mother's father?	(great grandfather)
5. your father's sister's daughter?	(first cousin)
6. your grandfather's sister?	(great aunt)
7. your aunt's granddaughter?	(first cousin, once removed)
8. your uncle's great-grandson?	(first cousin, twice removed)
9. your wife's (an only child) brother-in-law's, grandfather's son?	(father)

Famous Families ■ Hand out this quiz. The object is to match the last name with the first name of members of these famous families. The correct answers are in parentheses.

FAMOUS FAMILIES

_____ Flintstone (n)	a. Ozzie
_____ Clinton (c)	b. Cliff
_____ Corleone (e)	c. Hillary
_____ Taylor (m)	d. Jed
_____ Mountbatten (h)	e. "Don"
_____ Addams (i)	f. Tito
_____ Clampett (d)	g. Donny
_____ Cleaver (o)	h. Andrew
_____ Huxtable (b)	i. "Thing"
_____ Nelson (a)	j. Coretta
_____ Jackson (f)	k. Kara
_____ Osmond (g)	l. Maria
_____ Carter (p)	m. Tim
_____ King (j)	n. Pebbles
_____ Van Trapp (l)	o. Wally
_____ Veerman (k)	p. Miss Lillian

Famous Fathers and Marvelous Mothers ■ If possible, use pictures of the following parents. Otherwise, print as a fill-in-the-blank quiz, or mix up the names in each column and use as a matching quiz. The object is to match the parent with his or her child. Add more contemporary examples and some from your group.

Parent	Child
Jimmy Carter	Amy
Miss Lillian	Jimmy Carter
Ronald Reagan	Ron, Jr.
Fred Flintstone	Pebbles
Ryan O'Neal	Tatum
You	daughter/son
Mary	Jesus
Henry Fonda	Jane
Heathcliff Huxtable	Rudy
Pat Boone	Debbie
Abraham	Ishmael
Bill Clinton	Chelsea

Finger Painting ■ This will require advance preparation and should be staged in a "safe" part of the building. Bring a set of finger paints and papers and let your group create their masterpieces. This can be somewhat serious (pictures or symbols of Christian themes, etc.) or just fun. Do it as an individual or team activity. Let the paintings dry and display them after the meeting.

He Ain't My Brother, He's Just Heavy ■ This is a team relay, and the object is for each person to be carried from the team's starting point to the other end of the room. (Be careful of hurting the feelings of an overweight person.) The first person in each team must carry (with no feet touching the ground) the second person to the finish line. Then the person just carried must return and carry the next person who, in turn, returns and carries the next one, and so on. The team to move everyone first wins. When a person who is being carried slips and touches the ground before the line, he or she and the carrier must begin again.

Obviously it would help for the teams to have a line-up strategy.

Key Words ■ Ask for the specific parts of speech written in parentheses in each line and fill in their answers. Tell the group to be creative. Then read their edited clichés about the family. Afterwards, note how important those key words were to the meaning of the phrases. In the same way, our words can make a difference in our homes. Here are some lines to use:

• Show me the _____ (noun) to go home.

• Take me _____ (noun), _____ (adjective) roads.

• Home is where the _____ (body part) is.

• _____ (Verb) your _____ (body part) toward home.

• Home _____ (adjective) home.

• A _____ (place) away from home.

• There's no _____ (noun) like home.

Lean on Me ■ This can be done as a competition between teams or as a noncompetitive group event. Choose a person to be the "leanee" and place him or her in the center of the room. One at a time the other group members should come up and lean on him or her. "Leaning" means standing at such an angle that if he or she were to leave, the person leaning would fall down. The object is to see how many people can lean at one time; hopefully, everyone in the group. If you do this as a competitive game, the first team to lean everyone wins. (Teams should have at least 10 members.) Note: this game can illustrate how we lean on our parents for support.

Perfect Parents ■ Choose a boy and a girl to participate. Tell them and the audience that they are to play the roles of perfect parents. Their relationship is so close and their minds so united that they know what the other person is thinking and can anticipate his or her answers. To prove this they will be fielding questions from the audience. Have them stand side-by-side, facing the crowd. As each question is asked, they should answer by alternating their words.

Sample question: "Why did you decide to have children?"

Answer: M: "Well"
            F: "we"
            M: "just"
            F: "thought"
            M: "it"
            F: "would"
            M: "be"
            F: "a"
            M: "weird"
            F: "experience."

There's no way to predict what their answers will be, but the process and the results will be unusual. As a variation, expand them to "the perfect family" by adding a son and a daughter. All four of them would then have to respond, one word at a time.

Sib-links ■ Use the following as a quiz—either hand it out and have everyone compete, or divide into teams and have kids jump to their feet when they know the celebrity's brother or sister. The goal is to name the brother or sister of each of the following celebrities. The correct answers are in parentheses.

• Donny Osmond's sister (Marie)

• Michael Jackson's sister (Janet)

• Michael Jordan's brother (Larry)

• Jimmy Carter's brother (Billy)

• Barbara Mandrell's sister (Louise, Erline)

• Warren Beatty's sister (Shirley MacLaine)

• Orville Wright's brother (Wilbur)

• Rudy Huxtable's brother (Theo)

• Jerry VanDyke's brother (Dick)

• John Belushi's brother (Jim)

• Zsa Zsa Gabor's sister (Eva)

• Bart Simpson's sister (Lisa, Maggie)

• Apostle John's brother (James)

• Cain's brother (Abel)

• Esau's brother (Jacob)

• Jesus' half-brother (James, Jude)

Top Pops ■ This is a fill-in-the-blank or a matching quiz. Reprint it without the answers (in parentheses). Add current examples where appropriate.

FAMOUS FATHERS

Actor	TV Show
1. Danny Thomas	(Make Room for Daddy)
2. Ozzie Nelson	(Ozzie and Harriet)
3. Robert Young	(Father Knows Best)
4. John Goodman	(Roseanne)
5. John Forsythe	(Dynasty)
6. Carroll O'Connor	(All in the Family)
7. Redd Foxx	(Sanford and Son)
8. Bill Cosby	(The Cosby Show)
9. Michael Gross	(Family Ties)

10. Tim Allen   (Home Improvement)

Comic Strip Dads   *Names*
   1. Blondie's husband   (Dagwood)
   2. Pebbles' daddy   (Fred Flintstone)
   3. Annie's daddy   (Oliver Warbucks)
   4. Winnie Winkle's husband (Bill Wright)
   5. Hamlet's father   (Hagar the Horrible)
   6. Lois' husband   (Hi)

Father's Famous Phrases
   1. This (hurts) me more than it (hurts) you.
   2. When I was (your age) . . .
   3. I'll give you (something) to (cry) about!
   4. If I've told you (once), I've told you (1,000 times) . . .
   5. I'm going to (count) to (10) . . .

Child   *Father*
   1. Luke Skywalker   (Darth Vader)
   2. Amy   (Jimmy Carter)
   3. John John   (John F. Kennedy)
   4. Julie Eisenhower   (Richard M. Nixon)
   5. Jeff Bridges   (Lloyd Bridges)
   6. Michael Douglas   (Kirk Douglas)
   7. Debbie Boone   (Pat Boone)
   8. Emilio Estevez   (Martin Sheen)
   9. Superman   (Jor-el)
  10. Smurfette   (Papa Smurf)
  11. Prince Charles   (Philip)
  12. Solomon   (David)
  13. Ken Griffey, Jr.   (Ken Griffey)
  14. Dana and Kara   (Dave Veerman)

Walk a Mile in Their Shoes ■ Divide into two teams with each team having an equal number of members. Organize the teams along one wall with a bit of distance between them. Next, have everyone remove their shoes and place them in a pile next to their team. Then, have the teams change places, leaving their piles of shoes behind (team A should be with team B's shoes and vice versa). These may be put into large boxes. Explain that at your signal, the first person on each team should grab any two shoes in the pile, put them on (as much as possible) and then "run" to the other team where he or she should leave the shoes behind and then run back to his or her own team. The next person follows suit and so on until all the shoes are transferred. When shoes are brought to a team, they should be put aside by their owners. No one can take two shoes out of the pile or box until the previous team member returns. The first team to deliver all the shoes, wins. (Note: this is an illustration of how it might be helpful to "walk in our parents' shoes"—to see life from their perspectives.)

DISCUSSION STARTERS

Action ■ The week before you do this, hand out stamped envelopes, paper, and pens. Then have each person write a letter to his or her parents, thanking them for specific attitudes, actions, and activities that they appreciate. At your next meeting you can discuss how their parents responded.

Assignment ■ Tell your students that during the next two weeks each person is to make an appointment with Mom and another one with Dad. They should ask their parents the following questions:

Mom:

a. What do you enjoy about being a mother?

b. What is the most frustrating area of your life?

c. Before you and Dad were married, I'm sure you had an idea of what life would be like. What have been your greatest surprises?

d. What has been the happiest moment of your life so far?

e. How can I best demonstrate my love for you?

Dad:

a. What kinds of pressures do you feel as a father?

b. What goals that you set as a young man for yourself, family, and career have you achieved?

c. What are your dreams and goals for me?

d. What advice would you give someone who is going to become a father?

e. How can I demonstrate my love for you?

After two weeks, discuss this experience in your group.

The Card ■ Bring out pieces of cardboard, magazines, scissors, tape, markers, crayons, etc. Explain that each person should make a Mother's Day and/or a Father's Day card for their parent(s). They may cut out pictures, write poems, use humor, be serious, or whatever they want to express their feelings of love and appreciation. If possible, the pictures and written expressions should also focus on good times they've had together. Explain that they can give these cards right away or wait until the official day.

Classified ■ Hand out pieces of paper and pens. Ask group members to imagine that their parents are placing a want ad for a teenager in the local paper. Their job is to write that ad. Have a number of the ads read aloud. Discuss the ads.

Clichés ■ Ask for the typical clichés used in homes by Mom, Dad, and the children. List them on a chalkboard or poster board. Possible answers could include:

• When I was your age . . .

• This is going to hurt me more than it will hurt you!

• Everybody's doing it.

• _____'s parents let her.

• I don't love you anymore!

Discuss why these phrases are used and what they really mean.

Create a Family ■ Before the meeting, prepare slips of paper with specific family members written on them. Make sure to have enough slips so that everyone can participate. Just under two thirds of these slips should be children, and most of the rest should be parents. Indicate sex, ages, and any other characteristics you wish. For a group of 30, 19 could be children, ranging in age from 3–17 years old; 9 could be parents, ranging in age from 30–50; 2 could be grandparents.

Have everyone get into groups of 3–5 (the groups do not have to be the same size). Then have each person draw a slip of paper. The only stipulations are that each group (family) must have at least one adult and no more than two parents. And if a family gets two parents, one must be male and the other female. Obviously the combinations could range anywhere from 4 young children and 1 grandparent, to 1 child and his or her 2 original parents.

Have the families sit in a circle on the floor and hold a family meeting to discuss chores and allowances.

After a few minutes, have everyone put their slips of paper back in the box, form new groups, and draw new slips. Have these families sit and have a family meeting to discuss family rules and discipline.

Afterward, discuss their experience—how the make-up of the families mirrored real life, how they decided who was in charge, how they got into their roles, how they acted similar or different from how they would really act, and how they would design a family if they were in charge.

Declaration of Independence ■ Distribute pieces of paper and pens or pencils to the group. Tell them to write their own declarations of independence from home. They should include a preamble (their reasons), a time-table, the type of independence they desire, and a list of the "rights and privileges." Afterward, have a few of the declarations read aloud. Then discuss them and the process of writing them.

Evidence ■ Have everyone be seated and look through their possessions for evidence of independence from or dependence on their parents. One at a time they should point to the object or display it and explain its relevance. Here are some examples:

• Shoes—"My mom bought these for me." (dependence)

• Money—"I earned this on my job. It's mine to spend as I wish." (independence)

• Family picture "I need my family's love." (dependence)

• Car keys—"In a few minutes, I can be miles away from home." (independence)

• Braces—"My dad pays for these." (dependence)

• Report card—"School is preparing me to be on my own." (independence)

Family Feud ■ Divide into pairs and label one person in each pair person A and the other one person B. Have B explain his or her last fight (argument) with parents at home. Next, have each pair role play that incident with A playing the parent. Give them a few minutes and then repeat the process with A's last fight. Afterward ask:

• What were the "fights" about?

• What did the pretend parent say that was similar to how your mom or dad responded?

• What could you do to resolve those conflicts?

Family-ness ■ Distribute 8 1/2 X 11 sheets of paper and pens or pencils. Have everyone divide the papers into three columns. The first column should be about 2 inches wide and the middle one 1/2 to 1 inch. The third column will take the rest of the paper.

Discuss as a group the advantages of being part of a loving family. Everyone should list these advantages in the first column (possible answers: support, care, love, acceptance, opportunities to learn, place to let off steam and show feelings, place to be yourself, etc.). Next, have them label the center column "My Family" and check which of the advantages they see in their families. Then have them label the third column,

"What I Can Do." In the spaces after the advantages that they *did not* check, they should take a few minutes to write specific actions that they can take to improve the situations. Afterward, discuss the experience and challenge students to begin to make those advantages a reality in their families.

Follow-up ■ Plan a Parent Appreciation Night where students bring their parents to your meeting. The program could include skits where children and parents reverse roles, crazy crowd-breakers, and a presentation of a special "care package" to each set of parents. This package could include "love coupons," the doctored photo (see Family Picture), and a gift.

How Much Do You Know? ■ The purpose of this quiz is to see how much your young people know about their parents. Have them write the answers to these questions:

1. When is your dad's birthday?

2. When is your parents' wedding anniversary?

3. What is your mom's favorite food?

4. When your parents were your age, what were their goals for their lives?

5. How old is your mom? Your dad? What are some of the pressures they feel because they are that age?

6. What's the biggest problem facing your folks?

7. How do your parents feel about you?

(Add a couple more questions appropriate for your group.)

Afterward, discuss how they felt about the questions and how well they think they know their parents. Don't discuss their answers to the quiz.

Instant Family ■ Divide the crowd into groups of three, making sure that each group has at least one guy and one girl. Next, have each group designate one person as the mother, one as the father, and one as the son or daughter. Set up these situations, one at a time, that the groups should role play.

a. Last night the son or daughter came home an hour late. It's breakfast, and the subject is being discussed.

b. The three of you are discussing the son or daughter's future. The parents see college, but the child wants to get a job.

c. The subject of dating has come up. The parents have heard about the new morality and peer pressure and are worried about their son or daughter's steady dating.

d. The son or daughter has just expressed doubts about God. The parents react.

Use as many situations as you wish, perhaps forming new groups of three for each one.

Interview ■ Bring a parent or two to the meeting. If possible, they should be strangers to your group (certainly not parents of anyone present). Ask them about what it means to be a parent: their biggest fears, most frustrating moments, goals when they were in high school, what they would do differently if they could start adulthood over, their biggest surprises about life, and so on.

Mamas and Papas ■ The object of this starter is to see parents as people with feelings, just like us, and to try to see life from their points of view. Ask the group:

1. How did your father feel when . . .

   a. he got married?

   b. he found out your mom was pregnant for the first time?

   c. you crawled up into his lap and said, "I love you, Daddy"?

   d. he turned forty?

2. How did your mother feel when . . .

   a. you were born?

   b. she had to punish you for breaking something?

   c. she had a loud fight with your father?

   d. she saw your last report card?

3. When was your father really happy? Your mom?

4. How do you think you will feel in these situations?

Media ■ Use a chalkboard or a piece of poster board and record the answers so all can see. Ask group members to think of television shows and movies that center around families. Some of their answers may include: "Father Knows Best," "Growing Pains," "Rosanne," "Full House," "Family Ties," "The Bill Cosby Show," "Kramer vs. Kramer," "A River Runs through It," "Dennis the Menace," "Ordinary People," "The Color Purple," "Back to the Future," "Home Improvement," etc.

After compiling a fairly long list, go back and briefly discuss each one asking these questions and others:

• How is the family depicted? Is it a realistic picture?

• How are the parents pictured?

• Which one is most like your home? Why?

Parent Case Studies ■ Distribute sheets of paper with the following case studies printed on them. Read and discuss them one at a time.

Mary is 38 years old and lives with her two daughters in a two bedroom apartment (where it's a little crowded). The divorce was five years ago, but the pain is still fresh in her mind. It hasn't been easy, raising a family while holding a full-time job. Both girls are now in high school (a junior and a freshman), and that has brought new problems. They want more freedom and money for involvement in school activities. In addition, Mary is very aware of the temptations they face and of her limitations for control and discipline. She knows that when her youngest graduates in a few short years, she will be alone.

• How would you feel?

• What would you do?

Frank has worked hard to become executive vice-president of the company. It took long hours, much travel, and quite a few moves around the country, but now he feels secure in his position and salary. Frank knows that his career has taken its toll on his family, but after all, they are why he has worked so hard. He has wanted to provide for them as he should. Recently, however, Frank has had the feeling that he is living with strangers. His son (15) and daughter (12) have grown, but so far, he has missed most of it. Lately there have been arguments, especially with his son. Frank wants to be their father and friend, but he doesn't know how.

• How would you feel?

• What would you do?

Parent Measure ■ Distribute sheets with the following categories listed at the top. Tell group members to list first the qualities of the ideal parent. Next, they should check where each of their parents matches. Then they should add a column entitled "me" and rate themselves by the same ideal standards.

IDEAL QUALITIES	HOW THEY MATCH UP		
	MOM	DAD	ME

Pressures ■ Distribute papers and pens. As a group, discuss the pressures and needs that adults have. Students should list these on one side of their papers. When you have a fairly exhaustive list, have them turn the papers over and draw a picture, diagram, graph, or other symbol to represent what it means to be an adult. After a few minutes, have students display their symbols giving each person a chance to explain his or hers. Then discuss how they can help parents cope with adult pressures and needs.

Situations ■ Read the following situations aloud. After each one, have the group discuss and decide on a compromise solution.

1. Bob is a senior in high school and wants to work after school and on weekends. His father forbids it because he wants Bob to stay on the basketball team and to be involved in other school and church activities.

2. Mary has a small allowance, but she really can't buy much of anything with it. She wants to choose and to buy her own clothes. Mary is a freshman in high school.

3. Patti's curfew is 11 P.M. on weekends. She just turned 16 and thinks that she ought to be able to stay out till 1 A.M. or so, like most of her friends.

4. Albert wants a car. He has saved some money and has a part-time job to help pay for the car and its expenses. Mom and Dad say no.

5. Mr. and Mrs. Brentacre want the vacation to include the whole family—this means Teri. But Teri thinks family vacations are boring and would rather spend time with friends in the town where she used to live.

Some Total! ■ Give each person a blank piece of paper. After dividing it down the middle, they should write on the upper left, *What my parents have done for me this week.* Next, on the right side they should write, *What I have done for my parents this week.* After they make their lists, compare and discuss them.

Survey ■ Hand out cards and pencils and give the group your version of a Gallup Family Poll. Tell students not to put their names on the surveys and that their answers will be confidential. Ask:

• With how many of your parents do you live?

• How do your parents get along—great, good, OK, not so good, or bad?

• What three things does your family do together regularly?

• Which one of these do you enjoy the most?

• On a scale of 1–10, rate your family with 10 as the best and 1 as the worst.

Collect the cards, tabulate the results, and discuss your findings together. Ask:

• What does this survey tell us about our families?

• How well does your family communicate?

• To whom in your family do you turn when you have a problem? Why?

• What can you do to make your family better?

Tell the Truth ■ Choose three outgoing and creative kids to participate in an experiment. Seat them in front of the group and explain that you are going to give each one a card containing special instructions. One of the cards will read, *You should always tell the truth.* Another card will say, *You should always lie.* And the third one will read, *You should sometimes tell the truth and sometimes lie.* Explain that you will shuffle the cards so that no one will know who has which card, not even you; then you will ask a series of questions that they should answer according to the instructions on their cards (Note: encourage those who lie to be creative but not outrageous with their answers). Next, hand out the cards and have the participants read them and put them away. Then ask the following questions, giving each person a chance to respond to each one.

• What was the best vacation you ever took with your family?

• What do you like most about Easter?

• What public figure do you admire most and why?

• What is the most difficult task your mom and dad have as parents?

• On a scale of 1–5, with one being the worst, how do you rate yourself regarding how well you obey your parents? Why?

• If you came home an hour late after curfew because after the game you went to a party (that your parents said you couldn't attend), and your parents asked where you had been, what would you say?

• What do you think it takes to gain your parents' trust?

Afterward, see if the audience can guess who was always telling the truth, always lying, etc. Use this to lead into a discussion of how lying can erode and destroy trust between kids and parents.

There's No Place Like Home ■ This may be done individually or in small groups.

Give everyone a piece of scratch paper and a pencil or pen. Have them write the phrase "There's No Place Like Home" across the top. Tell them that by using those letters, they should write all the words they can that have some relevance to them about "home" or "family." After a few minutes, see who has the longest list. Ask that person to read his or her list aloud and to explain some of the words for the group. Repeat with others. Here are some possibilities:

• pet (our dog is like a member of the family)

• me (home is where I love to be)

• lace (my mother loves to put lace on things)

• pointers (Dad is always giving me these)

• I'm there

• please (my parents insist that I am polite . . . and I want to please them)

• hike (we took one of these on our family vacation)

• ham (Mom loves to cook and eat ham)

• real (home is the place where I can be myself)

• others (we are encouraged to bring friends home)

Time Line ■ Distribute paper and pencils and have group members draw a time line for their parents. For each parent they should draw a horizontal line about nine inches long. At the right end they should write the parent's present age and on the left end, the age that she or he left home (high school graduation, job, marriage, etc.). Next, on the lines have them mark the decade birthdays (30, 40, 50, etc.). Then they should mark other major events in their parents' lives (marriage, births, deaths, new jobs, moves).

Compare lines and discuss what feelings parents have when faced with life's crises, how they feel when they hit the decade birthdays, how they feel about aging, what they are going through now, and how children can help their parents go through tough times.

Typical Family ■ Take a poll of your group and do an instant statistical analysis. Ask each question, total the answers, and divide by the number of people to get your answers. Then read and discuss your results.

Questions (add others):

1. How many parents are in your home?

2. How old is your mother? Father?

3. How many daughters are in the family? Sons?

4. How many cars does your family have?

5. How many hours a week is your family together?

6. What triggered your last fight (majority answer)?

DISCUSSIONS AND WRAP-UPS

Dos and Don'ts ■ Use the following acronyms to help students remember what they should and shouldn't do when their parents are fighting. Don't BITE: B = Blame yourself; I = Interfere; T = Take sides; E = Explode (don't blow up at them or keep your feelings bottled up inside). Do PAT: P = Pray; A = Act in love toward both parents; T = Talk to a friend. Explain and elaborate on each point as you give it.

Good Family ■ Ask the following questions and be prepared to share from your own life:

• What makes a family "good"?

• What lessons have you learned from your parents for raising children?

• What would you like to change in your home?

• How can you make things even better?

Memories ■ Lead group members through the following discussion:

• Describe your favorite family vacation.

• When did you really pull together as a family?

• Who is your favorite relative?

• What factors (attitudes, activities, etc.) in your family do you hope to have in your home when you are a parent? Why?

No Place ■ The object of this is to help students understand their roles in making their homes better places in which to live. Introduce this by explaining that people say that "there's no place like home." Then ask:

• What do you think that phrase means?

• What should be found in the "ideal" home?

• What changes should be made in your home and family to make it more "ideal"?

• What changes can you make to help?

Run Away ■ Point out that every year thousands of young people run away from home. Ask:

• Why do kids run away?

• Do you know anyone who just "took off"? Why? How did it work out?

• Do you think running away is a good idea? Why or why not?

Trust Busters ■ Ask what kinds of things destroy trust between parents and kids. They should quickly give you categories that you should write on the board. These categories will include: lying, disobeying, complaining, not following through with respon- sibilities, hiding information from them, etc. As kids give these categories, have an associate write them on index cards (one category per card but more than one card for each category). Then distribute the cards among the group so that each person gets one card. Tell everyone to write one example of an action that a young person might take in that category that would destroy parental trust. Collect the cards, shuffle them, and read their answers aloud. Then discuss what each person could do to regain his or her parents' trust after doing each specific trust-busting action.

BIBLE STUDIES

Being an Example ■ Have everyone turn to 1 Timothy 4:12. Explain that Paul wrote this to a young leader in the church, Timothy, to help him build trust and solid relationships with older Christians. Timothy was told to "set an example . . . in speech, in life, in love, in faith, and in purity." Discuss together how these categories can be applied to their home situations and to building trust with their parents. In other words, how can they build trust by how they talk, how they live, how they show love, how they demonstrate faith, and how they act on dates?

Biblical Families ■ Hand out work sheets with these Bible verses listed. The material in parentheses is for your reference; don't include it on the sheet. After each Bible reference have group members write what it teaches about the family and what change should be made in their homes to better conform to these biblical principles.

VERSE	TEACHING	CHANGE
Exodus 20:12	(Respect your parents.)	
Proverbs 10:1	(Act wisely.)	
Proverbs 13:1	(Follow your parents' instructions.)	
Proverbs 15:5	(Submit to parental discipline.)	
Matthew 10:37	(Put Christ first in your life.)	
Matthew 18:6-7	(Parents should not lead children into sin.)	
Romans 1:28-32	(Obey your parents.)	
1 Corinthians 13:4-7, 13	(Love each other.)	
Ephesians 6:1-4	(Children and parents should respect each other.)	
1 Timothy 5:8	(Parents should provide for the family.)	

Father-Son ■ Before the meeting, choose two boys to act out the father-son drama found in Genesis 22:1-14. If this is too difficult, read the story aloud or tell it dramatically in your own words. Afterward ask:

• How do you think Abraham felt about Isaac? Why?

• Describe the relationship between father and son.

• If Abraham loved Isaac so much, why was he willing to kill him? Could you do that? Why or Why not?

• Where was Sarah?

Jesus' Parents ■ Have someone read aloud Luke 2:41-52. Then ask:

• How did Jesus' parents feel about Him?

• Why did Mary say what she did in verse 48?

• How do you feel about Jesus' response in verse 49?

• Note verse 51. How do you think Mary and Jesus felt? Why did Jesus obey?

Next read John 2:1-11 and ask:

• Jesus is now thirty. How has His relationship to His mother changed from the previous passage?

• How did He feel (verse 4)? How about Mary (verses 3 and 5)?

• Why did Jesus turn the water into wine?

• What can we learn about our relationships with our parents from these two stories?

Love Study ■ Have everyone look up the following verses, one at a time, while you have them read aloud. Do not comment about the verses.

• Matthew 7:12 (Golden Rule)

• Luke 6:27-36 ("Love your enemies.")

• John 13:34-35 ("By this will all men know you are My disciples.")

• Romans 13:8-10 ("Owe no one anything, except to love.")

• 1 Corinthians 13:4-7 ("Love is . . .")

• Philippians 2:3-8 (humility)

• Colossians 4:6 (gracious speech)

• 1 Timothy 4:12 ("Let no one despise your youth.")

• 1 Peter 2:1 ("Put away all malice.")

• 1 John 2:9-11 (loving your brother)

When you have finished reading verses, ask:

• What do you remember from those verses?

• What do they all have in common? (They deal with relationships.)

• With whom is it toughest to follow through with these exhortations? How about parents?

• Why is it so difficult to love our parents? Do our parents need our love? Why or why not?

Our Father ■ Have everyone stand and repeat the first two words of the Lord's Prayer: "Our Father . . ." Ask: What does it mean to call God "Father"? Refer to the following passages as you discuss answers:

1. John 3:3-15—We are His children. Ask: *What does it take to become a child of God?* (We are born and adopted into His family—the Bible uses both these pictures.)

Say: *You call God "Father," but are you even His child?*

2. Matthew 7:21—There is authority and obedience. Ask: *As our Father, what has God asked us to do?* (List several commands.) *What excuses do we use for not obeying Him?* (We don't have time; it's too hard; we're not sure He knows best, etc.) Say: *You call God "Father," but do you obey Him?*

3. Romans 8:29—There is a family resemblance. Say: *Paul says to be "conformed to the image of Christ." What does it mean to be like Jesus?* (priorities—see Matthew 6:33-34; humility—see Philippians 2:5-8; love—see John 13:24-35.) Continue: *You call God "Father," but do you bear the family resemblance? Do others see Jesus in you?*

4. 1 John 4:19-21—There is a family with brothers and sisters. Ask: *Who are our brothers and sisters?* (others who also know Christ as Savior) Say: *Often we have been unaccepting and unloving with them. But if God is our Father, He has every right to tell us who our brothers and sisters are. You call God "Father," but do you accept your brothers and sisters?*

Hand out cards and pencils. Take a few minutes for silent prayer and personal inventory. Have each person write his or her name and the main area of concern about his or her relationship to God as Father (being a child of God, obedience, family resemblance, accepting brothers and sisters). Collect the cards and promise to meet with each person individually during the next week or two to discuss each one's needs and to pray together. End by reciting the Lord's Prayer together.

Prodigal ■ Have someone read aloud the story of the Prodigal Son from *The Living Bible* (Luke 15:11-32). Afterward ask:

• Why did the son leave home?

• Was it a good decision? Why or why not?

• What was the older brother like? Why? Was he dependent or independent? Why do you say that?

Break into groups of five to six and have them write a modern version of the story. Share the results of their efforts.

Relating ■ Type the following verses out of *The Living Bible* in a continuous narrative form: Ephesians 6:4; Luke 18:16-17, beginning with "Let . . ."; Ephesians 6:1-3; 1 John 4:7-8; 1 Corinthians 13:4-7, 13. Be sure to note the references on the top.

Pass out copies and have everyone read them in unison. Then ask:

• These verses have been put together to convey a message; what is the message?

• What part of the reading especially spoke to you?

- When is it tough to obey your parents? Why?
- How can we honor God in our families?

Solid Families ■ Pass out cards with the following passages on them (one per card) and have students read the passages aloud one at a time. After each passage is read, ask what lesson can be inferred about the family. (Possible answers are in parentheses.)

- Psalm 68:6 ("Family" is God's cure for loneliness.)
- Genesis 28:14 (All the "families" of the world have been blessed through Abraham because of his descendant, Jesus.)
- John 19:27 (A family is for caring, and Jesus gave His mother to another family to care for her.)
- 1 Timothy 5:4 (Children should take care of needy parents and grandparents.)
- Proverbs 31:27 (A good wife watches her home carefully.)
- Joshua 24:15 (The family should serve God together.)
- Proverbs 22:6 (Parents should teach their children the right way to live.)
- 1 Timothy 3:4 (Having a solid family is a prerequisite for church leaders.)
- Numbers 14:18 (Parents' mistakes will affect their children.)
- Leviticus 20:9 (It is very serious to curse one's parents.)
- Psalm 27:10 (To be abandoned by father and mother would be tough, but God would be there.)
- Psalm 103:13 (God is loving and kind to us, like a great father.)
- Proverbs 15:20 (Children should make their parents happy.)
- Ezekiel 22:6-7 (It is a terrible sin to ignore one's parents.)

FRIENDS

CROWD-BREAKERS

A Building Process ■ This game involves two competing pairs and two sets of blocks. Seat one member from each pair next to each other behind a card table and place a pile of blocks in front of them. Explain that each person's goal should be to build the highest stack of blocks. They may only use one hand and touch one block at a time. They may build their own stack *or* remove blocks from their competitor's stack (knocking down a stack is not permitted—minus 200 points if it happens). Then blindfold both competitors and give the signal to begin. After a minute, stop the contest and total the points (100 points for each block stacked and 200 points for each row of height). Repeat with the other halves of the couples or with new teams.

A Nice Reflection ■ This game uses mirrors to illustrate the concept that we reflect to others information that they use to build their self-images. Divide into teams; this activity may be done as a relay or with team representatives. Give each team a small mirror and a script. The scripts for each team should be stories about high school kids (such as articles from Campus Life magazine) and should have lots of short paragraphs. The stories should be different for each team but of equal length. Have each team choose a mirror holder and a script holder. At your signal, the first person runs to the front and stands between the mirror and the script, facing the mirror. He or she looks into the mirror and reads the script aloud as quickly as possible. (This will be difficult because the words will be backward.) The contestant completes a

paragraph, then returns to the team. Then the next person comes and reads the next paragraph, and so on. The team to finish reading the story first wins.

Close Knit ■ Depending on the projected size of your group, before the meeting decide the number of teams you will be able to have. Each team should have a minimum of ten members. Next, purchase the same number of different colors of yarn (one color per team), and cut 2–3 foot lengths so that you will have one piece for each person. As group members enter the room, give each person a length of yarn, making sure that the colors are evenly distributed. Explain that at your signal, they should find the others with the same yarn color, tie the pieces together to form one long string, and totally wrap up their group in the yarn. (Everyone must be in the center, surrounded by the yarn.) The first group finished wins. Then use these teams for other events.

Connections ■ Distribute cards and pencils to everyone. Have students record the following facts about themselves (you may add to these but be sure that the facts are not too broad or too specific): placement in the family birth order, father's name, favorite dessert, career plans, month of birth, hobby. Next, explain that their assignment is to find someone else with whom they have one of these individual characteristics in common (for example, both fathers are named Fred). When a connection is made, they should join hands and continue to search for others who can connect with one chain's free hands. Continue the game until almost everyone is part of the chain of connections. While students continue to hold hands, have them explain, person by person, their connecting links. (Note: many of the connections will involve stretching the facts a bit—an architect linking with a housewife because both try to make the home a nice place, etc. When this happens, ask why they did it and how it parallels life.)

Cooperation ■ Choose couples to compete. These may be pairs of friends or team representatives. Give each couple a bucket and a balloon. Explain that the goal of the game is to see how many times a team can catch the balloon in its bucket . . . in two minutes. Here's how it works. A person from each couple stands at one end of the room. This person is the catcher and he or she holds the bucket. As a balloon approaches, he or she may reach or bend at the waist. but must not move his or her feet and must always keep both hands on the bucket. The other person from each couple stands about 10 feet away, behind a line. He or she has a balloon that, at your signal, he or she should bat toward the bucket. The balloon may only be batted with the hands—it may not be picked up or held. After a couple's balloon has been batted to the catcher and caught in the bucket, the catcher and batter should change positions and roles. This continues until time has expired. The couple catching the balloons the most times, wins. Note: be sure to assign a staff person to each couple to count their catches.

Entrance Exam ■ As kids enter the room, give each one a *Youth Group Entrance Exam* and a pencil or pen. Explain with mock seriousness that they need to do well on this exam to be part of the group. After a few minutes, give the correct answers (some are in parentheses). Congratulate the top 75% students and use the bottom 25% for the next activity.

YOUTH GROUP ENTRANCE EXAM

1. What was the topic of our last meeting?
2. Without asking anyone, write the first names of 10 members of the youth group in this space.

_____

3. Who won the Super Bowl that was played in 1994? (Dallas Cowboys)
4. What soft drink is our group's favorite beverage?
5. Who wrote the book *1984*? (George Orwell)
6. Who was President of the United States in 1984? (Ronald Reagan)
7. Who won the Super Bowl in 1984? (Raiders)
8. How old were you in 1984?
9. What junior highs or middle schools feed into _____ high school?
10. When was this building built?

11. Who is the mayor of this city?
12. What athletic shoe company is our group's favorite?
13. How does someone join our group?
14. How do we know that someone is in our group?
15. Who is the senior pastor of this church?
16. Why do you feel more like you do right now than you have all day? (because you're you)
17. Is it not true that a true answer to this question would be false?
18. List three movies starring Kevin Kostner. (for example, *Field of Dreams, Dances with Wolves, Robin Hood Prince of Thieves, JFK, Bodyguard, A Perfect World,* etc.)
19. What is our group's favorite fast-food restaurant?
20. What is our group's "official" color?

Later, use this quiz and the group's feelings when they were filling it out to bridge to a discussion of how outsiders should be welcomed and included.

Famous Pairs ■ Hand this out as a fill-in-the-blank quiz. Tell group members that every answer contains the "pair" sound (most begin with it). The answers are in parentheses.

1. chapter division (paragraph)
2. protects from a fall (parachute)
3. alongside, never meeting (parallel)
4. on the first day of Christmas (pear tree)
5. French water (Perrier)
6. persecution delusion (paranoid)
7. umbrella (parasol)
8. cut (pare)
9. place of beauty (paradise)
10. living off another (parasite)
11. story (parable)
12. apparent contradiction (paradox)
13. make helpless (paralyze)
14. capital on the Seine (Paris)
15. a local church (parish)
16. to die (perish)
17. imitation (parody)
18. colorful bird (parrot)
19. ward off (parry)
20. obvious (apparent)
21. fix (repair)

After you give the answers, have group members write

a sentence using as many of the words as possible. Read their creations. Award a pack of Doublemint gum to the person with the most correct answers.

Friend Hunt ■ Choose individuals to compete and have them come to the front of the room. Explain that you will tell them a specific kind of person to find. Then, they should go into the large group, find the person, and bring him or her back to you. The first one back with the right person wins that round. Repeat for about ten rounds and declare a winner. Possible "friends":

1. someone you dated recently
2. someone you'd like to date (different from #1)
3. a person with at least three brothers and sisters (four total siblings)
4. a friend who will tell you a secret (Have the secret whispered to the person and then to you.)
5. someone with a special talent (If possible, have the talent demonstrated.)
6. a very intelligent person
7. a very shy person
8. a girl with a great personality
9. a boy with a great sense of humor
10. a person who throws a great party

Friend Words ■ As kids enter the room, give each person an index card with one half of a word that relates to friendship written on it. At your signal, they should try to find the other half and complete their word. Use these pairs for other games and activities. Here are possible friend words to use and how you can divide them:

tog-ether	insep-arable	tru-sting	fait-hful
acce-pting	list-ener	hon-est	ki-nd
consi-derate	lo-yal	fu-n	comp-anion
sacri-ficial	op-en	clo-se	avai-lable

Later you could use these words in a discussion of what it takes to be a best friend.

Impersonations ■ Choose three volunteers to impersonate someone in the group. Then have an adult helper take them out of the room "to talk it over and to practice." When they are out of the room, the helper should tell the volunteers that all three will impersonate the same person (an adult leader or sponsor). Each person should do the best he or she can without consulting the other two. Explain to the large group that they are to guess who the volunteers are impersonating. It will be interesting to see three versions and which personal qualities, habits, and

mannerisms are highlighted. (Bring the volunteers into the room one at a time.)

In Common ■ Explain that friends often have a lot in common and that right now you want to see how much everyone in the group has in common with each other. Distribute pencils or pens and copies of the *We Have a Lot in Common* work sheet (see below). Tell students to get as many signatures as possible for each category. Afterwards, see who had the most signatures for any one category and who had the most signatures for the whole sheet. Note: when you make up this sheet, be sure to leave room for the signatures.

WE HAVE A LOT IN COMMON!

1. Someone with a birthday in the same month as yours
2. Someone who has lived in the same city as you, previous to this one
3. Someone who has one of the same names as you (first, middle, or last)
4. Someone with the same initials as you (first and last)
5. Someone whose mother or father has the same first name as your mother or father
6. Someone who has the same hobby as you
7. Someone who is the same height (within 1/2 inch) or weight (within 2 lbs.) as you
8. Someone who is wearing the same brand of shoes as you
9. Someone who saw the same movie last that you did
10. Someone who this past year has read three of the books that you read (not for school)

In-Crowd Improvisation ■ Choose three members of the group to come to the front to participate. Explain that their assignment is to speak about the in-crowd at their respective schools. Number the speakers and explain that they must speak in that order. Number one will begin, followed by number two, etc. The only catch, however, is that whenever you clap your hands, the next person must take up the speech immediately where the last person stopped (this may be in mid-sentence . . . wherever). Vote on the best talker and give a penalty to the loser. This can be done with any number of people and/or subjects.

Inflated Self ■ This game uses balloons and trench coats, so be sure to get these before the meeting. Give each team a trench coat and 15 balloons. Then have them choose someone (preferably a small person) to don the coat. Explain that at your signal, the teams should inflate all the balloons and stuff them into their trench coats (no balloons should escape or be popped). After the balloons have been stuffed, the contestants must do 15 jumping jacks (escaped balloons must be restuffed) and then run around a predetermined course with obstacles that must be ducked under and jumped over. When the contestants return to the starting line, they must pop all their balloons. The first team finished wins. As they race, play up-tempo music.

Inseparable ■ Divide the group into pairs; then have all the pairs stand back-to-back and link arms along a starting line. Next, take all their shoes and make a pile in the middle of the room. Explain that at your signal, the pairs must "run" to the pile of shoes, find theirs, put them on, and return to the starting line, all without unlinking their arms. The first team finished wins.

Matchless Friends ■ Give each person a slip of paper with one half of a famous pair of friends. Then tell them to find their partners without talking and without showing anyone their pieces of paper. To add motivation, penalize the last two. Here are some famous friends.

Laurel and Hardy

Hawkeye and B.J.

Abbot and Costello

The Lone Ranger and Tonto

Roy Rogers and Trigger

Cisco and Pancho

Johnny Carson and Ed McMahon

Siskel and Ebert

Snoopy and Woodstock

Heckle and Jeckle

Mickey Mouse and Donald Duck

Bob Hope and Bing Crosby

Dan Ackroyd and John Belushi

Norm Peterson and Cliff Claven

Cheetah and Tarzan

Herb and Dagwood

Odie and Garfield

Holmes and Watson

Proctor and Gamble

Mutt and Jeff

Sears and Roebuck

Simon and Garfunkle

Ralph Cramden and Ed Norton

Middle Name Scramble ■ Distribute pieces of paper and have everyone write their middle names on them. Collect all the names and put them into a box. Next have everyone draw out a name, find the person with that name, and link arms with him or her. In a few minutes you will have chains of kids (the larger the crowd, the better this will work). Spend a few minutes finding out the most common middle names, the most unusual ones, the source of the names, and the feelings about their middle names.

My Child, the ■ Before the meeting, contact several parents and have them give you a list of their child's strengths and abilities. This list may be supplemented by input from other adults. Read the lists, one at a time, and have the group identify the person being described.

Name That Kid! ■ This is a take-off on "Name That Tune." Use a series of contestants, two at a time, and seat them at one end of the room. Then describe a person, one characteristic at a time. When a contestant thinks he or she knows who you are describing, he or she should jump up, run to the other end, and ring a bell (or blow a whistle). This may be done with just two contestants or with teams using new team representatives for each round. Begin with celebrities and then move to kids in the room. To make this most effective, you will need specific information about the kids. Ask their parents about childhood nicknames, birthmarks, hidden talents, awards, famous quotes, etc.

Pairs ■ Divide into couples and give each one a sheet of paper and pen. Tell them to list things that always come in pairs. Physical characteristics such as arms or eyes are ineligible. The longest list wins. Here are some possibilities: shoes, socks, gloves, earrings, dice, bookends, skis, glasses, pants, twins, scissors, pliers, sheets, headlights, goal posts, guards, tackles, forwards, duets, etc.

Pass Word ■ Choose sets of best friends to compete in a version of *Password*. This is the game where one person is given a word to communicate to his or her partner by using *other* words (synonyms, opposites, clichés, fill in the blank, etc.). Bring the sets of friends to the front and have them designate one person in each set as the sender and the other as the receiver. Explain that each set will get 60 seconds to guess as many words as they can out of a list that you will give them. Each time the receiver guesses a correct word, you will ring a bell so that they can move on to another word. If they give up on any word, they can say "pass" and move to the next one.

Choose a set to begin and blindfold the receiver. The receiver should sit, blindfolded, facing the audience. The sender should sit facing him or her. Post the list of words on the wall behind them so that the sender and the audience can read the words. (Write words on poster board before the meeting.) Then give the signal to begin. Have an assistant check off the words on the board when they are correctly guessed. Use as many sets of friends as you wish and have time for. With a small group, use two sets and then reverse roles for round two. The set guessing the most words, wins. Here are some words to use: together, buddies, friendship, sharing, long-lasting, closeness, help, loyalty, relationship, cooperation, love, communicate, confide, give, listen, and so forth. All these words relate to friendship.

Peas in a Pod ■ Use teams of two and line them up next to each other along one wall. (If the room is small, do this in heats.) At the opposite wall, for each team, place a small tray or cup containing 10 peas. Next give each pair a straw and a card with a two-inch (diameter) circle drawn on it. At the signal, one team member runs to his or her cup of peas, picks up one with the straw without touching the pea with the fingers, runs back to the partner holding the pea on the end of the straw with suction, and deposits the pea on the card within the circle. The first pair finished wins. (The holder of the card may use his or her fingers to pick up peas if they fall on the floor but should not touch them while they are on the card.)

People Chase ■ Distribute People Chase sheets and pencils. Tell group members they have five minutes to gather as much information as possible. After the time is up, see who has the most and award a prize to the winner. Note: when you make these sheets, leave room for the answers.

PEOPLE CHASE

From people in this room . . .

1. Record as many middle names as possible.
2. Write the name of the person who was born the farthest from here.
3. Write the name of the person whose birthday is closest to yours.
4. Write the names of all the sophomores.
5. Without asking anyone, list as many names from people in the youth group as you can.
6. Record the names of three people with whom you have at least three personal characteristics in common (physical, personality, past, etc.).
7. List everyone under five feet tall.
8. Find one person whose initials spell something.
9. List five friends who are not in the room (but should be).
10. List the names of all the adults.

Scrunch ■ Explain that you will be yelling out a number at which time everyone is to organize into groups of that size. Then each group will be measured with a hula hoop. The groups who cannot fit will be eliminated. (The hoop must be able to pass over the entire group from top to bottom.) With a small crowd, begin with one and move up one number at a time. With a large crowd, go by two's. Continue until you determine the winning group.

Siamese Strut ■ Have everyone find a partner. Form the group into a circle with partners standing side by side. Explain that they are such good friends that they are almost like Siamese twins. So as they walk clockwise with their partners, you will call out ways that they are joined together. They should touch their partners at those spots and keep walking. Get everyone walking clockwise and call out the following connections:

• joined at the hip, left to right
• joined at the tip of the shoulders, one shoulder each
• joined at the foot
• joined at the shoulder blades

If you want to make this a bit more rowdy and competitive, form two concentric circles with the partners. Have one circle move clockwise while the other one moves counter-clockwise As you call out the connections, kids should get to their partners and stand there, connected. Each time, eliminate the last set of partners to connect. Here are some possible connections:

• knee to knee
• fist to nose
• forehead to forehead
• foot to seat
• little finger to little finger
• big toe to armpit

Continue until you have a winning pair. Give them the "Best Friends" award.

Siamese Twins ■ For this you will need very large sweatshirts designed to hold two people. You can buy shirts like this or you can make your own by sewing together two old sweatshirts for each set of twins. Be sure to cut and reattach the sweatshirts along the side and leave both collar openings intact. Explain that you are going to form "Siamese twins," attached along the sides. Choose two couples (or more depending on your crowd) to compete and have them don their sweatshirt outfits. (When dressed, there will be two heads for each set of "twins" but only one left and one right arm.) Next, seat them at a table facing the audience (four chairs will be needed), and place before each set a large bowl of cereal with milk and two spoons. The contest is to see who can eat all their cereal first. Note: the right hand must feed the left mouth and the left hand, the right mouth.

Stand Up, Sit Down, Fight, Fight, Fight ■ Get everyone seated in rows and lead them in the old football cheer, "Lean to the left, lean to the right, stand up, sit down, fight, fight, fight!" Make sure that everyone moves together, leaning way to the left, etc. Begin slowly and then pick up the pace until everyone is moving through the cheer together, rapidly. Now designate the odd-numbered rows as team one and the even-numbered rows as team two. Explain that you will be repeating the cheer except that the even team will be doing the opposite of the odd team. They will be standing, and their cheer and movements will be, "Lean to the right, lean to the left, sit down, stand up, we're the best!" Be sure to have this new version written and displayed on poster board so they can read it as they yell it. Next have both teams cheer and move at the same time.

Toss-up ■ Arrange the group into circles of eight to ten. Appoint a leader for each circle and give him or her a bag of items to toss one at a time to a person across the circle. Then, each group should decide a progression of tossing; that is, John (the leader) will always toss to Betty (across the circle) who will always toss to Pat who will toss to Bill who will toss to Mike who will toss to Suzanne who will toss to Marlene who will toss to Renae who will toss to John (who will toss to Betty, etc.). John begins the process by tossing one item. Everyone should go slowly until they get the idea. See how fast they can go, and then add items. Items to toss could include: tennis ball, small pillow, knotted sock, damp sponge, stocking cap, tennis shoe, banana, Ping Pong ball, etc.

Who's Who ■ See who can name the most people in the room. If the group is small, move to round two: first and last names. The finalists could participate in round three: father's first names (or middle names or mother's names, etc.).

DISCUSSION STARTERS

Affirm Foundation ■ Give each person two small cards on which they should write their names. Then pass around a box and have everyone deposit their cards. Pass around the box again and have them draw out two cards, making sure that neither one is their own. Their assignment is to write a note of affirmation during the week to each of the persons they have drawn, including an appropriate Bible verse.

Best Friends ■ Design a quiz to determine how much kids know about their friends. Have them write the name of a good friend on the top of the paper and then write the answers to the following questions:

• What is his or her middle name?
• Who is his or her favorite relative?
• What are his or her vocational goals?
• Who is his or her favorite musician or music group?
• What does he or she think about God?
• What would he or she say is your goal in life?

Afterwards, discuss whether or not they really have *best friends* who know them thoroughly and whom they know. And decide as a group what makes a good friend and how they can develop strong, deep, and lasting friendships.

Building Boxes ■ Ask: *What are the building blocks for a solid friendship? What's the foundation?* When an answer is given, discuss it with the group until you reach a consensus that the quality or characteristic mentioned is very important to friendship. Each time you agree on one, write it on an index card or a 4" X 6" piece of paper and tape it to the front of a small box. Place the boxes on a table so that students can see them and read the qualities. The qualities should include: commonality, communication, caring, commitment (loyalty), counsel, confidentiality, comedy (having fun together), etc.

Next, ask for other qualities that are built on those foundational ones. Put those boxes on the ones forming the foundation so that everyone can see them. Discuss how solid friendship are *built*, they don't just happen

Create a Hurt ■ Distribute sheets of paper with the following persons listed on the left-hand side: boyfriend/girlfriend, Mom, Dad, teacher, employer, classmate, friend, God. Explain that after each one they are to write how they have been hurt by each person. These sheets should be anonymous; no names should be used anywhere on them. Collect the sheets and read aloud a few of the hurts in each category. (Don't include details which give the person's identity away.) Then discuss what forgiveness would cost.

Getting to Know You ■ Have the group break into pairs, preferably with someone they don't know very well. Hand out the following questionnaire and lead them through it step by step. (When you reproduce the questionnaire, leave room for the answers.)

GETTING TO KNOW YOU

1. For two minutes, take a good look at your partner. Do not converse. Write down everything you know about him or her.

2. For the next minute, look into each others' eyes. (Try not to laugh.) Try to imagine what he or she is really like. Write down a couple of your ideas.

3. Talk to each other for two minutes. Try to remember what he or she tells you. Now write down everything you can remember.

4. If you had the time, what would you like to ask your partner to find out what he or she is really like?

5. If you got to know this person very well, what kinds of things would you share about yourself?

Collect the questionnaires (no names should be on them). Read a few of the answers for each question without comment. Then discuss how we really get to know others and how we build relationships.

Give and Take ■ Give everyone six cards and tell them to write one thing on each card that they would like to give to other members of the group. These can be tangible things (for example, money, music, good grades, and so forth) or intangible ones (for example, happiness, good health, long life, etc.). After everyone has finished, have them walk around the room and trade cards with each other. These must be blind trades, and the cards received should be added to their supply. Also, they should draw only one card from each person.

After a few minutes, seat and quiet everyone and ask:

• What cards do you have?

• What did you write on your cards? Why?

• What similarities did you find between the cards you gave and the cards you took?

• What is meant by the phrase "give and take"?

• How does "give and take" apply to relationships?

Give Him the Slip ■ Before this activity, select a

victim—someone who seems reasonably self-confident and popular. As kids enter the room, give each person a slip of paper that reads, "During the first activity, ignore _____ (the victim). P.S. Don't let him (or her) see this paper." Give the victim a slip of paper that says, "During the first activity, meet as many people as possible and write down their names." For the first activity, then, explain that you have given a dollar to a person (do this, of course) who will surrender it to the 15th person who introduces himself or herself to the secret money-holder. Then tell them to begin. After a winner has been determined, stop the game and ask the victim how he or she felt. Explain what you were doing, and ask whether he or she knew that there was a conspiracy to ignore him or her. (What were the clues?) And ask how it would feel to know that he or she always would be treated that way. Then ask everyone else how they felt knowing that _____ was purposely being avoided, how they feel knowing that there are lots of kids at school who are treated every day like that person was, and how they can help those kids.

I'm Sorry ■ Read the following phrases with the voice inflection implied by the parenthetical statements and discuss, one at a time, how they're used and how they relate to forgiveness.

a. "I'm sorry." (said casually)

b. "I'm so sorry." (sincerely, after hearing of a death)

c. "Sorry about that." (with Maxwell Smart accent)

d. "I apologize." (said formally)

e. "I blew it!" (said like you failed a big test)

f. "Pardon me." (one person trying to get past another)

g. "Excu-u-u-u-se me!" (Steve Martin style)

h. "Oops!" (said in a cutesy manner)

i. "Don't sweat it." (said casually)

j. "That's OK." (said like you don't mean it)

h. "I forgive you." (said condescendingly)

Just Friends ■ Give each person a card and a pencil and ask them to write the names of everyone in the room with whom they have a relationship. Next, tell them to turn over the card and write down the names of those in the room whom they don't know very well. Then have them rate the depth of the relationship with each of their friends listed on side one—"5" for very deep, down to "1" for very shallow. Finally, have them total their numbers. Make sure they don't share their rating with anyone in the group. Discuss this by asking:

• How did you determine the rating for each person?

• What does it take to build a strong friendship?

• Look at the other side of your card. What would it take for you to establish a friendship with someone listed there?

• We talk a lot about "friendship with God." How can you start a friendship with Him? How can you deepen it?

Mirror, Mirror ■ Divide the group into pairs and have the young people stand facing each other with one person in every pair facing the front of the room. Explain that those with their backs to the front must copy every move of their partners. Begin by having everyone facing the front place their hands up in front of them, palms out, about three inches from the partners' hands. Then explain that as you stand at the front moving your hands slowly, the leaders of each twosome must make the same moves you and their partners must follow. Use only your hands, moving them in circles, backward, forward, up, and down. Then repeat with the other person in each pair watching you.

Then have them mirror each other without following your lead, by looking into each other's eyes with person A being the leader. Repeat with person B as the leader.

Afterward ask:

• How did it feel being the follower, watching your partner for clues? What pattern did you see in the leadership?

• How did it feel to follow while looking into each other's eyes? Why was this more difficult or easier?

• During the last round, who took the lead? Why?

Pats on the Back ■ Have group members pair up with someone they don't know very well. Explain that their job is to "PATS." That is, they should *P*ick a person (which they have already done); *A*sk him or her "Who was the last person you praised and for what?" *T*ell him or her what you praise or what quality you most appreciate in people; and *S*hare with the whole group one attribute in your partner for which you are most thankful.

Playing the Role ■ Have everyone find a partner, and designate one person in each pair as A and the other as B. Then give them the following roles to act out. Allow only a few minutes for each role.

• Person A has just experienced a death in the family. Person B finds him or her and begins to talk about it.

• The two of you are talking about a recent failed romance of Person B and discussing dating in general.

• Person A has to break the news to his or her best friend, Person B, that he or she will be moving out of town in a month.

• You two are seeing each other in the school hallway for the first time since a bad argument between you.

• *If you are the same sex*, you both want to date the same person and are trying to work out the situation. *If you are different sexes*—boy, the girl whom you consider a very good friend, recently had a date with a friend of yours; you both feel kind of funny about the whole thing.

Practical Thought ■ Distribute papers and have everyone list areas, problems, and/or situations where they need God's forgiveness. Then break into groups of two or three and have students share these concerns and pray together. After everyone has prayed, have them think of someone whom they need to ask for forgiveness and someone they need to forgive.

Quick Pick-me-up ■ Take a few students out of the room and instruct them privately that they will be lying on the floor, each in the center of a circle of 10 students. Without changing their basic positions, they are to silently communicate to the circle to pick them up and set them on their feet. While you are out of the room with these students, have another staff person arrange the rest of the group into circles of 8–10, without telling them anything about what will be happening. Then bring in the kids and place each one on the floor in the center of a circle. (You may want to place them in a variety of positions—on the back, on the side, on the stomach, etc.) Observe the nonverbal methods of communication and how the circles respond. After a few minutes, debrief and ask:

• What do you think the circles represented? (the pits)

• When have you felt really down, at the bottom, in the pits?

• How do you get out of the pits? How do you tell others how you feel and ask them to help?

Survey ■ Pass out the following surveys and pencils. After group members fill them out, collect, read, discuss, and summarize your findings.

BEST FRIENDS

My best friend is:

a. a neighbor

b. a relative

c. a classmate

d. other

During an average week, we spend:

a. 10 hours together

b. 20 hours

c. 30 hours

d. other _____

We usually talk about _____.

What I appreciate most about my friend is _____

_____.

My friend and I have these important things in common: _____, _____, _____, _____.

Symbolic ■ Bring a number of appropriate sculpture materials. These can include Styrofoam cups, Play Doh, wire, paper, tape, etc. Show group members the materials and have everyone create symbols of friendship. After a few minutes, display and discuss.

Symbols ■ Hand out magazines and newspapers and have group members look for symbols or stories of forgiveness (smile, embrace, handshake, etc.). Then display and discuss.

Ultimate Care Package ■ Divide into groups and give each group a sheet of paper and a pen or pencil. Hold up a one foot square box and say something like: *Suppose you have a friend who is isolated and lonely. What could you put in this box to help him or her? How would you assemble the ultimate care package?*

After a few minutes, have the teams report what they wrote. Compliment them on their concern for their friends. Then ask:

• How would prayer help your friends?

• Why might your friends need prayer?

• Why do we fail to pray for our friends?

Unforgiveness Is . . . ■ Give each person a piece of paper and a pen and have them write an ending to "Unforgiveness is . . ." Collect, read, and discuss the "forgiving" alternatives.

Walls or Doors ■ This involves three or four competitors who will have to move from point A in the room to point B while blindfolded. The problem is that the others in the room will have arranged themselves in a configuration of lines (walls—side by side with arms outstretched) and openings (doors). They can only walk through the doors. Also, there will be a guide who will tell them which way to go. Explain that the object is to get to point B as quickly as possible. After the competitors are taken from the room, set up a configuration of walls and doors,

appoint a guide, and explain that a wall may become a door when the person bumps into it three times. Bring the competitors in one at a time and proceed, timing their journey from A to B. Afterward ask:

• What could "wails" and "windows" symbolize in our relationships with others?

• When have you felt like the blindfolded person?

• Whose role did the guide symbolize?

• How might he or she have been more effective?

• How does this relate to loneliness?

DISCUSSIONS AND WRAP-UPS

Best Friends ■ Ask:

• Who was your best friend in preschool? Grade school? Junior high?

• What caused your friendships to change?

• What do you appreciate in friends today?

Point out that often our first friendships are directly related to geography. That is, kids our age who live in our neighborhood tend to be our friends. As we grow older, however, the basis of our friendships changes to common interests: but, these are still limited somewhat by distance. In high school, when we can drive and when we have very specific interests, our friendships can become quite strong and can cut across all sorts of barriers.

Building Relationships ■ Use the following outline to guide your discussion. These are the basics for building good relationships.

1. *Communication*—being open, honest, and vulnerable. It means listening to what a person says and means.

2. *Compromise*—willing to give in to what the other person wants and to admit wrong.

3. *Commonality*—spending time together.

4. *Consultation*—asking the other person for help . . . allowing him or her to become involved in your life.

5. *Care/Concern/Consideration*—showing love and helping to meet the other person's needs.

6. *Commitment*—sticking by someone, no matter what—not being ashamed of that person, trusting him or her totally.

Challenge ■ Read aloud 1 Corinthians 13:4-7. Explain how this passage emphasizes respect, trust, honesty, and sensitivity. Then give students the following statements to ponder:

• *When you have decided that you are headed in the same direction, with the same destination, it makes sense to travel together.* (The point is that to build a positive and lasting relationship, the two people must be headed in the same direction, toward the same destination.)

• *Respect, trust, honesty, and sensitivity can be seen as bridges. The more bridges you have, the more you can fall back on if one collapses. If you only have one bridge, what do you do if it collapses?* (Challenge students to be bridge builders in their relationships.)

Classic Friends ■ See who can find sets of friends in the Bible. Some of them include: Joshua and Caleb; Deborah and Barak; Ruth and Naomi; David and Jonathan; Shadrack, Meshack, and Abednego; Jesus and Lazarus; Jesus, Mary, and Martha; Peter and John; Paul and Barnabas; Barnabas and Mark; Paul and Silas; Paul, Aquilla, and Priscilla; Paul and Phoebe; Paul and Timothy; Paul and Philemon.

Christian Friends ■ Explain that Christians should make the best friends because they have the Holy Spirit living inside them. Therefore, they can exhibit the fruit of the Spirit: love, joy, peace, patience, kindness, goodness, faithfulness, gentleness, and self-control (Galatians 5:22-23). Briefly explain how each quality would affect a friendship. Be sure to explain, however, that strains may come in a friendship when one person is a Christian and the other one isn't. That doesn't mean we shouldn't have non-Christian friends; it does mean that we should beware of giving in to pressures to compromise our values and beliefs.

Different ■ Ask: *In what ways are Christian friendships different? In other words, what should be part of Christian friendships that probably can't happen in general friendships?* (possible answers: praying together, vulnerability, spiritual sharing, ministry together, Bible study together, etc.)

Next ask: *What kinds of problems might arise when one person in the friendship is a Christian and the other person isn't?* (possible answers: different values and goals, disagreement over activities to do, different direction in life, conflict over compromises to make to maintain the friendship, etc.)

Then ask: *What special gifts can a Christian bring to a friendship?* (possible answers: sensitivity, hope, encouragement, good choices, sharing, biblical answers, guidance, love, etc.)

Gift Boxes ■ Give everyone a shoe box. Tell them to use the box to give a special gift to a friend this week. They might want to fill the box with cookies, put a note in it, use it to mail a "Care Package" to a friend out of town, put a friendship diorama in it, and so on.

Gifts of Friendship ■ Ask which of these gifts students have given to their friends:

• something tangible
• something emotional
• something personally costly
• something humorous
• something old
• something new
• something unique

I'll Know ■ Hand out pieces of paper and pencils or pens. Tell everyone to finish the following sentences:

• *I'll know you respect me if . . .*
• *I'll know you trust me if . . .*
• *I'll know you are honest with me if . . .*
• *I'll know you are sensitive if . . .*

Collect the papers and read aloud several answers for each sentence.

Improvements ■ Explain that no two people on the earth, in history, got along all the time. All human beings are finite and fallible, and they are sinners. So disagreements, misunderstandings, and even "fights" are normal. And sometimes being a good friend means confronting the friend with what he or she is doing wrong. But good friends, especially Christian friends, should be able to work out and work through their problems.

Explain that to improve a friendship, a person can . . .

• do something special for him or her
• talk to the friend about everything—be a good listener
• be loyal to the friend
• try to understand what the friend is going through
• be quick to forgive—assume the best of the friend
• be honest with the friend
• respect the friend
• be positive, upbeat with the friend and not jealous of his or her success

Relationship ■ Ask: What does it take to really get to know someone? In other words, how do we build real, solid relationships? (We spend time together; we talk; we're honest with each other; we experience things together; we go through tough times together; we share our feelings; we keep confidences; we pray for each other; etc.)

Split List ■ Ask for possible problems that might come between friends and list them on the board. Answers might include: misunderstanding, both like the same boy or girl, hurt feelings, competition, and so forth. Then ask:

• Think about when you were in junior high—who was your best friend? What caused you to split up or to move away from that person?

• What caused your last disagreement with your best friend? How did you resolve it?

• What causes people to become friends? Best friends?

• Why do people who really like and care for each other sometimes hurt each other?

BIBLE STUDIES

Great Friends ■ Study the relationship between David and Jonathan as found in 1 Samuel 18:1-4; 23:16-18; etc. Explain that their friendship was deep and close because it was based on their commitment to God, not just to each other; they let nothing come between them, not even career or family problems; they drew closer together when their friendship was tested; they were able to remain friends to the end. Later, Jonathan, the prince of Israel, realized that David and not he would become the next king. But that didn't weaken his love for David. Jonathan would rather lose the throne than his closest friend.

Jesus On Friendship ■ Have students turn to the following passages to discover what Jesus said about friendship.

• Luke 11:5-8—Jesus on prayer . . . and the limits of friendship

• Luke 14:7-14—Jesus on friendship . . . and reaching out to strangers

• John 15:13-15—Jesus on friendship . . . with Him

Love List ■ Have everyone turn to 1 Corinthians 13. After everyone has read the chapter silently, ask students to give you principles that suggest what friends can do to strengthen their relationships.

Proverbs ■ Read these Proverbs about friendship and discuss their implications: 17:17 (a friend loves at all times); 18:24 (there is a friend who is closer than a brother); 19:4 (real friendship); 22:24 (don't make

friends with people who have bad tempers); 27:6 (faithful are the wounds of a friend); 27:9-10 (a friend's counsel is pleasant—be faithful to your friends and your parents); 27:17 (iron sharpens iron).

Togetherness ■ Read the following passages together and discuss each one.

1. Genesis 2:18

• What does this passage tell us about the way God created us?

• How is this relevant to our discussion of relationships?

2. Hebrews 10:24-25

• What should be the purpose of "assembling together"?

• Obviously this verse relates to churches, but how can it apply to our other groups?

3. James 2:1-9

• When have you seen or experienced this kind of "partiality"?

• Everyone seems to be exclusive with their groups; why should we expect Christians to be different?

4. 1 Samuel 16:7

• When have your first impressions of someone been wrong?

• Why do you think we judge others by their outward appearance? Is it fair? When has this happened to you?

5. Luke 6:32-36

• This passage talks about those who aren't good "on the inside." How should we relate to people like that?

• Is there a Christian clique at school (perhaps this youth group)? Are there those who actively oppose Christians? In either case, what should we do? How should we respond?

Verses, Versus ■ Give six people one verse each and then place them in various parts of the room. Explain to the group that they should visit all six people, hear their verses, and then choose the verse that most represents their need. The six verses and what they represent are:

1. John 13:34-35 (love others unconditionally)

2. Proverbs 18:24 (be a true friend)

3. Ephesians 4:2 (be patient with others)

4. Galatians 5:13 (serve one another)

5. Philippians 2:19-22 (encourage others)

6. Hebrews 10:25 (become involved in church)

After choosing a group, students should sit and wait until everyone else has chosen. Then, each group should study the set of verses relating to their group and discuss them. Put all the sets on one sheet. (Possible answers for your use are in parentheses.)

1. *Love others unconditionally.*

• Romans 5:8—How did God show His love for us? (He sent His Son to die for us.)

• John 13:35—What is the ultimate evidence of a follower of Jesus? (love for each other)

• Matthew 5:44—What about enemies? (love them too)

• Matthew 5:48—Are we ever exempted from this? (no)

2. *Be a true friend.* List the qualities of friendship given in these verses:

• Exodus 33:11 (directness, meeting face to face)

• Proverbs 17:17 (love)

• Proverbs 27:9-10 (good advice, loyalty)

• Proverbs 28:23 (honesty)

• John 15:13-15 (sacrificial love)

• Hebrews 10:24 (helping each other to be better people)

3. *Be patient with others.*

• How do we receive patience? Galatians 5:22 (from the Holy Spirit)

• What does "being patient" mean? Colossians 3:12-13 (being forgiving, not holding grudges)

• What are the characteristics of real love? 1 Corinthians 13:4-8 (patience, kindness, humility, forgiveness, trustfulness)

• How does patience grow? James 1:2-4 (through trials—difficult situations)

4. *Serve one another.* How can we serve others according to these verses?

• Proverbs 3:27-28 (Give them what they need.)

• Proverbs 15:1 (Speak patiently.)

• Matthew 5:40-42 (Give more than asked.)

• Matthew 25:34-39 (Be aware of needs and help meet them.)

• Acts 20:35 (Give.)

• Philippians 2:3-4 (Put others before yourself.)

• James 2:14-16 (Act on your faith.)

• 1 Peter 4:9 (Be hospitable.)

5. *Encourage others.* What is the main point of each of these verses or how do they illustrate encouragement?

• Proverbs 15:4 (Encouraging words build up others.)

• Proverbs 16:24 (Positive words bring healing.)

• Proverbs 25:20 (Insensitivity can harm others.)

• 1 Corinthians 1:4-6 (Paul thanks the Corinthians for

their strength.)

• 1 Corinthians 16:16-18 (Do everything to encourage those who work hard.)

• 2 Timothy 4:11 (Mark's help would encourage Paul.)

• Revelation 2:1-3 (God affirms the good qualities in the church at Ephesus.)

6. *Become involved in church.* How should church involvement help us deal with loneliness in ourselves and others? Check out the example of the early church.

• Acts 2:44-47 (People shared their time and money.)

• Acts 4:23 (Believers shared good news with each other.)

• Acts 12:1-5 (They prayed for each other.)

• Acts 14:19-28 (The early church supported Paul's missionary work.)

• Acts 16:40 (Church leaders encouraged the body of believers.)

• Acts 20:17-28 (Paul and the Ephesians had a strong bond of love.)

• Acts 28:11-15 (The early church encouraged Paul and helped meet his needs.)

Words and Marks ■ Read the passages and discuss the questions.

1. James 3:1-12

• How can our words hurt others? (by cutting them down—directly or through gossip)

• What kind of words should come out of the mouths of Christians? (words of praise, words that build others up, etc.)

2. 1 John 4:7-10

• What is the mark of a Christian? (love)

• How do we show that we love God? (by loving others)

• How can we love others? (put love into action; consider the needs of others and strive to meet those needs)

VALUES AND PRIORITIES

CROWD-BREAKERS

A Cut Above ■ Have contestants guess the prices of types of elective surgery. Beforehand, arrange to have various kids act as models for the types of surgery. Each time, have one parade between the audience and the contestants, emphasizing the part of the anatomy that is to be fixed. Whenever possible, use the technical name. Then, after the bidding, explain what the surgery is. After each surgery is presented, each contestant should guess the cost, writing the guess on a card. Then the cards should be displayed, one contestant at a time (begin with a different contestant each time). The winner is the person who comes closest without going over the actual amount. Here are some surgeries and their average costs in 1995.

- hair transplant—$5000
- nose job—$3500
- liposuction—$3000
- pace maker installed (batteries not included)—$9000
- orthoscopic knee surgery—$12,500
- MRI—$1000
- face lift—$6000
- otoplasty (ear job)—$2000
- mentoplasty (chin tuck)—$17,500
- blepharoplasty (eye tucks)—$3500
- heart by-pass—$37,000

Concentration ■ Use two decks of cards and place them face down in the center of the floor in a large square. Have a team on each side of the square, and play a large version of Concentration. First, two cards are turned over so that everyone can see them. The cards are then returned to their face-down positions. The next person then turns over two cards, and so on. The goal is to find two identical cards. When this happens, they are picked up and the person continues until a mismatch occurs. Continue until all the cards are gone and determine the winning team.

Drop Everything ■ This is a relay, and so you will need teams and a set of boxes for each team. After you divide into teams, give each a pile of boxes of varying shapes and sizes. The boxes should be closed so that they cannot fit inside each other. Explain that the first person should pick up one box and carry it to the other end of the room and back. He or she should then hand the box to the next person who should pick up another one, carry both boxes to the other end of the room and back, and give them to the third person who should add a third box to the stack and so on. The race continues until one team has successfully transported all of the boxes, at one time, down and back. If any of the boxes are dropped, the person dropping them must return to the end of his or her team's line. The next team member must then retrieve the boxes and continue that leg of the relay from that point. As a surprise ingredient, explain that whenever your assistant blows a whistle, the participants, wherever they are, must drop everything and return to the end of their lines. Then the next team members must pick up the boxes and continue the relay. Make sure that your whistle-blowing assistant is behind a screen or a wall and cannot see the relay as it progresses. He or she should blow the whistle at about 45 second to one-minute intervals, early in the contest. This game can be used to make a point about how we feel as we try to carry too many responsibilities and fulfill too many demands on our time and the chaos caused when we are asked to "drop everything" to do something else.

Juggler Vein ■ Bring a juggler to the meeting to teach the whole group how to juggle. Be sure you have enough sets of items to juggle so that everyone can participate. If you have a large crowd, use items that they have in their pockets, purses, etc. or have volunteers come to the front to participate. Possible juggling items could include: Ping Pong balls, coins, oranges, tennis balls, etc. Make sure the items are not breakable or messy. This game illustrates how we often feel about our interests and activities—trying to juggle our schedules to keep everything in the air.

Quitting Time ■ This is a physical contest often used by wrestling coaches to toughen up their athletes. Have everyone find a place along one of the walls. Then they should assume a type of squatting position with their feet directly below their knees and their backs leaning against the wall. At first this will be easy, but soon it will be difficult to maintain the position. See who can stay in that position the longest without quitting; then give him or her a prize. This game highlights the concept of knowing when to quit.

Schedule ■ Before the meeting, write out the following activities on individual pieces of paper and make a number of sets so you have one for each team.

quiet time	eat breakfast
study	call boy/girlfriend
attend school classes	eat dinner
watch television	attend school classes
practice sport	jog
kiss Mom good-bye	go shopping
feed dog	write term paper
go to youth group	sleep
eat lunch	read book

With a maximum of ten people per team, there will be more activities than people. Place the slips of paper in boxes (one set and box per team). At your signal, everyone should rush to their team's box and pull out a piece of paper. Next, they should arrange themselves in the order that they should do the activities and then sit down in line. (Example: "eat breakfast" should go before "eat lunch.") The first team seated in an order that makes sense wins that round. After each round, everyone should return their papers to their team's box. Repeat for four or five rounds.

Time Trial ■ Before the meeting, hide $10 in the room and design or write about 20 treasure maps. Some of these maps should be false, some should be very complicated, and three or four should be correct and relatively easy to understand. The maps could be a sketch, a list of clues, a series of steps to take, a poem, etc. In addition, prepare a set of time cards—a deck of cards with an amount of time (ranging from 30 seconds to 3 minutes) taped to each card. Most of the times should fall in the 60–90 second range.

Arrange the group in a circle around the pile of maps that are face down on the floor. Explain that you have hidden $10 in the room and that you will give some of them the chance to find it. Choose your first searcher and have him or her draw a time card out of the deck; this tells how much time he or she will have to search for the treasure. Explain that the maps will help guide the search, and have the first searcher select a map. Repeat with about four or five kids or until the treasure is found. (Note: The treasure probably will not be found; however, you should be willing to part with the money just in case it is.)

This game illustrates how we use our time and how we solve problems. The most successful treasure-seeker will be the person who carefully looks over all the maps used so far, noting similarities, etc. and then looks for the treasure. He or she will also use information gleaned by watching previous searchers.

Treasure Hunt ■ Distribute magazines throughout the room, making sure that each student has at least one. Call out various items and see who can find them first. If you don't need the magazines, have kids tear out the items and hold them up. The first person to hold up the item wins that round. You could ask for:

- a bottle
- a beauty enhancement product
- great looking shoes
- a hot car
- something very expensive
- perfume
- sports equipment
- pleasure
- love
- happiness
- something guaranteed to bring popularity
- something that God doesn't like
- something that God approves of

Upside Down and Inside Out ■ This is a relay using teams. It will serve as a visual object lesson of the fact that biblical values are often the opposite of society's. Before the meeting, prepare slips of paper giving specific instructions for each person's actions. Make four sets of these instructions (one for each team) and put them in separate paper bags. Line up the teams at one end of the room and explain that this will be a relay where each person has to perform a specific task that will be drawn out of the team's bag. When the first person finishes his or her task, the next person may proceed until all the tasks are completed. The first team done wins. You will need appropriate props for the following possible tasks:

1. Run to the other end of the room, pick up the paper and pen, and print your full name (including middle name) upside down and backward.

2. Take off your shoes, lie on your back, and scoot across the room and back. (Provide towels to scoot on if the floor is dirty.)

3. Run to the other end and drink a Coke upside down (leaning against the wall with your feet in the air, supported by another team member).

4. Run to the other end of the room, pick up the book, open it to the marked paragraph, turn it *upside down*, and read it aloud.

5. Choose an article of clothing that you are wearing (sock, shirt, jacket, etc.), run to the other end of the room, take it off and put it back on inside out, and return to your team.

6. Run to the other end of the room and shout out the alphabet backward, one letter at a time from Z to A.

7. Run to the other end of the room and back as fast as you can while making three complete revolutions on the way down and on the way back.

8. Line up your team from shortest to tallest and then from tallest to shortest.

9. Run to the other end of the room, take the new and unopened plastic garbage bag and turn it inside out.

10. Run to the other end of the room, take a piece of poster board and marker and draw a skiing scene with mountain, house, and skier, upside down.

Whodunit ■ Before the meeting, prepare papers divided into four equal sections labeled "Who," "Where," "What," and "When." On the back of the sheets, write "Why." Give everyone a piece of paper and a pen. Tell them to use their imaginations and to write a creative answer to the question "Why" on their papers. Tell them that someone did something unusual, and so they should write out an unusual explanation (e.g., "because her boyfriend warned her that she better not go to the movies with her girlfriends" . . . or "because last Thursday, flying saucers were spotted near the school cafeteria.")

Next they should fold the papers in fourths so the "Who" section is showing. Collect the papers and redistribute them right away or at a later point in the meeting. Then have everyone write an imaginative answer to "Who" (e.g., "Strawberry Shortcake," "Bill Clinton," "Spiderman," etc.). Repeat the folding, redistributing, and writing process until all the sections are filled. Then collect and read them aloud, beginning with "Who" and going through "Why." This could be tied into a humorous look at lifestyles.

DISCUSSION STARTERS

Evidence ■ Bring two strangers to the group. These should be Christian students from another church and school. If they are similar in style of dress and interests, have one of them dress like another type of kid at school (for example, burn-out, punker, nerd, jock, etc.).

Give everyone a piece of paper and a pencil or pen. Then introduce your guests. Ask them to walk through the crowd, and tell the crowd to write down what they think these kids are like. Obviously they will be forming their opinions simply by the clothes, pins, hairstyles, make-up, etc. that they see.

Collect the papers and put them aside. Then tell the audience that they may ask these kids questions to help them determine what they are really like. Have an assistant record the questions asked.

After the questioning, read some of the written descriptions of your guests. Then ask the audience if they think those descriptions are accurate in light of what they have just learned through questioning. Next, ask why they used the questions they did—why did they think those questions would help? Then ask the audience what they think of your guests' spiritual lives (for example: Are the guests Christians? How do they know?). Conclude by telling the truth about your guests. Then challenge your kids to think about what sets them apart as Christians (actions, values, etc.).

Fashion Show ■ Have a fashion show with the clothes being modeled all worn inside out. Use this to illustrate how Jesus' values turn the world's values inside out. Here are some examples:

- Jesus says serve; the world says be served
- Jesus say give glory; the world says get glory
- Jesus says do your best; the world says win at all costs
- Jesus says money is a means; the world says money is the end
- Jesus says be last; the world says be first

Goals ■ Pass out 8 1/2" X 11" sheets of paper and pencils and have everyone divide the papers into four sections, labeled Physical, Social, Spiritual, and Mental. Ask students to write near the top of each of these sections, one goal for improving their lives in that area. The goal should be specific and measurable (for example, "I will lose 15 pounds" or "I will help Mom around the house" or "I will read the Bible through in a year," etc.). Beneath each goal, they should write a three or four step strategy for achieving it (for example, "cut out candy breaks," "jog every day," "don't eat seconds," etc.) Challenge students to keep these goals posted in their rooms or in their notebooks as constant reminders of what they want to accomplish.

Good, Better, Best ■ This may be used as a discussion starter or as part of your wrap-up. Summarize the meeting, explaining what the games were meant to illustrate. Have everyone look at their lists of things to do, now prioritized, and explain that part of their responsibility as Christians is to use their time well. Often they will have to make difficult choices concerning which activities to do, which clubs to join, and which responsibilities to accept. These choices may be between good and bad, but usually they will involve all good things. Then they must choose the best over the merely good or even the better. Emphasize that self-discipline and knowing how to use time are very important in this process. Offer to have a seminar on using time.

House of Cards ■ Using playing cards, shuffle them and deal them out so that everyone has six cards. Explain that "clubs" stand for activities, interests, and mental abilities; "spades" stand for health and physical abilities; "diamonds" represent possessions, money, and jobs; "hearts" represent relationships, social standing, and popularity. (Note: it would be helpful to post these instructions on the wall.) Tell kids to write one specific thing, person, or ability they have on each corresponding card (something they have).

Discuss how they feel about the cards they have been dealt (for example, perhaps someone received no "hearts," etc.) and why this may or may not be like life. Then give everyone the opportunity to trade for other cards. (Have extras of each at the front.) Any

card may be traded for another card, but no one may have more than six cards. Discuss what they traded and why.

Next, have everyone shuffle their six cards and place the cards on the floor, face down, in front of them. Go around the room and take a card from everyone. Then have them look at their remaining cards. Discuss how they felt about losing *those* cards and why this experience is a good example of what often happens in a terrible disaster like a hurricane, tornado, or an earthquake.

Invest ■ Before the meeting, choose four associates or student leaders to be team captains. Explain that you will be giving them roles to play during the meeting. They may be creative, but they should stay within their designated roles which are:

- *Businessman*—come dressed in a three-piece suit and tie, carrying a briefcase. Your goal is to make as much money as possible.
- *Athlete or movie star*—come dressed in sports equipment or in a glamorous outfit. Your goal is to be as famous as possible.
- *Mother Teresa type*—come dressed in rags or in an outfit implying service. Your goal is to help as many people as possible.
- *Handicapped person*—come in a wheelchair and/or with another obvious handicap (blindfolded, hand tied behind back, etc.). You may choose your goal (any of the others).

These captains' first task is to recruit members for their teams. Give each one his or her own place in the room, and then have them recruit members as kids enter the room. Don't worry about the relative size of the teams. Each captain should try to recruit as many as possible. Later in the meeting you will discuss why individuals chose particular teams.

Once everyone has gathered in their groups with their leaders, explain that there will be three rounds during which each group must design a plan to invest for the purpose of being successful whatever you give them. It should be their plan; they can write whatever they want within the allotted time. (During this activity, the team leaders should stay in character—businessman, athlete or "star," Mother Teresa type, handicapped person—trying to persuade their teams to follow their lead; but the teams may go in any direction that they choose. Paper and poster board will be needed for the teams.) Here are the rounds:

Round 1: *Money.* Give the teams a hypothetical $3 per person (businessman), $2 per person (athlete/star), $1 per person (Mother Teresa type), and $.50 per person (handicapped).

Round 2: *Abilities*. They should use the abilities that the team members possess. Don't weight any of them.

Round 3: *Time*. Give each team a personal life span of 50 more years.

Groups should plot their investment plans on the poster board. For each of these rounds, the teams should agree on a team strategy. If consensus is impossible, they may have a minority report later. Have each team give its report one round at a time. In other words, begin with "money," and have the teams report; then move to "abilities," and so on. During these reports, be careful not to make any value judgments or to interject your own values. Instead, clarify what the students mean and probe for their rationale and motivations. Also, if a minority of any team did not agree with the majority decision on any round, give them the opportunity to explain their feelings and investment plans.

Once everyone has committed to certain values, either by words or actions, lead the following discussion:

1. Why did you choose your team? What attracted you to it? Why is your leader dressed the way he or she is dressed?

2. You were instructed to "invest for the purpose of being successful." How did your team define success? Why? What kind of influence was your leader? Do you agree with your team's definition of success? Why or why not?

3. (Have the team leaders explain their hidden agendas, what their goals were.) The "handicapped" group was different from the rest; your leader had the freedom to choose any of the other goals. Why did you choose the one(s) you did?

4. What did you think about when you discussed "invest," especially regarding "abilities" and "time"?

5. What are some biblical principles that relate to this discussion?

Just a Minute ■ Choose three or four volunteers. They should be seated at the front of the room, blindfolded. Their assignment is to estimate a one-minute passage of time. You will tell them when to start and they should stand up when they think a minute has passed. Do three rounds: one in silence, one with a background of rock music, and one with someone counting backward from 100 in a monotone voice. Have someone timing a minute and see who is the closest to being correct. Discuss how time is relative, depending on the situation and distractions.

Just What I Always Wanted ■ Before the meeting, collect a box full of old toys, tools, clothes, etc. (you can find a great selection at garage sales). Your collection could include: a shirt with a spot on it; a pair of pants with a hole in the knee; a rusty saw; a used toothbrush, an open Coke can; a child's puzzle with a piece missing; a stale loaf of bread; and other similar items. Determine a couple of prices for each item—what it would cost new and what it is worth now (or what you paid for it at the garage sale).

Explain that you are going to play a game of "The Price Is Right," and choose three kids to compete. Explain that the object is to see who can come the closest to the price of the item when it was *new*, without going over the correct amount. Then bring out the first item and take their bids. Afterward, reveal the winning price and give that person 1000 points. Offer bonus points to whomever can come closest to the "used" price. Repeat with a new set of kids for each item. Play this until your time and/or the interest runs out. Afterwards, give the highest point winners their choice of the items as prizes.

Ask:

• What made the difference in price between new and used?

• What kinds of expensive items lose their value the quickest? Why?

• Remember saying "Just what I always wanted" when you received a prized gift for Christmas or your birthday? Why didn't that gift satisfy you for very long?

• What kind of things do you tend to think of being "just what I always wanted"?

• What in this world has lasting value? Why?

List ■ Hand out pieces of paper and pencils and ask everyone to list everything that they have to do during the next week. First they should list major responsibilities (school, work, clubs, sports, etc.); then they should write down special assignments (homework, chores, etc.); next, they should list required events that they have to attend (church, dates, brother's soccer game, etc.); finally, their lists should include desired activities—what they want to do if they can (shopping, listening to records, watching favorite TV programs, etc.) and miscellaneous items—little specific things which may come up during the week (call friend, write letters, plant flowers, etc.). These lists will be quite long. Then ask:

• How do you find time for all these things?

• For which category do you usually make time? Why?

• How do you decide which things to do and which

ones to drop or put off?

Nick of Time ■ Hand out papers and pens to everyone. Have group members list the following activities (or have them preprinted on the sheet).

school	dates
Bible reading	worship
fun with friends	meals
sports	reading for fun
shopping	talks with friends
church activities	talks with others about God
prayer	work
work outs	homework
talks on the phone	meditation/contemplation

Next, have students write to the left of each item the approximate number of hours they spend in a typical week doing each activity. Then ask group members to analyze their sheets to evaluate their lives. Ask:

• What does this little exercise tell you about your priorities?

• What *should* be your priorities?

• What can you do to change?

• Besides time spent on them, what other measurements are there for our interests? (money spent, thought life, effects of the activities, etc.)

• When do you feel as though you are just going through the motions? How can this change?

Shopping Spree ■ Distribute pencils or pens and sheets of paper with the following items listed down the left side and blanks after each one.

[ ] happy family _____

[ ] successful career _____

[ ] fame/popularity _____

[ ] wealth _____

[ ] sex _____

[ ] strong relationship with God _____

[ ] fun/pleasure/good feelings _____

[ ] good looks _____

[ ] athletic skill _____

[ ] solid marriage _____

Down the left side, in the boxes, students should rate these items in order of priority, 1–10. Then have them imagine that they have $1,000,000 to spend. They should divide it among the various items as bids. Explain that each item will go to the person who bids the highest for it.

Allow a few minutes for everyone to write their

bids in the blanks to the right of each item. Then go through the items one at a time and award them to the highest bidders. In case of equal bids, award the items to all those bidding that amount. Students should circle the items that they have won.

After you have awarded all the items, ask everyone how they felt about the items they won, how those items matched up with their priorities, and how they decided on the amounts to bid.

Time Limit ■ To demonstrate the relativity of time, do the following:

• Bring a ticking clock or timer, and have group members compete against the clock for a prize or penalty. Have the contestants assemble a child's toy or something similar, in one minute. (This shows that in some cases time feels very short.)

• Ask two or three volunteers to stand in front of the group on one leg while blindfolded. Everyone should be quiet. Each volunteer should lower his or her leg when he or she thinks a minute has passed. (This shows that in some cases time feels long.)

To Do List ■ Give everyone a piece of paper and a pencil. Then have students write down all the activities, assignments, and responsibilities that they have in the next few days. Next, have them rate the items on their relative importance using a 1-5 rating system, 5 being for items of most importance. Discuss how they determined the importance of the items. Next, discuss where they would be most tempted to procrastinate. Finally, encourage group members to design an action plan that would involve doing the most important things first (regardless of how distasteful they may be).

Valuables ■ Distribute pencils and cards and tell each group member to describe his or her most valuable possession (call it an MVP). They should not only write what it is, but why it is their MVP. Also, make sure that they describe a possession—a thing (not a person, a relationship, or a concept). For instance, "dog" would be all right, but "God" or "love" would not. After a minute or two, collect the cards and read a few of them aloud. The cards will probably contain some serious and some humorous answers.

Comment on how interesting their MVPs were. Then ask students to summarize the "why" answers that you read. Ask: *What makes something valuable to us? What criteria do we use?* Ask why some of these items were more valuable to certain people than the original cost. Emphasize the fact that worth is a value that we place on something. List the "worth" criteria on a piece of poster board or the chalkboard. The list will probably include: "It is valuable to me because . . ."

- "I have invested in it." (money, time, self, etc.)
- "It serves a special, necessary service to me."
- "There is 'love' attached to it."
- "In the past, it was good or helpful."

Next ask: *What gives you "worth" to God?* Use the previous criteria as discussion points.

Winning Hand ■ Before the meeting, get a stack of 3"x 5" cards and write on each one a specific item, quality, or personality characteristic. These could include: a new car, a perfect complexion, beautiful hair, a great singing voice, 135 IQ, a great body, a state-of-the-art stereo system, $1,000 in cash, a new wardrobe, a condo in Europe, etc. Also include a few just average things like "job in a factory," "a used car," "two weeks vacation a year," and others.

Give each person five cards and instructions to not show them to anyone else. After everyone has the cards, explain that this game is played like Pit where you trade an equal number of cards with another person by yelling out the number of cards you have to trade (for example, "three, three!"). The cards don't have to contain the same items to be traded, just the same number. The idea is to try to come up with "a winning hand." (Note: at this point you will be asked what determines "winning." Don't answer the question—just begin the game.)

After five minutes or so, stop the game, seat everyone, and discuss the experience. Have a few kids explain why their hands are "winning" ones. Ask others why they traded certain cards and what they hoped to get in return. Be sure to discover what they used as criteria for "winning" and "value."

DISCUSSIONS AND WRAP-UPS

Talk-to ■ Use these points as a wrap-up to the meeting, discussing each point briefly.

1. *God's values are the opposite of the world's.* Jesus said that "the first must be last, the servant," "the greatest will be least," and "you'll find your life when you lose it."

2. *Real success is doing what God wants.* This means "seeking first His kingdom."

3. *God commands us to be good stewards of our lives.* We are to invest our lives wisely for Him.

4. *All of life must come under God's control.* This includes your present and your future.

5. *What you are right now will determine what you will become.* How are you investing your life?

The End ■ Ask: *When does time seem to fly?* Possible answers might include: the last minute of a game when your team is losing; the last day of vacation; the last hours with a boyfriend or girlfriend; etc.

Ask: *When does time seem to crawl?* Possible answers: when you're running a marathon; the last minute of a game when you're winning by a close margin; the months and days when you are apart from a loved one; when you're sitting in a boring class; etc.

BIBLE STUDIES

Assignment ■ Give everyone the assignment of reading Matthew 25:14-30 and writing down any questions they have about it (this is the Parable of the Talents). Offer to discuss their questions personally or at a future meeting.

Bible Search ■ Divide into four groups and give each group a passage to discuss. Each group should choose a person to lead the discussion and report to the large group their answers. If possible, have handouts with all the passages and questions available so everyone can take notes on other groups' findings.

Passages:

1. Mark 9:33-37; 10:17-21

2. Matthew 20:1-16; Luke 13:22-30

3. Matthew 6:31-34; John 13:12-17

4. Matthew 25:14-30

Questions:

1. List the biblical principle(s) contained in your verses.

2. What are the values taught or implied?

3. What definition of success is taught or implied?

4. How do biblical values and success compare to the world's?

5. How should these passages affect your future (career choice, relationships)?

Birds and Treasure ■ Distribute copies of Luke 12:22-34 (or have everyone turn to the passage) and read the verses together. Have group members underline words or statements that say something about our value to God. Discuss the underlined portions. Then ask:

- How is life "more than food" and the body "more

than clothes"? What does that statement mean? (We have more than physical needs.)

• What does it mean that we are "more valuable than birds" to God? Why are we more valuable? What should be our response to this truth? (See verses 22, 25, 26, 29.)

• If God really loves us this much, what should be our response? (See verses 29-33.)

• Explain this statement, "Where your treasure is, there your heart will be also." Where is your treasure?

Priorities ■ Have group members read Ecclesiastes 3:1-8 and Ephesians 5:15-17. Then ask:

• How do these verses apply to how we use our time?

• In light of this, what changes should you make in your schedule?

• How do you determine your priorities?

Principles and Priorities ■ Discuss the following Bible passages, one at a time, discovering the principle that is being taught and asking how it applies to group members' schedules and choices. The biblical principle is in parentheses after each passage. After the discussion, explain the principle.

1. Matthew 6:33-34 (A person's relationship with God should be the number one priority in his or her life.)

2. Ephesians 5:15-17 (We must be careful how we use our time.)

3. John 9:4 and James 4:14 (Our time is limited; we must use it wisely.)

4. Colossians 3:23-24 (We must work hard at all we do; we are really working for Christ.)

Time ■ Have group members read James 1:22-24 and 2:14-18. Then ask:

• How do these verses relate to our use of time? Procrastination?

• What would it take for you to discipline yourself to get things done?

True Treasures ■ Ask a student to read Matthew 6:19-24 aloud as everyone follows along. Discuss the passage using the following questions:

Verses 19-21

• What treasures do people "store up" on earth? How? Why?

• Explain this: "Where your treasure is, there your heart will be also."

Verse 24

• What do people do that shows that they love and serve money?

• Why is it impossible to serve both God and money?

• Why are people so obsessed with money?

Verses 22-23

• Why do you think these verses are sandwiched between the thoughts of 19-21 and 24?

• What do they mean? (Answer: Eyes refer to vision, a way of seeing. Christians have the ability to see life from God's perspective. The world's point of view is quite different; in fact, it's often the opposite. The way we look at life and the world will determine whether we have God's values and live by His standards or not, whether we are filled with light or darkness.)

• How do you think God would have wanted you to order your priorities in life?

Worry ■ Have group members read Matthew 6:25-34. Then ask:

• What causes you to worry?

• Which of these categories represent your worries: food, drink, or clothes?

• How can we "seek first the kingdom of God"?

• What are the "other things" that will be given to us?

• What does verse 34 mean? How can this apply to us today?

GOD'S WILL AND THE FUTURE

CROWD-BREAKERS

Ash in a Flash ■ You'll need a large area for this activity. Divide into teams of two and instruct team members to lock arms, back-to-back, and race to the end of the room and back. Explain that during this "arms race," periodically you will activate a flash (using a strobe flash unit). Whenever they see the flash, they must hit the floor. Then they can get back up (with arms locked) and continue the race. The first team back wins.

Back to the Future ■ Before the meeting, write a number of descriptions on cards for each of four categories: marriage and family, career, environment (home, neighborhood, etc.), and hobbies and leisure activities. These descriptions should range from the normal and mundane to the creative and off-the-wall. For example, for *career*, some of the cards could read: horticulturist, stunt pilot, smell engineer (received PhD in armpit physiology), mad scientist (studies anger), cotton-pickin-finger-lickin-chicken-plucker, and so forth. Place the cards into four boxes or envelopes.

Explain that they may be worried or fearful about the future, but you have the gift of prophecy and have perfected a way for them to find out what they will become. Have each person draw one card out of each box. Then have them the cards aloud. The futures will include such gems as:

• *married at 42 to much younger spouse (13)–have three boys, five girls, and two gerbils*

• *professional roller coaster tester–life has its ups and downs*

• *lives in a Quonset hut overlooking Dreary Gulch in*

central Utah

• *collects stamps and sky dives . . . at the same time*

Career Path ■ Before the meeting, prepare 50 index cards with the following information. Write one line on each card and the same line on the number of cards noted in parentheses:

• graduate from high school (15 cards)

• get accepted at the right college (8 cards)

• graduate from college (7 cards)

• get advanced degree (5 cards)

• get job as apprentice (5 cards)

• go to night school to get degree (3 cards)

• work in family business (2 cards)

• get married (5 cards)

• note: you may want to add a bunch of dead-end cards like, "drop out of high school," "watch TV all day," "buy lottery tickets and hope to hit it big," "lift weights," "buy a hot car," etc.

In addition, make "career" cards with occupations written on them. Make sure that you have enough for every person to have one.

Shuffle the "career" cards and distribute them to everyone. Then shuffle the "path" cards and distribute them so that everyone has the same amount. Explain that their goal should be to hold cards that describe a career path that will lead them to a good career. They may trade any number of cards with anyone, but the cards must be traded face down. In other words, these should be blind trades. The trading will continue for five minutes.

Give the signal to begin. After five minutes, ask everyone to be quiet. Then have volunteers explain the careers they chose and the path they acquired for getting there. Discuss whether these career paths are realistic or not and why.

End of Your Rope ■ Divide into teams. Then have everyone sit at random in single file columns on the floor. (Teams will be interspersed throughout the columns.) Give each column a length of rope. Each person must be seated with both hands on the rope. The game is played like musical chairs. When the music plays, everyone scoots along the floor from one end of their rope to the other. When a person gets to the end of the rope, he or she should stand, run to the beginning, and begin moving down the rope again. When the music stops, everyone should freeze in place. Those standing count as points against their teams. At the end, the team with the lowest number of points wins.

Fallout ■ Hand out small paper bags to everyone. Then explain that in a few minutes there will be a "nuclear explosion." Each person's job is to try to catch the most "fallout"—little Styrofoam pieces that are used for packing fragile items. Next, turn out the lights and tell everyone to get ready to catch and to put their fallout in their bags. Turn on a strobe light and then throw out the Styrofoam pieces (by handfuls) over their heads. They should remain seated while they catch. After a few minutes, turn on the lights and have everyone count their fallout pieces; the one with the most wins.

Following Directions ■ Give everyone the same set of construction materials. Then read a pre-written set of building instructions. Group members may not ask questions or be told what they are making. Find a simple craft made with paper, cardboard, tape, etc. Read the directions slowly, giving everyone time to follow them. It will be very interesting to see who comes the closest to making what they were supposed to. (These crafts may be found in *Highlights* magazines or various Sunday School materials.)

You may also hand out paper and pencils and describe, step by step, a picture or design they will draw. Again, don't tell them what they're drawing.

The Future ■ Distribute index cards and pens or pencils. Tell everyone to write their names on the top of the cards. Afterwards, collect the cards and shuffle them. Pass the cards out again, making sure that no one gets his or her own card. Tell students to write a future prediction for the person whose name is on the card they received. Note: these predictions should not be insulting.

After a few minutes, collect the cards. Read them aloud, without telling who is being described and see if the group can guess whose future is being described.

Future Telling ■ Before the meeting, ask a few parents about some of the little-known future plans of their young people. At the meeting, introduce the great Swami, teller of the future, and have him or her make specific predictions about these group members. Be sure to sprinkle in some off-the-wall humorous predictions.

Guidance ■ This will work best with four to six couples. They may compete as team representatives or simply as couples. In any case, have one member of each team stand behind a long table in front of the room. Have the other member of each couple kneel on the floor in front of his or her partner. Next, give each person standing behind the table a bag of Legos. (These may be purchased as small "kits," each of which will form a specific vehicle, person, building, etc.) At no time should the "builders" be told or have any idea what they are building. Then give the kneeling partners the instructions. At your signal, the kneelers should read the instructions to the standers. The couple to build the correct Legos' project first wins.

Head I Win, Tails You Lose ■ This is an outdoor activity in a neighborhood. Divide into two teams. Explain that both teams will start at the same point on the sidewalk but will face opposite directions. When you say go, they should begin to walk. At every corner, the team leader should flip a coin. If it lands on heads, they should turn right; if tails, they should turn left. After ten to twelve minutes, you will sound a loud signal (whistle, church bell, boat horn, etc.). When they hear the signal, they should run back to the meeting place. The first team to return wins. (If they don't hear the signal, they should return after fifteen minutes.) When the groups return, have them tell about their journeys, where they ended up, and how they felt about the process.

Highways and Byways ■ Bring the same number of copies of a map as the number of teams you will have in the meeting. Beforehand, choose an obscure location on the map and write a series of map-oriented descriptions of the mystery place. Give each team a map and explain that their job is to find the mystery location. Then read the descriptions aloud, one at a time. The first team to find the exact location wins. Repeat if you have time with another mystery location. Here are some sample directions:

about fifty miles from Madison; about ten miles from a lake; near a railroad; two miles from the intersection of two state highways; fourteen miles from a state park; etc.

Landing a Job ■ Before the meeting, take pieces of cardboard or poster board (approximately the number of kids who will be attending) and tape or write an occupation on each one. Scatter the boards around the room, face down. Then have everyone find a place to stand in the room, without touching any of the pieces of cardboard. Explain that this game is like musical chairs. When the music stops, they should try to land on a job (stand on a piece of cardboard)—the person getting to the cardboard first (or, in case of a tie, covering most of it), gets that job for that round. Anyone not landing a job is eliminated from the game. Here are some possible occupations to use: architect, engineer, doctor, electrician, accountants, business executive, geologist, manufacturer's sales representative, clerk, car sales person, banker writer, youth minister, actor, police officer, elected official, X-ray technician, secretary, soldier, garbage collector, teacher, insurance broker, government bureaucrat, cashier, photographer, realtor, travel agent, truck driver, telephone operator, small business owner, retail sales clerk, scientist, interior decorator, carpenter, janitor, TV camera operator.

After each round, eliminate a job or two by explaining a difficult circumstance (let those who have been eliminated—now unemployed—decide on which jobs should be taken away). Here are some difficult circumstances to use:

• high interest rates

• inflation

• population shift

• recession

• new taxes

• corruption in high places

• natural disaster

• new technology rendering product obsolete

• glut in the marketplace

• etc.

Orders from Headquarters ■ Have everyone stand and distribute the following sheet of instructions. Tell them to follow the instructions **exactly** as printed. Although everyone will have the same instructions, each person will achieve quite different results.

ORDERS

1. Face your house.

2. Turn to the right.

3. Take five steps and turn around 180 degrees.

4. Stand shoulder to shoulder with the person closest to you.

5. Take ten steps, heel to toe, toward the wall farthest away from you.

6. Turn to your left and take two giant steps (as far as you can stretch).

7. Sit down and yell, "I'm done!"

Plate Pendulum ■ Choose three representatives from each team and designate one as the sender, one the receiver, and one the swinger. Construct a plate-pendulum using a pie tin, suspended by a length of string attached to the center of the tin. The sender and receiver are seated six feet apart with the swinger standing between them. The swinger swings the plate like a pendulum between the two team members. The object of the game is to see how quickly the sender can transfer a stack of items, one at a time, to his or her receiver without losing any items and without touching the plate. Possible items to be passed: popcorn kernels, Ping Pong ball, tissue paper, wet piece of soap, etc. The quickest time wins.

Predictions ■ Pass out paper and pens and have everyone write down his or her predictions for twenty years from now for the following:

1. Madonna

2. Super Bowl winners

3. Popular hairstyles

4. President of the U.S.

5. Space travel

6. Most popular fast food restaurant

7. The occupations of three people in the room

Collect the papers and read the predictions aloud.

Radioactivity ■ This is "musical chairs" with a new name and twist. Set up chairs in a circle facing out with one less chair than you have participants. If possible, plug in the radio to a socket controlled by the wall switch that also controls the lights. When you play the radio, group members should walk clockwise around the circle of chairs. When you turn out the lights and the radio, they should scramble for an empty chair. After a moment or two, turn on the lights. The person without a chair is eliminated from the game. Remove another chair and repeat. Continue until only one person is left and declare him or her the champion.

The Right Turns ■ Make up a dance where the predominant move is a right turn. For example, on a 4/4 count, they could take a step to the right side on 1, a step to the left side on 2, pivot to the right on 3, then clap and bring the left foot up even with the right one on 4.

The Seer ■ Before the meeting, write out a bunch of "fortunes" and put them in a box painted black with white question marks all over it. Have a staff member or a student dress-up like a fortune teller, complete with robe and turban. Introduce him or her as the "Great Swami Salomi" who will tell their futures. Then, one at a time, have students approach the front. The "Swami" should touch them on the forehead, take their pulse, look intently into their eyes, or do some other melodramatic act. Then he or she should reach into the future box, pull out a fortune, and read it. Some of these fortunes should be fulfilled immediately or at another time during the meeting. Here are some possibilities:

•*You will drop out of school, marry a witch doctor (which doctor? . . . Yes, that's the one), and tour the remote areas of Zambia looking for happiness.*

•*You will become rich and famous . . . but then lose it all in a stock swindle . . . but then inherit a bundle from a long lost aunt . . . but then gamble it all away in Las Vegas . . . but then win the Magazine Sweepstakes . . . but then. . . .*

•*You will be surprised, very soon.* (Later, in the meeting, pull a surprise on this person.)

•*In four days, you will have a nightmare which will happen one week later.*

•*Soon you will receive a very disturbing phone call.* (Have someone call this person a few minutes later.)

•*Your next date will be _very_ interesting. This person will go out with you only because he or she feels sorry for you, but then will realize what a wonderful person you are and want to get very serious.*

•*In the next 24 hours, you will have to make three _very big_ decisions.* (Later, in the meeting, use this person in a game that involves decisions.)

•*You will give me $5 right now!*

Sneak A-tack ■ Obtain a large map of the world and post it on a bulletin board or a piece of cork board. Divide into two teams and designate one as Russia and the other as the USA (or two other countries of comparable size). Explain that this game is much like Pin the Tail on the Donkey, except that each person will be pinning *bombs* on the other country. These bombs should be color-coded

pushpins. The game begins with team #1 sending their first "bomber" to the map. While blindfolded, the bomber walks to the map and pushes the pin into it, trying to land on enemy territory. Next, team #2's bomber attacks. Proceed until everyone has dropped a bomb or until one team scores a direct hit on the other's capital city. To determine the winning team, count the number of pins in each country of both colors. The country with the least number of pins in it wins.

Steer Crazy ■ If you meet in a gym or large room, use Big Wheels or tricycles for this race. In a home or smaller room, have the racers crawl. Lay out a race course in the room. The course should vary in width along the way, beginning at about six feet and narrowing down to two feet at a couple of places. Use orange cones, cardboard boxes, or masking tape on the floor as the outside borders of the course. The course should have at least two turns in it. Mark out areas for "pit stops," one per team.

Divide into teams and have each team choose a competitor. Line up the competitors, side by side, at the starting line and line the non-racing team members along the course (the teams should kneel outside the boundaries of the course). Before you give the starting signal, explain that the racers must compete *blindfolded* and that they should listen to their team members shout instructions as they "drive" the course. Also show where the pit stops are for each team and explain that each driver must make a pit stop on the way to the finish where they will be handed a spray can of deodorant that they must spray in each "pit." Then blindfold the competitors and let the race begin. Note: to determine the winner, award 1000 points for finishing first, 500 for second, etc., and deduct 100 points for each time the racer goes off the course. When a racer goes off course (crosses one of the lines on either side), he or she must re-enter the course no more than three feet down the course from where he or she left. Also, if you have a short course, you may want to have the racers go around it more than once.

If you have time, repeat with a new set of competitors and keep a running point total to determine the winning team.

Stockpile ■ Divide into teams and give each team a section of the room as its territory. Explain that you will give teams 90 seconds to build the highest stockpile using any items that they can find on their assorted team members. (They can't use the members themselves.) Give the signal to begin, and after 90 seconds, measure the piles to determine the winning team.

Treasure Hunt ■ This may be done inside or outside, in cars or on foot, depending on your space and time limitations. Before the meeting, hide a treasure and a series of clues leading to the treasure. Each clue should be a riddle that will lead the team or individual to the next clue and so on until the treasure is found. Although this will take more work, you can make the hunt more exciting by giving a different set of clues to each team. The last clue for all the teams should be the same, however, because it will lead to the treasure. Letter and number the clues so that team members will know if they have found the right clues for their team. Team A, for example, would be handed clue A-1 which would lead them to A-2, etc. Before the hunt begins, be sure to explain the ground rules (geographical parameters, phone number for additional help, maximum time limit, etc.). Here are a few sample clues: "A place with class, to fail or pass; a winter cheer, may be heard here." (the entrance to the high school gym); "I never sausage activity; it's a real slice; certainly a sign of the times." (the pizza place, under the sign); "After hours delivery assured; at this wordy place, volumes will be heard." (the public library night depository).

What's Our Will ■ Take three or four kids out of the room. While they're out, decide on a specific action that the group wants an individual to take (for example, place both hands on the right hip, stand on one foot, give someone a high five, put fingers in both ears, kneel in a praying position, etc.).

Bring the first person back into the room. Explain that the group has a specific action that they want him or her to do, something involving hands and feet. The audience will applaud if the person is moving toward the desired position or action and will respond with a standing ovation when the desired position or action is reached.

Repeat with the others, with new actions each time.

Will I? ■ Have kids match these famous "wills." The correct answers are parentheses.

will-ful	____ (e)	a. lithe
will-ilwaw	____ (n)	b. legal document
will	____ (b)	c. wasteland
wil-debeest	____ (h)	d. favorably disposed
will-ies	____ (l)	e. stubborn
will-ing	____ (d)	f. type of carpet
will-ow	____ (k)	g. droop

wil-derness	____ (c)	h. Gnu
will-owy	____ (a)	i. Bill
will-power	____ (j)	j. strength of mind
wil-t	____ (g)	k. with narrow leaves
Wil-son	____ (m)	l. nervous
Wil-ton	____ (f)	m. Woodrow
Will-iam	____ (i)	n. violent, cold wind

DISCUSSION STARTERS

Bloody Sunday ■ In a meeting on "future fear," use the song *Sunday, Bloody Sunday* by U2. There is also a video of this available. Play the song (or show the video) and discuss it.

Epithets ■ Use a chalk board or a piece of poster board and ask students for familiar phrases that have "hell" in them. Answers will include: "It was hell!", "Like hell you do!", "Go to hell!", "Damn you!", "Hell no!", "Like a bat out of hell!", "When hell freezes over!", and others.

Then ask for familiar phrases using "heaven." The list will be much shorter and will include: "For heavens sake!", "You look divine," "It was heavenly," and others. Compare and discuss the two lists. Ask what these phrases reveal about how people view heaven and hell, why they use "hell" so much more than "heaven," and why they can be so casual about hell if they think it is really bad. Also discuss how the reality of heaven and hell should affect the way they look at the future.

Getting In ■ Divide into groups of 5–7 and tell them to create a brief skit about getting into heaven. These can be humorous or serious and should last just a couple of minutes each. After a few minutes of preparation time, have them perform the skits. Afterwards, ask why they chose the approach they did, how they feel about heaven, how most people view heaven, and what it really takes to get in.

Guidance Evidence ■ Distribute papers and pens or pencils and have students take a few minutes to look around the room for "evidence of God's guidance." They should record this evidence on one side of their papers. The room itself, objects, people, clothes, and personal belongings—anything in the room is fair game. Then have students turn over their papers and write the answer to this question: *What proof do you have that God has an agenda for your life and future?*

Take time to discuss the lists and students' answers.

Predictions ■ Distribute the following sheet. Be sure to leave room for answers when you reproduce it.

One thing I predict for:	school	family	church	country
one month from now	_____	_____	_____	_____
one year from now	_____	_____	_____	_____
one decade from now	_____	_____	_____	_____
one century from now	_____	_____	_____	_____

Collect the papers. Read them aloud, and discuss their answers.

Read It and Weep ■ Read a few literary descriptions of hell and discuss them as a group. These could include portions of Milton's *Paradise Lost*, Dante's *Inferno*, C. S. Lewis' *The Great Divorce*, Satre's *No Exit*, Myra's *No Man in Eden*, and others. Discuss briefly why these writers pictured hell the way they did and what contemporary ideas of hell are. Then read biblical descriptions. End the discussion by emphasizing the fact that hell is the ultimate horror—being totally alone and separated from God and love forever.

Signs of the Times ■ Distribute newspapers to the group and have everyone find news items that possibly could be related to events prophesied in the Bible (for example, world powers, the world getting worse, nuclear threats, etc.) or that speak of the end times (for example, themes of movies, cult leaders talking about the end of the earth, etc.). Have students explain and display their findings and discuss them as a group.

DISCUSSIONS AND WRAP-UPS

Cards ■ Hand out index cards and pencils or pens. Have everyone write the word "me" at the bottom of the card (when held vertically). Next, have them each write a goal at the top of the card (for example: *have a good career, be a good wife and mother, marry the right person*, etc.). Then have everyone write a possible "route" in the middle of the card, with possible steps to take them from now to that future goal, following

God's guidelines mentioned earlier in the meeting. Close by having kids spend time talking with God about knowing His will and reaching the goals they wrote on their cards.

Future Fear ■ Use the following outline as a guide for a discussion or for a wrap-up.

• Teenagers seem to have a lot of fears. Almost every time a survey on fear is taken, "nuclear war" and "the future" are near the top of the list.

• Uncertainty and the possibility of imminent death is a gnawing reality, and it hangs over our heads. Your parents may have practiced air raid drills in school. There was always a chance of surviving an air raid (like in England during World War II). In a nuclear war, however, survival is very unlikely. The television shows of a few years ago, *Special Bulletin* and *The Day After*, dramatized this reality.

• The future is always beyond the realm of knowing (despite "Back to the Future"); this heightens our fears.

• The Bible provides the pieces to our future puzzle and the final chapter of the book of our world's history. We can know who wins and to some extent how.

• No matter what happens, we can be assured of being on the winning side if we are Christians. And, we can be in touch with the God who is over all the future. As someone has said, "I may not know what the future holds, but I know who holds the future."

• Romans 8:28 and 38-39 give us tremendous promises about our futures. God will work all things together for our good if we trust Him and live for Him. No matter what, we can never be lost to His love.

Futures ■ To discuss future fears, ask:

• What about the future seems frightening?

• Why do we have future fears?

• How do we know what God wants us to do with our lives?

• What can a person do to overcome future fear?

Future Glimpses ■ Ask:

• What do people do to try to find out what will happen in the future? (possible answers: see fortune tellers, check astrology charts, use Ouija boards, read tea leaves, etc.)

• Every year, people spend tons of time and money trying to see into the future . . . why? Why do people want to know what will happen to them?

• What one fact would you like to know about the future? How would knowing that affect the way you live now?

God's Will ■ Use the following points as a discussion guide or an outline for a meeting on God's will.

• Finding God's will is often like a treasure hunt—one clue leads to another. Instead of demanding the treasure, we should follow the clues that we have which will lead us to the treasure.

• Often we want to know the future way ahead, but God reveals His will for us a step and a day at a time. We should determine to live each day in His will.

• Sometimes our choices and God's will seem to be chance or fate. Instead, everything happens for a purpose. God is in control of the universe.

• Often God gives us guidance, but we don't follow His instructions or we don't know what He means. We must be obedient to what He has already told us and continue to search the Bible and ask knowledgeable elders when we aren't sure.

• Sometimes we may receive the same instructions as other people, but the specific applications and directions will vary considerably.

According to the Bible, to find God's will we must:

1. Focus on God (Matthew 6:33-34).

2. Obey what God has already told us to do (Romans 13:8).

3. Pray (Philippians 4:6).

4. Study the Bible (2 Timothy 3:16-17).

5. Seek counsel from others (Proverbs 20:5, 18).

6. Think (Romans 12:2).

7. Act in confidence (Hebrews 11:6; James 1:5, 8).

Remember, God is working in us "helping us want to obey Him and then helping us do what He wants" (Philippians 2:13, TLB). God gives us the "will" and then the "way" (see also Psalm 37:4 and Philippians 4:6-7). We must be careful that we really want God's will and not our own or others'.

Good News! ■ Lead a discussion based on the following questions:

• Is the return of Christ good news or bad news to most people? Why would it be bad? (end of fun, judgment, proof that the Bible is true, etc.)

• Why should Christ's second coming be good news for Christians? (vindication, release, redemption, completion, fulfillment, etc.)

• What does the Bible phrase "our blessed hope" mean? (the second coming of Christ: fulfillment, reunion with a loved one—not escape from troubles and persecution.)

• How do you feel about Jesus' return?

Heaven and Hell ■ Ask:

• What do you think heaven is like? What is hell like? How do you know?

• How do these ideas differ from what your friends think? Why?

• What does it take to get into hell? Into heaven? How can a person be sure that he or she will go to heaven? Why?

• Why do people choose to go to hell? What can you do to help them go to heaven?

How Would You Feel? ■ Ask:

• How would you feel if someone said the world would end on Tuesday?

• What if someone said that Jesus will be returning next month?

• What if you heard that Jesus had already returned in the next town?

Note: after each answer ask: *What would you do?*

Knowing the Future ■ Ask:

• Would you like to know your future, or would you to be surprised? Why?

• If you could have one question answered about your future, what would it be? Why?

Planning Our Futures ■ Explain that James 4:13-17 gives three basic facts of life that we should remember when planning our futures:

1. *God is in control* ("if it is the Lord's will")—we must depend totally on Him.

2. *Life is a daily gift* ("we will live")—we must make the most of the time we have.

3. *All our plans should include points one and two* ("go . . . and do . . .")—when we know what God wants, we must do it.

Talk ■ Have everyone turn to Colossians 1:9-10 and follow along as you make these points:

1. Verse 9a—*We need help and understanding of what God wants us to do.*

2. Verse 9b—*We need help in becoming wise about spiritual things.*

3. Verse 10—*We need help in making God's will our way of living by:*

pleasing God

honoring God

doing good for others

knowing God better

Explain that God gives us these general directions and then let's us choose the route. So if we want to know and do God's will, we ought to ask God to show us and then make sure that what we do pleases and honors him, helps others, and helps us know God better.

Thoughts ■ Use the following thoughts as a discussion guide or as an outline for your wrap-up for a meeting on the end of the world.

The concept of the end of the world makes sense to Christians because we believe in a "linear view of history." That is, there is a beginning and an end (as opposed to "cyclical"). The Bible records history beginning at Creation (Genesis 1:1) and ending at Jesus' Second Coming (1 Thessalonians 5:10).

The exact date of Jesus' return is unknown (Matthew 25:13), but for centuries, people have tried to set dates. Because of fulfilled prophecies and other "signs of the times," it has always seemed as though He was coming very soon. Bible prophecy, however, is like a mountain range. Looking at the mountain peaks from a distance, they seem lined up tightly, one right behind the other. Actually, deep valleys lay in between, stretching for many miles. The same is true for prophecy. Even if ninety-nine out of one hundred prophecies have been fulfilled, there still may be a long valley to experience until the last peak. Jesus' return has always seemed imminent.

Over the centuries, since the Bible's prophecies were given, the Church has been sharply divided over specific interpretations. This is especially true regarding the timing of the return of Jesus and the "millennium" (1,000-year reign) mentioned in the book of Revelation. The three main millennial views are "Premillennial" (Jesus will return before His 1,000-year reign on the earth); "Postmillennial" (Jesus will return after and as the culmination of a 1,000-year period of peace and love on the earth); and "Amillennial" (Jesus will return, but the "1,000 year reign" is symbolic of Christ's reign in the hearts of Christians). Sincere, Bible-believing, evangelical Christian scholars, preachers, and lay people believe each of these positions. Unfortunately, many churches have chosen eschatology as a watershed of belief, and church splits have resulted.

Instead, we should affirm the clear and unifying teachings of Scripture. These are:
* *The world is getting worse (Matthew 24:5-35).*
* *Jesus is coming back (Matthew 24:27, 44; John 14:1-3; Acts 1:11; Philippians 3:20; 1 Thessalonians 4:13-17; 5:23; Titus 2:13; Revelation 1:7).*
* *Judgment is sure (Matthew 25:31-46; 1 Corinthians 3:13-15; 2 Corinthians 5:10; Revelation 20:11-15).*

* *We must be ready (Matthew 25:36-44).*
* *There will be a resurrection of the body–for believers a glorified body (Acts 17:31; 1 Corinthians 15:35-38; Philippians 3:20-21; 1 John 3:2).*

BIBLE STUDIES

The Bible and Future Fear ■ Have kids read the following passages aloud, one at a time:
* Luke 12:22-32
* Luke 11:11-13
* Hebrews 13:8

Discuss how each passage relates to future fears.

Choices ■ Divide into small groups of 5–7 each. Give each group the following list of Bible verses that they are to look up and then answer the following questions. (Note: some of the possible answers are in parentheses.)
* What does this passage tell us about "God's will"?
* According to this passage, how can we know what God wants for our lives?
* What should we look for or avoid?

1. Romans 12:1-2 (Our minds are important in finding God's perfect will.)
2. Matthew 6:33-34 (We should seek God first, then live one day at a time.)
3. Matthew 4:7 (We shouldn't put God to the test.)
4. Proverbs 3:5-6 (We shouldn't depend totally– "lean"–on our own understanding.)
5. Psalm 90:12 (We should live "daily.")
6. 2 Timothy 3:16-17 (The Bible will direct us to what God wants.)
7. Hebrews 11:6 (We should live by faith.)
8. Romans 13:8 (We should obey what God has already told us to do.)
9. Philippians 4:6 (We should pray.)
10. Proverbs 20:5, 18 (We should seek the counsel of others.)
11. James 1:5-8 (We should ask for wisdom and act with confidence.)

Bring everyone back together and proceed with the discussion. Tell them to use the appropriate verses to help answer the following questions when they apply. Ask:

* Because God is in control, are we only puppets who are forced to do what God wants us to do, or do we have real choices to make? Why do you feel that way?

• How can a person know God's will?

• In what situations can we know God's will for sure?

• What do people mean when they say, "God told me"?

Double-minded ■ Have everyone turn to James 1:5-7. Read the passage aloud as they follow along. Then ask:

• What does this passage imply about God's will?

• What can a person do to find out what God wants him or her to do?

• In what situations are you tempted to be "double-minded"?

Next, have everyone turn to Colossians 1:9-10. After they read it silently, ask:

• What did Paul continue to ask God to do for the Colossian Christians?

• Why is it important to know God's will?

• What actions are mentioned in this passage that Paul says are God's will for us? (answer: "live a life worthy of the Lord," "please him in every way," "bear fruit in every good work," "grow in the knowledge of God")

Faith in the Future ■ Distribute pencils and paper and have students jot down the following Scripture references. Each one should look up the passages and summarize how the message of each passage applies to his or her own life. When everyone has finished, discuss how the Scripture promises apply to you personally, and encourage students to do the same.

1. Deuteronomy 31:6

2. Joshua 1:5

3. Jeremiah 29:11

4. Psalm 37:37

5. Matthew 6:33-34

Lettuce ■ Read Hebrews 10:19-25 and explain that in this passage, God gives us a spiritual "lettuce salad" that will help us deal with all our fears, especially those about the future. Here are the "let-us leaves" (explain each one as you read it):

• "let us draw near to God . . ." (verse 22)

• "Let us hold unswervingly to the hope we profess . . ." (verse 23)

• "let us consider how we may spur one another on toward love and good deeds." (verse 24)

• "Let us not give up meeting together . . ." (verse 25)

• "let us encourage one another . . ." (verse 25)

No Guarantees ■ Have everyone turn to James 4:13-17 and follow as you read the passage aloud.

Then ask:

• What's wrong with being confident about where we will go and what we will do tomorrow?

• According to this passage, what's wrong with bragging?

• What evidence do you have that life is "a mist that appears for a little while and then vanishes"? How should knowing that affect the way we live?

• If life is short and we have no guarantees about tomorrow, why should we plan for the future at all?

• How does verse 17 relate to the rest of the passage?

• How can we know what God wants us to do?

Scripture and Prayer ■ Divide into groups of five and have each group read Romans 8:18-39 around the circle, with each person reading a verse in succession. Afterward, have each person share one future fear. Then have the groups close with a time of prayer for each person in their group.

8
LOVE AND SEX

CROWD-BREAKERS

Beauty Contest ■ Bring a box full of women's and men's clothing (three or four sets of each). Then choose three for four guys to dress up as girls and three or four girls to dress-up as guys, to compete in a "beauty contest." Let the other guys help dress and make up the girls and the other girls help dress and make up the guys. Then have the girls (dressed as guys) parade one at a time while the other girls rate them on a scale of 1–10. Follow this with the guys (dressed as girls) parading while the other guys judge them. Add up the scores and determine the winners.

Body Language ■ Explain the concept of body language and nonverbal communication. Divide into pairs and designate one person A and the other B. A is the sculptor, and B is the clay. Explain that you will give them a situation or an emotion and A should sculpt B" (including facial expressions, arms, legs, head, stance, etc.) to best show that emotion. Alternate sculptors and clay with each emotion. Here are some possible emotions and situations to use: depression, acting cool, fear, anger, looking sexy, joy, love, etc.

Dear Abby ■ Before the meeting choose a guy and girl to be your advice columnists. Have the crowd write out their love and romance questions that you will submit to your panel of "experts" (don't reveal their identities). Collect the questions, introduce the experts (they should be dressed appropriately), and have them give creative and humorous (or serious) answers.

Food Rally ■ Before the meeting, arrange food stations around the room(s). Each food station should be a paper plate with a number of pieces of the same type of food; for example, marshmallows, apple slices, cherries, strawberry halves, cake, pineapple slices, prunes, and so forth. Note: This will work best if you can spread the food stations among several rooms.

Divide into teams and distribute toothpicks to everyone. At your signal, the first person from each team should run around to the food stations where he or she should pick up a piece of food using his or her toothpick, eat the food, and then go to the next station. When he or she returns to the team, the next person should do the same. The first team to have everyone spear and eat all the food, wins.

Fortune Kisses ■ Buy a couple of bags of Hershey Kisses (or one of Kisses and one of Hugs). Before the meeting, place a fortune inside each one. This can be done by typing on narrow slips of paper, inserting them in the foil, and re-wrapping the candy. During the meeting, distribute the Kisses (and Hugs). Have students open and read the fortunes. These fortunes will be funny and will provide "volunteers" for your next game. (Two matching fortunes may compete as a couple.) To be sure that guys and girls get the appropriate fortunes, dedicate a bag to each sex and distribute accordingly.

Possible fortunes:

"Your girlfriend has eyes for another man"–guy.

"Your next date is seated near you right now"–either.

"The girl on your right has a crush on you"–guy.

"The tall guy across the room will ask you out"–girl.

"Right now, tell him how you really feel"–girl.

"You're looking for your secret admirer"–either.

"You are the secret admirer"–either.

Heart Chain ■ Divide into pairs and give each pair three or four sheets of red construction paper, a roll of tape, and a pair of scissors. Give them three minutes to see which pair can cut out and tape the longest chain of hearts. After they display their chains and you determine the winner, put the chains on the wall for decoration.

Heart to Heart ■ Before the meeting cut out three large hearts from separate sheets of poster board. The hearts should be three different colors (such as red, white, and pink). Then, cut each heart into puzzle pieces. Make the pieces large or small–just so you have enough for every person who comes to the meeting. As group members enter the room, give each one a puzzle piece. Then, after everyone has arrived, tell them to find the other members of their teams and put their puzzles together. If you have extra puzzle pieces, give them to the appropriate groups after they have begun to work on their puzzles. The first team to complete their puzzle, wins.

I Can't Express My Love ■ Choose two couples to compete for a great prize (e.g., concert tickets, dinner for two, etc.). Explain that they will sit facing their partners and will share their deepest feelings of love for each other out loud. These expressions will be written on cue cards that your associates will hold up for them to read. They must say each phrase with as much feeling and sincerity as possible. The lines will alternate guy-girl-guy-girl and so on. The only catch, however, is that each person will have a bag of large marshmallows that they will feed each other, one marshmallow at a time, before each line. Chewing and/or swallowing the marshmallows is prohibited, so be sure to have a bag for depositing the used marshmallows when they've had enough. The couple to drop out first (due to an inability to speak) loses.

Possible lines:

• "You are so beautiful"–guy says to girl

• "You are so strong"–girl says to guy

• "I love the way you laugh"–guy to girl

• "You are ruggedly handsome"–girl to guy

• "I've never met a girl like you"–guy to girl

• "You make me feel like a woman"–girl to guy

• "I love you, my darling"–guy to girl

• "I love you too much to lose you"–girl to guy

• "My love for you knows no boundaries"–guy to girl

• "I'll love you with all my heart, forever"–girl to guy

If You Love Me ■ This is an adaptation of an old game. Everyone sits in a circle with the "it" person in the middle. He or she chooses a person, sits on his or her lap, looks him or her in the eye, and says, "If you love me, _____ (here he or she should address the victim in a creative way, such as "you big hunk of a man," "liver lips," "sweetie pie," etc.), smile." The person must respond without smiling, "_____ (using the same descriptive phrase) loves you, but I just can't smile." If the victim smiles, he or she becomes "it." If not, the person in the center continues with another victim.

Leg Men ■ Choose four or five guys to participate in a "best legs" contest. Roll their pants legs up to their knees, remove their shoes and socks, and have them stand behind a sheet so that no one in the audience knows which legs belong to which person. One pair at a time, point to the legs and have each person pose (flex, wiggle toes, display various features, etc.). Then vote on the best pair of legs. To add to the difficulty and interest, you may want to have all the legs in nylons and/or slip a girl secretly into the contest.

Love Letters ■ Using teams or individual competitors, give them romantic words or phrases to spell out using their bodies. One at a time, the competitors come to the front and draw a piece of paper with a word or phrase written on it. Then he or she should spell out the word with his or her body, arms, and legs (not the fingers) as the audience (or that person's team) guesses. See how long it takes each person to communicate the word or phrase. Romantic words could include: precious, darling, honey, lovey dovey, lover boy, cutie pie, be mine, babycakes, I love you, you're beautiful, I can't live without you, all my love, and so on.

Love Letters in the Hand ■ Purchase a bag of those small, candy hearts that have special Valentine's Day sayings written on them. Distribute the candy hearts, one to each person, and tell everyone not to eat them. Now, using teams, give them the task of writing a love letter or a love story using all of the team's sayings. Of course, they should be allowed to fill in missing words. After about five minutes, have team representatives read the stories or letters to the rest of the group. As each story is read, kids should stand and read their "heart sayings" when they fit in.

Love Songs ■ Choose a number of guys and girls and pair them up at random. One at a time the girl must sit on the guy's lap while he sings her a short and simple love song (or reads her a love poem). They must keep straight faces. Laughers lose and must face a penalty. Possible songs could include "Let Me Call You Sweetheart," or "By the Light of the Silvery Moon."

Love Words ■ Divide into groups of five. Give each group a few sheets of scratch paper and a pen or pencil. Then have them draw five words out of an envelope. Their assignment is to write a poem about love that uses these words. Allow about five minutes for the poems to be composed. Then have the groups, one at a time, read their words and then their poems to the whole group. Here are possible words to use: lips, hair, figure, personality, grace, charm, muscles, like, special, (name of female leader), (name of male leader), heart, broken, future, marry, steady, date, forever, break-up, romantic, flowers, sweetie, first fight, etc.

Lust Appeal ■ Bring a stack of newspapers and magazines and have everyone look for advertisements that appeal to lustful desires. These could be ads for everything from movies to cars, from clothing to flowers. Use this to illustrate the pervasiveness of lust in our society.

Mine, Mine ■ Give each team a bag of spring-powered clothespins. Have them distribute the pins among team members and then choose a male representative to stand at the front. At your signal, they are to see which team can pin all their clothespins on the person's shirt the fastest. Determine the winning team for this first round.

Next, explain that you want to see how many clothespins team members can grab off their representative and pin on themselves. They can only take clothespins off the team representatives. Blow the whistle and watch the chaos. The focus of the last part of this game is self-centeredness.

No, No, Never, Never, Uh, Uh, Uh! ■ This is a group activity that will be fun and will reinforce the idea of saying "No!" The key to it is the rhythm of the phrase, "no, no, never, never, uh, uh, uh." If you were to beat this out slowly in 2/4 time, it would be like this: "no" (quarter note), "no" (quarter note), "ne" (eighth), "ver" (eighth), "ne" (eighth), "ver" (eighth), "uh" (sixteenth), "uh" (dotted eighth), "uh" (quarter). Make sure you know the phrase and the rhythm before you try to teach it to the group.

Give the phrase to the group and have them repeat it together a few times so they get the hang of it. After they seem to have it, add hand motions—they could cross their hands back and forth over each other, right hands over left, as they say the first "no, no." Then

they could repeat the motion with the left hands over the right as they say "never, never." Then they could shake their right index fingers in front of them as they say "uh, uh, uh!"

After they do this a couple of times, explain that you will be providing verses in the form of questions. After each verse, they should repeat the phrase. Note: when you do the verses, be sure to say them in rhythm. Here are some possible verses to use.

• *What do you say when he wants his way?* ("No, no, never, never, uh, uh, uh!")
• *What do you say when she says, "Let's play"?*
• *What do you say when his hands begin to stray?*
• *What do you say when she says it's okay?*
• *What do you say when he wants to lay?*
• *What do you say when she says, "Please stay"?*
• *What do you say when she says, "Do it or you're gay"?*
• *What do you say about a roll in the hay?*
• *What do you say when she mocks your "nay"?*

Another way to do this would be to divide the group into boys and girls. Then alternate verses with each side shouting their answer to the other.

Not the Same Old Line ■ This can be done guys versus girls or with two teams. The teams send up representatives (one each) who sit in chairs facing each other. Their challenge is to say to each other, alternating back and forth, a familiar line that you will give them. The catch is that they must convey the same meaning as the line they have been given using different key word(s) each time. Each person is given 10 seconds to respond. If they repeat a line or go over the time limit, the other team wins that round. Continue for as many rounds as you need. Here's how it works. The first line could be, "I *love* you with all my *heart*!" (Key words are italicized.)

Person A	Person B

"I *like* you *extremely much* with all my *soul*!"

"I *adore* you with all my *being*!"

"I *think the world of you* with all my *mind*!"

"I am *extremely fond of you* with all my *liver*!"

Other lines could include: "Your eyes are like pools"; "You're the nicest person I know"; "You make me feel like a real man (woman)"; "I've never met anyone like you before"; etc.

Opening Moves ■ Collect a number of products that are difficult to open (for example: catsup packet, saltines in cellophane, childproof medicine bottle filled with water, candy bar, potato chips bag, hand-twist-top bottle of pop, Capri Sun drink, Planters peanuts bag, Dentyne gum packet, and frozen Fudgesicle). Divide into teams and have a relay with each person running to the front, reaching into his or her team's bag, pulling out one item, opening it, and eating the contents. The first team finished wins. (Be sure to have a full set of products for each team.)

Poems ■ Hand out paper and pens and have group members write trite or cute love poems. Example: "Roses are red, grass is green, if you date me, I won't be mean." Collect and read.

Pure ■ Bring two white handkerchiefs and two sets of soiling ingredients. Divide into two teams and seat them together on the floor. On the table in front of the room, place two clean, white handkerchiefs and two bags of various soiling and staining materials (for example, ketchup, dirt, grape juice, peanut butter, prunes, etc.). Explain that you want kids to come to the table, one from each team, and use one soiling ingredient from their supply to rub into the handkerchief. After about 15 seconds, have the next two come up. Continue until all the ingredients have been used or all the team members have had a chance. Then bring out two bowls of water and some liquid soap. Have each team choose a person to come forward and try to clean the handkerchief that was soiled by the other team. Allow about a minute for this. The team with the cleanest handkerchief wins.

Use this to illustrate how easy it is to make something dirty and how difficult it can be to get clean again (better to stay pure in the first place).

Really Appealing ■ Explain that you're going to find out who is the most appealing member of the group. Then choose eight contestants (guy and girl from each class or four from each of two teams; use as many contestants as you have supplies). Bring the contestants to the front and give each one an orange and a pair of work gloves. The contest is to see who can peel the orange the quickest and best while wearing the work gloves. This can be messy, so be prepared with drop cloth and towels. Declare the winner and pronounce him or her as the most "a-peeling" person you know. Another twist to this would be to give each person a knife and an orange and see who can peel the orange in one continuous peeling.

Seeing Red ■ Divide into teams. Then explain that they are going to compete in a quick scavenger hunt, looking for special "love" items. Hand out lists of the necessary items and allow only five minutes to find as many as possible. Encourage students to use their imaginations and creativity. Here are some possible items to create or find: sweetheart, cupid, poem, love song, red, gift, "truly," "be mine," "love at first sight." After students have found their items, have each team display, act out, or explain each one.

Sex Appeal ■ Make a list of products advertised on TV, "guaranteed" to enhance one's "sex appeal." These could include toothpaste, mouthwash, deodorant, shaving cream, gum, after-shave lotion, shampoo, perfume, etc. Bring three or four sets of these to use in a relay. Be sure to choose an "indestructible" part of the room or bring a drop cloth and towels to avoid harming the furniture or carpet.

Using teams, have each team select a male representative (these guys should have fairly strong egos) who "needs help" with his sex appeal. Bring the team representatives to the front and seat them side by side. (Place the towels, etc. in the appropriate places.) In front of each person, place his bag of "surefire sex-appeal" products. Explain that you know they'll work because you've seen them on TV.

The game proceeds like a relay with the girls from each team coming up one at a time, reaching into the bag, grabbing a product, and using it on their man. Each girl has only 15 seconds to do her task. Every time you blow the whistle, the girls must run back to their teams and the next members take their turns. The products may be applied in any order except that shaving must come after the shaving cream. Here's a possible order:

1. Close-up (toothpaste and brush tied loosely together)

2. Sure deodorant

3. Edge shaving cream

4. Certs breath mints (eats all of them)

5. hair spray (with comb loosely taped to can)

6. razor (without blade)

7. Scope mouthwash

8. Mennen Skin Bracer (featuring a slap across the face)

Play a popular song in the background. When the time is up, choose the "sexiest" man and award an appropriate prize, such as all the leftover products.

Note: this game illustrates how we use sex to sell everything and how this destroys our ideas about sex and love.

Strings Attached ■ Divide into two teams and choose four members from each team to participate.

This game will have two rounds. In round one, team A will have its representatives lined up side by side, on their knees, facing team B. Between the two teams will be four lengths of thread. The one end will be tied around a marshmallow, lying on the floor in front of team A's people. The B'ers will hold the other ends in their right hands. At the signal, the B team will pull their strings toward them by using only the fingers on the right hand (no pulling with their arms). Meanwhile, A-team members are trying to catch the marshmallows with their mouths. The object is to see how many marshmallows are captured by A-team members (and how short the strings are when they catch them). Repeat the process with round two and reverse the roles.

The Right Moves ■ Choose six students to participate, three guys and three girls. Send four of them out of the room with a staff member. Using a couch or a bench, seat the remaining girl at one end and the guy on the other. Next, bring in a girl from the other room. Explain to her that this "couple" is interested in each other and that she should make one change in their situation to get them more romantically involved. After she makes the change (for example, moving the guy closer to the girl), tell her that she must take the place of the girl in the couple. Next, bring in a guy and repeat the process. What makes this game work is the fact that the person who is rearranging the couple must then become part of the new arrangement. (Caution: watch out for heavy sexual innuendoes. Make sure that they begin far apart and that each person only makes one move. Also, alternate guys and girls. If things begin to get carried away, stop the game and move on.)

Valentines ■ Bring red construction paper, scissors, tape, other paper, crayons or multicolored felt-tip pens, and other materials. Give everyone time to create two or more valentines. One must be for someone in the room and the other may be for anyone. Allow about ten minutes and then have a few displayed and explained (those who want to do this). Award prizes for the most creative, most romantic, most meaningful, and so on.

Weight Wait ■ Divide into teams, give each team a bag of balloons, and have each choose a person to compete in a "weighty" contest. These competitors should lie on their backs on the floor with their team members surrounding them. Explain that the object of this game is to see which team can be the first to have their person totally supported by unpopped balloons. At your signal, the team members should inflate their balloons and then place them under their

team representative. They may lift the person while the balloon is being put into place but may only place one balloon at a time under him or her. When you have a winner, break all those balloons and repeat with new competitors.

DISCUSSION STARTERS

A Gift ■ Distribute cards to the group and have them write down the possession that is most important to them. (Let them know that it should be a thing, not an idea, person, goal, or quality.) Next, have them mill around the room and find someone with whom they can trade cards (possessions) or someone to whom they would be willing to give their card. After a few minutes, discuss their experience. Ask what their conditions were for giving away their valuable and prized possessions (probe for serious answers).

Point out the parallels to sex. That is, do we give it away to just anyone, or are there special conditions? The hedonistic approach is that sex is merely a route to pleasure. The Christian answer is that sex in the context of marriage is part of a person's journey toward fulfillment. How you view life and the value of sex, therefore, will determine when and how you give it away.

Aliens ■ Choose two drama students or kids who are kind of crazy and make sure they practice this before the meeting. Have them dress up like two aliens, give them a fictitious planet and creative names, and introduce them to the audience. Without using any off-color references or sexual terms, they should have a typical locker room conversation. The only catch is that on their planet, sex is brushing their teeth. They also should not use the words teeth, molars, etc. Afterward, ask the group for reactions and see if they could figure out what the aliens were discussing.

Basic Questions ■ Before the meeting, write on a poster board these five questions.

1. How can I find love without falling into tragedy?

2. How can I control myself?

3. How can I experience forgiveness and healing?

4. How can I escape being lonely?

5. How do I get guidance to make the right choices?

Pass out papers and pencils and ask everyone to choose one of the questions and write down a nugget of insight that would be part of a helpful answer. (Each should put the number of the question next to his or her answer.) Everyone should be serious.

Collect the papers and put them in piles according to the question. Next, read the questions, one at a time, and then the nuggets for that specific question. After each, have group members comment briefly about the appropriateness and relevance of the answers.

Bon Appetit ■ This should be practiced before the meeting. Dress two actors as very overweight people (do not use people who really are overweight) and have them look at the latest issue of *Bon Appetit* or another food magazine. They should "ooh" and "aah" just like guys do when viewing a skin magazine like *Playboy*. Afterward, ask what these two were doing that paralleled someone reading a sex magazine. Ask:

• How would you react if you went to a theater filled with hungry people and saw a "striptease" show with food?

• Would you conclude that the people were hungry or sick? Why?

• What do you think about our society's obsession with sex?

Celebri-tease ■ Read the names of celebrities, and after each one, have the crowd give the masculine and feminine qualities that each person exhibits. Afterward, discuss how they determined which characteristics were "male" and which ones were "female" and whether these qualities are absolutes or relative to culture. Possible celebrities could include: Mariah Carey, Billy Joel, David Letterman, Madonna, Cindy Crawford, Bill Clinton, Michael Jordan, Jesse Jackson, Michael Jackson, Oprah Winfrey, Santa Claus, Shaquille O'Neal, and others.

Headlines ■ Distribute a few copies of the latest newspapers and have group members find stories that somehow deal with sex. These could include rape, incest, abortion, unwed mothers, adultery, etc. Read Genesis 1, emphasizing God's pronouncement after creation that "it was very good." Then ask:

• What happened? If sex, procreation, and all of creation were good, why is our world filled with so much of what we have just read?

• How do sin and Satan distort love and sex?

• What is God's "good" idea for sex?

How to Say "No" ■ Divide into groups of three and give each one a piece of paper and a pencil or pen. Tell everyone that their assignment is to think of a creative way to say "no" to someone (a boyfriend, girlfriend, date) who is pressuring them to get involved sexually. To get them started, give them a few of these phrases: *Get lost!; Buzz off!; Forget it"; "Negatory"; "It doesn't compute"; "Cool it!"; "No way,*

Jose"; etc.

Explain that these are possibilities, but their answers should be much more creative. After a few minutes, collect their papers. Then read them aloud.

Afterward, ask:

• Which of these ways of saying "no" are realistic? Why?

• How can you say "no" in a loving way?

• Why is it difficult to say "no"?

• Why would it be helpful to think through ways to say "no" ahead of time?

Love Lists ■ Distribute pieces of paper and pencils. Have group members write down as many ways as they can imagine to express love to another person. Share and compare their lists. Then ask:

•Which of these ways to express love are realistic?

•Which of them apply to parents? Brothers and sisters? Girl or boyfriend? God?

• What's the difference between "like" and "love"?

• What's the difference between "love" and "lust"?

Mine, Mime ■ Using teams, have each team define one of these words: "power," "lust," or "love." They should then design a pantomime or skit to demonstrate their definition. Allow a few minutes for preparation and then have them act out their pantomimes and skits. See if anyone on the other teams can guess what is being enacted. Next, have each group read their definitions. After they have finished, read the dictionary definition for each word. Discuss the similarities between power and lust and the differences between those and love. (This should have been obvious in the skits.)

The Quiz ■ Explain that you are going to give everyone a quiz to see how well they know what's going on in the world around them. Then distribute a quiz with questions that you have designed as suggested below (or read the quiz and see who can give the correct answer first).

1. Ask for the main characters in the most popular soap opera in your town.

2. Ask for a summary of the plot on the last episode of a popular and sexy, prime time TV show.

3. Ask for the name of the artist who recorded a recent popular song with a sexual theme.

4. Ask for the name of the most popular, dirty-talking disc jockey.

5. Ask what magazine has annual "swim suit edition."

6. Ask them to give you the names of three sexually

oriented "men's" magazines.

7. Watch television and record the themes from three ads that use sex to sell their products. See if they can identify the products by the songs.

8. Ask for the name of the popular woman on "Wheel of Fortune."

9. Ask for the occupation of Dr. Ruth.

10. Ask them to name three beauty pageants.

Kids should have no trouble answering these questions. This will be a dramatic demonstration of how our lives are saturated with sexual influences, thoughts, and pressures.

Sex Ads ■ Distribute magazines and have groups or individuals tear out ads that use sex to sell their products. Display the ads one at a time and list the products. (Be sure to screen the magazines first.) The variety is amazing. Your list will include clothes, after-shave lotion, cars, stereos, rental cars, hotels, wine, computers, food, and many others. Ask why advertisers use sex to sell and discuss how and why our culture is obsessed with sex.

Sex Appeal ■ Distribute cards and pens, and ask everyone to write down three main characteristics of sex appeal. In other words, what three things more than any others give a person sex appeal? (Note: with a large crowd, you may want to have them list only one or two.) Next, collect the cards and read them aloud, listing the results on a chalkboard or piece of poster board. If you wish, compile a separate list for men and women. Pass out cards again and have everyone write down the top ten characteristics determined by your poll. Then have group members rate themselves, confidentially, on their sex appeal, by checking each characteristic that they feel is true of them. Afterward ask:

• By giving each characteristic one point, how did you do on a scale of one to ten? Don't give the answer.

• What do you think of our little scale? Are these valid qualities for rating? Why or why not?

• How do you feel about being rated? How do you feel about rating someone else?

• What is sex appeal? (What does the phrase mean?)

• Why is sex appeal so important anyway?

Survey ■ Pass out cards and ask these two statements:

1. Agree/Disagree: Christian kids usually go farther sexually than they thought they would.

2. The best advice I heard on how far to go is . . .

Collect the cards, shuffle them, and read the answers aloud. Then discuss each question.

Top 40 ■ Bring a Top 40 list (from a local radio station or record store) and play a reverse version of Name That Tune. Using teams or the whole group, read off a title. The first person to stand and then sing the correct first line of the song (or a familiar part of the song) wins that round. Continue for at least ten songs and then award an album to the winner. Discuss the songs, noting how many deal with sex and love. Also talk about MTV. How do group members feel about the heavy emphasis on sex in music and videos? Ask: *What does this tell us about our society? About us? How does this affect us?*

Vulnerability ■ You will need to set up this activity before the meeting. Bring at least two blindfolds and be sure to prepare a separate room for the experience (remove all breakables, etc.). The idea is for each individual to experience what it means to be completely vulnerable. Try to have as many kids as possible participate. But if size and time limit you, choose volunteers and make most of them male.

Explain that each person will be blindfolded and led into another room where they must find their way out with only the knowledge that in the room there is "one thing you want to find and two things you don't want to find." (Have a person in the room with candy and place a couple of harmless stumbling blocks or barriers in the way.) Also ask participants to say nothing about the experience until the discussion.

Lead the kids into the room, one at a time (more than one can be in the room at a time). During this time, give the rest of the crowd the announcements or tell them a story of personal vulnerability. As the participants exit, remove the blindfolds and have them sit quietly with the rest of the group to wait for the discussion.

After everyone has finished, have them share their feelings with the rest of the group. Make sure they tell what it felt like to be totally at the mercy of you and your assistants in the other room. Ask how this feeling of vulnerability compares to how a girl often feels on a date or walking alone at night.

Wet T-shirts ■ If you're brave enough and won't have a public relations nightmare, advertise that at your next meeting there will be a wet T-shirt contest for guys (with a great prize for the winner). When the contest begins, designate a girl as the "sponge-ette." Her responsibility is to soak down each guy before he parades before the judges. These judges, other girls, should rate each contestant on a 1–10 scale, like the gymnastic judges. Be sure to have a "ringer" in the group—a small, skinny guy wearing a great T-shirt (sequins, etc.).

Your kids will probably assume that this is a physique contest, and so athletes and other macho-types will enter. The catch is that it actually is a T-shirt contest, not a body contest, so your winner should be the one with the best-looking T-shirt, perhaps even your skinny contestant. Afterward, discuss the contest and the group's expectations. Undoubtedly they will have made sexual/physical comments, etc.

Who Loves You, Baby? ■ Have each individual make a list of every person in this world who loves him or her. After each name, they should write why they are loved. For example:

• Mom—because I'm her son.

• Joann—because I love her.

Afterward, have them share some of the reasons that they have on their papers. Discuss them relative to the nature of real love.

DISCUSSIONS AND WRAP-UPS

Difficulties ■ Ask for ideas on why it is difficult to wait—why sexual pressure is so strong. Possible answers will include: love for the other person, natural sex drives and desires, constant exposure to sexual ideas and pictures on TV, in movies, and in songs, pressure from friends to prove one's manhood or womanhood, need to be loved, not wanting to be left out or to be ridiculed. Then ask for ideas on how to resist and defeat these pressures.

Disrespect ■ Divide groups by sex. Appoint an adult leader to each group and have them lead a discussion (and have someone record the answers) with the following questions:

• How do you experience disrespect from members of the opposite sex?

• What words imply disrespect? What actions? Why?

Then bring the whole group back together and have the leaders report the results of the discussions on their experiences of disrespect. This is very important, so make sure that everyone takes the answers seriously. As you proceed, be sure to ask why we, as men and women, are hateful or disrespectful toward each other and how we can show more respect.

Note: this discussion fits with the "Respect" Bible

study that appears later in this chapter.

Lies ■ To illustrate the fact that the idea of safe sex outside of marriage is a myth, a lie, discuss these often used statements that we hope are not lies:

• Your secret is safe with me.

• I love you.

• We'll always be friends.

• No, I'm not mad at you.

• It won't cost much at all.

• You can't get into trouble.

• Don't worry, no one will ever know.

• You can trust me.

Love Clues ■ Have everyone write down their answers individually or discuss them as a group.

• How can you tell that your parents love you? (Possible answers: "They tell me," "They give me things," "They cook my meals and provide a home," etc.)

• How can your parents tell that you love them?

• How can you tell that your brother(s) and/or sister(s) love you?

• How can they tell that you love them?

• How can you tell that your boyfriend or girlfriend loves you?

• How can you tell that God loves you?

• How can He tell that you love Him?

Lust Talk ■ Use these points for a talk on lust. We have problems with lust because:

1. We underestimate the importance of purity.

2. We underestimate the pain of lust.

3. We underestimate the power that lust has in our lives.

Lust is the opposite of love: lust is self-centered while love is other-centered; lust is grasping while love is giving; lust is impatient while love is patient; lust burns while love warms. Challenge kids to reject the emphasis on sex, greed, and self-centeredness in society and to love instead.

Maturity ■ Explain that one definition of maturity is: *The ability to postpone gratification.* Ask for examples of how babies and little children refuse to wait for *anything* (for example, eating, going to the bathroom, taking, etc.). Have students explain how they have improved in the ability to wait (for example, sit still in church, wait turn to speak, eat only at meals, etc.). Then discuss how waiting for marriage to have sex is a sign of maturity and how not waiting is a sign of immaturity and selfishness.

Prayers and Promises ■ Because sex sins are so damaging emotionally and make us feel so guilty, the subject of forgiveness must be handled with care. Explain that God stands ready to forgive us if we have a personal relationship with Him and are truly sorry for what we have done (1 John 1:9). Jesus died for *sin* and for our sins. And God's forgiveness is complete—He forgives and forgets our sins, totally, wiping the slate clean.

Next, distribute pieces of paper and tell students to write on the papers the sins for which they want to be forgiven and that weigh heavily on their minds. Spend a few moments in silent prayer, giving everyone the chance to talk to God seriously, sincerely, and privately.

Then explain that you want them to come to the front of the room, one at a time, and drop their pieces of paper into the fire in the fireplace where the papers will be burned. The smoke will symbolize their prayers ascending to God, and the fire will symbolize God's total forgiveness as He destroys every evidence of their sins.

Sexual Identity ■ Use the following outline as a guide for a discussion or for a wrap-up.

A. We experience anxiety about our sexual identities.

1. Performance—*Am I acting like a man or a woman?*

2. Existence—*Am I really a real man/woman?*

B. Certain factors heighten this anxiety.

1. The women's movement—saying there is no difference between the sexes, except physiological.

2. The gay movement—saying there is no moral difference in sexual "preference" and that a person is destined to be the way he or she was born; that is, with that sexual preference.

3. The breakdown of marriage—with more emphasis on sex outside of marriage and eliminating sexual role models.

C. In light of these problems, what can we do? How can we react?

1. We can return to traditional values. This is good except that it could mean a return to stereotyping as well.

2. We can understand our identity and freedom in Christ. The Bible says little about sexual roles, but it does tell us that God has a special person in mind for each person to become. Sex is part of our identities, and God wants to make something beautiful out of *all* of us.

D. We aren't what we should be yet, but we must live with the difference between our real selves and our ideal selves, understanding these biblical guidelines:

1. The Bible says that sexual intercourse is to be experienced *only* within marriage, but it doesn't say that sexual intercourse is ultimate pleasure.

2. The Bible says that there are sexual differences, but it doesn't say much about roles (many of these are from culture).

3. The Bible says that we should be grateful for our sexual identity, but it also says that heterosexual activity outside of marriage and homosexual activity are wrong.

4. The Bible says that our ultimate fulfillment as persons can be found in a personal relationship with God.

Waiting ■ Use a chalkboard or a piece of poster board and on the right half write the answers to the following question: *In life, when is it important to wait?* Possible answers could include: *When you plant flowers or other plants–it takes time for the seed or bulb to grow, mature, and bloom. It would hurt or kill the plant to keep digging up the seed to see how it's doing.* (On the board you could write "plant seeds."); *When you're cooking–recipes require a certain length of time to cook for it to turn out right; In education–certain things take time to learn; As an athlete–proper training takes time–there are no shortcuts; You have to wait to read the conclusion of a book–if you jump right to the end, you miss the whole story–and the punch line of a joke.; etc.*

Then on the left side of the board, record their answers to the question: *When is it important not to wait?* Possible answers could include: *When you're in a race–you should start when the gun goes off; If you have to make a decision–sometimes we put it off indefinitely; When someone is in trouble and needs your help or to do something else that you know is right; If you are in pain or have other symptoms of sickness, you should see a doctor right away.*

Then say: *We talk about waiting when it comes to sex. Which of these situations is sex most like, and how?*

Answer: *Waiting to have sex at the right time is like allowing the plant to mature, preparing and mixing the recipe's ingredients correctly, training for the important contest, and reading the story to really appreciate the conclusion. Taking impatient shortcuts ruins the plant, cake, and story, and you will be the loser.*

Then explain that God knows us and what it will take for us to be happy, satisfied, and fulfilled. Certain matters take time . . . and patience.

What's the Difference? ■ Ask:

• What's the difference between guys and girls? No, not the obvious physical differences . . . the other ones? (emotional, social, etc.)

• In our society, what are some of the traditional roles of women? . . . of men? Where did we get these differences?

• How do our perceived differences affect us—the way we see ourselves and the way we act?

BIBLE STUDIES

The Best Sex ■ Divide into four groups. Give each group one of the following passages: Ecclesiastes 2:1-11; 3:1-8; 1 Corinthians 6:12-20; 1 Thessalonians 4:3-8. Tell them to discuss what the passage teaches about our bodies, pleasure, sex, and marriage. They also should answer the question: *What can a person do to have the best sex?* After a few minutes, have each group report their answers to everyone.

Bible and Sex ■ Divide into groups and give each group a question to answer by looking up the appropriate Scriptures. Use their conclusions as your wrap-up.

1. Who thought up the idea of sex, and what is its purpose? See Genesis 1:26-28, 31; 2:18, 21-25; Hebrews 13:4.

2. How does God feel about sexual relations between unmarried people? See 1 Corinthians 6:15-20; Galatians 5:19; Ephesians 5:5; 1 Thessalonians 4:3-5.

3. How does God feel about sexual relations between a married person and someone other than his or her spouse? See Exodus 20:14; Luke 18:20; Romans 13:9; James 2:11; 4:4.

4. What does God think about divorce, homosexuality, etc.? See Romans 1:18-29; Matthew 5:31-32; 19:9; Romans 7:2-3; Matthew 5:28; Philippians 4:8.

5. What should be the relationship between husband and wife? See Hebrews 13:4; Ephesians 5:21-33; 1 Corinthians 7:1-5.

6. How can we resist the temptations that surround us? See Luke 4:3-12; 1 Corinthians 10:13; James 1:2-6.

The Cure ■ Have everyone turn to Matthew 5:27-32. Read the passage aloud as they follow along. Then ask:

• What's wrong with adultery?

• In what ways is lust the same as adultery? How is it different?

• What is Jesus telling us to do about lust?

• What is Jesus teaching about adultery?

Have someone read aloud Mark 7:14:23. Then ask:

• Where does lust come from?

• How can we control our tendency to lust?

Escape ■ Read and discuss 1 Corinthians 10:12-13. Ask students how they can protect themselves from giving in to temptation, what promise verse 13 holds, what "ways of escape" they can think of, and how they can resist temptation.

Look It Up ■ Have kids read the following passages aloud. After each one, comment briefly on what the Bible is teaching about sex.

• Psalm 19:13—guilt and shame accompany sexual sin

• Proverbs 5:1-21—sexual sin causes scars and pain

• Romans 6:1-14—believers should not be involved in sexual sin

• 1 Corinthians 3:19-20—God doesn't care if "everybody's doing it"

• Philippians 2:12-16—the secret to staying pure

• 1 Thessalonians 4:1-8—staying pure before marriage

• 1 Timothy 6:11-12—run from temptation

• Hebrews 13:4—the marriage bed should be kept pure

• 2 Peter 3:14—say no to premarital sex

No Strings Attached ■ Before the meeting, write the following Bible verses on index cards, attach each one to a string, and lay them in a box with the strings hanging out.

Have kids come up to the box, one at a time, take a string and pull out the card. As the person takes the cards in his or her hand, cut the string with a scissors. Then have the person read the verse aloud.

After all the verses have been read, ask what they had in common. Then ask what you were symbolizing by cutting the strings.

• John 3:16

• Romans 8:35-36

• John 10:11

• Luke 12:7

• Luke 15:3-6

• Ephesians 3:17-19

• 1 John 4:8

• 1 John 4:9-10

• 1 John 4:16

• John 13:34-35

- 1 Corinthians 13:4-7, 13
- Ephesians 2:4-7
- 1 John 3:1-3

Respect ■ This study goes with the "Disrespect" discussion mentioned previously. Hand out sheets with 1 Thessalonians 4:1-12 written on them (the whole passage). Then, take your lists of disrespect and together look for specific answers in these verses (words, phrases, or principles that relate). As you discuss each, write the answers on the chalkboard (or a piece of poster board) and have students underline them on their sheets. Here are some examples: "live in order to please God," "each of you should learn to control his own body," "no one should wrong his brother or take advantage of him," "love each other," "lead a quiet life," "win the respect of outsiders," etc. Next, ask for ways that we can show respect to each other.

Then have someone read John 13:34-35 and 1 Corinthians 13. Emphasize that each person is responsible, before God, for his or her actions, that as Christians we are to obey God, and that Christian love is an action, not a feeling. Explain that respect for each other is not optional; it is a requirement, and that it is active, not passive. Have everyone turn over their sheets and write on the back the words or phrases from the Bible that apply directly to them in their relationships with members of the opposite sex. After a minute or so, explain that they may have to go to certain people and ask for forgiveness; certainly their actions must change.

Sex and Self ■ Work through the following passages together as a group.

1. Read Romans 12:3-8 and ask:

- What does verse 3 tell us about our self-concepts?
- When have you thought of yourself "more highly" than you ought to?
- How does this teaching affect your relationships?
- What do these other verses imply about our relationships with others?

2. Read Proverbs 11:4 and 24:5-6 and ask:

- What do these verses mean?
- What does "safety" mean?
- Who are some possible counselors? How can they help?
- Why do we try to do things on our own?

3. Read Hebrews 4:14-16 and ask:

- What has Jesus done for us?

- What difference does this make in our relationship with God?
- What does verse 16 teach?
- How does this apply to "love and sex"?

Sexual Identity ■ Ask the group what they think the Bible says about our sexual identity and roles. (They should give specific references if possible.) Then look up and discuss the following passages together: Genesis 2:15-25; Proverbs 31:10-31; Galatians 3:28; Romans 1:24-34; Ephesians 5:21-33; 1 Corinthians 6:13-20.

Sex within Marriage ■ Divide into groups and give each group a passage of Scripture to discuss. Explain that each one of these passages is an important part of what the Bible teaches about sex. After reading the verse(s), they should ask: *What does this verse(s) mean? How does it relate to sex before marriage? In marriage?*

1. Genesis 2:24—Sex is good. Implication: God invented sex, not modern pornographers, and He made human beings sexual, on purpose.

2. 1 Corinthians 6:13, 18-19—Sexual sin is never right. Our bodies were not made for that. No other sin affects the body as this one does. Implication: We should avoid *all* sexual sin.

3. Exodus 20:14 and 17—Adultery is forbidden.

4. Hebrews 13:4—*The marriage bed is undefiled.* Implication: This means that sex is good within marriage, but it does not teach that "anything goes."

5. 1 Corinthians 13:4-5—*Love is patient and kind . . . it does not demand it's own way.* Implication: Love is not something we "make" by "making" someone else give us pleasure.

6. 1 Corinthians 7:5—Sex must only be withheld for the purpose of prayer and fasting, and then only by mutual consent.

The Loving Thing ■ Read each case study aloud. After each one ask, "What would be the most loving response?"

- George and Bill are roommates in college, but they don't get along. They always seem to be at each other, bickering and making life miserable. One night, Bill comes home and sees that George has worn one of his shirts without asking and has left it on the floor. Bill is furious, but he wants to do the loving thing.
- Sally's mom has just finished chewing her out for something she hasn't done. Sally is hurt, but she wants to respond with love.
- Ellen and Beth are sisters. Ellen has just told her

mom that Beth, the older one, deliberately disobeyed Mom. It is not true, and Beth wants to strike back. What would be the *loving* response?

• Art has been witnessing to his friend Tom for a couple of months. Art has witnessed through his lifestyle and—when the opportunity has arisen—by his words. Today, Tom just laughed at Art and told him to forget all that religion stuff. How can Art respond in love?

BIBLE

CROWD-BREAKERS

Bible Race ■ Do this with teams or everyone competing as individuals. Make sure that everyone has a Bible; then explain that this will be a race to see who (or which team) can find each answer first. Ask them to find the following:

• a promise

• a commandment

• a question

• a warning

• a prayer

• a statement about the future

• a condemnation

• praise

• a story

• a good example to follow

• a miracle

• an object lesson

Use this to teach what the Bible contains.

Conventional Wisdom ■ Divide into teams and seat them in parallel columns facing the front of the room. Each time you ask a question, the first people in each team compete to come up with the correct answer. The first person to blurt out the correct answer wins that round. Then the competitors move to the back of their respective teams while everyone moves up a position. The idea is to complete each well-known phrase. Here are some phrases to use (answers are in parentheses):

• You can't have your cake . . . (and eat it too).

• A bird in the hand . . . (is worth two in the bush).

• He who hesitates . . . (is lost).

• A watched pot . . . (never boils).

• Haste makes . . . (waste).

• Curiosity . . . (killed the cat).

• Every cloud has . . . (a silver lining).

• Waste not . . . (want not).

• Birds of a feather . . . (flock together).

• All that glitters . . . (is not gold).

• The proof of the pudding . . . (is in the eating).

• Don't count your chickens . . . (before they hatch).

• Strike while . . . (the iron's hot).

• Where there's a will . . . (there's a way).

• A word to the wise . . . (is sufficient).

• A fool and his money . . . (are soon parted).

Another possibility would be to phrase these in the form of questions. For example:

• What can't you have and eat? (your cake)

• Who is lost? (he who hesitates)

• What never boils? (a watched pot)

• Where is the proof of the pudding? (in the eating)

• What should you do while the iron's hot? (strike)

• When shouldn't you count your chickens? (before they hatch)

You may want to do a separate contest with well-known Bible wisdom, or you could mix these phrases in with the others. Check Proverbs for others.

- The truth shall . . . (set you free).
- A house divided against itself . . . (cannot stand).
- Wise as serpents . . . (harmless as doves).
- Turn the other . . . (cheek).
- Sheep without a . . . (shepherd)

Following Directions ■ Have everyone stand in a large circle. Then read the following verses while the entire group attempts to follow along with their actions. Read (sing) this to the rhythm and tune of the *Hokey Pokey*.

Warm up (go at a pace that everyone can follow easily):

Lift your left foot up,
*   stick your right hand out,*
Grab your neighbor's hand
*   and shake it all about.*
Now hold on to your ear lobes
*   as you turn yourself around*
That's what it's all about.

Repeat if they are having a difficult time following you. You also may want to have several kids demonstrate their unique interpretations.

Now that the group is warmed up, go on to the main event (read this at a faster pace or go through it twice):

Point your right hand up,
*   point your right hand down*
Point your left hand up;
*   now bend and tap the ground.*
Take a big step forward,
*   take a big step back;*
Then give a mighty clap.

Quickly form a circle;
*   do a wave around the place,*
And if somehow it faded,
*   put a smile back on your face!*
Just put your left hand out
*   and spread your fingers wide;*
Then slap your neighbor's high five!

The Light Brigade ■ Seat teams in parallel columns. Give the last person in each team a small flashlight. Explain that this will be a race. In a moment, you will turn off the lights—that will be their signal to begin. The first person should turn the flashlight on, stand up, make a 360 degree turn, turn off the flashlight, and hand it to the next person. That person should stay seated, turn on the flashlight, make a 360 degree turn, turn off the flashlight, and hand it to the next person. The process should continue all the way down the line, alternating between standing and sitting. When the light gets to the front of the line, the first person should run to the end and start the process over, standing up. The first team to go through the entire team, ending in the original position, wins.

Olive You ■ Bring contestants to the front and have them stand behind a table. Give each one a jar of olives. Explain that they will have two minutes to make a hill out of the olives. The person with the highest hill, wins. Afterwards, explain that each one was making a "mound of olives." This should help them remember the "Mount of Olives" where Jesus gave the Sermon on the Mount. Note: you could do a second round with the contestants blindfolded.

Passages ■ Using teams, give each team a fairly lengthy Bible passage to memorize together. They can take up to ten minutes to learn it (quizzing each other, using memory gimmicks, etc.). Then they must recite it one person at a time to a judge. Award points for the team members who successfully recite the verses.

Recipe ■ Before the meeting, find a relatively simple recipe for a dessert (such as cookies or brownies), make copies of the recipe, and collect all the necessary ingredients, plus a few others. Place the ingredients on a table in front of the group and have teams choose a boy "chef" to whip up dessert for them. Have the chefs stand behind the table and give each one a bowl. Read the directions as they are written on the recipe. The chefs must follow your instructions with no help from the audience. (No one can explain what the abbreviations tbs., tsp., c., pt., and so forth mean or what utensils they should use to measure and mix.) After the time is up, have each one form his "cookies" on a cookie sheet or put the dough in a pan, then bake them in the oven. Serve these as refreshments later (if you dare).

This illustrates what it means to follow directions, the importance of directions, and what a person must know to follow them correctly.

Revelation ■ Before the meeting, find or build four or five unusual objects. Lay them on the floor or on a table and make sure that they are individually, completely concealed under blankets.

Explain that this will be a contest to see who can guess the identity of the objects under the blankets.

Begin with object #1 and reveal just about two inches of it—see if anyone wants to venture a guess. Continue to reveal two or three inches at a time until someone gives the correct answer. Here are possible objects to use:

- a large, macrame flower pot holder
- a golf ball retriever (reveal the grip end first)
- a dog "pooper-scooper" (reveal the grip end first)
- a power, lawn trimmer (reveal the grip end first)
- a camera tripod
- a sump pump
- a toilet bowl snake

Use this as an example of "revelation"—making something known. Then explain how the Bible is God's special revelation of Himself—by reading it we can know about Him, His plan for the world, and His will for our lives.

Right, Writing ■ Give each person a piece of paper with a part of speech written on it. Then tell everyone to write a creative word on their piece of paper in that part of speech. Divide the crowd into teams. Then have each team arrange themselves into one long sentence using as many of the words as possible (they cannot change any of the words that they have written or write new ones). Read the sentences and determine the winning team. For round two, have them see how many complete sentences they can form with their words.

This game can help you make a point about the use and meaning of words.

Scavenger Hunt ■ Divide into as many teams as you wish, but be sure that they have an equal number of Bibles and resource books. Explain that you are going to have a scavenger hunt and that all of the items can be found in the Bible. Next, hand out the scavenger hunt sheets and let them begin. Print the sheets without the answers listed in the parentheses. Most of these items can be found in more than one verse.

SCAVENGER SHEET

Item (or person)	Verse(s)
1. Phoebe	(Romans 16:1)
2. camel	(Genesis 24:30)
3. fleece	(Judges 6:37)
4. Ichabod	(1 Samuel 4:21)
5. axhead	(2 Kings 6:5)
6. barber	(Ezekiel 5:1)
7. fountain	(Proverbs 13:14)
8. Boaz	(Ruth 2:1)
9. Sosthenes	(Acts 18:17)
10. sparrow	(Matthew 10:29, 31)
11. Susanna	(Luke 8:3)
12. lips	(Song of Songs 4:11)
13. girdle	(Isaiah 11:5)
14. moth	(Matthew 6:19)
15. mother-in-law	(Ruth 2:11)
16. Laban	(Genesis 24:29)
17. jaw bone	(Judges 15:15-17)
18. Hittite	(Genesis 25:9)
19. vomit	(Proverbs 26:11)
20. perfume	(Exodus 30:35)

Whoever has all the answers first is the winner.

Throw the Books at Them ■ Put names of all the books of the Bible on pieces of paper (add a few fakes like "Hesitations" and "Hezekiah"). Use teams of any size. At your signal, each person on each team should draw out a book. Then the team members should arrange themselves in the correct order. Replace the papers and repeat for two or three rounds.

Verses Versus ■ Using teams, have each team choose one representative who will recite a long passage of Scripture from memory. Explain that the winner will be the person who can recite the longest passage (number of words). Give students a couple of minutes to huddle as teams to determine who knows which Bible verses and who should be the team's representative. Then have the contestants stand before the whole group and recite.

Wiz Quiz ■ Distribute the quizzes (see below)—without the answers. Allow a few minutes for everyone to try to answer the questions. Then give the answers (in parentheses).

WIZ QUIZ

1. How many Division One college football players does it take to change a light bulb? (answer: one, but he gets two hours credit for it)

2. How many three-cent stamps are in a dozen? (answer: twelve)

3. The television show that has contestants answer with questions. (answer: What is Jeopardy?)

4. Why was Goliath so surprised when David hurled the small smooth stone at him? (answer: because such a thing had never entered his head before)

5. Who is the closest relative who is the sister of your father's brother-in-law? (answer: your mother)

6. What Jewish king's older brother died as a result of adultery and murder in the family? (answer: Solomon)

7. If the Vice President were to die, who would be President? (answer: the President)

8. Name the three wise men mentioned in the Bible who followed the star to Jesus. (answer: no names are given—we don't even know there were three)

9. What gets wet as it dries? (answer: a towel)

10. What can go up the chimney down but not down the chimney up? (answer: an umbrella)

11. Whose wife will she be on the day of resurrection?

Congratulate everyone on how they did on the quiz and for not groaning too loud when you gave the correct answers. Explain that the meeting is about finding God's wisdom.

Words-worth ■ Before the meeting, prepare pieces of paper to be distributed to group members as they enter the room. Each piece of paper will have a number on one side and a part of speech on the other. Each person should write a creative word corresponding to the part of speech on his or her piece of paper (e.g., "adjective"—slimy). To prepare these papers, choose a familiar, simple sentence, such as, "The quick brown fox jumped over the lazy dog." . . . or, "I regret that I have but one life to give for my country." Then, instead of those specific words, assign each one a number and a part of speech. The first sentence would be: "1—article; 2—adjective; 3—adjective; 4—animal; 5—past tense action verb; 6—preposition; 7—article; 8—adjective; 9—noun." The second sentence would be: "1—personal pronoun; verb; 3—impersonal pronoun; 4—personal pronoun; 5—verb; 6—number; 7—noun; 8—infinitive verb; 9—preposition; 10—possessive pronoun; 11—noun."

With a large group, use only one sentence but more than one copy of it, or use both sentences with the second one using letters instead of numbers. In either case, when everyone has written their specific words on their papers, call for the numbers, in order, to come to the front. Then read the sentence that they form and compare it to the original sentence. This game draws attention to the use and meaning of words.

DISCUSSION STARTERS

Bible Acts ■ Before the meeting, prepare slips of paper with Bible stories/situations written on them. Break into groups of three or four members each.

Have each group draw a Bible situation that they are to act out for the others. The rest of the group should try to guess the characters. Here are some possibilities.

• Eutychus and Paul—Acts 20:7-12
• Paul and Silas—Acts 16:22-34
• Peter's escape—Acts 12:6-17
• Agabus—Acts 21:10-14
• Vineyard and workers—Matthew 20:1-16
• Balaam—Numbers 22:21-35
• Naaman and Elijah—2 Kings 5:1-14
• David and Nathan—2 Samuel 12:1-7

Characters ■ Read a few characters from Frederick Beuchner's *Peculiar Treasures* (Harper and Row), or Personality Profiles from the *Life Application Bible* or the *Life Application Bible for Students* (Tyndale House Publishers). Discuss these individuals in terms of how we are like them and the principles that we can apply to our lives.

Context ■ Distribute Bibles and talk about the kinds of literature contained in the Bible: history, poetry, story, parable, prophecy, teaching, letter. Then explain how context is so important in determining the meaning of any word or sentence in any book and why it is especially important in studying Scripture. Give examples of the types of context: immediate (the surrounding verses), larger (the chapter and surrounding chapters), book (the specific book of the Bible), the whole Bible, cultural, historical, etc. Pull verses out of context to show how the meaning is drastically changed. Finally, give group members a work sheet of verses that they should read for meaning by checking the context.

Helps ■ Bring a number of Bible study reference books and explain how to use them. These could include: Bible dictionary, concordance, parallel version of the New Testament, Gospel harmony, one volume commentary, study Bible (for example, the *Life Application Bible*), etc.

Next, distribute the books to individuals or small groups and have them research material on a specific passage like the Sermon on the Mount, specifically the Beatitudes in Matthew 5:1-12. Have each group report what they learned about the setting, people, time, and so on. Then, discuss the meaning of the various verses and how they are relevant to today.

Repeat the process with a passage from the Epistles and then one from a historical book like 1 Kings.

You could take a small group to a Christian bookstore to show where they can find each kind of

Bible help. You can give almost any size group a tour of the church library.

If All the Bibles Were Destroyed . . . ■ Give everyone a piece of paper and a pen. Tell them, *Let's suppose that all our Bibles were destroyed. I wonder how much Scripture we know. For the next five minutes, I want you to write down all the Bible verses you can remember. Come as close as possible to the exact wording and include the references if you can.*

After the time is up, post the references on the wall in the sections of the Bible where they belong—Law, History, Poetry, Prophets, Gospels, Epistles. Ask:

• How difficult was this exercise?

• Where are the gaps in our Bible knowledge? We don't have much of a Bible here, do we?

• What difference should the Bible make in our lives? (See 2 Timothy 3:16.) What stops us from studying and learning it?

Memory ■ Ask students to quote from memory anything they know Jesus said when He was on earth. Be prepared for amazement or disappointment. Compliment those who know many of Jesus' statements, and encourage those who don't know what Jesus said to learn more. Point out that the consensus of human opinion about Jesus ought to be enough to encourage us to know what He said. Too often, however, Christians have only a fuzzy idea of Jesus' teachings.

What Did He Say? ■ Hand out the following list of subjects, *omitting the references*. Introduce the activity by saying: *The Sermon on the Mount is one of the best known sections of the Bible, and it covers three chapters of Matthew (5–7). How many of the following subjects do you think Jesus touched on in those chapters? Circle the ones that you are sure he talked about.*

Food	6:31-34	Murder	5:21-22
Clothes	6:28-30	Adultery	5:27-28
Birds	6:26	Money	6:19-21
Commit-ments	5:33-37	Spiritual dieting	6:16-18
Worry	6:25-27	Criticism	7:3-5
Salt	5:13	Fruit	7:17-20
Anger	5:21-22	Divorce	5:31-32
Light	5:14	Getting even	5:38-41
Doing what's right	5:17-20	The Lord's Prayer	6:9-13
Humility	5:3	Lust	5:27-29
Peacemaking	5:9	Weather	7:24-27

Helping others	6:1-4	Obedience	7:24-27
Prayer	6:5-8	Enemies	5:43-45
Mourning	5:4	Persistence	7:7-8
Friends	5:43-47	Heaven	7:13-14
Parenting	7:9-12	Bad Teachers	7:15-16
Construction	7:24-27	Love	5:43-47
Law suits	5:23-26	Priorities	6:22-24
Forgiveness	6:14-15	Defamation of character	7:1-2

After students have finished, ask them to mention some of the topics in the list they felt Jesus *did not* talk about. As each one is mentioned, ask if anyone can think of something Jesus said about that specific topic. Afterwards, explain that Jesus touched on *all* of these topics in the Sermon on the Mount, and give the references.

DISCUSSIONS AND WRAP-UPS

Application ■ Have everyone turn to James 1:22-25. Then ask: *What does this passage mean? Why isn't it enough to read the Bible every day? What else must we do?* The point is that God has revealed Himself in the pages of the Bible, His holy Word, His special revelation. The Bible is God-breathed, inspired, and as we read it, the Holy Spirit illumines it, showing us the meaning and what we should do. But the action is up to us. We must follow God's directions, putting the message of the Bible into practice in our lives. This is application.

Illumination ■ Explain that this word means "to throw light on." Give examples of how we "illumine" objects in our lives. Then ask how God illumines the Bible for us. Explain that in Christian theology, this word describes the activity of the Holy Spirit as we read God's Word. He shows us the meaning and application. Read aloud John 16:12-15 and discuss its meaning.

Inspiration ■ Explain that we use this word to describe how we feel when filled with awe (when watching a sunset, hearing a great piece of music, being challenged by a great speech, and so forth) or to describe our motivation. In Christianity, however, the word "inspiration" has a limited, technical meaning referring to the process used by God to reveal Himself in the Bible (His special revelation). The Bible is not merely a great piece of literature written by human beings about God. And it is not a book *dictated* by God to human secretaries. Instead, the Bible was uniquely written by God through human instruments. Scripture is *God-breathed.* God gave the human authors His thoughts and guided their writing to keep it from error.

Have everyone look up 2 Peter 1:20-21 and follow along as you read the passage aloud. Then have them turn to 2 Timothy 3:16-17, and read this aloud. Discuss what these verses mean.

Listening to Jesus (talk) ■ Say that there are two reasons for listening to what Jesus says:

1. Because what He said was true, whether we like it or not (refer to the wise and foolish builders at the end of Matthew 7).

2. Because what Jesus said relates to where we live, the problems we face. All of us probably can identify with at least one of the issues in the Sermon on the Mount.

Explain that if we call ourselves "Christians," we should know what Christ said, and then do it. Because many of Christ's strongest teachings are in the Sermon on the Mount, we should study it thoroughly.

Revelation ■ Ask for a simple definition of "revelation." According to the dictionary, it means, "an act of revealing to view" or "making known." Have group members give examples of everyday "revelation." Explain that "revelation" in relation to God means "God making Himself known." Then ask: How has God revealed Himself to us? The correct answer is threefold (have individuals read each passage aloud):

• in nature (natural or general revelation)—Romans 1:18-20

• in Scripture (special or specific revelation)—2 Peter 1:16-21

• in Christ (perfect revelation)—Hebrews 1:1-3

If you use all of the previous discussions in one meeting, take them in reverse alphabetical order. In other words, begin with "Revelation," and then move to "Inspiration," "Illumination," and "Application."

Wise School ■ Ask students what they think the difference is between wisdom and foolishness. Then ask them to imagine a "wise school." What subjects would be taught there. What would be the main textbook? Why?

BIBLE STUDIES

Application ■ Teach your group members how to apply the Bible to their lives by asking the right questions and designing an action plan. Work through a specific passage together asking these questions:

1. *How is this relevant?* In other words, does a similar situation exist today? Are the people to whom this was written like anyone we know? In what ways is the society similar to ours? Who and how?

2. *Can I put myself in the passage?* That is, how can we identify personally with the people or the message?

3. *What should I do?* This is where the Holy Spirit will begin to "convict" us, helping us see changes that must be made in our lives. For example, He could be saying, "Improve your relationship with Mom and Dad."

4. *How can I do it?* What steps can we take to do what we answered for question number three? Here's where we think of specific actions to take and then write them down.

5. *What first step can I take today?* This is where we become very specific and commit to actually doing what God has been telling us.

Application is not just making a passage relevant by bringing it into the twentieth century. It is not just seeing oneself in the passage and realizing how it applies personally. It is even more than knowing what God wants done. Application means doing; it involves action. When we really apply Scripture to our lives, we *do* the Bible (James 1:22).

Bible about the Bible ■ Divide into groups and give each one 2 Timothy 3:16-17 and one additional passage to discuss: Hebrews 4:12; John 10:35; James 1:22-23; Luke 16:17; 2 Peter 1:20-21; 2 Timothy 2:15; Matthew 5:17-20. They should ask:

A. What do these verses tell us about the Bible?

B. How does Scripture teach? Correct? Train in righteousness?

C. What will be the ultimate result of our studying the Bible?

D. How do we misuse the Bible?

Paraphrase ■ Break into groups of four or five and give each group one of the following passages to paraphrase. They should put the passages into their own words with local and personal applications.

• Romans 8:38-39

• Matthew 5:13-16

- 1 Corinthians 13:4-12
- Hebrews 13:1-3
- James 1:2-8
- Philippians 4:4-7

Quiet Time ■ Give group members a pattern for daily devotions. This can be an outline with questions to ask or the "Spark" study from *Campus Life* magazine. An excellent "quiet time" resource is *Alive* by S. Rickly Christian (Zondervan Publishing). Other devotional books are available from Christian bookstores. Bill Sanders has written *Out-takes* and *Goal Posts*, published by Revell, and Kevin Johnson has written devotional books for junior highers, published by Bethany House.

Read It Through ■ Involve your whole group in a project to read the Bible through in a year. There are many reading plans available, but perhaps the most easy to follow is the special edition of *The Living Bible* published by Tyndale House. Entitled *The One Year Bible,* this book contains the entire Bible arranged in 365 daily readings. January 1, for example, has Genesis 1:1—2:25; Matthew 1:1—2:21; Psalm 1:1-6; and Proverbs 1:1-6. When you finish the book, you will have read the entire Bible. These are available at any Christian bookstore.

Worksheet Using 2 Timothy 3:16-17, dictate the following worksheet (or distribute copies).

IT WORKS!

Useful for . . .	This means . . .	I need to . . .
1. Teaching		
2. Rebuking		
3. Correcting		
4. Training		
5. Equipping		

Work through the "This means . . ." column with the group. Then allow a few minutes for everyone to fill in the "I need to . . ." column privately. Explain that this column refers to actions that they know God has been telling them to take in each of these areas during their past Bible studies or in Bible lessons they have heard.

10
BALANCED LIFE

CROWD-BREAKERS

Balanced Teams ■ Write the words "physical," "social," "spiritual," and "mental" on individual slips of paper. Divide the group into four teams and have each team choose a representative to draw one of the papers. The four teams would be named after the aspect of life they drew. Then assign them the task of creating a theme song, a nickname, and a cheer for their respective teams (e.g., *social*: song —"Friends"; *nickname*—"luv-bugs"; cheer—"party hardy"). Allow a maximum of 10 minutes for creating and then have each team sing, cheer, and chant. (They could also choose a celebrity mascot.) Give them 10 more minutes to invent a competitive game for all the teams featuring their team's theme (e.g., "physical"—an eating race). Follow this with all the teams competing in the four games.

Balancing Act ■ Divide into teams and have them line up behind the starting line. At the "go" signal, the first person should walk as quickly as possible to another line and back while balancing an item. If the item falls, the person must start over. The next person may leave only when the previous one has returned. Here are a few "balancing acts"; add others so that you have one per person. Items must be *balanced*, not held.

• book on head

• pencil on bridge of nose

• Ping Pong ball on back of hand

• beanbag on top of one shoe

• golf ball on spoon in mouth

• stick, vertical in the palm of one hand

Cats in the Hats ■ This improvisation activity draws on "social" skills. Collect a number of hats that symbolize types of people. Bring the hats in a large box. Next, number the whole group; then have them come two at a time, in order, don hats, and act as characters who would wear those hats. After about thirty seconds, stop that couple, have them drop their hats into another box, and call up the next two. Possible hats:

• Physical—football helmet, hard hat, baseball cap, boxing head gear

• Social—French beret, Easter bonnet, top hat, party hat

• Spiritual—nun's cap, army helmet with cross on it, yarmulke, prayer shawl

• Mental—graduation hat, derby, "thinking cap," dunce cap

• Miscellaneous—chef's hat, police officer's hat, crown, cowboy hat, straw hat, sombrero, etc.

Dictionary ■ This game requires mental abilities, and it is played in teams. One team (or a person from a team) chooses a little-known word from the dictionary and announces it to the whole group. The other teams (or everyone) then writes down a "definition" on a strip of paper. These are collected by the first team's captain, and he or she mixes in the correct definition. Next, the team captain reads the definitions slowly, one at a time. Everyone chooses what he or she thinks is the correct definition (as a team or as individuals). Then reveal the correct definition, and award points. Give 10 points to everyone who guesses the correct definition and 10 points to the "word chooser" for each person he or she fools. Continue for as many rounds as you can, making sure that all the teams get an equal number of times to choose a word.

Exercise ■ Bring kids to the front and have them demonstrate their form in running, walking, and swimming . . . in slow motion.

Flex Relay ■ Divide into teams and have them sit in parallel columns. Give each team two grapefruits. Explain that this is a relay that involves flexing their biceps. Here's how it works. The first person in line places the grapefruit on his or her arm between bicep and forearm (each arm should have a grapefruit). Then the person walks to the end of the room and back and gives the grapefruit to the next person in line who must follow suit. If a grapefruit falls, the person must begin his or her leg of the race over. Only the person racing at that time may touch the grapefruit. In other words, no one may help him or her put the grapefruit on his or her arms, etc. The first team to have everyone complete the course, wins. For round two, use oranges or, if the room can get messy, use tomatoes. For round three, use golf balls.

Get a Grip ■ (This is a "physical" contest.) Bring a hand exerciser—the type with finger grooves that one squeezes to strengthen a forearm and grip. Throw out a challenge to the crowd for anyone to squeeze the hand grip, holding a dime between the two handles for one minute without letting the dime fall. (It's tough!) If you have some who accomplish it, have a "grip off" to determine the winner. If you don't have a hand exerciser, use the "sledgehammer challenge." This is where the individual holds a hammer straight up with his hand at the end of the handle and his or her arm fully extended. Then the person must lower the head of the hammer slowly to his or her nose and back (using only the wrist—keeping the arm extended).

Indoor Marathon ■ Divide into teams and explain that you will be having a race around an indoor course. Depending on the configuration of your room, lay out a circular course with a few turns in it if possible. Next, have each team choose four racers who will go to the start; the rest of the team members should line the sides of the course. Explain that the race will involve *crawling blindfolded*. As the first person from each team finishes the course, he or she should remove the blindfold and give it to the next person who races, and so on. Have them remove their shoes for safety, and use easily removable blindfolds, such as paper-filled swimming goggles, masks with covered eye holes, etc.

Medicine Man ■ Using teams, explain that this is a "good health" relay. The idea is to transport valuable medicine from one location to another, as quickly as possible. Then give each team an eye dropper and a glass of colored liquid (each team should have a different color). At the other end of the room, set an empty glass for each team. Explain that at your signal, the first person should fill up his or her dropper with "medicine," run to the team's glass at the other end, empty the dropper into the glass, and return to the team, handing the dropper to the next team member, and so on. Allow about two minutes for the race, and then measure the liquid in each glass to determine the winning team.

Muscle Beach ■ Bring two bags of balloons and two oversize sweatshirts. Choose two guys to compete and have each one choose two helpers. Put the sweatshirts on the competitors and give the balloons to the helpers. Explain that this is a contest to see which team can make their competitor the most muscular by blowing up the balloons and stuffing them in the appropriate spots under his sweatshirt. After a few minutes, have the "muscular men" parade in front of the crowd, assuming various body building poses along the way. Have the crowd judge the winner. For round two, see which boy can pop all his balloons the quickest.

One Hundred ■ (This is a contest using mental skills.) This game is played in pairs, so divide the group into twos. The idea is for the pair to alternate adding numbers between 1 and 10 until one person is able to reach 100. That person "wins." Here's how it works. Person A begins by choosing a number between 1 and 10 which he or she says out loud (for example, "8"). Person B adds a number to A's number, in his or her head and says the total out loud (for example, "15"). Person A then adds a number and says the total (for example, "25"), and so on until the winner is determined. Run this like a single elimination tournament where the losers sit down and the winners pair up and play again. Of course there's a system to the game to guarantee a win. See if anyone figures it out.

Popeye Challenge ■ Using teams, have each one choose its *strongest* guy and a girl to participate in a contest. Bring the volunteers to the front and introduce them as "Popeye" and "Olive Oyl." Then, using plastic spoons, have the girls feed their men each a jar of strained spinach after which they must bend a metal bar (use tubing or coat hangers) while singing the Popeye song. ("I'm Popeye the sailor man, I'm Popeye the sailor man. I'm strong to the finish 'cause I eat my spinach, I'm Popeye the sailor man—toot, toot.")

Ski Exercise ■ (This is a contest of physical endurance.) An exercise for getting the thighs in shape for skiing calls for a person to lean against a wall in a sitting position (thighs parallel with the floor) and to hold that position for a long time. It's rough; the legs tire quickly. As a game, have everyone find a spot against the walls around the room. Say "go" and see who can hold the position the longest. As a variation of this, choose team representatives and place shaving cream pies on the floor underneath them.

The Price Is Right ■ Run this game like the TV show with contestants from the audience or competitors from the teams. Instead of prices, however, they are to guess the total amount of calories in an item or group of food items. (Use a calorie book as your reference.) Begin with simple and common foods and drinks (for example, a packet of sugar and a bottle of pop). Next use unusual ones (for example, one French fry, a glass of Gatorade, a catsup packet, or an ice cream bar) or a small combination (for example, a hot fudge sundae or a Big Mac). Finally, use large combinations (for example, a salad with Thousand Island dressing, hot tea with sugar, and a sour cream and bacon baked potato; steak dinner; Chinese dinner).

For most of these items, use vivid verbal descriptions and show a picture. For a few, bring samples of the foods. Keep track of who wins the rounds and award a fat prize (such as a box of chocolates) to the winner. (This may also be done with the whole crowd, with each person marking his or her answers on a sheet of paper.)

The Right Stuff ■ Bring all the ingredients for two or three fast foods and lay them out on a table in front of the room. Run this as a relay with each team member coming to the table, doing one of the tasks, and returning to the team. The last person eats the food. Here are some possible really-fast foods:

Hamburger	Taco
bun opened	shell prepared
lettuce	beef
tomato	tomatoes
mayo	lettuce
mustard	onions
catsup	olives

Hamburger, cont.	Taco, cont.
onions	sour cream
pickles	
beef	
top put on	

Ham and Cheese on Toast

bread toasted

mayo

lettuce

ham

cheese

mustard

top put on

If these ingredients cost too much, buy a few Big Macs and have team members separate the ingredients, one by one. For round two, they can put the fast foods together again and gobble them down.

The Whole Thing ■ This would be a good game to use to break into teams for later activities and to illustrate the concept of "wholeness." Bring four puzzles with equal numbers of pieces (the total being what you expect your attendance to be). Give every person a puzzle piece and tell group members to find the puzzle in which it belongs. Place the puzzle shells in four corners of the room. The first group to complete their puzzle, wins. (The four puzzle groups can become the teams for later activities.)

Trivial Pursuit ■ (This is a game of mental skill.) This popular game could take the entire meeting time. For use as a crowd-breaker, set up a "college bowl" format with each team sending one or more representatives. Use the questions from "Trivial Pursuit" (go from one category to the next), and keep score. For the bonus rounds, use trivia questions that you have written about the youth group that year or about their high school.

Tug-of-War ■ (This is a "physical" game.) Using four teams and a large rope tied into a circle and shaped into a square have a four-corner "tug-of-war." Each team gets on a corner and tries to move the rope a short distance. With a small group you could play the traditional tug-of-war.

Waitress Relay ■ Give each team a box of items (prepare identical sets for all the teams) and a circular serving tray. The idea is for the team members, one at a time, to run with the serving tray down to the box, place an item on the tray, run back to the team, and hand the tray to the next person who repeats the process. The trays must be carried over the head with one hand, with the items accumulated on them (none are removed). The first team to carry all the items (or the last one to drop them), wins. Possible items could include: silverware, cup of water, paper plate, tennis ball, stack of books, golf ball, piece of paper, etc. This illustrates the importance of balance.

Weight a Minute! ■ Using teams, have each one choose three members to be their weight representatives. Their weights should be totaled and recorded on a piece of paper. Next, one team at a time, have the "weight reps" parade in front of the other teams who make a team guess. Award 1,000 points to the team coming the closest to the actual weight of the three. For round two, use 5 members from each team. For both of these rounds, each group of "weight reps" should consist of a mixture of males and females. For a tie breaker, do the whole team. Obviously it would be good to use kids who don't look their weight. Note: if you use two teams, make it a challenge—the team guessing closest to the weight of the other team's representatives wins the round. Also, bring a scale in case of challenges.

Words-worth ■ (This is a "mental" game.) Before the meeting, choose about 25 words with unusual meanings from the dictionary. Type up these words with their definitions and make five copies. During the meeting, choose five kids to compete in a "vocabulary improvement test." Give each one a copy of the word list and three minutes to study it thoroughly.

After the study time, line them up side by side and explain that their goal is to get to a line (or wall) some distance away. They can get there by knowing the word for the definition that you will read. For every correct answer given, they can take one step forward. Begin at one end of the line and ask the first person to answer the question. If he or she answers correctly, he or she can take a step. Either way, move to the next person with the next definition. If he or she answers incorrectly, he or she may not move, and you can repeat the same definition with the next person. Continue until you have a winner.

Note: More "Social" crowd-breakers can be found in the chapter entitled *Relationships and Friends* and "spiritual" ones in the chapter *About the Bible*.

DISCUSSION STARTERS

Finding Faith ■ Give students the following sentences to decipher. The trick is to remove the extra letters F A I T H.

1. Waill yiotu gof wihth met? (Will you go with me?)

2. It realily fliked tahe movihe. (I really liked the movie.)

3. Thist his ai wifird meieting. (This is a weird meeting.)

4. Wihat at verfy satrange lehader! (What a very strange leader!)

5. Whahit wifll thappen nexat? (What will happen next?)

Afterwards, discuss how faith fits into every aspect of life.

Fitness Day ■ Organize a fitness day (or half day) where the emphasis will be fitness in all areas of life. Blend all four areas together during the day. Here are suggestions for each:

Physical:	have an aerobic workout
	have fruit and juice available
	serve health food for lunch
	have a mile walk, run, or swim
Social:	analyze friendships
	interact in small groups
	write letters to loved ones
Mental:	teach how to study
	set up a personal plan of priorities and actions
	read a book and discuss it (e.g., *The Screwtape Letters*)
Spiritual:	each do "quiet time"
	worship together
	spend time *alone* with God, in meditation

Labels and Boxes ■ (This is a "social" discussion starter.) Explain how we often label people. Then ask them what kinds of labels are used at their schools. Next, bring out sheets of blank, computer labels and make sure that each person receives one. Instruct them to write a "new" label, one that they haven't heard before (for example, "Pack man—someone carrying a book pack). After a few minutes, have students bring their labels to the front, one at a time, stick them to a large box, and explain them. Discuss, using the following questions:

• Why do we label people? (so we don't have to think

about them)

• What labels have you had?

• How do you feel when people pin a label on you?

• How did people try to label Jesus? (teacher, son of a carpenter, rebel, blasphemer, miracle worker)

• What kinds of labels do people give Him today? (great teacher, moral example, lunatic)

P./S./M./Sp. ■ Divide into four groups and give each group some Bibles and one section of life—physical, social, mental, and spiritual. Their assignment is to find a Bible character who needed to apply (or applied) his or her faith to that specific area of life. Samson, for example, eventually used his strength for God; Paul used his mind in presenting the Gospel to the philosophers on Mars Hill in Athens; David wrote beautiful songs; King Saul needed work on his people skills; Naomi's faith was "caught" by her daughter-in-law, Ruth; Barnabas encouraged people; etc. They should also find two passages that relate to that specific area (for example, Romans 12:2—"renewing your minds"; Colossians 3:23—"work for God"; 1 Corinthians 13—"love"; etc.). After a few minutes, bring everyone back together and have the group report.

Stations ■ Designate areas around the room or building as stations. Have as many as you need for the size of the group, but be sure to divide the stations evenly between spiritual, social, physical, and mental. At each one, there should be a leader who will supervise the activities there. Hand out scoring sheets and pens, and explain the procedure and rules. (At each station they should perform a task or take a test and then record their points on the score sheets. After they've finished a station, they move to the next one.) Distribute students equally among the various stations and begin. After everyone has completed all the stations, total the scores and find out who is most "balanced."

Possible "station drills":

Physical

1. Shoot free throws. See how many are made out of 10 tries giving five points each.

2. Do sit-ups and push-ups—1 point each; maximum 50 points.

Spiritual

1. Write down the books of the Bible—1 point for every one correctly spelled; maximum 50 points.

2. Recite the Lord's Prayer—1 point per word; maximum 50 points.

Mental

1. Take a 25-question "trivia" test—2 points for every correct answer.

2. Define 10 unique words with five points per definition.

Social

1. List all your friends (first and last names)—1 point each; maximum 50 points.

2. Name the other members of the entire group—2 points per correct name; maximum 50 points.

After you've totaled the scores, announced the winners, and awarded the prizes, ask:

• In what areas did you score the most points? Why?

• How does this game make you look? Is it an accurate picture? Why or why not?

• Where does your Christian faith fit into each of these areas? What difference should a relationship with God make in the social area? Physical? Mental? Spiritual?

Read Matthew 6:25-33 aloud, and challenge students to put Christ at the center of their lives.

Time Capsule ■ Pass out secular magazines (*Time, People, Seventeen, Redbook*, etc.) to the crowd with two or three persons per magazine. Explain that you are going to put together a "time capsule" to let people centuries from now know what our culture was really like. They should tear out ads and articles in the four areas: mental, physical, religious/spiritual, and social. After a few minutes, have the items displayed and put into a pile for each specific area. Discuss:

• Which area was easiest to find?

• Which one was the most difficult?

• What would future civilizations think about us if all they knew were these articles and ads? Would they have an accurate picture? Why or why not?

• What did you find (if anything) that would give clues concerning Christianity? Where would a person have to look to find information about Christ? Why?

DISCUSSIONS AND WRAP-UPS

Balance ■ Use this as part of a wrap-up or as a guide for a discussion.

Most Americans, especially teenagers, tend to emphasize one area of their lives while virtually ignoring the others. The typical "jock" eats, drinks, and sleeps sports. His or her grades suffer, and socially, the parties must revolve around the person's sport, or he or she doesn't go.

To the social butterfly, popularity, friends, and partying are everything. Physical abuse through drinking, smoking, and drugs is common, and academics aren't a priority.

Then, of course, there are the "intellectuals." They spend their time in the library, at the chess club, or in games of "Dungeons and Dragons."

Obviously, the most neglected area of all is the spiritual.

Because most kids stop going to church after confirmation, there's not much happening in this area.

Often we live compartmentalized lives, acting differently depending on the circumstances and the crowd.

It is important to be "balanced"—to see ourselves as whole people and to develop in all areas of life. And God wants to bring wholeness, working in us to develop each area and to integrate all the areas. God is not confined to the "religious" compartment and must be the center of our lives.

So whether you eat or drink or whatever you do, do it all for the glory of God (1 Corinthians 10:31), making all things new (2 Corinthians 5:17).

(See Luke 2:52 and Romans 12:1-2 where the four areas of life are mentioned; also see Colossians 3:23.)

Compartments ■ Explain how we tend to compartmentalize and segment our lives. Then ask:

• Where do you see overlap between the four areas of life (physical, social, mental, spiritual)?

• How does one area affect the others?

• If we grouped everyone here on the basis of what they were really like (regarding their emphasis on physical, social, mental, or spiritual), how would the groups look?

• Where would your friends at school fit in? How do you see yourself?

• Where does God fit in?

F - A - I - T - H ■ Use the following acrostic to help show how faith fits into all areas of life.

F — family, friends, future

A — attitudes, actions activities

I — interests, intellect, income

T — thoughts, talents, talk

H — health, habits, heroes

Ask for other words to add.

Fast Foods ■ (This is a "fitness" discussion.) Ask:

• What do you think about the TV ads for Burger King, McDonald's, and Wendy's? Which is your favorite ad?

• What is your favorite fast food? Why? How often do you have it?

• What meal(s) do you count on for nutrition?

Young Thinking ■ Explain how easy it is when we're young to feel as though we're immortal—that we can do anything and life will never end. Then explain how it's a problem of perspective.

The entire world, for a baby, is her crib. But, standing outside and looking in at her, we know that there is the bedroom, the upstairs, the whole house, the neighborhood, the city, the state, the country, the world—a lot more out there that she doesn't see. Our age and experience have broadened our perspective—we know there's more.

In the same way, for too many young people, right now is all there is and nothing else counts. But life is much more than that, and how we live now can affect us and our children for generations to come. (Ask any older person about his or her youth and about how fast time flies.) A sign of maturity is the ability to see the big picture; to do what is right *now* because of what it will mean in the future—to wait or just say no.

Challenge kids to look at ways that they may be tempted to sacrifice the future for now (for example, drinking and popularity, sex and acceptance, cheating and grades, etc.).

BIBLE STUDIES

Balanced Life ■ Say: *Not much is recorded in the Bible about Jesus' life from His birth until His public ministry at age thirty. There is one situation; remember the incident at the temple where Jesus was discussing theology with the clergy? Right after that, Luke summarizes Jesus' teenage years by saying, "And Jesus grew in wisdom and stature, and in favor with God and men" (Luke 2:52). What kind of picture does this verse give you of Jesus?* (Discuss.)

Jesus grew in "wisdom"—that's the mental area; "stature"—the physical area; "favor with God"—spiritual; and "favor with man"—social. Luke is telling us that Jesus was a whole person, maturing in all areas of life. How can a person become unbalanced in his or her life? Give examples of situations or people you have known. (Discuss.) *What corrective action can we take to become fit in each area?* (Discuss.)

Divide into four groups and give each one a set of verses. They will correspond to the four areas of life: physical, social, mental, and spiritual. Each group should read the verses and answer these questions: *What does this passage teach us? How does this relate to this year in our lives?* After a few minutes, have each group report.

• Physical—1 Corinthians 6:19-20; 9:26-27; Philippians 4:5; 1 Timothy 4:8

• Social—1 Corinthians 13:4-7; Colossians 3:17, 23; 1 Peter 3:15; 1 John 4:19-21

• Mental—Psalms 1:2; 46:10; Proverbs 23:7; Romans 12:1-2; Philippians 1:9-10; 2:5; 4:8

• Spiritual—Philippians 4:6-7; 1 Thessalonians 5:17; 2 Timothy 3:15-17; 1 Peter 3:15; 1 John 5:3

Body Use ■ Distribute copies of 1 Corinthians 6:19-20 from *The Living Bible*, or read it aloud. Then ask:

1. Why does it say that our bodies are the home of the Holy Spirit? (The Holy Spirit lives within us if we are Christians.)

2. Why don't our bodies belong to us? Who owns them? Why? How does this differ from what we hear in society? (God created us. When we become Christians He sends His Holy Spirit to live in us. Society says that we are the lords of our own bodies—we can do anything we want with our bodies.)

3. How can we use "every part" of our bodies to give glory to God? . . . minds? . . . mouths? . . . eyes? . . . hands? . . . legs? . . . stomachs? . . . sexual organs? . . . desires? . . . other? How do health and appearance relate to this discussion?

Focus ■ Divide into four groups and give each a set of passages to look up and discuss:

• Physical—1 Corinthians 6:19-20; 9:27; 1 Timothy 4:8, 12

• Social—John 13:34-35; Romans 12:9-21; 14:15; Colossians 3:17

• Mental—Proverbs 23:7; 1 Corinthians 4:5; Philippians 2:5; 4:8

• Spiritual—Philippians 4:5-6; 1 Thessalonians 5:17; 2 Timothy 3:15-17; 1 Peter 3:15; 1 John 5:3

Look It Up ■ Have students look up the following verses. After each one is read aloud, ask the group how that passage relates to how we should take care of our bodies.

• Matthew 6:33-34 (God should be the center of our lives—nothing else.)

• Matthew 25:14-30 (We are to use well what God has entrusted to our care, and that includes our bodies.)

• Luke 2:52 (The balanced life—Jesus matured in all areas of life.)

• Romans 12:1-2 (We should present our bodies to God. The balanced life is also implied in this passage.)

• 1 Corinthians 6:12-13 (Our bodies are God's temples; therefore, we should take good care of them.)

• 3 John 1:2 (God wants our bodies and our souls to be well.)

Note: another passage to use would be the story of Jacob and Esau in Genesis 25:27-34. Esau was willing to sacrifice his future for present satisfaction.

Not Confined ■ Emphasize the fact that God is not confined to a religious box in our lives and only interested in church, theology, and saints. Instead, He wants to be intimately involved in all areas of our lives, in every part. Read four selected verses relating to the four areas:

• 1 Corinthians 6:19-20—physical

• 1 Corinthians 11:27-3—spiritual

• 1 Corinthians 13:4-8—social

• 1 Corinthians 14:20—mental.

Then challenge students to put Christ in the very center of their lives, allowing Him to change them from the inside out. Close by reading 2 Corinthians 5:17 and Ephesians 3:17-19 aloud.

The Whole Story ■ Have everyone turn to Colossians 3 and lead them on a short journey through this passage. Explain how this chapter emphasizes the necessity of improving every area of life: physical, social, mental, and spiritual. Use this outline for the study.

1. Colossians 3:1-4—mental: "set your mind on things above."

2. Colossians 3:5-7—physical: these are obvious physical vices.

3. Colossians 3:8-14—social: these qualities affect all relationships.

4. Colossians 3:15-17—spiritual: this section emphasizes prayer, Bible study, singing, and fellowship.

SALVATION, GRACE, AND FORGIVENESS

Note: Many of these crowd-breakers are illustrations of "sin," featuring "missing the mark," or of "grace," featuring impossible tasks.

CROWD-BREAKERS

Balloon Box ■ Bring a good supply of balloons, divided equally between two colors. Throw them into the crowd to be blown up and tied. Next, have two people stand at opposite sides of the crowd, each holding a large box. Assign a color (matching the balloons) to each box and explain that the object of the game is to see how quickly they can get all the balloons into their matching boxes without breaking any of them and only hitting them while seated. Try this a couple of times to get them competing against the clock. (Be sure to have extra balloons to replace those that break.) Next, repeat the contest with the lights off and using a strobe light. This will make the task almost impossible, but it will be a lot of fun.

Barrel of Monkeys ■ This is a very inexpensive toy that can be found in most toy stores. Inside a plastic barrel are a dozen or so plastic monkeys with arms outstretched (one curled upward and one downward). The idea is to dump out all the monkeys into a pile and then to pick them all up in a continuous chain by linking the arms. The first monkey is the only one held. At first this seems easy, but as the chain lengthens, it becomes increasingly difficult. Finally, the last monkey is flat on the table and is a real challenge to pick up. Do this as a team relay or as an individual race against the clock.

Batter-up ■ For this game you will need a Nerf ball and a strobe light. Divide into teams and have them choose two or three representatives (depending on the number of teams) to compete in a "home run derby." Explain that you will be the pitcher and, one at a time, they will be the batters (hands will serve as "bats"). Mark out home plate and the line over which they must hit the ball for a home run, and then begin the game. One at a time, have the batters step up to the plate. Give each one ten swings at the Nerf ball to see how many home runs he or she can hit. (Have someone keep score.) After everyone has had a turn, announce the score and then explain that you are now ready to move into the second "inning." This time you will see how many home runs they can hit while the strobe light is flashing. Turn off the regular lights and turn on the strobe at a fast pace. Then pitch the ball slowly, giving each batter 10 swings as before. It is very difficult to make contact during the strobe.

This illustrates "missing the mark." We also miss the mark when we try to perform well (sinlessly) in our lives. Our perception has been distorted and our ability impaired.

Carbon Copy ■ Choose three pairs of kids to compete. (These may be representatives from teams, couples, friends; any combination will work.) Explain that one person in each pair will be the artist who will draw a diagram as described by his or her partner. Give each pair a piece of poster board and a magic marker. Seat them side by side, by pairs, with their backs to the audience and the poster board in their laps so that everyone can see the boards. Then explain that the "artists" will have to be blindfolded. After blindfolding them, tape the diagrams for each couple on the wall and have the "describer" of each couple stand between his or her diagram and the partner's poster board. (The artist shouldn't be able to see what the partner is drawing.) Tell the describers to begin giving instructions and the artists to begin drawing. Here are some possible diagrams:

Allow about three minutes for the artists to complete their work. Afterward, vote on the best copy of the original and award prizes.

Note: The point of this game is that it is virtually impossible to make an accurate copy of the original, especially considering the handicaps. Even without blindfolds, good pictures would have been very difficult. Matthew 5:48 states: *Be perfect, therefore, as your Heavenly Father is perfect*, but none of us attain this standard, handicapped by sin in our lives and in the world.

Come Clean ■ This is a relay involving clean laundry. Divide into equal size teams and give each team a box of various laundry items. The boxes should contain identical sets. Laundry items could include three pairs of socks of varying colors, a T-shirt, two towels, three handkerchiefs, a pillow case, two sets of shoe laces, and a large sheet (preferably the fitted type).

The teams should sit in parallel lines with their boxes at one end and a table at the other. At your signal, the first person in line should pull out of the box an item or a set that he or she should then pass down the line, person-to-person, to the last person. Note: socks and shoe laces must be pulled and sent in matching pairs. Also, an adult helper should stand behind the table to judge whether the item has been folded correctly—socks should be rolled and stuffed.

When the item reaches the last person, he or she must fold it correctly, place it on the table, run to the front of the line and pull out the next item or set. The items may be pulled from the box in any order *except* for the sheet which must be the last item sent down the line. The first team to finish, wins.

This illustrates how God's forgiveness is like being laundered, being made completely clean.

Here Comes the Judge ■ Choose three girls from the audience to model football uniforms. Have them dress in another room, and then bring them in one at a time so they can walk in front of the audience while three judges (football guys) rate them on a scale of 1–10. (A "10" is perfect.) Total the numbers and announce the winner. Then, surprise everyone by turning the tables and appointing the girl contestants as judges and the previous judges as contestants. Each "macho man" must don a tutu and then perform four ballet moves (one person at a time for each move). The new judges rate them 1–10 each time. The moves could include a pirouette, an arabesque, or a jeté.

Note: This illustrates the truth that we should "judge not that we be not judged" and that God has every right to judge us by the standards we use to judge others.

Hitting It on the Nose ■ Choose four guys and let them choose girl partners. Explain that you are going to see who is the best shot among the girls, and then give each girl a water pistol. Drape towels over the guys' shoulders (and on the floor if necessary), have the girls stand six to eight feet from their partners, and place a ball of shaving cream on each guy's nose. At your signal, the girls are to use their squirt guns and try to shoot off the shaving cream. The first couple to finish wins.

Lifeguard Training Course ■ Use volunteers from the crowd or team representatives. Explain that they are potential lifeguards and will have to go through a grueling training course before they can be certified. Explain that the person completing the course the fastest will be declared *Champion Lifeguard* and receive a prize. Then lay out the following course in the room (complete with volunteer "victims") and explain it to the competitors and the rest of the group. Note: if you have enough room, the competitors could compete at the same time. It would be chaotic and fun.

1. Throw out a life-line from point A, into a box at point B.

2. Recoil the life-line and "swim" the breast stroke (on the floor) from point A to point B.

3. Take the whistle out of the box and blow it three times.

4. "Swim" the back stroke (on the floor) from point B to point C.

5. Pick up a victim at point C and carry him or her to point D.

6. At point D, blow up a balloon until it pops (to simulate mouth-to-mouth resuscitation).

7. Drag the victim from point D back to point A.

Opposites ■ Divide into teams and seat them in parallel columns facing the front of the room. Explain that you will say a word, and the first person in each team should shout the word that is opposite. The first person to shout the correct word, wins that round for his or her team. After each round, the people in front should go to the back, with the columns moving up. Begin with easy words; then move to more difficult ones. Here are some words to use and their opposites:

left	—	right
up	—	down
north	—	south
evil	—	good
love	—	hate
terrible	—	great
empty	—	full
fire	—	ice
Republican	—	Democrat
southwest	—	northeast
liberal	—	conservative
God	—	Satan
synonym	—	antonym
phony	—	genuine

The team to win the most rounds wins the game.

Paddle Ball ■ Divide into teams and give each one a paddle ball (the ageless toy wooden paddle with a rubber ball attached by an elastic string). When you say "go," the first person on each team should run to the front, pick up the paddle, and swing the ball out and back five times (trying to hit the ball with the paddle, of course). Then the first person runs back to his or her team and is replaced by the next person who swings the paddle, and so on through the team. The process continues until one team reaches the combined total of fifty hits (or less, depending on how coordinated and skillful your kids are). Obviously you will need to have an official hit counter for each team. Afterward, see if anyone can hit the ball five times in succession.

Piece, Peace ■ Using teams, have them choose two representatives each to compete in a contest to see who can assemble a puzzle the quickest. After the competitors have been chosen, bring out the puzzles. They should be very simple, children's puzzles. Explain that one person will put the puzzle together while the other gives verbal instructions. The catch is that the "assembler" will be blindfolded. If possible,

use a different puzzle for each team. The team to complete the puzzle the fastest wins. Only voice instructions may be given—no touching—and only the designated person may speak.

Quick Change Artist ■ Bring two sets of clothes in garbage bags or old suitcases. Include a variety of clothing items in assorted sizes. The sets don't have to be identical, but they should contain similar items. Divide the crowd into two teams and explain that you are going to have a relay. Form the teams into parallel columns and give the first person in each a bag of clothes. When you say "go," he or she must carry the bag to the other end of the room, dump out the clothes, put them all on (over the clothes which he or she is wearing), run back (with the bag) to his or her team, take off the game clothes, put them back in the bag, and give the bag to the next team member who repeats the process. The first team to have everyone dress and undress wins. (If the group is large, choose 10 representatives per team or have more teams and sets of clothes.) Possible clothing articles could include: extra large pants, small T-shirt, gloves, nylon stockings, boots, overcoat, earmuffs, and hat.

Note: This activity can be used to illustrate being *clothed in righteousness* (Psalm 132:9).

Scrabble Scramble ■ The best way to do this game is with two sets of children's magnetic letters with metal chalkboards. If these aren't available, make two sets of letters (the alphabet twice-individual letters on small pieces of paper) and put each set in a bag. Also, give each team a roll of tape and a poster board on the wall on which they can tape their letters.

Divide into two teams and have them form parallel columns beginning about six to eight feet from the front of the room. At the signal to start, the first person from each team should run to the front, pull out a letter, and put it on the board. After he or she returns, the next person follows suit. The idea is to build as many words as possible in the time allotted. If a letter doesn't fit into a word right away, it may be put to the side and used later. The letters may be used like a Scrabble game or crossword puzzle where one letter can be used in two words, but they don't have to connect. After the time is up (approximately three minutes), check out the validity of the words and award points: two for each letter used in each word, three bonus points for each letter used in two words, and two bonus points for using Q , Z, and X.

Slate ■ Divide into two teams and give each team chalk and a chalkboard to use. Have the teams line up in columns facing the chalk boards, about eight feet away from them. Explain that the goal of this game is to see which team can more completely fill their chalkboard with writing, within a time limit. The two rules are: only words may be written (no scribbling), and everyone on each team must write something. Explain that the time limit is one minute and 17 seconds.

Designate an adult helper or two to serve as judges (to make sure that the rules are obeyed) and give the teams a few seconds to get organized. Then give the signal for the race to begin. When the time is up, stop the writing and display the chalkboards, one at a time, for all to see. Have the judges declare the winning team *for round one.*

Next, explain that for round two, they must erase their opponent's filled-in chalkboard, again in one minute and 17 seconds. The team to do the most complete job of erasing will win that round. The rules are: each person may only take *one* swipe with the eraser at a time, and everyone on each team must participate within the time limit. Allow a few seconds for the teams to determine their strategies; then give the erasers and the signal to begin. Afterwards, declare the winning team—the one with the cleanest chalk board.

Note: this game illustrates the fact that God's forgiveness wipes the slate of our lives clean.

Take Aim ■ Set up a target at the front of the room. This can be a circle through which the items must be thrown, or a box into which the items must be thrown. Choose five or six contestants and give them each a bag full of items that are difficult to aim and to "fire" accurately. Then have them, one at a time, shoot or throw their items toward the target from a distance of at least six feet. Keep track of successful hits and determine the winner. As a team game, have a target for each team and make sure that each team member receives a different item to throw. To heighten the tension, include penalties for the losing team or individuals. Possible ammunition items could include: sugar packet, inflated long balloon, rubber band (shot with one hand), Ping Pong ball (blown out of the mouth), 3"x 5" card, drinking straw, Styrofoam cup, cotton ball, paper airplane, paper plate, leaf, etc.

Target Practice ■ This is similar to the game above. Make a variety of targets that the group must hit with a variety of missiles. Then give everyone their missiles and let them try to hit the targets, one at a time. Here are some possibilities:

• batting a balloon through a hula hoop from at least six feet away

• landing a paper airplane in a wastebasket

• throwing a wadded-up piece of paper through a circle that is swinging back and forth

• shooting a cotton swab with a straw, off the ceiling and into a box that you are holding in front of you at about shoulder height

• bowling a golf ball to knock down 10 "pins" (golf tees)

• shooting a rubber band at a dart board

Note: This illustrates "missing the mark," one definition of sin.

The Test ■ Explain that you have a special IQ test for everyone, and those who flunk (score less than 75 percent) will have to experience a penalty. Distribute the following test that has impossible questions (most answers are in parentheses). After the test, have group members exchange papers and grade them. Then determine those who flunked (most of them), and suspend the penalty (illustrating "grace").

ARE YOU AN INTELLI-GENT (OR LADY)?

1. What is the capital of Afghanistan? (Kabul)

2. Who was Barry Goldwater's running mate? (William Miller)

3. In Mississippi, why can't a man marry his widow's sister? (because he's dead)

4. Name two of Ronald Reagan's old movies. (*Bedtime for Bonzo, Knute Rockne–All American, Santa Fe Trail, King's Row, Desperate Journey, This Is the Army, The Killers,* etc.)

5. True or False: Is it not true that a true answer to this question would be false? (Yes, it is not true.)

6. How many angels can dance on the head of a pin?

7. True or False: The statement, "God helps those who help themselves" is in the Bible. (False—Ben Franklin said it)

8. Who lost the Super Bowl of the 1993-94 season? (Buffalo Bills)

9. How many three-cent stamps in a dozen? (12)

10. True or False: You feel more like you do right now than you have all day.

11. In what city did the TV show "Cheers" take place? (Boston)

12. What does N.A.S.A. stand for? (National Aeronautics and Space Administration)

13. Who was the shortest man in the Bible? ("Knee-high Miah" [Nehemiah] or Bildad, because he was only a shoe height [the Shuhite])

Turn Around ■ Choose two kids to compete (they

could be team representatives). Stand them in front of the room, facing each other, about four to six feet apart. Give one person an inflated balloon. At your signal, he or she should bat the balloon toward the other person. (You may want to use a plastic toy bat.) That person must do a 360 degree turn before hitting the balloon back. After the first "balloon bat," each person must do a 360 degree turn before hitting the balloon back. The first person to miss the balloon, allowing it to hit the floor, loses. If you have the room, divide the whole group into twos, distribute a lot of balloons, and have everyone compete at the same time. Run it like a tournament.

Turned Around ■ Do this in a large room. Make sure that everyone has a coin and have them stand at one end of the room and face the wall. Have everyone hold their coins in their hands. Tell them to flip their coins. If they get *heads*, they should turn 45 degrees to the right and take one step forward. If they get *tails*, they should turn 45 degrees to the left and take one step forward. Explain that you will have them do a series of coin flips, all together, when you tell them to. The idea is to see who can get to you first (you should be standing at the other end of the room), simply by flipping coins and following your instructions. (If they run into a wall, they should wait until a flip takes them away from it.) It will also be interesting to see how long it takes.

Note: this can be used to illustrate how confused and directionless people can be *or* the necessity to be "turned around" by Christ.

DISCUSSION STARTERS

Amazing Grace ■ Summarize the story of John Newton, the writer of the song *Amazing Grace*, found in *101 Hymn Stories* by Kenneth W. Osbeck, Kregel, 1982. Read the stanzas, and then sing the song together.

Before and After ■ Give everyone a card or piece of paper and a pen or pencil. Have them draw a line down the middle. At the top of the left side they should write *B.C.*, and on the right, *A.D.*

Explain that *B.C.* means *Before Christ*, and that *A.D.* means *After Decision*. Tell them to write what they were like before they accepted Christ as Savior, on the one side, and then what they are like now, on the other. Everyone should be honest and not put their names on the tops of their cards. Make a few comments about how Christ changes lives, including

ours. Then collect the cards, mix them up, and read a few (concealing the identity of the writers) to illustrate the truth. Make the point that we don't have to have a dramatic conversion experience (from being depraved to becoming a super-saint) to have new life in Christ. Some of the less obvious changes could include: desire to read the Bible and pray; desire to tell others about Christ; increased sensitivity to others; desire to help others, etc.

This exercise illustrates how Christ changes lives.

Catalog ■ Using sheets of paper and pens, have everyone list as many sins as they can think of in two minutes. Explain that this is not a contest, nor does it reflect on their personal lives. The idea is to see what they consider to be sins. Take a few moments to see what types of sins made their lists and discuss various definitions of sin ("missing the mark," breaking a law, rebelling/disobeying, failing to do what is right, being self-centered, etc.)

Escape! ■ Bring a pair of handcuffs and hold them up in front of the crowd. Explain that you want volunteers to put them on and then try to get out. There is a trick to it, but it is possible to escape. As an incentive to try, offer a T-shirt or other good prize to the first person who can escape within 30 seconds.

Bring up the first contestant, put on the handcuffs, and watch him or her squirm. When 30 seconds are up, unlock the cuffs, remove them, and repeat with the next person. (Note: These should be real handcuffs that only can be removed by using the key.) If none of these volunteers can figure out how to escape, bring up a staff member who knows how. Put the cuffs on him or her and say "go." Then he or she should simply say, "Will you please let me out?" That's the trick! All the person had to do was ask. Then, unlock the handcuffs and release him or her.

Afterward, ask how this is an illustration of how we are saved. Trapped in our sins, we can try all sorts of ways to extricate ourselves. But the truth is that only Christ holds the key. He is ready and willing to release us from our sins; all we have to do is ask.

Excu-u-u-u-u-se Me ■ Choose eight kids to role play the following situations. Each play takes two actors.

• *Person 1*—You have just been pulled over by a policeman for going 50 mph in a 20 mph school zone, running a red light, and having an expired vehicle registration. In addition, your driver's license has expired.

Person 2—You are the policeman.

• *Person 1*—You have just walked in the door an hour after your parents' curfew.

Person 2—You are the father or mother. You have waited up for your son or daughter. On your way home, you saw your child's car or date's car parked on a side street with the windows fogged up.

• *Person 1*—Your teacher has suddenly stepped back into the room during a test and has accused you of cheating.

Person 2—You are the teacher.

• *Person 1*—You are going steady with person 2. He or she has seen you flirting with another person and is confronting you about it.

Discuss the guilt and grace in these situations. That is, which persons were guilty and why? How could they receive forgiveness?

Forgiveness Game ■ Give each person five index cards. On one they should write something bad that they did in grade school, and at the bottom of the card they should write "5 points." On their second cards, have them describe a similar incident during junior high, and on the bottom write "10 points." On the third card they should write something from high school and "15 points." Their last two cards should be blank. No names should be written on the cards.

At your signal, everyone should mill around the room and trade cards with other kids (blind draw). The object is to collect as few points as possible within the time limit. After six or seven minutes, stop the game, total the points, and determine the winner.

Next, have some of the "confessions" from each age period read aloud. Discuss those incidents and how real forgiveness relates to the game (for example, "What did you have to do to get rid of your points? How is this similar to what Jesus did for us?").

Free ■ Check the newspapers and your mail and collect the "free" offers that you find. Bring them to the meeting and discuss them, one at a time, along the following lines:

•Is this really free? Why or why not?

•What do we have to do to get it? What strings are attached?

•Why are we attracted to "free" offers?

Fresh Starts ■ Give each person a piece of paper and a pen or pencil and have them list the "fresh starts" they have had in their lives. Beneath each fresh start they should write the main benefit to them. Their fresh starts could include: new semester in school, new job, new town, new relationship, new house, new year, new season in sports, etc.

Discuss how God's forgiveness gives us a fresh start in life.

God and Humans ■ This skit will require set-up and practice before the meeting.

Two guys enter the room. One is wearing a sign around his neck that reads, "God," and he has a Burger King crown on his head. The other person is wearing a Mickey Mouse shirt (or something similar) and a sign reading "human." "God" is standing on a short platform (like a wooden box or chair). Scattered on the floor are a number of boxes of varying sizes. On one side of each box is written a sin and on the other side, an emotional effect of that sin. (For example, jealousy=anger, adultery=shame, stealing=guilt, lying=insecurity.)

"God" and "human" begin by talking about life. Then "human" notices the boxes on the floor; he asks "God" what they are and if he can try them. "God" explains lovingly and carefully, and advises against using them, but he says that it's "human's" choice. After looking at the boxes, thinking about them, and talking a bit more to "God" about it, "human" stoops down and picks up a box. As he checks it out, he experiences the emotional effect. "Human" continues to pick up boxes (he doesn't drop any of them), and his communication with "God" progressively deteriorates until he is blaming "God" for all his problems and the fact that they are weighing him down. Finally "human" is on his knees on the floor, overwhelmed by the collective weight of the boxes. "God" asks if "human" wants help. "Human" responds with a desperate, "Yes, please help me!" "God" then reaches down, lifts off the boxes, and throws them back over his shoulder. "Human" stands and embraces "God."

Afterward, discuss how this illustrates grace, and how a person comes into a relationship with God.

Grace ■ Distribute copies of the following worksheet and pencils. Have everyone fill them out with a possible offense, penalty, and by grace what the penalty could be for each authority figure. Then discuss their answers.

Authority Figure	Offense Deserved	Penalty	Grace
Judge			
Parents			
God			
Teacher			
Police Officer			
Employer			

Grace Is . . . ■ Hand out papers and pens. Have everyone finish the sentence, *Grace is . . .* Collect and read. (Both humorous and serious answers are all right.) Then discuss what grace means.

Grace Project ■ As a group, determine a fitting gift for a needy family. Pray, collect the money, purchase the gift, and deliver it secretly and anonymously. The needy family should never know the source of the gift.

On an individual basis, have each person choose a person who has wronged them the most or who is always giving them grief. Then tell them to give these "grief-givers" an anonymous, good gift.

These projects teach grace from God's point of view—love with no strings attached.

Guilt Trip ■ Explain that you are taking a survey to determine the guilt or innocence of the group. Students should close their eyes while you read the following situations. At the conclusion of each situation, you will ask for a show of hands to see who has been guilty of similar behavior. (They don't have to fit the situation exactly, but they should raise their hands if they can identify with it.) Situations:

1. You and your parents are at the high school open house. Your teacher has just explained your work and grades, and then tells your parents, "Your child is doing all right, but could do so much better. He or she is just not performing up to his or her *potential*."

2. Your brother (or sister or friend) was supposed to pick you up at 3:00 sharp from school. It is now 3:30, and there is still no sign of him. You know he's been goofing off and are so mad you could spit! He finally pulls up, and you let him have a verbal barrage! You then discover that he had a *very good* reason for being late.

3. You've had a rough day (pop quiz, boy/girlfriend squabbles, late for class or detention, coach on your back, etc.), and you are in a bad mood when you get home: kicking at the cat, throwing your little brother's stuff back into his room, muttering through your teeth, and slamming your door. The climax comes when you scream at your mom after she asks about your homework. At dinner you realize that Mom has fixed a surprise meal for you with your favorite dessert.

4. (Guys) You're on a date with a girl you really like. You're in a secluded spot, and you put your arms around her and try to kiss her. She stops you and says, "How could you do such a thing. I thought you were different and really liked me."

(Girls) You know you've been flirting with this guy at school and leading him on, but you're really not that interested in him. He calls you to ask you out, but you make up a silly excuse.

Afterward, comment on how many hands were raised; then discuss how this game illustrates our real guilt and need for grace and mercy.

Hurt List ■ Hand out sheets of paper and pens or pencils. Tell students to use one side of their papers and to write down all the ways that others have hurt them. These hurts may have occurred at any time during their lifetimes. They should list the general categories and not be specific with detailed descriptions and names (for example, "lied to me," "stole my bike," "ignored me," etc.). After everyone has finished, have them turn their papers over and write all the ways that they have hurt God. Again, these should be general categories (for example, "disobeyed Him," "ignored Him," "haven't prayed for a long time," etc.). After everyone has finished, discuss the similarities and differences between the two lists. Then ask how God has responded and how He presently responds to our sins and hurts against Him. The answers will describe Jesus coming to earth and dying for us and the fact that total forgiveness is available to us (1 John 1:9). Then ask how this should influence how we forgive others; that is, what should we do about the hurts we have received. After the discussion, destroy the papers together.

Majoring on Minors ■ Distribute papers and pencils and have everyone list what they consider to be minor sins and those that they wish weren't sins. Afterward, discuss their reasons for both designations.

New and Improved ■ Divide into groups and give each group paper and a pen or pencil. Explain that each group is a research and development department of a major corporation. Their assignment is to design a *new* and *improved* product that you will give them. They should brainstorm ideas and then write them down, ready to report to the whole group. Give each group one of the following "products": automobile, kitchen, computer, television, airplane, camera, and college.

After a few minutes, have the groups report what they designed. Then ask the whole group to brainstorm how they would design and market a new and improved human being.

Quiz ■ Before the meeting, choose and instruct one or two questioners and make a pile of "bricks" (these can be shoe boxes or smaller boxes). Ask for a volunteer to participate in an interview. Seat this person on one side of a table with the questioner (interviewer) on the other and the boxes on the floor. Let the interview begin with the interviewer asking questions and the volunteer giving the answers. Every time the answerer uses "I," "me," or another "self" pronoun, the interviewer should put a box on the table and build a wall between the two of them. (Do not explain that it is a wall.) The interview should continue until all the boxes have been used or until the interviewer runs out of questions. This can be repeated as many times as you wish until the audience figures out what you are doing. If no one guesses what has been going on, ask the group why the boxes were placed on the table, what caused them to be placed there, etc. This game illustrates how much of what we do and say is self-centered; the essence of sin is "self-centeredness." Possible situations for the interviewer and interviewee to discuss are:

• a recent sports event on television or at school

• the American economy or political situation

• the quality of Japanese products vs. American products

• problems and pressures in dating

• differences between junior and senior high

Note: Have the interviewer try to avoid leading questions (for example, What do you think?).

Symbols ■ Distribute magazines and tell students to find pictures that illustrate or symbolize forgiveness. Possibilities could include a waterfall, soap, a baby, an eraser, an artist, a blanket or other covering, a judge, a chalkboard, a wastebasket, etc. Have individuals explain their symbols. Then tell how God's forgiveness "covers our sin," "cleans us up," "declares us 'not guilty'," "gives us a fresh start," "discards all of our past mistakes," etc.

The Great Divorce ■ There is a beautiful section dealing with grace and forgiveness in chapter four of C.S. Lewis' *The Great Divorce* that could be read and discussed.

Total Forgiveness ■ Divide into teams and give each team a felt-tipped pen and a poster board with the word *FORGIVENESS* printed across the top. Tell each team to appoint a "recorder" and a "reporter." Then explain that they should form words from the letters in *forgiveness* that illustrate what it means to forgive and to be forgiven. The recorder should write the words on the poster board, and the reporter should be ready to explain their meanings to the rest of the group.

Allow about three minutes for everyone to find and write the words. Then have the teams report their

findings, alternating back and forth. Here are some possible words: I, give, for, forge, sin, fire, son, rev, fig, vine, sieve, never, go, given, govern, giver, finger, if, or, sing, ring, nor, siren, fire, fern, sign, sever, and ignore(s).

Wronged ■ Pass out scratch paper and pens and ask everyone to visualize someone who has wronged them. Next, they should each write a list of the offenses and how they felt. After a few minutes ask: *What would be your conditions for forgiving this person?*

Next ask them to take another piece of paper and list all the ways that they have wronged God, according to the Bible. Then ask what it would take (or took) for God to forgive them. Discuss this briefly. Then read Jeremiah 31:33-34, emphasizing the phrase, *I will remember their sin no more.*

Ask: *In light of what God has done for you, could you tear up your list of "wrongs" and forgive with no conditions?*

DISCUSSIONS AND WRAP-UPS

Effects ■ Discuss the effects of sin by asking what our sin does to us (besides separate us from God) and to others. Then ask what has been done about sin and what we can and should do about it.

Forgiveness ■ Use the following as content for a discussion or a wrap-up on God's forgiveness.

It is virtually impossible for us to understand the forgiveness of God with our finite minds. "Forgiveness" is the action resulting from God's attributes of love, grace, and mercy and must be balanced with His justice and righteousness.

God has loved us and continues to love us unconditionally; however, He has given us the ability to reject His love and to live apart from Him.

Because of our choices, we have separated ourselves from God. Our sin and rebellion leave us under His judgment, but His love continues. God stands, like the loving father in the story of "The Prodigal Son," waiting for us to return.

Jesus' death and resurrection make it possible for us to come "boldly" into God's presence. We need only accept Jesus' sacrifice for sin and, by faith, receive Him as our personal Savior. Thus, when we confess our sins (1 John 1:9), we are not pleading with God to forgive us—He already forgives us—rather, we are removing the sin barrier that we constructed in the relationship, and we are experiencing the reality of His forgiveness.

God's forgiveness frees us from the guilt of the past and frees us to live in vital union with Him.

Grace ■ Use these thoughts on grace for a discussion or wrap-up.

Grace is foundational to our faith and is what makes Christianity unique among religions. Religion emphasizes attainment of "oneness with God" through personal effort and good works. These works may include eating prescribed foods, praying regularly, traveling to sacred sites, doing good deeds, and a myriad of spiritual exercises. Christianity says that there is nothing we can do to earn God's favor; it is a gift because of what Jesus has done for us. Grace has been defined as "undeserved favor," and it is because of God's grace that Jesus came, died, and rose from death. Ephesians 2:8-9 states that it is by God's "grace you have been saved, through faith—and this is not from yourselves, it is the gift of God—not by works, so that no one can boast." In other words, our salvation rests totally on grace.

The flip side of "grace" is "mercy." Grace means getting what we don't deserve (a positive act from God), and mercy is not getting what we really deserve. The dynamic interplay of grace and mercy in the plan of God culminated in the Incarnation. Humanity stood (and we stood) guilty before the righteous Creator, deserving eternal death and separation from Him. Instead, God sent Jesus to take what we deserve, to die for our sin, in our place. As we repent and accept by faith what Jesus has done for us, we realize personal redemption, forgiveness, justification, and salvation.

Memory Device ■ To help students remember the lessons learned about forgiveness, give each one a small eraser at the end of the meeting. Buy erasers with unusual and creative shapes and sizes.

Past-Present-Future ■ Explain that God's forgiveness is complete. Then ask how His forgiveness of past sins should affect us in the present and in the future.

The Price ■ Explain that forgiveness always costs the person who does the forgiving. Then ask what it will cost to forgive . . .

• someone who owes you $100?

• someone who borrowed your shirt and ripped it?

• someone who insulted you?

• someone who embarrassed you in front of your friends?

• someone who spread lies about you?

• someone who dented your car?

• someone who hurt you physically?

Explain that forgiveness may cost the forgiver money or a material item, and it will always cost the forgiver vengeance or retribution. Then ask what forgiving us costs God.

React ■ Distribute cards and pencils to everyone. Have them write their names and phone numbers on the cards. Then ask them to seriously consider whether or not they have ever truly given their lives to Christ—received His free gift of salvation and become "saved." If not, and they would like to talk more about it, have them write "yes" underneath their phone numbers. Assure them that you will call and set up a time when you can get together. Then have everyone write a one-sentence reaction to the meeting, and collect the cards.

Repentance ■ Explain that no matter what we've done, God stands ready to forgive and forget. But the key is repentance. This is a word used in the Bible over and over. It means being sorry for our sins, confessing them, and turning away from them. Guilt is not the same as repentance—that's an important first step. Say something like: *Guilt is feeling bad that we got caught. Guilt is feeling bad that we did we did something wrong. Guilt is feeling separate from goodness. But guilt rarely changes behavior. Repentance moves from our realizing that we broke the rules to realizing that we have offended the Ruler. Sin affects many areas of life and many relationships, but its deepest effect is to strike out against God.*

Read Psalm 51 aloud, emphasizing verse 4: *Against you, you only, have I sinned and done what is evil in your sight . . ."*

Starting Over ■ Ask: *If you could start over, what would you erase?* The answers could focus on certain relationships (for example, with parents, with boyfriend or girlfriend, etc.), reputation (for example, in the neighborhood, at school, at work, at church, etc.), grades and school work, and other sensitive areas. Then have students apply this question to their relationship with God (For example: How could they start over with Him? What would this mean for their lives?).

BIBLE STUDIES

Action Application ■ Read Matthew 18:21-35 and 1 John 3:11-18; 4:7-21. Say: *We see clearly from this passage that we ought to be forgiving others the way God forgives us. As Christ's followers we are overwhelmed by the reality of His love and grace. It is our responsibility to emulate Christ's example and to love others as He has loved us. Is there someone who has wronged you or who owes you* *some debt? Write down their names. Ask God to give you His grace and power to forgive them, no strings attached. This is not easy and may take a personal struggle and a lot of prayer. Is there someone you have wronged or to whom you owe a debt? Go to that person as soon as possible and straighten it out. Go in God's strength.*

Buy It! ■ Use teams and give each team one of the Bible passages listed below. Explain that their task is to create an advertisement to "sell" the result/ concept/idea presented in the passages. Here are the passages and their results/concepts/ideas.

• Isaiah 1:18 (scarlet and red sins changed to white and wool)

• John 8:1-11 (a fresh start—condemned no more)

• John 4:1-26 (living water)

• 2 Corinthians 5:17 (made totally new)

• 1 John 1:9 (confession leads to forgiveness)

Have the groups present their advertisements and then read the verses aloud.

Crud ■ Have everyone turn to 2 Samuel 11. Read and summarize the story of David and Bathsheba. Talk about the crud in David's life. As you do this, you may want to dirty a mirror as an object lesson, adding dirt with each of David's sins.

Have someone read Psalm 51 aloud. Explain that David wrote this psalm after being confronted about his sin by Nathan.

Then have someone read Psalm 130:3-4 aloud. Explain that if someone as *dirty* and *soiled* as David could be forgiven, so can we.

Then read Isaiah 43:25 aloud and explain the fact that God forgives and *forgets*.

Gift of God ■ Divide the crowd into three groups. Give each group a key word or phrase from Ephesians 2:8-9 and the assignment to think of a creative way to demonstrate the meaning of this concept to the whole group. It could be a game, role play, puzzle, task, drama, etc. The idea is to help everyone experience the truth of their concept (word). The three words and phrases for the group are "grace," "faith," and "gift of God."

Allow time for students to decide what the word means in the context of the passage and to create their demonstrations. Then, have each group lead the whole crowd through its experience.

After all three concepts have been demonstrated and experienced, ask:

• Putting all these concepts together, what do they mean? Put the answer in *your own* words.

• *How* does this happen? In other words, how does a person receive, by faith, God's gift of salvation?

• What kinds of works do people do to try to be saved?

• When and how did you become a Christian? (Have two or three kids share their testimonies.)

God's Forgiveness ■ Break into groups and give each one a passage or two. Have students write down everything they can discover about God's forgiveness. Then have them report and discuss together their answers.

• 1 John 1:9

• Isaiah 43:25

• Psalm 103:11-12

• Hebrews 10:17

• Matthew 18:21-35

• 1 Corinthians 13:5

• Romans 8:1-4

Good News, Bad News ■ The format of this study is "good news—bad news—good news." The first section, "good news," focuses on the holiness of God. God is perfect, totally without limitations or imperfections, and is completely good. This is good news because:

• *God is in control.* Although events may seem chaotic to us, a sovereign God is working His plan.

• *God is unlimited.* God's power and knowledge mean that He can do and change anything, and that we can never be lost to Him (Psalm 139).

• *God's will is best for us.* We can trust completely in Him.

The second section, "bad news," emphasizes our sinfulness. We are imperfect, finite, full of sin; therefore, we fall short (qualitatively) from God's glorious ideal (Romans 3:23). Our sin separates us from Him, and so we cannot experience His presence, love, and direction. Even worse, we fall under judgment, and the "wages of sin is death" (Romans 6:23).

The third section, "good news," explains the Gospel—that Jesus, the holy, sinless Son of God, became sin, took our sins on Himself, paid the penalty for our sins on the cross, and rose victorious over sin and death. Now, through faith in Christ, we can be justified, forgiven, and free to draw near to God. We can experience God's love and plan in our lives . . . and heaven too.

Good News

Copy the following verses on cards and distribute them. Have selected students read the verses aloud, one right after another, without comment: Leviticus 11:44; 1 Samuel 2:2; Psalm 99:1-5; Isaiah 6:3; Revelation 4:8. Then ask:

• What is the key word mentioned in all of these passages that best summarizes their message? (Holy.)

• What does it mean that God is *holy*? (He is perfect, without sin, etc.)

• How does this make you feel about God? How could this fact about God (His holiness) be good news for us?

Bad News

Next, have everyone look up the following verses together, one at a time, and follow along as a designated student reads each one. After each verse, ask the discussion questions listed below.

1. Ephesians 1:4; 1 Peter 1:15

• What does God expect of us? (to be holy, just like Him)

• Is anyone here perfect? When do we become "imperfect" and "unholy"? (at birth)

• Why is it impossible to fulfill the requirements of the verses we read? (because sin gets in the way)

2. Romans 3:9-20, 23

• These verses seem to emphasize what we've already discussed. What do they say? (no one is righteous or holy; all have sinned)

• What are the consequences of all of this "unholiness"? (separation from God, judgment, and hell)

• Why is this bad news? (no one escapes; everyone deserves hell)

Good News

Say something like: *I once asked someone, "Do you think heaven's perfect?" He responded, "Yes, of course, because God is there. If it weren't perfect, it wouldn't be heaven." Then I asked, "Are you perfect?" He answered, "No, of course not." "Well," I responded, "how do you expect to fit in?"*

That's the real issue. So far, we have looked at the good news of God's holiness and the bad news of our sinfulness and separation from Him. Now let's look at the rest of the story.

Read Romans 3:24-26 and ask:

• Remember these verses follow the ones we just read about sin. What does "justified freely by His grace as a gift through the redemption that came by Christ Jesus" (v. 24) mean? (we are made right with God through Christ who paid the price of sin)

• What does Jesus' blood have to do with all of this? (He died for our sins)

Read Romans 5:9-11 aloud and ask:

• What's the good news about this passage? (we are saved from God's wrath)

• What does "reconciled" mean? (brought back into friendship and fellowship)

• What does Jesus' resurrection mean in all of this? (it is proof that the Gospel is true and that Christ lives today to intervene for us)

Read Romans 6:20-23 aloud and ask:

• What is the free gift? (salvation, eternal life)

• Why is it free? (we don't have to earn it)

• Who paid the price? (Jesus paid the penalty for sin)

• How can we obtain the gift and have our unholiness and sins covered? (we need only ask for it)

Close with an evangelistic appeal, inviting group members to accept God's free gift by giving their lives to Christ.

Grace ■ Read Ephesians 2:8-9 and ask for a definition of "grace." Review what you've done in the meeting and relate the activities to these scriptural principles.

• "All have sinned and fall short" (Romans 3:23).

• Salvation is a gift. We are saved by what God has done, not anything we have done or can do (see Romans 6:23; Ephesians 2:8-9).

• Because God's grace extends to us, we should also extend "grace" to others (see Matthew 18:21-35).

If you have a number of non-Christians in attendance, explain how a person trusts Christ, and give them the opportunity to respond.

I Deserve It! ■ Read Matthew 20:1-16 aloud; then ask:

• What do you think is the point of the parable?

• Was the employer fair? Why or why not?

• Why do you think the employer paid the workers in that order so that everyone could see how much the late arrivals were being paid?

• What does Jesus mean by "the last shall be first and the first last"?

• How does this relate to "salvation by grace"?

Lord's Prayer ■ Repeat the Lord's Prayer together, aloud (Luke 11:1-4). Stop after the phrase, "Forgive us our sins, for we also forgive everyone who sins against us." Ask: *Do we really mean that?* (Some may admit they never really thought about having to forgive others to the extent they are forgiven.) *How good are we at forgiving others?* (Share from your own experience about a time you had trouble forgiving.) *Does this mean we should forgive everyone?* (Yes.) *When would that be really tough?* (Often it's difficult to forgive when the person won't acknowledge he or she needs us to forgive him or her.)

New Life ■ Use the following Bible references in a game or have kids look them up and read them aloud one at a time. These verses discuss new life in Christ.

• Matthew 1:21

• Luke 3:16

• Luke 19:8-10

• John 1:12-13

• John 3:3-8, 16-17, 36

• John 5:24

• John 8:11

• John 13:35

• John 15:5-8

• Acts 17:6

• Romans 6:5-11

• Romans 7:4

• 2 Corinthians 5:16-21

• Galatians 5:22-26

• Colossians 2:9-15

• Colossians 3:1-8

• Hebrews 10:19-25

• 1 John 3:7-10

Nobody's Perfect ■ Read Romans 3:23 aloud; then ask:

• What does it mean that all have sinned? What about Mother Teresa, Martin Luther King, Jr., the Pope, the Apostle Peter, Billy Graham? (No person is good enough to be accepted by a holy God.)

• What does the word "sin" mean? (transgression, self-centeredness, missing the mark, not doing what you're supposed to do, disobeying God, etc.)

• What does "fall short of the glory of God" mean? (inability to measure up to perfection)

• Are some "sins" more serious than others? (Any sin is serious enough to merit death. Some sins have more earthly consequences than others.)

• How do we rationalize our sinfulness? (We often make comparisons or excuses.)

• Do you know anyone who says he or she hasn't sinned? (Only Christ led a sinless life.)

Then read Romans 6:23 aloud and ask:

• What do we deserve for our sin? (death)

• What does this mean? (eternal separation from God)

• What is the "gift"? (the path to salvation—eternal life through Jesus' death)

• How do "grace" and "mercy" relate to this verse? (Eternal life is a gift that cannot be earned, but God's grace allows us to obtain it.)

Prodigal Son ■ (Luke 15:11-31) Summarize the story of the Prodigal Son, and then read Luke 15:17-24 aloud. Afterward, ask:

• How did the father demonstrate his love for his son? (freedom, acceptance, compassion, celebration, etc.)

• What did the son have to do to obtain his father's forgiveness? (nothing)

• What did the son do to realize and experience his father's forgiveness? (return and confess)

• Which character(s) are you most like? Father? Older brother? Prodigal?

12

A WORLD AT WAR

CROWD-BREAKERS

Arms Race ■ Divide into two teams and give each team a set of boxes (all different sizes—the same amount and sizes for each team). The teams are to line up at one end of the room and "stockpile" the boxes at the other end (stack them, one at a time). This is a relay, so team members leave when the previous one has returned. The trick is that the boxes may only be carried with the arms (between the wrists and shoulders). If the boxes fall, those that are unstacked must be brought back and carried again. The first team to finish their stockpile wins the arms race.

Checkers ■ Before the meeting, mark out a checkerboard on the gym floor or yard (use chalk or masking tape to outline the squares and removable stickers to signify the colors). Divide the group into two "armies," choose a "commander-in-chief" for each one, and assign their colors (red and black). Next, line up the armies and begin a giant game of checkers with the commander-in-chief making the moves and team members serving as the checker pieces. Designate areas for prisoners of war. If the game goes quickly and the "board" is still visible, play another round.

Command Performance ■ While everyone is seated, bring two or three kids to the front to demonstrate marching and following commands. Use simple commands like "right face," "left face," "about face," "forward march," "to the rear march," etc. (Ask a local R.O.T.C. officer or a veteran for the commands and how to deliver them.) Go slowly at first and then pick up the pace. It will be a hilarious and confusing sight.

Computer, Video ■ Hold a tournament on a personal computer or Nintendo-type system with one or more of the war games. Or go to a video arcade and use their games. Many of the video games feature shooting and war situations.

Defuse the Bomb ■ Divide into two teams, give each team a mouse trap, a pair of tweezers, and ten small items (for example, cheese, piece of thread, paper clip, match, piece of paper, bread crust, cloth, straight pin, rubber band, pebble). During a set amount of time, they are to set the trap (bomb), using all 10 items if possible. Then the other team will have to defuse it. Using the tweezers and going one person at a time, they should try to remove as many items as possible from the trap without triggering it. Award five points for every item removed (and for every item not used by the setting team). Repeat the game for two or three rounds.

Drill Team (skit) ■ Have seven or eight group members form a mock, precision drill team. Introduce "The United States Academy Precision Drill Team," and have them perform. This can be very funny if they have uniforms, keep straight faces, march right behind each other in short, little steps, and perform ridiculous drills to the unintelligible commands of their leader.

Dying Soldier (skit) ■ Characters needed: soldier (lying on the floor), nurse (bending over him), and announcer. The announcer begins by explaining, "We now take you to World War II and the battlefields of

Europe where we find a wounded soldier and a nurse. The soldier speaks."

<u>Soldier</u>: "Ooooooh!" *(long groan)*

<u>Nurse</u>: "Dying soldier, dying soldier; tell me your name, so I can tell the folks back home."

<u>Soldier</u>: "Noooo!" *(painful, prolonged "no")*

<u>Nurse</u>: *(more insistent)* "Dying soldier, dying soldier; tell me your name, so I can tell your folks back home!"

<u>Soldier</u>: *(writhes in pain and responds)* "Nooo!"

The nurse continues to plead, and the soldier continues to say no. Each time he says no, however, our lovely nurse becomes increasingly irritated and, finally, downright angry and physically abusive. (She hits him, jumps on him, etc.)

Finally the nurse in her frustration and desperation says:

<u>Nurse</u>: "But why? Why won't you tell me your name so I can tell your folks back home?"

After a pause, the soldier responds (here's the punch line)

<u>Soldier</u>: ". . . (pause) because . . . (pause) they already know my name."

Note: This skit can also be performed by one person playing all three parts. As the narrator, he or she may sit on a stool and face the audience; as the nurse, he or she dons a nurse's cap and stands; as the soldier, he or she wears an army hat or helmet and lies on the floor.

German Soldiers ■ This is a skit that will take only brief preparation beforehand. The Captain marches his squad of six soldiers into the room. Suddenly the last person sneezes. The Captain quickly halts the squad and approaches the first soldier. Looking him square in the eye, he demands, *Did you sneeze?* (with a German accent, of course).

The soldier timidly replies, *Nein, Capitan.*

Then the Captain yells, *You lie!*, pulls out a gun, and shoots the soldier who falls to the floor.

The Captain repeats the interrogation with the other soldiers, with the same result each time. Finally he comes to the last soldier and again demands, *Did you sneeze?*

The soldier replies, *Ya, Capitan.*

The Captain smiles and replies, *Geshundheit!*

Hot Spots ■ Hand out papers, as printed below, with a list of war-torn countries on the left. Explain that to the right of each country, they should write the problem or the name of a divisive group in that country. Throw in a couple of humorous ones and/or

fake countries to lighten it up. Possible answers are in parentheses.)

Country	Problem
Northern Ireland	(Civil War)
Somalia	(war lords)
Lebanon	(Civil War)
Israel	(Arab terrorists)
Switzerland	(the "Alpos")
Iraq	(Iran)
Belgium	(the "Waffles")
Italy	(the Red Brigade)
Turkey	(the Kurds)
Ham on Rye	(the Mustard Corps)
Nicaragua	(the Sandinistas)
Bosnia	(the Moslems or Serbs)
Iceland	(the "Fridges")
Iran	(Shiite Moslems)
I Walked	(Grumblers)
Philippines	(Communists)

Infantry (skit) ■ Three kids rush into the room (one at a time, about five seconds apart) gasping for breath and with urgency in their voices, *The infantry is coming . . . the infantry is coming!* Eventually another person enters holding a small seedling or sapling. He or she announces, *Here is the infant tree; where do I plant it?"*

Mail Call (skit) ■ The sergeant lines up the troops and gives out the mail. He calls out a couple of names after which the soldiers shout "yo" and step forward to get their mail. Then he says:

	(Answer)
"Smith"	"Yo!"
"Jones"	"Yo!"
"Occupant"	"Yo!"
"Duncan"	"Yo, Yo!"

Marching Orders ■ Have everyone stand and then lead them through a series of typical orders that are given to soldiers as they march together. Here are a few:

• *Forward, march!*
• *To the rear, march!*
• *Halt!*
• *Left face!*
• *About face!*
• *Change step, march!*
• *Rout step, march!*

- *Eyes right!*
- *Parade rest!*
- *At ease.*
- *etc.*

M.A.S.H. Night ■ This is a little dated, but it will still work. Have everyone come dressed in army fatigues or as their favorite M.A.S.H. character (the "Klingers" could get a bit bizarre). Have a character parade; then divide into groups of three to four and give each group a skit to perform. The skits should be short, simple, and written out and should center on war and doctors. (Four skits are included in this section.)

Pass the Ammunition ■ Do this as a relay. Break into teams and have members sit in columns. Give each team a stack of cards and a pen and explain that the first person is the sender (and the manufacturer), and the last one is the receiver. Those in between are relayers. The object of the game is for a team to draw, pass, and receive as many different types of ammunition as possible in two minutes. At your signal to begin, the sender draws a picture of one type of ammunition on a card and sends it down the line. When it reaches the receiver, he or she must write on the card what it is (without any help). Then the receiver runs to the beginning and becomes the sender. The game ends when the time is up. Duplicates and unintelligible pictures are discarded. Display the ammo that has been drawn and declare the winner.

Pillow Womp ■ Clear out the center of the floor and bring out a 2"x 4" board and two cinder blocks on which to rest it. (Be sure to protect the floor.) Next, have two competitors stand on the board facing each other and give each one a pillow to use as a weapon. The idea is to knock the other person off his or her perch while not being knocked off yourself or losing your balance and falling off. Continue with other challengers until you have a champion. You may want to make a rule against hitting an opponent in the head.

Tanks a Lot ■ This should be done outside or in a gymnasium. Bring three or four refrigerator boxes with both ends removed on each one. Line them up on their sides and put two or three kids inside each box. At the signal, they are to race to a designated line and back by rolling the box. The boxes move like tank treads, rolling along on the cardboard sides. Obviously the propulsion comes from the insiders who walk inside the box with their hands extended and roll their "tank."

Ultimate Weapon ■ Explain that over the years we've heard about AWACs, MX, Stealth Bombers, Patriot Missiles, Star Wars, Rambo, Neutron Bombs, and The Terminator, but today we will be designing the most advanced weapon of all—one of their own creation. Then break into groups of two or three and give them paper and pens. Their task is to draw and explain the "ultimate weapon." After a few minutes, have the groups display and explain their devastating creations.

What's In a Name? ■ Hand out the following quiz. Students should match the name of the group with the country. Some countries may have more than one group. And the groups may no longer be active. Possible answers are in parentheses. Add new countries with current problems and groups.

Country	Problem
Northern Ireland (f, h)	a. Pol Pot
Palestine (d, k)	b. Red Brigade
Vietnam (e)	c. Kurds
Thailand (a, l)	d. Zionists
Nicaragua (i, n)	e. Vietcong
Iran (g)	f. IRA
Lebanon (g)	g. Phalangists
Poland (j)	h. Ulster Volunteer Force
Italy (b)	i. Sandinistas
Philippines (m)	j. Solidarity
	k. PLO
	l. Khmer Rouge
	m. Communists
	n. Contras

War ■ Play a version of the "War" card game. Bring enough playing cards so that you have at least one for every person in the meeting. Place a card table in front of the room and place the cards on the table in two equal stacks. Divide into two teams and seat them in parallel columns on the floor, in front of the table and perpendicular to it. Kids should come to the table two at a time, one from each team. Each one should turn over the top card in his or her team's stack. The person with the lowest card is eliminated from the game and should sit on the sideline and root for his or her team. The person with the highest card wins and goes to the back of the team to wait for the second round. The winning team also gets both cards each time. These cards should be put face down alongside the original stacks.

For the second round, shuffle the new stacks, place them in the original position, and go through the teams again. This time, however, each person should take two cards off his or her stack and turn them over (the bottom card is the one that counts).

For the third round, have them turn over three cards, and so forth. The first team to run out of players or cards, loses. Note: make sure this moves along.

DISCUSSION STARTERS

Cartoons ■ Video tape small segments of a number of Saturday morning cartoon shows that feature war and violence. After showing the tape, ask:

•Why are these shows popular?

•What do kids learn from watching them?

•What would Jesus say about television shows like these? Why?

Headlines ■ Pass out recent copies of the newspaper and have the students find everything about war in the world (events, features, ads, movies, etc.). Discuss their findings. Ask about the causes of each conflict, what it will take to end it, and what it will take to end all wars.

Letters ■ Pass out paper and pens and tell students to write a letter to a very young child, explaining war. Collect and read a number of the letters aloud. Then discuss what they wrote and how they felt when writing the letters.

"Neighbors" ■ This is an old movie, but it is still available through Pyramid Films and other rental companies. This 10-minute film focuses on the relationship between two neighbors who have a beautiful flower growing on their property line. Because each person wants to possess the flower for himself, fences are built and torn down, until a full-scale conflict ensues. This film is an excellent illustration of the seeds of war. Show it and discuss the message.

Prayer ■ List the world's hot spots and assign them to specific kids for daily prayer for a week. Close the meeting by praying conversationally for the personal "warring" attitudes of group members.

Refugee ■ If your church or high school has a refugee family, see if one or more family members can come to a meeting to share their experiences and to answer questions. They could be from Cuba, Thailand, Poland, Romania, Vietnam, Haiti, etc. This should give group members views of war and oppression from eyewitnesses.

Sounds of Silence ■ Tell everyone to get very, very quiet so that it is completely silent. After about a minute, ask what they were thinking about. Then have everyone get totally silent again. This time tell them to listen carefully. After a minute, ask what they heard. Then discuss what the Bible means by "peace," how peace relates to "quiet," and how a person can have peace in the midst of chaos.

Toys ■ Buy a couple of new toy guns. Play a game with them like "target practice" or "quick draw." Then discuss violence in our society. An addition or alternate to this would be to bring a toy catalog and read about the toys that feature violence (for example, G.I. Joe and Rambo dolls; soldiers and other toys; board games; guns, grenades, rockets, laser guns, and other weapons; Nintendo and other video games).

What If . . . ■ Break into groups of three and give each group a slip of paper with a "What if . . ." situation to discuss. After a few minutes, bring the whole group back together and compare notes. Here are some possible situations:

1. The U.S. became involved in a war in Central America, and you were drafted. What would you do? Why?

2. You were in the U.S. Marine Corps and were about to be shipped to Somalia right after the U.S. soldiers had been killed. What would you have done? How would you have felt? Why?

3. You were living in a country village, and the rebels were insisting that you join them to fight the government. (They threaten to harm you and your family if you refuse.) But you don't want to be a soldier. What would you do? Why?

4. You're against war and don't want to be in the army, but you have just turned eighteen and are supposed to register for the draft. One of your friends has decided not to register. What will you do? Why?

Note: If you have a large group, add other situations.

DISCUSSIONS AND WRAP-UPS

Causes ■ Ask:

• What causes war? How about in Bosnia? South

Africa? Kuwait? Somalia? Russia? Vietnam? Our Revolutionary War? World War I? World War II? Northern Ireland? Korea?

• When do you think the United States will go to war again? Why should we ever declare war? (is it ever justified?) How are we different from the former Soviet Union?

• In what ways are the causes of war similar to the conflicts that you face with family, friends, and enemies? What should you do about those conflicts?

Christians and War ■ Ask:

• What does the Bible say about war? (See "Bible Studies" for related Scripture.)

• How would Jesus respond if He were confronted with a war situation or with violence? (Note: He was— Roman occupational army, oppression of His people, the cross, etc.)

• When does Jesus' teaching of "turning the other cheek" apply?

• Why do you think Christians should or should not go to war?

Rambo ■ Discuss the "Rambo syndrome" and ask:

• Why are these movies and similar ones so popular?

• How do they picture war? Is the picture accurate? Why or why not?

• What subtle messages do these movies give about violence? About morality? About the value of human life? About America?

• How should a Christian respond to this?

Revenge ■ Ask:

• What part does revenge play in continuing wars? (Northern Ireland, Israel, Lebanon, Rwanda, etc.)

• What would it take to stop this revenge cycle?

• How would you react if you were involved personally?

• How does Jesus' command to "turn the other cheek" relate to this?

BIBLE STUDIES

Fightings ■ Read James 4:1-10 aloud. Then ask:

•According to James, what causes war? (wrong motives, envy, selfish desires)

•What other situations, besides national conflicts, are affected by these causes? (interpersonal conflicts)

•How can we solve these problems in ourselves? (We can submit to God and obey Him.)

Peace in the Bible ■ Distribute cards with these references on them.

- 2 Chronicles 14:1-6
- Psalm 34:14
- Psalm 122:6-9
- Matthew 5:9
- John 14:27
- Romans 5:1
- Ephesians 2:14
- Colossians 3:15
- Psalm 3:1-8
- Psalm 120:1-7
- Isaiah 26:3
- Luke 2:14
- John 16:33
- 1 Corinthians 1:3
- Philippians 4:7
- 1 Peter 3:11

Have students look up the verses and think about what they teach about peace. Then have kids read the passages aloud, one at a time, and comment on them. Be sure to discuss the difference between the peace of God and peace with God, and how peace relates to conflict.

Submission ■ Have someone read Romans 13:1-7 aloud. Then ask:

• What does it mean to "submit" to the governing authorities?

• When shouldn't a person submit?

• When are revolution and war justified?

• When is violence justified?

• How does this apply to the draft, war, and conscientious objectors?

• How does the commandment "You shall not murder" (Exodus 20:13) apply to this? What about Matthew 5:21-22?

13
CHRISTMAS

CROWD-BREAKERS

All I Want for Christmas ■ Give each person a famous character and the assignment to write a Christmas list for him or her (tell them to use their creative imaginations). Possible characters could include: Scrooge, Atilla the Hun, Frankenstein, Rudolph the Red-nosed Reindeer, Spiderman, Bill Clinton, Michael Jordan, Julia Roberts, Billy Joel, Arsenio Hall, etc. Then have them read their lists aloud, one at a time.

Body Language ■ Have a game of charades with a Christmas twist. Use the following items which must be *acted out* (letters, syllables, or sounds may not be given as clues). Here are some possible words to use: wrapping, carols, wreaths, reindeer, ornament, stocking, candles, tinsel, Santa, wisemen, angels, red and green, spirit, snow, presents.

Carol Trivia ■ This quiz has clues to the titles of familiar carols. The correct answers are in parentheses.

CAROL QUIZ

1. These two carols begin with the word "angel" (*Angels We Have Heard on High*; *Angels from the Realms of Glory*)

2. A carol that mentions 12 A.M. (*It Came upon a Midnight Clear*)

3. Adeste Fideles (*O Come, All Ye Faithful*)

4. This one describes the city where Jesus was born (*O Little Town of Bethlehem*)

5. A carol to the tune of *Greensleeves* (*What Child Is This?*)

6. The wisemen's song (*We Three Kings*)

7. A carol about the quietness of Christmas (*Silent Night*)

8. A carol that runs down the scale at the start (*Joy to the World*)

9. What carol uses "Hark!"? (*Hark the Herald Angels Sing*)

10. A song that shouts the good news (*Go Tell It on the Mountain*)

11. A unique cradle carol (*Away in a Manger*)

You also could use *I Wonder as I Wander, O Christmas Tree, O Holy Night, The First Noel, There's a Song in the Air, While Shepherds Watched Their Flocks, Bring a Torch Jeannette Isabella, I Saw Three Ships Come Sailing.*

Christmas Collage ■ Use teams and give each team a stack of old magazines, a piece of poster board, a pair of scissors, and a roll of cellophane tape. Explain that you want them to make a collage using pictures from the magazines. These should be *Christmas* collages. In other words, the pictures should represent Christmas. In addition, they should have at least one picture that beings with each letter in Christmas (for example, <u>c</u>andy, <u>h</u>olly, <u>r</u>inging bell, <u>i</u>ncense, <u>s</u>tocking, <u>t</u>insel, <u>m</u>usic, <u>a</u>ngel, <u>S</u>anta). After cleaning up the scraps and collecting the scissors and tape, have the groups display and explain their collages.

Christmas Daze ■ Divide into groups of three or four and assign each group a "day" of Christmas (1–12). Tell groups to dream up a new, creative, modern gift that *my true love gave to me*. In another room, place a tape recorder, a tape, a pitch pipe, and a volunteer. After the groups have decided on their gifts, have them go to the room (one group at a time, in reverse numerical order), rehearse their line of the song, and then record it. They should not be permitted to hear the recording of the previous groups. They may sing their phrase in any style, rhythm, and meter, but they should try to begin on pitch and should enunciate clearly. After all the groups have finished, play the entire song for the whole crowd. It could go something like this, *On the twelfth day of Christmas my true love gave to me: 12 Game Boys playing, 11 teachers flunking, 10 football games winning, 9 confused freshmen, 8 thousand dollars, 7 dates this Saturday evening, 6 straight-A classes, 5 steak dinners with all the trimmings, 4 years of college scholarship, 3 dozen records, 2 brand-new sports cars, and a year without any homework!*

Christmas Hunt ■ Here are two Christmas scavenger hunts. The idea in both is for individuals or teams to use their imaginations and bring back items that most closely resemble those on the list.

CHRISTMAS SIGNS

1. manger	2. Santa	3. red and green
4. stocking	5. sash	6. Christmas spirit
7. cheer	8. joyful noise	9. jingle bells
10. wrapping	11. beard	12. silent night
13. wisemen	14. scent	15. wisemen
16. myrh		

THE NIGHT BEFORE

1. mama	2. St.	3. "twas"
4. sash	5. sugar plums	6. kerchief
7. clatter	8. miniature	9. "with care"
10. nose	11. luster	12. "with a jerk"
13. shook	14. Blitzen	15. "a good night"
16. "new fallen"	17. non-stirring creature	

Christmas Poem ■ Divide into teams and give each team scratch paper and a pen or pencil. One person from each team should come to the front and draw six words out of an envelope. Then the teams should write a song or poem using those words in it. All the words must be used in the team's creation. Here are possible words to print on individual slips of paper and put into an envelope: tree, yuletide, snow, stockings, elf, Santa, shepherds, star, gift, sugar plums, Jack Frost, myrrh, manger, holly, red and green, good little boys, holy night, (name of youth leader), (name of pastor), Grinch, blessings, Scrooge, carol,

dreaming, ho ho ho, list, naughty, incarnation, and others.

After about five minutes, have the teams come to the front one at a time. They should tell everyone what their words are and then present their song or poem.

Christmas Quiz ■ Distribute the following quiz. The correct answers are in parentheses.

1. Where did the wise men find Jesus? (in a house)
2. In what country did the writer of "Silent Night" live? (Austria)
3. How many angels spoke to the shepherds? (one)
4. What pictures are on this year's Christmas stamps? (Check this one ahead of time.)
5. What does Santa do in his garden? (Hoe, hoe, ho!)
6. Who wrote "The Christmas Song"? (Mel Tormé)
7. What movies featured the song "White Christmas"? ("White Christmas" and "Holiday Inn")
8. What does "Noel" mean? (Merry Christmas)
9. What do Santa's wife and a sea gull have in common? (sandy claws)
10. Who is the last reindeer in "The Night Before Christmas?" (Blitzen)
11. What perfumes have you heard or seen advertised lately?
12. In the Bible, what animals are mentioned present at Jesus' birth? (none)
13. How did the "X" get in "Xmas"? (It's the Greek letter that is the first letter of "Christ.")
14. An elf with his eyes closed slipped on the sidewalk. What did he say? ("Icy"—"I see!")
15. What Christmas carol's first line comes down the scale eight notes? ("Joy to the World")
16. What did Santa say "as he rode out of sight"? ("Happy Christmas to all and to all a good night.")
17. Who worked for Scrooge? (Bob Cratchet)
18. What are the names of the wise men from the East? (Unknown—no names are in the Bible.)
19. What does "Adeste Fidelis" mean? ("O Come, All Ye Faithful")
20. What was your all-time favorite Christmas present?

Give the correct answers and award a prize to the person with the most right. You may want to comment on the legends and misconceptions that have grown around Christmas.

December Quiz ■ Divide into teams and seat the teams together. Explain that you will be reading a series of questions about December. If they think they know the answer, they should jump to their feet. The first person to stand will get the chance to answer. If he or she answers correctly, he or she wins 200 points for his or her team. But every incorrect answer receives minus 100 points. And every person who yells out the answer before being called on loses 100 points too. Here are the questions for the quiz. The answers to some of the questions are in parentheses.

1. How many Fridays are in this December?
2. What infamous historical event occurred on December 7? (the bombing of Pearl Harbor)
3. How many Tuesdays are in this December?
4. What is the date of New Year's Eve? (December 31)
5. How many Saturdays are in this December?
6. What date is Hanukkah? (Check calendar beforehand—it changes every year)
7. How many Mondays are in this December?
8. On what day are there only 12 shopping days till Christmas?
9. What day of the week is December 17th?
10. What date is December's third Thursday?
11. What day of the week is Christmas Eve?
12. Name three December birthdays.

Dramatic Reading ■ Introduce this as a serious event—a dramatic reading by a well-known personality. Then have a guy (who has practiced) read "The Night Before Christmas" as Mr. T (for example, "I pity the fool mouse who stirs!"), Rocky (for example, "Yo, we was all sleepin'"), Bill Clinton (for example, "Fellow Americans—no child should have to go to bed with merely sugarplums dancing in their heads"), or another well-known character and voice.

Elf Control ■ Create a tiny person (the elf) by using two kids in the following manner. One person forms the elf's legs by putting his or her arms through a pair of children's shorts and his or her hands into small socks and shoes. This person is also the elf's head. Next, place a jacket (or extra large sweatshirt with a slit up the back), backwards, over the front of this person, and fasten the collar in the back, leaving the jacket open. The second person, then, should stand behind the first one and place his or her arms around the person's arms and through the jacket forming the arms and hands of the elf. Place a table under the elf's feet and "hide" the extra body parts of your two participants by draping sheets over the table and over the head of the "arms person." What makes this person so funny is the way that he or she looks, the

fact that the head has no control over the arms, and the fact that the "arms person" cannot see what is on the table.

Introduce this person as one of Santa's elves and interview him or her. Be sure to ask questions that must be answered by some sort of physical movement by the face, arms, and/or legs. Use your imagination. Here are some possibilities:

• What do you do to keep in shape up there at the North Pole? (The elf should then demonstrate various exercises such as jumping jacks, leg lifts, push-ups, etc.)
• What kinds of food do you eat since it is too cold to grow your own? (The elf should eat yogurt, pop, etc.)
• How do you put together all those beautiful toys? (The elf should try to build a toy from various materials lying on the table.)
• What do you to get ready for the big night? (The elf will put on deodorant, brush teeth, shaved, etc.)

Feudal Pursuit ■ Play a special Christmas version of *Family Feud*. Before the meeting, take a poll of your group (if it's large) or of at least 20 kids at a local high school or mall. Use their answers as the information base for the game. Here are some categories to use:

• tree decorations
• favorite Christmas carols
• names of Santa's reindeer
• hot toys
• favorite movies
• Christmas TV specials

Make a poster board for each category, listing the top six answers and how many people gave each one. Then cover each answer with dark paper that can be ripped off at the right time. Divide the group into teams and let them compete. Instead of using a buzzer, flip a coin to see who gets to go first. The team with the highest point total wins.

Gift List ■ Give everyone a piece of paper and a pen and ask them to write their Christmas lists, making sure not to put their names on the papers. Collect the lists and then read them aloud, one at a time, with the group trying to guess the identity of each author.

Just What They Always Wanted ■ Using teams, hold this unique version of "charades." A team member comes to the front and draws the name of a celebrity out of an envelope. He or she then must decide on an appropriate Christmas gift for that person and then, using body language and the traditional charades signals, communicate the gift to the team who tries to guess the celebrity. The team to take the least amount of time for all their celebrities wins. Possible celebrities could include: Richard Gere, Mother Teresa, Miss Iowa, Amy Grant, Emmit Smith, Magic Johnson, Tim Taylor, Peter Pan, Terminator, Oprah Winfrey, etc.

Living Presents ■ Divide into four or more groups (each group should have 7-10 members). Explain that their assignment is to make a toy using all their members as the parts. Allow about ten minutes to plan and build their toys. Then have each group demonstrate their unique present. Possible toys could include a tricycle, doll, video game, puzzle, board game, etc. If your group would find the creative aspect of this a bit difficult, have them draw the toy out of an envelope.

Man for All Seasons ■ Fill your meeting with special games and activities that are usually featured at other holidays, but adapt them for Christmas. For example, you could have a "Christmas Egg Hunt," make "Christmas Valentine cards," sing "Happy Birthday" to Jesus, use noisemakers to celebrate a New Year for serving Christ, shoot off Party Poppers to celebrate independence from sin, etc.

Miracle Appliance ■ Explain that we have all seen those television ads where a small kitchen utensil is being demonstrated: "It dices, it cuts, it peels! By Ronco!" The idea here is for each team to create its own miracle appliance. It doesn't have to be limited to the kitchen. They should come up with the basic idea and then write an advertisement for it. For example: a car that shovels your walk in winter and cuts the lawn in the summer—by remote control—for $9.95; a TV that does your hair and nails while you sit and watch the soaps; an alarm clock that wakes you up by gently vibrating the bed and then takes your blood pressure and other vital signs and prescribes the diet for the day; a book you can sleep on and learn from.

Ornament Hunt ■ Bring out a Christmas tree (for the youth room, the church, or the home where you are meeting) and announce that you are going to decorate it. The only catch is that they will have to go out and get the "trimmings." Run this like a door-to-door scavenger hunt with lists of items and a time limit. After the teams return, collect their ornaments and items, declare the winning team, and decorate the tree. If you have three or four teams, here is a possible list of decorations to find:

- two ball ornaments
- two handfuls of tinsel
- two Christmas tree ornaments
- a string of lights
- a star
- four bows
- three candy canes
- three unique ornaments

If you do this with a lot of teams or with individ- uals, ask for one of each item and eliminate the lights (bring your own).

Person Present ■ Divide into teams and give each team a set of wrapping supplies (for example, cardboard, tape, paper, bows, string, and so forth). Tell kids to choose a person that they would like to present to the world. Explain that the contest is to see which team can gift-wrap their person the best—the contest is quality, not speed. Stress creativity. After about 10 minutes, have each group present their gift to everyone else, describing its unique features, etc. Be sure to take pictures of these masterpieces.

Santa Clause ■ Divide into teams and give each one a box of supplies including cotton, coat, hat, pants, "stuffing," etc. (Or you may want to put all the supplies in a pile in the middle of the room.) Explain that their task is to choose someone from the team and dress him or her as "Santa" using only the materials provided. Because their Santas will look different than the traditional one, they should write a story about him or her, relating to the costume, and explain what kind of gifts he or she gives.

Note: To really make this fun, have a variety of costumes available such as a sombrero, baseball cap, helmet, sports coat, tennis shoes, Hawaiian shirt, and so forth. After a few minutes, have each team introduce its Santa and tell his or her story.

Santa's Helpers ■ Divide into groups of three or four each. On a table place piles of raw materials: cotton balls, string, paper, aluminum foil, tennis balls, balloons, crepe paper, magazines, toothpicks, index cards, rubber bands, newspapers, coat hangers, cloth, and tools such as tape, scissors, felt-tip markers, glue, and so on. Explain that we are all familiar with the television advertisements during the Christmas season that expound the virtues of super toys, exciting games, fantastic dolls, and miracle appliances. Then explain that by using the materials and tools on the table, each group should build its own unique product. Also, they should create an ad for it. After they everyone has finished, have students display their products and give their sales spiels.

Sing . . . along? ■ Divide your crowd into 10 groups and give each group a section of "The Christmas Song" by Mel Torme. Their assignment is to act out the imagery (chestnuts roasting on an open fire, etc.). Then put the whole song together with each group acting out its part in sequence.

Special Specials ■ Explain that every holiday season there are a multitude of television specials. It seems as though everyone has a Christmas program, from the Muppets to Johnny Cash; from "Frosty" to the "Donkey with the Droopy Ears." Then say something like: In fact every possible special has been shown. Right?" "Wrong, rancid holly breath! Right now, your assignment is to create a unique, new, Christmas special." Then divide into teams, give students paper and pencils, and let them create. After about five minutes, have everyone describe their shows to the rest of the group. The descriptions can include sound effects, special guests, story line, etc.

Team Wrap ■ Divide into teams and give each one a large box (same size for each team), wrapping paper, scissors, tape, ribbon, and a bow. Line up the teams in columns and explain that at your signal, the first person should run to the front and begin to wrap the box. After 15 seconds, you will blow a whistle; then he or she should run back and be replaced by the next team member who should continue the wrapping process. End the relay when everyone on each team has had one turn, and then judge the best wrap. Or see which team can wrap its box completely, using paper, ribbon, and bow.

TV Specials ■ For a few weeks preceding your meeting, tape just a short portion of each of the dozen or so Christmas specials. At the meeting, hold a contest to see who can correctly identify the specials as they are shown. If you can't find a VCR, pick up a couple of TV listings and just read the descriptions for your contestants.

Wrapping Wrace ■ Divide into teams and give each team an identical set of gift wrapping supplies. These supplies should include boxes (about four per team, of varying sizes), wrapping paper (use newspapers), scissors, tape, crayons, ribbons, bows, cards, pens, etc. Each team should be formed as an assembly line with each person in the line having one job to accomplish on each box. One box must be totally wrapped before the next one can proceed down the line. At your signal, the race begins—the first team to wrap all its presents, wins.

Here's how it works: The first person runs to his or her team's pile of boxes, chooses a box, and brings it

back to the next person in line who has the paper. This person chooses the right piece of paper and hands it, with the box, to the next person who has the scissors. This person, then, cuts the paper to the right size and passes it and the box to the next person who tapes the paper around the box. The next person decorates the present with his or her crayons; the next one wraps and ties a ribbon around it; the next one attaches a bow; the next one writes and attaches a card; the last one takes the present and runs it to the table.

DISCUSSION STARTERS

Ants ■ If possible, bring some ants to the meeting. If this is not possible, bring pictures of ants. Use these as an illustration of the incarnation. Show everyone the ants and say: *Let's suppose that for some reason you love these ants, and you want to tell them how you feel and that you want to help them. What are some ways you could try to communicate with them?*

If no one says this, explain that the perfect way would be to become an ant. Have them see how disgusting that would be—to become an ugly, creeping, crawling ant. Explain that that is how we are in comparison with God (we're even worse), yet that's what Jesus did, becoming a tiny speck in the universe He had created—a man. Tell everyone to think of Christmas every time they see an ant.

Born in a Barn ■ Hold your meeting in a barn. It will provide a great opportunity for discussion of where and how Jesus was born. If you can't get a barn, try to borrow a lamb for an object lesson. Discuss what the Bible means when Jesus is called "the Lamb of God."

Cookie Sale ■ For a few weeks before Christmas, have group members bake Christmas cookies. They could even do this together at a member's home. Then hold a bake sale. Send the profits to a charity that helps needy kids. Later, discuss the experience.

Court ■ Tell this story (you'll have to embellish with a few lines). *It's Christmas Eve and a woman has just been taken before the judge for shoplifting (she was getting presents for her children). Because it is Christmas, the judge decides to let her off. The shopkeeper from whom she had stolen is incensed, however. After all, his merchandise has been taken and "used," and he has to bear the brunt of the cost.*

The fact is, someone has to pay! This is very similar to what God has done for us. We stand guilty, and someone has to pay. Like the judge, God declares us "not guilty." The difference is that He also paid the price. Our penalty was death, but Jesus came to earth to pay the penalty. This is what Christmas is all about—God's reaching out to us through His Son.

The Emptying ■ Divide into teams and place a glass of colored water on a table in front of each team. Then give each team a Styrofoam cup that the first person on each team should hold throughout the contest. Give the next person on each team a straw. Explain that this is a contest to see which team can empty the most water from their glass and transfer it to their cup in two minutes, by only using the capillary action in their straw.

At your signal, the second person on each team should run to the glass, put his or her straw into the water, place his or her finger over the top of the straw, go back to the team, and empty the water from the straw into the cup by removing the finger. Then the next person should take the straw and do the same. The process should continue until one of the glasses is empty or until the time is up. The winning team is the one with the most liquid in its cup.

Later, read Philippians 2:5-11 and explain that this passage is called, "The Emptying." Ask about the various ways that containers can be emptied. Then ask how someone could "empty himself" and how Christ emptied Himself.

Gifts ■ This will take a lot of preparation, but it's worth it. Collect a number of small boxes (enough for each member of the group) and in each one place a symbol of a gift that God gives us. Wrap the boxes, place them in one large box, and wrap that box. During the meeting, announce that a large present was left for the group. Bring it into the room and have it opened. Have everyone come forward and take a small gift from the box. Next, everyone should open their boxes and hold on to the gifts that were inside. One by one, have each person display his or her gift and explain what it means and how it relates to God's gifts to us. Possible "gifts" could include: fruit of the Spirit, spiritual gifts, talents, the church, relationships, family, personality, Christ, eternal life, salvation, and others. Symbols for some of these gifts could include a family picture (for family), a cross (for salvation), a mirror (for each person's unique personality), alpha and omega (for eternal life), a heart (for love), a seed (for new life, faith, or nature), and so on.

Love Gifts ■ Before your meeting, compile a list of names and addresses of lonely people in the community. Pastors and other adults will usually be quite willing to supply these names. After your meeting, have students who want to participate in this project draw the names. Their assignment is to buy (or make) and deliver a very special and meaningful Christmas gift to their people. (Each individual should draw one name or family.) These gifts, however, should be given anonymously, and the people should never be told who the donors are. The cards should only be signed, "A Friend" or "Someone who cares." Discuss the experience at another meeting.

Missionary ■ Using a phone amplifying device (a special hook-up that you can purchase for a couple of dollars) and a P.A. system, call a missionary and talk to him or her about Christmas and the special customs of the country in which he or she is serving. If you know a missionary family with teenagers, put together a group Christmas "care package" and send it with notes from everyone.

Nursing Home ■ Take your group caroling to a nearby retirement village. As a special surprise, line up three or four of the residents to share "the greatest (most significant) gifts they ever received." This can be a very meaningful time and an experience of blessing each other.

Shopping ■ Plan a group shopping trip. Beforehand, spend time writing the "gift lists" together and discussing how they decide what to buy for whom.

The Very Best ■ Distribute paper and pens or pencils and have everyone describe the most meaningful gifts they ever received. Collect and read them aloud. Afterwards, discuss what the gifts had in common and what made them so meaningful. Chances are good that most of them will be tied to the feelings or the relationship behind the gift—the giver gave something of himself or herself. This can lead into a talk or a discussion of how they can give truly meaningful gifts this Christmas.

What's the Object? ■ Use teams or choose a pair of group members to compete. Have them come to the front, one couple at a time. Separate them so that the crowd can see both people in the couple, but they can't see each other. Give person A an object and person B paper and a hard surface on which to write. Explain that person A is to describe his or her object to person B who will draw it on the paper. The description, however, may only include shapes, lines, and relative distance (no names, functions, or other clues). Repeat with the other pairs. Possible objects could include pliers, can opener, level, wallpaper roller, catcher's mask, Christmas ornament, star, crêche, dictionary or other book, etc. Afterwards, see how the drawings compare to the described objects and then discuss how this relates to Christmas, the Incarnation, and God becoming man.

Will the Real Jesus Please Stand Up? ■ Bring in four guys and have each one introduce himself to the group. Each one should say, "My name is Jesus." Allow the audience to ask questions of each one to try to determine who is the real Jesus. Beforehand, brief the actors to respond to the questions *in character*, according to the following guidelines:

1. a very good and moral man, and someone who wanted to rock the religious establishment, but not God

2. fully God who lived on earth, but not a real human being

3. a religious leader, like a prophet, but not God

4. God in the flesh—the God-man

After about five minutes of questioning, have the audience vote on who they think the real Jesus is. Have kids explain the reasons for their choices. Then have the "real Jesus" stand up. Use this to lead into a discussion of Christ's true identity.

Wise Men ■ Begin a new tradition in your church. Instead of Santa Claus, have three high schoolers dress up as the wise men and have them visit the young children in Sunday School. They can listen to their gift requests, distribute small presents, and explain the meaning of their gifts to the Christ child.

Wreaths ■ Bring a supply of evergreen branches, pine cones, holly, etc., and wire, cutters, and other necessary tools. As a group, make Christmas wreaths to be distributed after the meeting to a nursing home nearby. Another option is to make Christmas ornaments for others or ornaments that symbolize students' lives. Styrofoam balls, glitter, ribbon, glue, and other materials will be needed for this.

DISCUSSIONS AND WRAP-UPS

Christmas Involvement ■ Explain that there are several examples in the Christmas story of people who took responsibility for the needs that crossed their paths:

• The *innkeeper* took responsibility for an unplanned meeting. Instead of turning Mary and Joseph away, he gave them a place to stay.

• The *shepherds* responded to a startling revelation and did something about it, instead of going back to their jobs.

• *Joseph and Mary* took responsibility for life's unexpected challenges and obeyed God, instead of merely thinking of themselves (which would have been much easier).

• The *wisemen* responded to the profound opportunities of life, following the star and seeking the newborn king.

Gifts ■ Ask:

• What kinds of gifts does God give to us?

• How should we respond to these gifts?

• What kinds of gifts do we have that we can share with others?

Presents ■ Explain that because it's Christmas and everyone gives and receives, you want to talk a little about presents. Then ask:

• What type of present would you give to the President? To a teacher? To an "enemy"? (Allow humorous answers but then press for serious ones.)

• What kind of present could you give your "enemy" that would heal the relationship? Why?

• What kind of present could you give to God?

Society ■ Ask:

• What makes you think that most people have lost the true meaning of Christmas? Give some examples of where people have caught the truth.

• What can you and I do to get closer to and to demonstrate the true meaning of Christmas?

"T" Party ■ Use the following outline for a wrap-up. Explain that you are going to have a "T" party to help everyone remember possible non-material gifts that they can give. After giving each word beginning with a "T," give an example from Jesus' life. Then give possibilities for them. Possible answers are in parentheses.

• **TIME** (helping, just being together, listening)

• **TRUTH** (support, affirmations, compliments, words of thanks; principles and promises from the Bible)

• **TALENT** (expertise, insight)

• **TRUST** (confidence in, great expectations for, friendship with)

• **TREASURE** (something valuable to you, help in time of need

BIBLE STUDIES

Bible Hunt ■ Make sure that everyone has a Bible. Explain that this will be a contest to see who can find Christmas verses in the Bible. You may want to do this as a team competition, but don't allow anyone to give more than two correct answers. As you read each event, have an assistant write it on the board. Here are the events to read:

• the announcement to the shepherds

• Christ's resurrection

• a prophecy about Jesus' birth

• Mary's song

• how to become a follower of Christ

• a statement about why Jesus came to earth

• Jesus' birth

• Jesus' death

• the visit of the wisemen

• another name or title for Jesus

• a story from Jesus' youth

Afterwards, see who can put these events and statements in the right chronological order. Say that *How to become a follower of Christ* will be last.

Afterward, explain why so many people miss the meaning of Christmas. Lost in the traditions and plastic, they miss Jesus. Also explain how even many Christians don't really know much about Christ . . . or where to find His story in the Bible.

Ask: *Why do people today find it hard to believe in Jesus?*

Emptying ■ Read Philippians 2:5-11 and ask:

• What does this say about who Jesus is?

• What does this say about what Jesus did?

• What does this say about what Jesus will do?

• What does this say about us?

Giving ■ Have everyone read John 13:1-17 and ask:

• How does this passage relate to Christmas?

• How do these verses relate to our gift-giving?

• What do verses 16 and 17 mean?

• Now look at 13:34-35. (Read the verses aloud.) How can we demonstrate Jesus' love this Christmas?

Giving of Gifts ■ Explain that the best way to understand the relationship between God and humankind is the giving of gifts. Then have them discover the gift mentioned in each of these passages. The answers are in parentheses.

1. Genesis 1:1 (Creation—God gave us life.)

2. Genesis 15:1-5 (Noah, Abraham, Moses, David—God gave us the covenant.)

3. Matthew 10:28-30 (God gives guidance and protection to His people.)

4. Acts 3:17-26 (God gave the prophets.)

5. Luke 2:1-20 (God gave His Son to be born as a baby and to live as a man.)

6. John 3:16 (Jesus gave His life, dying for us and paying the penalty for our sins.)

7. Romans 10:9-10 (God gave us the way to have eternal life through faith in Christ.)

8. John 14:15-17 (God gives the Holy Spirit to live in us.)

9. Galatians 5:22-23 (God gives us the fruit of the Spirit.)

10. 1 Corinthians 12:27-31 (God gives us spiritual gifts.)

11. Ephesians 5:25-27 (God gives us the church—other believers.)

12. 2 Peter 1:20-21 (God gave us His Word.)

13. 1 John 3:1-2 (God gives us the promise to make us like Christ.)

14. Romans 8:28 (God gives us guidance.)

Incarnation ■ Write the words of the following passages of Scripture on index cards with three or four words per card.

• Hebrews 2:9

• Philippians 2:5-8

• John 1:14

• 1 Peter 3:18

(Add verses for a large crowd.)

Distribute the cards randomly throughout the room. Explain that the cards contain parts of verses that speak of the incarnation, Jesus emptying Himself and becoming a man. When you give the signal, they should find the others in the room who have other words to the same passage and then form a group.

Like Jesus ■ Read Romans 8:19 and ask:

• What is the goal of the Christian life? (to be like Christ)

• Jesus became man (the Incarnation). How can we be like Jesus in that? (by going into our world, humbling ourselves, and giving our lives for others)

• What specific ways can we "incarnate" the Gospel?

Magi ■ Have everyone turn to Matthew 2. Tell them to find the different ways the Magi demonstrated what they thought of Jesus. Use this to discuss how people today demonstrate by their actions what they really think of Jesus.

Then explain that from the actions of the Magi, we can see that . . .

• Jesus was the reason for their journey

• Jesus was the answer to their search

• Jesus was deserving of gifts

• Jesus was worthy of worship

Ask students how *their* actions demonstrate what they truly believe about Christ. Do they really believe that Jesus is God? Do they really believe that Jesus is the Savior? Do they really believe that Jesus is the only way to heaven?

Memory ■ Encourage group members to memorize one of the following verses: John 14:6; Philippians 2:5-8; Colossians 2:9; Hebrews 4:15-16.

Messiah ■ Have everyone read silently Isaiah 52:13-15 and chapter 53. Then ask:

• What does this passage say about what God's servant looked like on earth? (53:1-3—"no beauty or majesty," "despised," "rejected," etc.)

• What do verses 4-6 say that He did? ("took up our infirmities," "carried our sorrows," "was pierced for our transgressions," etc.)

• How about verses 7-9? ("He was oppressed and afflicted"; He was killed.)

• These verses describe the promised Messiah; how were they fulfilled in Jesus? (Jesus was rejected by many; He died on the cross to pay the price for our sins.)

Special Delivery ■ Before the meeting, type the verses listed below on cards, place them in small boxes, and gift wrap the boxes. Then, during the meeting bring out the bag of gifts and distribute them at random. Have the gifts opened one at a time (no special order) and the verses read. Discuss each passage with the following questions.

2 Corinthians 9:6-15

• To what kind of "giving" is this passage referring? (tithes, offerings, collections, etc.)

• Who is the recipient of these gifts? (other Christians in need—the poor)

• What should be the giver's attitude? (cheerfulness)

• How do these verses relate to you and me?

Luke 6:38

• What will be the results of generosity? (You will receive as you have given.)

• Have you had an experience like this? (Be prepared to share from your own experiences.)

James 1:17

• What does this verse teach? (All good gifts come from God.)

• What "good" gifts have you received?

• What "good" gifts can you give others?

2 Corinthians 9:15; Ephesians 2:8-9; Romans 6:23

• How does God give? (perfectly)

• What are God's gifts? (salvation, life, talents, spiritual gifts, etc.)

• How can we obtain God's gifts? (only by faith) What does this imply about our giving and receiving from each other? (We should give from the heart, sacrificially, expecting nothing in return.)

Matthew 7:9-12

• What will God give to us? (good things)

• What do verses 9 and 10 mean? (A good parent won't give bad gifts to a child.)

• Verse 12 is the "Golden Rule." How should that affect our giving?

Acts 20:35

• What does this say about receiving? (It is good.)

• Why and in what ways is giving better than receiving?

The Real Story ■ Distribute sheets of paper with John 14:6-10, Philippians 2:3-9, Colossians 2:9, and Hebrews 4:14-16 from *The Living Bible* written on them. Explain that all these verses relate to the real meaning of Christmas. With their pencils, they should circle words or phrases that relate to Christmas (for example: "I am in the Father and the Father is in Me," "taking the disguise of a slave and becoming like men," "all of God in a human body," "understands our weaknesses," etc.). Spend a few moments asking for their circled phrases and listening to their explanations. Then ask what it means that Jesus was fully God and fully man.

DATING AND BREAKING UP

CROWD-BREAKERS

Ad ■ Distribute paper and pens and ask everyone to write a newspaper advertisement of 15 words or less for the girl or guy of their dreams. Collect these unique ads and read them aloud.

Alikes ■ Seat everyone in boy-girl pairs and give each person a Personal Quiz and pencil or pen. Tell them to answer the following questions honestly and privately.

PERSONAL QUIZ

1. What is your favorite type of music?
2. What is your favorite subject in school?
3. What kind of movie or video do you like to see?
4. Name a woman who is living whom you greatly admire.
5. Name a man who is living whom you greatly admire.
6. What's your favorite sport to watch?
7. What's your favorite sport to play?
8. List three to five of your favorite Bible verses.
9. How many years do you plan on going to school after high school?
10. Why did you come to this meeting?

Afterwards, have each couple compare their answers as you read the questions again. Tell them to give themselves 10 points for every time their answers matched exactly and 5 points for every time their answers were close. Then have them total their points. See which pair had the highest point total and declare them Mr. and Miss Compatibility.

All in Your Mind ■ This is a skit in which a boy goes to a hypnotist to improve his dating life. The hypnotist puts him under and gives him detailed instructions on how to talk to his date, converse with her father, open the door, eat at the restaurant, etc. After each one, the hypnotized boy repeats back the instruction verbatim. The hypnotist tells him to remember everything when he awakes and then snaps him out of it. The next scene is the date, but because the events happen out of order, the boy does everything wrong. For example, the father answers the door, so the boy has to talk to him first and gives the speech he learned for talking to the girl. Then they go to a movie and have popcorn instead of going to a restaurant, etc.

Attached ■ Attach competing couples with a length of string or cord, a length of thread, a balloon, a piece of elastic, and a length of yarn. Have them stand apart so that the balloon and elastic are taut. The contest is to untie the strings, with each person keeping one hand behind his or her back. The first couple finished, wins.

Note: they may work on untying their own knots and their partners'.

Another possibility is to have them free themselves of their bonds any way they can including breaking them. Again, the fastest team would win.

The Big Date ■ Bring two couples to the front and explain that this will be a contest to see which couple has the most sophistication. Seat the couples at separate card tables and make sure that their clothes are protected. Explain that this is a very expensive and exclusive French restaurant—the food is exotic and the atmosphere is thick (very dark). To make sure they get the feel for the atmosphere, all four participants must wear blindfolds. To make sure they get the feel for the food, they will have no utensils and only use their hands. And to make sure that they have togetherness, they must feed each other (no one may feed himself or herself). Explain that after you put the blindfolds on, you will bring out various plates of food (a five-course dinner) that they should feed each other. The first couple to eat all of a course (everything on a plate) will receive 1000 points for that course. You will also award 100 points to each couple for every compliment given during the meal (for example, *You have beautiful hair, I love the way you chew, Your breath smells divine*, etc.).

Here are the courses of food to use: a banana (unpeeled), a small bowl of Jello, potato chips and/or saltine crackers, spaghetti, M & Ms, and two cups of milk. Afterward, remove the blindfolds, help the contestants clean up, and proclaim the winning couple.

Blind Date ■ Choose two boys and two girls (or more couples if you want to make this competitive). Designate parts of the room as "rooms" on the date. Explain that one of the boys and one of the girls will be blindfolded and go on a "date" in the room. They will be guided verbally by the other boy and girl through their blind date. The rooms on the date can be the girl's home (boy must climb steps, ring bell, greet father, compliment girl, and escort her to the car); the car—a wagon pulled by a tricycle (boy must seat girl and "drive" them both to the restaurant); and the restaurant (they must pour Coke and drink it, eat cake, etc.). As a competitive event, have another set of couples repeat the procedure. The best time wins.

Blind Dates ■ Give every person a piece of paper reading, *Your name is _____. Your date's name is _____.* Choose boys' and girls' names at random, but make sure there are no duplications, except that all the names given to boys should be listed as dates on the girls' papers and vice versa. Also, be sure to separate the boys' and girls' papers. In other words, John should receive a piece of paper from the boy's pile. It reads, *Your name is Claude. Your date's name is Mildred.* Nanci could receive a paper that reads, *Your name is Suzanne. Your date's name is Ralph.*

Tell everyone to remember the names on their papers, their own and their date's. Then pass out blindfolds and make sure that everyone is blindfolded. (If you have a large group, just make sure

that the room is pitch black when you turn off the lights.) Explain that at your signal, they are to *crawl* around the room looking for their dates. When they get together, they should sit quietly and wait for instructions. They should not talk further to their dates until you tell them.

After everyone has found his or her partner, turn off the lights, or have everyone remove the blindfolds and have them discuss the following questions together:

• What's your real name? Describe your family.

• What was your favorite date (activity)? Why?

• Describe your ideal boy or girl.

• Have you ever been on a blind date? If so, what was it like?

Candy Kiss Hunt ■ Purchase a bag of Hershey's Kisses wrapped in the red and green foil. Insert a numbered slip of paper inside each wrapping. Make sure you have two of every number, and put one in a "green" kiss and the other in a "red" one (designate one color for boys and the other one for girls). Hide the candies around the room, making sure that none are in sight. Explain about the colored kisses and that each person can only have one. Also tell them about the numbers and that they should find their partners (the other person with the same number). Then have them get up and look for the kisses. Use these pairs in other games involving couples.

Circular Letter ■ Beforehand, write the following phrases at the tops of sheets of paper, one phrase per sheet: *This is a difficult letter for me to write because . . .* and *I'm afraid we'll have to break up because . . .*

Divide into groups of 8–10 and seat them in circles. Give every person a piece of paper, a pen or pencil, and a hard surface on which to write. Explain that when you give the signal, they should begin by writing, using their imaginations and writing anything they think would be appropriate. After about thirty seconds, have them pass their papers one person to the right. As soon as they receive the new paper, they should continue the story, again using imagination and creativity, until you tell them to pass the papers again. Allow about ten seconds more each time because they will need time to read what others have written. After everyone has written on seven or eight letters, announce that this will be the last one so they should end it. Then collect the letters, redistribute them, and have kids read them aloud. In a large group, have each circle decide on the funniest letter to read aloud to everyone.

Couples ■ Give girls slips of paper from the "A" envelope and give the guys slips of paper from the "B" envelope. Explain that the envelopes contain short jokes about girls or boys, but the jokes have been divided into two parts. When you give the signal, everyone should try to find his or her partner. Here are the jokes in their A and B segments:

- A—Because she was the truck driver's daughter,
  B—she was semi-sweet.
- A—Her father owned a laundry,
  B—so she took him to the cleaners.
- A—His father was a jockey,
  B—but he wasn't very stable.
- A—She was only the farmer's daughter,
  B—but all the horse manure.
- A—She was the moonshiner's daughter,
  B—and he loved her still.
- A—As he patted down the pony,
  B—he was feeling a little horse.
- A—She was a dentist, and he was a carpenter,
  B—so they fought tooth and nail.
- A—He worked in the shoe store
  B—and turned out to be a heel.
- A—Because his father was a surgeon,
  B—he was always making cutting remarks.
- A—She wanted to continue dating the optometrist,
  B—but he made a spectacle of himself.

Give the signal and give everyone time to find the right partner. (Note: use your adult helpers to fill in where needed.) Then have the pairs read their jokes aloud to the rest of the group, one pair at a time.

Couples Scavenger Hunt ■ Divide into boy-girl couples (couples of the same sex will be all right if the numbers are uneven) and have them sit together. Explain that you will call out an item, and whichever couple brings it to you first wins that round. They can use the contents of their purses and pockets and anything else they have on them. Possible scavenger items to call could include a shoelace, 97 cents in change, a ticket stub, a picture of a boyfriend or girlfriend, a gift from someone of the opposite sex, etc.

Date-O-Matic ■ Before the meeting, prepare two envelopes, one entitled *places* and one entitled *materials*. Write the places and materials on individual slips of paper and put them in the appropriate envelopes. Break into groups of 2–4. Explain that each group will draw a slip of paper from each envelope. Their task is to design a creative date using the place and materials they have drawn. Afterwards, have each group read its creative date for the rest of the group. Here are possible places and materials to use (add those that are appropriate for your area):

PLACES	MATERIALS
beach	volleyball
woods	camera and film
parking lot	pen and paper
gymnasium	snack food
a pick-up truck	$2.49 in change
K-Mart or other discount store	office supplies
downtown	crepe paper and balloons
playground	Gummy Bears

Date Relay ■ Divide into teams and have the teams sit in columns with a blindfolded male representative in front. Give each team a bag containing about 10 items that a girl could use in getting ready for a big date. The bags should contain identical items. At your signal, the last person should reach into the bag, pull out an item, and pass it to the front. The blindfolded boy at the front should then use that item and pass it back. When it reaches the end of the team, another item may be passed and so on until the bag is empty and the guys are made-up like girls. The first team finished wins. Items could include lipstick, eye shadow, blush, comb, blouse, dress, toothbrush and paste, mouthwash to gargle, perfume, fingernail polish, and fingernail clippers.

Dating Dreams ■ Divide into groups. Explain how we often dream dating experiences, and in our dreams, everything is in slow motion. Say that you want them to recreate those dreams. Then give each group a dating dream sequence that they should pantomime for the rest of the group. Give them a few minutes to prepare their pantomimes—everyone in the group should be in the act. Here are some dream sequences to use (add others):

- love at first sight, across a crowded dance floor
- a blind date
- a tearful farewell at the airport
- a date with someone when you see someone else you'd rather be with

Dating Game ■ Choose three dating couples and run this like television's "Newlywed Game." You can use questions like these:

- What attracted you to him?
- What will she say is her greatest strength?
- How long will he say he thinks you will go together?
- What does he do that really bugs you?
- On a scale of 1 to 10, rate your last date together.
- Who does she most resemble—Blondie, Oprah Winfrey, Madonna, Mother Theresa, Connie Chung, or Cindy Crawford?
- Who does he most resemble—Richard Gere, Sylvester Stallone, Tim Allen, Billy Graham, Steve Urkel, Michael Bolton, or Michael Jordan?

Dream Girl/Guy ■ Ask for the group to give the parts of speech that you need to fill in the blanks in the paragraphs below. Don't let them know what the stories are about until all the blanks are filled. Then give them the title and read their creations.

DREAM GIRL

The girl of my dreams has _____(adjective) _____(color) hair. Her _____ (plural noun) are _____(color), and when she _____(verb) them at me, I melt. Her figure is _____(adjective); her femininity is _____(adjective). And what a personality! She is _____ (adjective) and has a great sense of _____ (noun). As a matter of fact, she's one of the most _____(adjective) girls in school. The person most like this dream girl is _____ (name of girl in room).

DREAM GUY

My ideal guy is about _____(number) feet tall with _____("ing" adjective) muscles. Not only is he a great athlete, but he is also a _____ (adjective) student. Last semester, he got _____ (number) A's and only _____ (number) F's. He is always _____(adjective) and _____ (adjective) and very sensitive to my _____ (plural noun). He spares no expense on our dates—the last one cost $_____(number) when he took me to _____(place). As a matter of fact, the one guy who most reminds me of him is _____ (name of guy in room).

Here are a couple of additional scripts to use:

PERFECT GUY

My perfect man is a real _____ (noun). He's about _____(number) feet tall and has a _____(adjective) complexion. His hair is _____(adjective) and _____ (adjective). His sexy eyes are _____(color).

They remind me of _____ (plural noun). His _____(plural noun) ripple, and he has a _____(adjective) walk. This dream boat always treats me _____(adverb); he's so _____ (adjective) and _____(adjective).

PERFECT GIRL

This perfect girl has beautiful long flowing _____ (noun). When she _____ (verb) her eyes at me, I _____(verb). She has a perfect figure: _____(number), _____(number), _____ (number). She always wears such _____ (adjective) _____(plural noun) too . . . and what a _____(noun); her smile _____(verb) and lights up the room. She is a perfect example of _____ (noun) and _____(noun).

Finder of Lost Loves ■ This word game would be good for those who come to the meeting early or right on time. Give each person a puzzle in which to find the "lost loves." In your puzzle, mix in 9 or 10 dating and love words, hidden among other miscellaneous letters. The words may be written backward, forward, up, down, or diagonally. Be sure to list them on the sheet so the kids will know what to look for. The first person to find all the words wins. Here is a sample puzzle.

B	A	N	Y	I	H	L	R	I	G	S
O	R	B	E	L	E	I	K	L	O	I
Y	E	O	F	O	T	J	R	L	S	N
A	C	T	K	V	A	R	E	N	T	G
C	T	R	A	E	H	P	T	O	E	L
R	R	C	G	D	N	A	T	P	A	E
J	U	S	T	F	R	I	E	N	D	S
M	E	D	H	J	K	N	L	Q	Y	T

Hidden words: BROKEN, LOVE, HEART, TRUE, JUST FRIENDS, LETTER, DATE, GO STEADY, PAIN, HATE, BOY, GIRL, ME, SINGLE, SOLE

Flipside ■ Hand out the following list of desirable qualities in a potential mate. Then have everyone write the negative side of each quality. For example, "steady and sure" can also be "slow and boring," and "outgoing and effervescent" can become "flighty and scatterbrained." Afterward, discuss students' answers and talk about the implications for choosing or being a good date.

FLIPSIDE

1. beautiful hair—

2. great sense of humor—

3. a good mind, solid thinker—

4. spontaneous and exciting—

5. generous, a big spender—

6. sensitive—

7. musical, very talented—

8. very athletic—

9. a great figure—

10. polite and considerate—

11. quiet and thoughtful—

12. confident and self-assured—

Handle With Care ■ Set up a relay in which teams transport fragile items through an obstacle course. Possible items could include: wet tissue paper supporting a golf ball; a Ping-Pong ball balanced on a piece of cardboard; a spoon carrying a raw egg (an empty shell would be less messy); a balloon held between the knees; a plastic plate balanced on one finger; a cookie held between the elbows; ribbon candy held between the teeth; etc. This relay illustrates how relationships are fragile and must be handled with care.

Hit List ■ Distribute Hit Lists and tell students to get signatures from members of the opposite sex who fit the specific categories listed. A person may only sign a sheet once.

HIT LIST

1. Has been a blind date

_____

2. Needs a date

_____

3. Looks interesting

_____

4. Has recently broken up with boyfriend or girlfriend

_____

5. Is going out this weekend

_____

6. Is not going out yet this weekend

_____

7. Has used a dating service

_____

8. Has written a love note in the last two years

_____

9. Is easily embarrassed

_____

10. Would be willing to go "Dutch treat"

_____

See who can fill in the sheet the quickest. Then read and compare some of the names in the blanks.

Humpty Dumpty ■ Do this as a contest of speed and dexterity between two volunteers or team representatives (also it may be run as a relay). Explain that you have difficult puzzles for them to assemble—the first one finished will receive a prize and the last one, a penalty.

Seat the two contestants behind a table and give each one a roll of tape and some string to use to hold their puzzles together. Explain that when they have finished the first puzzle, you will give them another one and so on until you run out of puzzles. Keep your puzzles in separate bags so the pieces won't get mixed up. Here are possible puzzles, in order of difficulty.

1. a picture from a magazine, cut into 10 pieces

2. Tinker Toy or Lego pieces with pictures of the finished objects

3. a red, construction paper heart, cut into 15 pieces

4. an apple, cut into sections

5. a banana, peeled (with peel in two parts) and cut into 3 pieces

6. an egg shell, broken into a number of pieces (Use whole eggs with the contents blown out. Carefully break them into pieces as large as possible.)

The point is that after a breakup it's difficult to get yourself together again.

Ideal Date ■ Divide into 10 groups and give each group a part of the date. Tell them to write their idea of that specific part of an ideal date. Collect the parts and read them in order. Here are possible date parts: guy (description); guy (clothes); girl (description); girl (clothes); transportation; dinner (menu); dinner (place); main event; event location; date ending.

Love Is Blind ■ Divide into teams and have each team choose a couple (boy and girl) to compete for them. Bring all the couples to the front and blindfold them. Give each couple an identical set of items and explain that, while blindfolded, their job is to get their partners ready for a date and they have only three minutes to complete the job. The guys' bags should contain lipstick, hairbrush, hair spray, toothpaste, toothbrush, and necklace. The girls' bags should contain shaving cream, razor (without blade), mouthwash, comb, hair spray, and neck chain. Say "Go!" and watch the fun. Be sure to be prepared for the mess too.

May I Have This Dance? ■ Pair off your group into couples and choose one person in each couple to be the leader. Explain that you are going to have a group dance, so each couple should assume the waltz position. The idea in this dance is for the leader to lead and the follower to follow (this sounds easy enough). Then turn on the tape that you have prepared beforehand and watch the chaos and fun. (Note: The tape should have parts of a number of songs, ranging from easy-listening ballads to hard rock. You may also want to throw in parts of a polka and a waltz.) Whatever the style of music, your couples should dance facing each other in the waltz position. After a few minutes, reverse the leader and follower roles and continue the dance.

The Moves ■ Make sure that everyone is seated, packed pretty close to each other. Tell them to follow your instructions. That is, they should move the direction you indicate if the line you read applies to them. Note: if any place is already taken, they should sit on that person's lap. Then give the following instructions.

• move one place to your right if you had a date last night

• move one place backwards if you will go on a date this weekend

• move two places to the left if you haven't had a date in the last two weeks

• move two places forward if there's someone you'd like to date but you haven't been asked (or gotten up your nerve to ask) yet

• move three places to your left if you are tired of the whole dating scene

• stay in the same place and turn to your left if you're a girl

• stay in the same place and turn to your right if you're a guy

• move one place forward and one place to your right if there's someone in the room you'd like to date

• etc.

Partners ■ Have everyone choose a partner. This should be someone of the opposite sex if possible. Let them chat for a minute or two; then have them sit down, back to back. Emphasize the fact that they must not cheat, and then ask the following questions. Give each person 100 points for every correct answer.

1. Is this person wearing a class ring?

2. What is the color of his or her eyes?

3. Do his or her shoes tie?

4. What is the color of his or her shirt?

5. Is he or she wearing a watch?

Add other questions. The person with the most points wins.

Rotate-A-Date ■ Form two concentric circles with boys in one and the girls in the other. Then pair everyone up as much as possible (if there are more boys than girls or vice versa, explain that the extra people will have a bye for the first round, but they will get their chance to participate the next time). Then give all the pairs the following role play to act out.

• *Boy*: You've never asked a girl out before, but you really want to go out with her. You have just called her, and she has just answered the phone.

• *Girl*: You've seen him at school (actually you're in a couple of classes together), but you really don't know what he's like. You're not sure how to answer when he asks you out.

Have all the couples act out the beginning with the phone ringing. After a few minutes, have the girls move counter clockwise one person and the boys move clockwise one person (this should put them two people away from their previous partners). Then have the new couples act out the following situation:

• *Boy*: You and she have been going out for quite some time now, and you thought everything was going great. Today, however, she said that she had doubts and wasn't sure you should be getting so serious. You have asked to see her after school, to talk over your relationship.

• *Girl*: You really think that you ought to break-up. You still like him, but not the same as before. You'd rather just be friends. You have agreed to talk about it after school.

Again, have them play their roles and then move around the circle. Then have the new couples act out this situation.

• *Boy*: You *really* want to go out with her.

• *Girl*: You *really don't* want to go out with him. He spots you walking alone after school and comes along side. Then he asks you out for Saturday night.

Add two or three other situations.

Silence Is Broken ■ Before the meeting, tape-record a number of sounds of things breaking. During the meeting, play the tape and have the kids write down what they think the broken items are. Then play the sounds again and give the correct answers. Here are some possible sounds:

• light bulb breaking

- balloon popping
- paper tearing
- twig or pencil snapping
- wave breaking on the shore
- wood being chopped
- promise being broken (verbal—"I'm sorry. . . .")
- heart breaking (sound of crying)
- Styrofoam cup being squashed
- string or thread snapping

Afterward you could ask, What does breaking up sound like?

Strings Attached ■ Put all the girls on one side of the room and all the guys on the other. On the floor between them, place a number of strings. They should be about three feet long and should be crossed but not tangled. Tell each person to pick up an end to a piece of string. At a signal, they should find their respective partners (at the strings' other ends). Next, give them five minutes to discover the following information about each other: middle name, unique or hidden talent, best vacation spent, career goals, last time punished by parents and reason, and favorite dessert. Have them report the most unusual findings to the group. Note: If you prepare the strings ahead of time, lay them on the floor and cover them with a newspaper.

Watch Your Step ■ Beforehand, tape a number of sheets of paper on the floor, like a quilt or mosaic but with a few inches of space in between them. These sheets should be of various colors, and some should have letters or numbers on them. Determine a sequence that should be followed by someone walking from one end of the papers to the other, for example: red, 3, W, 17, blue, yellow, 99, N, T, etc.

Ask if the group can remember the Indiana Jones movie where Indiana has to walk over a tile floor in the right way or face certain death. If he stepped on some tiles, they would break away and send him falling into the chasm below. Other tiles would trigger spears, daggers, and so forth. Explain that these papers on the floor represent the tiles and that you are looking for a new Indiana Jones to walk successfully from one side of the tiles to the other. Then ask for volunteers. Let each volunteer keep walking if he or she follows the correct sequence, but blow a whistle and stop them if they make one false move. The idea is for those who follow to remember the correct sequence thus far, and then add new tiles.

Note: this activity illustrates the difficulty that kids often face in dating—it feels like walking through a mine field—with one false move destroying them.

DISCUSSION STARTERS

Advice ■ Distribute the following worksheet. Have the students check which source they would go to first for advice on each problem. Then discuss who they listen to the most and who they think is right.

Problem	Parents	Friend	TV/ Movie	God
1. Whom to date				
2. Kissing on a date				
3. Where to go				
4. Going steady				
5. Petting				
6. Marriage				
7. Sexual intercourse				

Assignment ■ Ask your students to talk to their parents during the week about dating. They should ask:

1. How did their parents meet?
2. What attracted each the most in the other person?
3. What was the biggest positive surprise in marriage?
4. What was the biggest negative surprise in marriage?

Tell students to come to the next meeting prepared to discuss what they learned.

Blind Date ■ Choose two volunteers who do not know each other (possibly from different schools) to go on a blind date. This truly will be a "blind date" because they both will be blindfolded the entire time. Have the staff chaperone (and guide) pick them up and introduce them to each other, using first names only. The guide should take them out to eat at a restaurant like Arby's or Burger King, and then to a park where they can spend time talking and playing a game (if there's snow, they could build a snowman). The whole date should last only about two hours. Then they should be brought to the meeting (on time), where the blindfolds will be removed and they will discuss their experience. You should also discuss how dating is usually based on looks and on what others think (and how this experience differs).

Breaking Up Is Hard to Do ■ Choose a few guys and girls to role play the following situations:

- You have been dating steadily for three months. Lately, however, things have been a little stale and you (the girl) have decided that you should break up. You still feel the same way about him, but you want the freedom to date around. The two of you are talking about your relationship.

• You (boy) have finally gotten up the courage to ask her out, and so you call her up and ask. You (girl) don't want to go out with him, and so you make up excuses.

• You (girl) have had a few dates with him and really like him a lot. Lately, how ever, he has been sort of avoiding you in the halls. You sit down next to him at lunch and begin to talk. You (boy) think she's OK, but you're really not that interested.

• You (girl) are trying to tell him that you want to be "just friends."

After each role play, discuss how realistic the situation and the acting were and what people can do to make dating and boy-girl relationships less tense and pressure-filled.

Break Up ■ Divide into boy-girl couples. (Extras may pair up with someone of the same sex.) Explain that they have one minute to find out as much as they can about each other. Then, when you give the signal, they should find another partner, preferably of the opposite sex, and find out as much as they can about that person in a minute. Each time you give the signal, they should change partners. Note: have them switch at least three times so that everyone will have spoken to at least four partners.

Afterward, have various kids stand and tell you as much as they can about their partners. Ask them what questions they asked and how the questions changed (or stayed the same) from person to person. Use this a starter to discuss how dating can provide opportunities for getting to know others.

Cards ■ If your discussion about sex has been quite heavy and personal, you will want to provide the opportunity for kids to receive counseling. Distribute cards and have everyone write their reactions to the topic of the meeting. Then have them write "yes" if they or friends have been involved in a date rape situation (the boy forced himself on the girl). This doesn't mean that intercourse necessarily happened, but that the pressure was there. Then ask them to write their names if they want to get together for a personal appointment with you or another sponsor to talk over their feelings and to get help. Assure them that no one else will see these cards and that you will respect their privacy. Collect the cards and put them out of sight until you can read them later.

Case Study ■ Write a case study of the typical, very serious, high school romance (for example, *John and*

Suzie are in love, and they've pledged to "love each other forever"–their names are carved on trees all over town. A silly misunderstanding leads to an argument which eventually leads to their breakup. After the breakup, they won't talk to each other, they say they hate each other, and they always put each other down).

Read the case study aloud and then ask:

• Who knows of a similar situation? (This can be answered by a show of hands.)

• Why do couples become so hateful?

• How can this whole scene be avoided?

• What are the differences between those couples who can break up in a friendly manner (and still be friends) and those who "hate" each other?

• Why do couples make the commitment of going "steady" in the first place?

Causes ■ Divide into three groups and give each group a piece of paper and a pencil or pen. Tell them to work together to write 10 questions that they would like to ask kids in high school about what causes couples to break up. Afterward, discuss their questions, and see who has answers.

Dear Best Buddy ■ Give everyone a piece of paper and a pencil and explain that each person has a letter to write. Here are the situations:

• Girls—Your best friend has been asked to go to a hotel party. She really doesn't want to go, either with the person who has asked her or to the party, but she wants to be popular and accepted by the group. Write good advice to her concerning what she should do and what she should tell the guy who asked her.

• Guys—Your best friend has told you that all of his buddies want him to go to that hotel party and chip in for the room, but he really doesn't want to go. Write and tell him what he should do.

Make sure the letters are anonymous. Collect, read aloud, and discuss them.

Dear John ■ Give everyone a piece of paper and a pen or pencil. Tell them to imagine that they have been going with a certain person for quite some time, but now they realize that they should break up. They want to be friends, but they want to break up kindly. Tell them each to write a letter to this person. The letters should begin with "Dear John" or "Dear Joanne." After a few minutes, collect the letters and read a few aloud. Then discuss how to break up kindly and how breaking up can affect a person's self esteem.

Double Standard ■ Choose two volunteers to participate in a role play. Be sure to have the necessary props on hand. In this role play, the guy will be playing the part of the girl and the girl, the part of the guy. Here's the situation. The guy (played by the girl, who will be using lines she has heard) is trying to ask out a girl over the phone. The girl (played by the guy) doesn't want to go out with him and is turning him down without lying. The guy persists. Afterward, discuss how realistic the scene was.

Falling in Like ■ Divide the group into two teams, seated on the two sides of the room. Explain that the contest is to see which team can remember and sing the most love songs with the word *love* in them. Team one will start by singing the first line to a love song. After a couple of measures, you will stop them and point to team two. Then they should sing a different song until you say "stop" and point back to team one. This process will continue until one of the teams cannot think of a new song with the word *love* in it or repeats a song already used. The only twist is that whenever the word *love* appears, they must sing *like* instead. For example, "Love me tender" would be "*Like* me tender, like me sweet, never let me go . . ."

Afterward, discuss the difference between *like* and *love* and how a person can know which is which. Explain how infatuation and our emotions can confuse us about real love and how some people are in love with love.

Interviews ■ Divide into couples. Give each person a pencil and a piece of paper and tell them that they have three minutes (90 seconds each) to interview each other about what they look for in someone to date. Have them report the results of the interviews. Compile a list and discuss the differences and similarities and why they look for what they do.

Ideal Index ■ Divide into boys and girls and send them to separate rooms. Make sure that each group has a leader (an adult sponsor would be good). This leader should distribute cards on which the following is written:

IDEAL INDEX

What is your idea of the ideal date? Answer with a person or statement. (Don't allow them to use members of the youth group for their answers.)

MIND like . . .

SKIN like . . .

LAUGHTER like . . .

BODY like . . .

EYES like . . .

VOICE like . . .

PERSONALITY like . . .

OTHER . . .

After everyone has filled out these cards, the leaders should collect them and have a brief discussion about why kids wrote what they did. Then, while still in separate rooms, the leaders should lead a discussion on the following questions (and have someone record the answers):

1. How do you experience disrespect from members of the opposite sex?

2. What words imply disrespect? Why?

3. What actions imply disrespect? Why?

Bring the whole group back together and have each leader read some of the "Ideal Index" cards. This will be light, so don't discuss the answers. Then have the leaders read the answers to their questions about disrespect. This is very important, so make sure that everyone takes the answers seriously. As you proceed, be sure to ask why we, as men and women, are hateful or disrespectful toward each other and how we can show more respect. Compare the "disrespect list" with their "ideal index," and ask where respect fits into the index.

Prayer ■ Because much guilt can surface in a discussion about dating and sex, spend time in silent prayer. Encourage everyone to use this time to talk to God about their guilt or to ask for help for themselves or those who are in destructive dating relationships.

Another way to facilitate this would be to have each person go to a different part of the room or building to spend time alone, talking over this whole area with God, asking for His forgiveness and direction.

Questions ■ Hand out index cards on which kids can write any questions about dating, date abuse, or breaking up that they would like you to attempt to answer at your next meeting.

Red Flags ■ Bring a large red towel or piece of cloth to the meeting. Have all the girls gather on one side of the room and all the guys on the other (in separate rooms if necessary). Give them two minutes to brainstorm all the ways that members of the opposite sex can create problems in dating situations.

Bring the groups back together and seat them on the floor facing each other. Give the girls the red flag first and invite them to tell the guys one of the things that they feel really creates problems on dates. Before the guys can defend themselves or deny the problem, interrupt with the ground rules, saying something like: *Let's assume that the accusation and problem are valid, at least some of the time . . . all right, all the time.*

What we want to accomplish is to arrive at some ways to eliminate or avoid this problem. Guys, any suggestions? Girls, any suggestion?

Don't exhaust the discussion and keep it on the specific matter at hand. Then switch topics by having the girls toss the red flag to the guys for their first contribution of a problem created by girls in dating situations. Continue for three or four problems for each side.

Role Play ■ Break into twos (boy-girl combinations as much as possible). Designate the taller person in each couple as person A and the other as B. Then give the following role plays for them to act out.

• A and B have been going out for quite a while. A begins the discussion with B, explaining that he or she is frustrated because their relationship seems to be in a rut.

• A and B went out for the first time last weekend, but it was not a very good date. B really likes A and would like to go out again. B begins the talk with A, asking him or her out and assuring him or her that this date will be different.

• A is really interested in B and wants to go out with her or him. A designs a creative date and asks B out.

• A and B have been set up to go on a blind date. They are talking on the phone. B is taking A out and has called him or her.

Romance Roles ■ Divide into groups of three with each threesome including at least one boy and one girl. Have them designate persons 1, 2, and 3 in each group. Then give the following role plays to act out with the numbers and their roles as given below. After each role play, the observer should give his or her observations about how realistic the acting was, how appropriate the lines were, etc.

Role Play #1—*Asking Out*

Person #1—boy; Person #2—girl; Person #3—observer

The boy is trying to ask the girl to go with him to a school event. He is really nervous and wants to make a good impression. The girl wants to go out with the boy, but she has a conflict on the day in question. She has to turn him down, but she wants to let him know that she isn't just giving him an excuse and would really like to go out another time.

Role Play #2—*Getting Asked Out*

Person #2—boy; Person #3—girl; Person #1—observer

The girl is trying to get the boy to ask her out. She is taking the initiative, but she doesn't want to seem too bold.

Role Play #3—*Expressing Feelings*

Person #3—boy; Person #1—girl; Person #2—observer

The boy and the girl had a date last night. They see each other in the hall and have a conversation. They both had a good time and want to let the other person know that (and they would like to go out again) . . . without being too obvious.

Afterward, discuss the situations and how realistic the role-playing was. Then discuss how dating can help or hinder romance and building relationships.

Warning Signs ■ Pass out index cards and have everyone finish the following sentence: *You know it's time to break up when . . .*

These cards should be anonymous. Explain that each person should write one creative and humorous ending and one serious ending. Collect the cards and read them aloud. Read the humorous answers first, skipping duplicates. Then read the serious answers. Discuss the answers together.

DISCUSSIONS AND WRAP-UPS

Attractions ■ Ask:

• What attracts guys to girls?

• What attracts girls to guys?

• Why do certain couples keep dating?

• What do you look for in a person to date? What kind of person do you want as your husband or wife? Why are the answers to those two questions different (or similar)?

• In relationships, what does the word *compatibility* mean?

Breaking Up ■ Begin by asking how many can think of a couple who has broken up recently (ask for a show of hands). Then say: *Now don't raise your hands, but how many of you have had the experience yourselves? It's no fun when it happens to you.* Then ask:

• What are some reasons for the breakups you have observed or experienced?

• How do couples break up? What lines are used?

• Can people who used to be serious be "just friends" after a breakup? Why or why not? How?

Challenge ■ Tell students to take dating seriously, especially any potential physical activity. Explain that although love is a matter of the heart, it must also involve the head; in other words, we must use our brains. Challenge them:

1. Be wise in who you date—stay away from potential trouble-causers.

2. Be wise in where you go—stay away from tempting and vulnerable situations.

3. Be wise in what you decide—determine your standards before you encounter the situations.

4. Be wise in following Christ—build healthy relationships, built on respect and trust.

Cruel and Unusual Punishment ■ Use this as a wrap-up or as a discussion guide.

Someone has said that dating is "cruel and unusual punishment," yet it is the only "mating ritual" we have. It's kind of scary, isn't it, to think that our dates prepare us for marriage? Of course, some people go in totally blind and are surprised at what they get. Some look for a person who will meet their emotional needs. Others use the trial-and-error method. If their marriage doesn't work out, they divorce and try again (until they get it right). Still others play the waiting game, expecting God to drop "Mr. or Ms. Right" in their laps. Most of us don't like the old idea of parents arranging our weddings, but maybe it would be a lot better than these other ways of choosing mates.

And then there is the whole matter of love. This is a subject for another whole meeting. Here let me just say that our idealized, romantic ideas of love tend to complicate the process. In America, we believe that you marry the person you love. In reality, no matter how you choose a mate, you have to learn to love the person you marry.

God wants us to take seriously this whole area of dating, love, and marriage. It's not a game, and marriage is the most important decision a person can make after the decision to accept Christ as Savior.

Are you dating with a purpose? Have you involved God in the process? Remember, He loves you and wants to be part of every decision you make.

Dating ■ Ask:

• How do you decide whom you will date?

• Why do most high school couples stay together?

• What is the purpose of dating?

• How can dating prepare a person for marriage?

Games ■ Ask:

• Is our system of dating good or bad? Why?

• Which is easier, asking someone out or being asked out? Why?

• What kind of "games" are played on dates? (for example, being cool, saying the right lines, trying to

find out what the other person thinks of you, etc.)

• What is "date abuse"?

• What is the answer to date abuse?

Loving the Wrong Type ■ Ask:

• It is said that love and compatibility are different. What do you think that means?

• What is the difference between love and dependence?

• What kind of qualities should you look for in the one you marry?

Mate Meeting ■ Ask:

• When do you think you will meet your "mate"? Describe the situation.

• How will you know that this is "the one"?

• What can you do now to help prepare you for this future scenario?

The Pain ■ Use this outline as a discussion guide or for a wrap-up.

1. Often we set ourselves up for painful breakups because we . . .

    a. rush into relationships

    b. expect too much—we're unrealistic or make too many demands

    c. commit ourselves too soon

    d. don't allow the relationship to grow

    e. get involved in an unbalanced relationship—emotional release, heavy physical involvement, etc.

2. Instead, we should . . .

    a. proceed slowly

    b. become friends first—get to know the other person

    c. date a variety of people in a variety of situations

    d. be honest about our feelings and take it a day at a time

    e. resist using the other person to meet our needs or playing on their emotions

3. And, most important of all, we should let Christ control this area of our lives by . . .

    a. committing each person and situation to Him

    b. acting in love toward our dates

    c. responding in love after any breakup

Strengths and Weaknesses ■ Ask:

• What are some strengths in people you know?

• What do you think it means that a person's strength is his or her weakness?

• How would this relate to marriage?

Taking Care ■ Explain that sometimes we get ourselves into problem situations on dates because we aren't careful or selective about who we date or because we aren't careful about actions or situations that can cause problems. It's like going into a date blind. Then ask:

• What precautions can a guy take to avoid having problems on a date? How about a girl?

• What's the difference between being friendly and flirting? Why can flirting be dangerous?

• Where would a person go on a date if he or she *wanted* to have problems with temptation? (possible answers: to a party where there's drinking; alone in a car on a dark road; to a boyfriend or girlfriend's house when the parents are gone; to a dirty movie; etc.)

• Where could a person go on a date where he or she would likely not have sexual pressures? (possible answers: on a double date with a trusted couple; to a Christian youth group activity; to a picnic or outdoor event, in the daylight, with a large group; to a G-rated movie; etc.)

• On a date, what constitutes sexual harassment?

• How can dates be spontaneous and fun when they're planned?

• What can guys and girls do to develop healthy relationships?

BIBLE STUDIES

Bible Dates ■ Work through the following passages together or break into groups and give each group a separate passage to discuss.

1. Read Genesis 2:18-25 and ask:

• Do you know anyone who expects to find his or her spouse this way? Explain.

• What do you think the phrase "made for each other" means?

• Do you think God has one person picked out for you? Why or why not?

2. Read Genesis 24:1-67 (or summarize) and ask:

• How did Isaac meet Rebekah?

• Have your parents ever tried to match you with anyone? If so, how did you respond?

• What advantages would there be in having your marriage "arranged"?

• Where does love fit into all of this?

3. Read 2 Samuel 11:1-5 and ask:

• What attracted David to his "date"?

• What TV shows have featured similar scenarios?

• What are the disadvantages to meeting this way?

• Where does love fit into all of this?

Love ■ Introduce this by saying that often we use the word *love* when we're dating. Sometimes we're trying to express our feelings, but sometimes our motives aren't that pure. Then read 1 Corinthians 13:4-7 and discuss each of these phrases (from *The Living Bible*):

• *patient and kind*

• *never jealous or envious*

• *never haughty or selfish or rude. Love does not demand its own way.*

• *If you love someone, you will be loyal to him no matter what the cost. You will always believe in him, always expect the best of him, and always stand your ground in defending him.*

Radical Respect ■ Explain that dating can be cruel and unusual punishment for teenagers—there are so many expectations, pressures, confused feelings, and games. But the key word to remember in any relationship with a member of the opposite sex is *respect*.

Have everyone turn to 1 Thessalonians 4:1-10 and have someone read the passage aloud. Explain that this passage has four keys for dating. Have someone read each verse and; after each, briefly discuss the verse and then make the point listed below.

1. Verse 3—avoid sexual immorality

2. Verse 4—practice self control

3. Verse 5—practice respect (don't wrong others)

4. Verse 6—practice love

Respect ■ Have someone read John 13:35 aloud. Have others read 1 Corinthians 13 and other passages about love. Then ask how these passages relate to dating. Emphasize that each person is responsible, before God, for his or her actions; that is, as Christians we must obey God, and Christian love is an action, not a feeling. Challenge them that respect for each other is not optional, it is a requirement, and that it is active, not passive. Give everyone a sheet of paper and have them write the words or phrases from the Bible that apply directly to them in their relationships with members of the opposite sex. After a minute or so, explain that they may have to go to certain people and ask for forgiveness; certainly their actions must change.

Where Is the Love? ■ Look up together the following passages on love. Read them and then ask how they relate to dating and breaking up.

1. Matthew 22:36-39 (love your neighbor)

2. Matthew 5:43-47 (love your enemies)

3. 1 Corinthians 13:4-7, 13 (love is the greatest)

4. 1 John 4:7-8 (love comes from God)

Ask students how they can respond in a loving way in a breakup instead of with hatred.

PEER PRESSURE AND POPULARITY

CROWD-BREAKERS

Acting School ■ Before the meeting, prepare slips of paper with the names of famous personalities or types of people written on them. During the meeting, using teams, have each team send a representative to draw a slip naming a person or type that he or she must act out for the group. This is like charades in that no words may be spoken, and the only clue that may be given is whether it is a "person" or "type." After that, the actor must play the role while his or her team tries to guess the correct answer. Keep track of the time it takes each team—the lowest total time wins. Here are some possible personalities and types; you can add names of people from school and church:

Personalities	Types
Sylvester Stallone	jock
Bill Cosby	nerd
Arsenio Hall	wimp
Jay Leno	"space cadet"
Tom Cruise	party animal
Madonna	druggie
Hillary Clinton	punk
the school principal	"in crowd"
the football coach	country
Charles Barkley	tough guy/girl
Frank Thomas	conceited
Bart Simpson	shy
Mr. Rogers	student body president
Steffi Graf	drunk with hangover

Tie in to the theme of peer pressure by noting how "types" can often be identified by their common actions or style of dress.

The Big Squeeze ■ Divide into teams of 8–10. Explain that you are going to call out a shape. When you do that, they should squeeze into that shape as quickly as possible, with everyone on the team involved. Call out the following shapes, one at a time. Award 1000 points to the team that forms each shape first.

• basketball
• football
• coffee cup
• ball point pen
• Big Mac sandwich
• piece of stuffed pizza
• New Orleans Superdome
• oil well
• sand castle

Later, use this as an example of how we can be *squeezed into a mold* (Romans 12:2).

The Big Squish ■ Bring a box of lemons and limes, two pairs of boxing gloves (or heavy work gloves), and two tall glasses. Choose two competitors (individuals or team representatives—use two guys; then repeat with two girls). Explain that they will be competing in "the big squeeze" and will be making homemade "limon" (a la Sprite). The object is to see who can squeeze the most lemon and lime juice into the glass in three minutes while wearing the boxing gloves. The loser will have to drink the winner's glass of juice.

This illustrates how we can feel squeezed, emptied, and cast aside by others. When have they felt like a squeezed lemon?

Bounce Back ■ Bring two paddle-and-ball toys to the meeting. These are the old toys that have a wooden paddle with a small rubber ball attached with a thin rubber string.

Divide into two teams (boys and girls will work well), and seat them in columns. Have the first person on each team stand in front, and give him or her one of the toys. Explain that each person on the team will have 15 seconds to see how many times he or she can hit the ball with the paddle. After 15 seconds, when you blow the whistle, the next person should jump up, come to the front, take the paddle, and begin hitting. The team to score the most hits, wins.

This illustrates the difficulty we often feel in "bouncing back" from giving in to pressure.

Copy Cat ■ Arrange everyone in a long line. Explain that this is a game of follow the leader except that they won't leave the room or even move around in it. Instead, you as the leader will make a certain motion that the first person in line should mimic. Then the second person should repeat what the first person just did, and so on down the line. They should always copy the motions of the person just before them in line. The idea is to see if you can get at least ten motions all the way down the line. When a person makes a mistake, he or she must go to the back of the line.

An advanced variation of this is to break into lines of ten. The first person in each line should do a motion. The second person should repeat that motion and add a new motion. This should continue until the tenth and last person is doing the correct ten motions in the right order. The first team to do this wins.

Crushed ■ Bring four girls to the front and give each one a glass and a can of orange or grape Crush pop. Explain that this is a race. At your signal, each person should open the cans, pour the pop into her glass, drink all the pop, and then crush the can with her hands.

This ties into the subject in two ways: (1) often kids give in to the pressure to drink, and (2) the brand name Crush describes how many of them feel after giving in.

Domino Effect ■ Bring a number of boxes of dominoes and create a group domino sculpture. When you're finished, take a picture of it, and then count down and push the first domino—and watch them fall.

Note: If you want to use this as a discussion starter, ask: What does the "domino effect" mean? How does this operate in your school? When have you felt like a domino?

Lip Sync ■ "Lip-syncing" (a person or group mimes and synchronizes the movement of their lips with a popular song) is quite popular. This will take preparation, but it can be a lot of fun. Have a couple of acts ready to go and spotlight them in the meeting. If you wish, use this as a springboard to introduce the subject of imitation and peer pressure.

Lost in the Crowd ■ Mark out a course with masking tape on the floor. You may want to position various penalties along the course or simply use a point system and run this as a contest. Either way, choose three or four volunteers. Explain that you will take them from the room. Then they will enter, one at a time, blindfolded, and try to walk the taped course (one foot in front of the other). They will know where to walk from the sounds of the rest of the crowd lined along the course. If they should take a step straight ahead, the group will hum quietly. If they should step to the right, the group will hum a higher pitch, and to the left, a lower pitch. The more severe the angle of the turn to be taken, the higher (or lower) the pitch. At the end of the course (or time limit), the blindfold will be removed, and they will be told their score (or receive their penalties and/or rewards).

Note: While they are walking, you should act as the choir director for the crowd.

Mr. Subliminal ■ This is a skit patterned after the character featured on Saturday Night Live. Two kids are talking: one is John Christian and the other is Joe Subliminal. Joe is trying to get John to do a number of things that are wrong, but his message is said quickly between the lines. The conversation could go something like this (the subliminal messages are in parentheses).

Joe: John! Good to see you (feels good). How's it going (tastes great)?

John: Great! Things couldn't be better.

Joe: That's good to hear (you'll love it). Hey, some of the guys (be popular) are going out after the game (girls too). Do you want to come along (in crowd)?

John: What're you gonna do?

Joe: Oh, just grab a pizza (beer) and go back to Ted's house (beer). Watch a video (rated R) and hang out (girls). It'll (beer) be fun (high). What do you say (accepted, popular, in)?

Quick Change Artist ■ Bring a large box of old clothes and other costumes and props. Ask for two volunteers to act out the characters in a script you will read. After they come to the front, explain that they will have to wear the appropriate costume that they will find in the box. Also, the two of them will play *all* the characters in the play and thus will have to change costumes quickly. So that they won't get confused, each person should play every other character as you read the script.

Once upon a time, there was a very mean KING who was married to a very ugly QUEEN. The KING ruled his kingdom with an iron hand so that everyone, even the QUEEN was afraid of him. Also living in the castle was their daughter, the gorgeous and very well-dressed PRINCESS. But she was lonely and would sit for hours gazing out the window, reading books, or talking to the QUEEN.

One day the PRINCESS was gazing out the window when she saw a handsome form on the horizon. Could it be? Yes, it was . . . PRINCE PASTA, her girlhood boyfriend was riding his horse toward the castle. As he came close, the PRINCESS called out, "Dismount, my love. I shall descend yon staircase and fall helplessly into thy arms so that thou shouldst carry me thither!"

Startled, the PRINCE reined in his horse, dismounted, and walked quite briskly toward the castle, only to be accosted suddenly by a fire-breathing DRAGON. Quickly the PRINCE drew his sword and thrust it at the DRAGON who bit it out of his hand. Then the PRINCE took out a gun and shot the DRAGON who bit the dust.

Suddenly, a GUARD appeared and tried to stop the PRINCE who tripped him and gave him a secret, wrestling sleeper hold. Next attacked a WOLF, and then a RABBIT, and then a DWARF. But the PRINCE dispatched them all. Finally he was in the castle, and there was the ugly QUEEN.

"I want to marry your daughter," said the PRINCE.

"I'll have to ask the king," said the QUEEN. The KING entered the room. "He wants to marry our daughter," said the QUEEN.

The KING answered with all the terror he could muster, "Oh he does, does he? Well, first he must kiss her."

With that the PRINCESS burst into the room. Seeing the PRINCE, she fell into his arms. She looked lovingly into his eyes, and he bravely kissed her on the lips. Suddenly the PRINCESS turned into a FROG and hopped out of the room. The PRINCE spit in disgust, the KING roared with laughter, and the QUEEN burst into tears.

THE END

Ping Pong Blow ■ This may be done with everyone or as a round-robin tournament with teams, depending on the size of the group. Use a Ping Pong table if possible, but a hard floor with boundaries marked as though it were a table will also work. Arrange your two teams around the table, one on each side and no one at either end. Place the Ping Pong ball in the middle. At your signal, the teams should try to blow the ball down the table and off their opponent's side (or across the boundary line on the floor). No hands may be used; and when the ball goes out of bounds on a side, it should be placed back in the middle of the table at the point where it went out.

This experience can relate to James 1:5-8, which describes a double-minded person blown about; often we feel that way when trying to please everyone.

Reversal ■ This game will emphasize the importance of turning peer pressure around.

Divide into teams and have each team choose two representatives who will act as a "worker" and a "teller." Explain that the goal of the workers is to complete a simple task that you will tell to the respective tellers. The tellers will shout the directions. The first worker to complete the task will win. The only catch is that the tellers' instructions will be exactly opposite what they should do; the workers should listen to what the tellers say and do exactly the opposite.

You can give all the teams the same task or different, but similar ones. Continue for as many rounds as you have time. Here are some possible tasks:

• Walk backward to the far wall; turn counterclockwise two times; print your name on a piece of paper, last name first; and then crawl forward back to the starting line.

• Get as low as possible; stretch as high as possible; say, "Wow," as loudly as you can; say, "All right," as quietly as you can; shake hands with everyone on your team whose last names begin with W or below in the alphabet.

Slow Motion ■ This is a skit that should be rehearsed ahead of time. Explain that because of all the talk about peer pressure, you went on campus with a hidden camera to record how some kids might be pressuring others. Right now you want to roll the tape so they can judge for themselves whether or not any undue pressure is being exerted.

The scene opens with a student standing by himself. A boy and a girl approach him and the boy says: *Say John, do you want to come to the party tonight?*

John answers: *No, I don't think so.*

The girl says: *Are you sure?*

John answers: *Okay, I'll go.*

Stop the action with everyone freezing in place. Explain that what the audience just observed was a blatant example of peer pressure, but the subtle nuances may not have been obvious to the untrained eye and ear. You will roll the tape back and play it again, this time in slow motion so they can see clearly what went on. Have the actors reverse themselves back to their original positions (as though the tape was being rewound).

The scene is the same, except that everything is in slow motion and there are the following additions. When the two kids approach John and the boy says his line, the girl should whisper loudly, in sexy tones, in John's ear, *Hey big boy . . . you can come with me!* After John declines, the girl should take out a knife and hold it to John's throat while the boy twists John's arm up behind his back, while the girl says her line. During the pause between lines, two other kids should come into the scene and threaten bodily harm to John and then leave. Finally John says, *Okay, I'll go.*

Squeeze Play Divide into teams. Bring out an inflated inner tube and explain that the goal of this game is to see which team can get all its members through the tube the fastest, one at a time. Time the teams and record their times. Then announce that for the second round, they must go through the tube by twos. For the third and final round, they can go through with any number at a time (allow time for them to determine a strategy).

Note: If your group is too small for teams, do this as a task to be accomplished by the whole group or as a contest between twos or threes (depending on the size of the tube), where they have to begin with the tube at the floor around their ankles and move it up over their heads without using any hands.

This can relate to Romans 12:1-2 in the Phillips version: "Don't let the world around you squeeze you into its own mold." Ask about the kind of molds they see in school and when and why they feel squeezed.

Who Sez Run this like the children's game "Simon Says," except that you should substitute your name for Simon. Then run the group through their paces, seeing who can follow your instructions accurately. Here are some possible instructions:

- stand up
- turn to the right
- wave your hand
- stop waving
- pat the person to your immediate right on the back
- stop patting
- hum softly . . . louder . . . louder . . . louder . . . higher
- stop humming
- recite your favorite poem
- stop reciting
- hold your breath
- start breathing naturally again
- bend at the waist
- put your left hand on your right ankle
- stand on your right leg only
- sit on the floor

Remember to begin most of the directions with "_____ says," but be sure to give other directions without any preface. When the game is over, you can ask the kids if they ever do things just because "So-and-so" says.

DISCUSSION STARTERS

Application To end a meeting, distribute paper and pencils and give everyone a minute or two to think of one or two kids who always seem to give in to peer pressure. Have the students write the names of those kids on their papers and commit themselves to pray each day for them and about how to respond to them.

Assignment To end a meeting, tell everyone to find another person (preferably same-sex) to make a covenant with. They should promise that:

- they will pray for each other every day
- they will affirm each other whenever possible
- they will correct each other in love, when necessary
- they will renew this covenant every two weeks

The Big Influence Ask for three volunteers. When they are out of the room, explain to the group that you will bring in the volunteers one at a time, and that half the group (on the left side of the room) should try to get the person to sit in the chair on the right, while the other half of the group (on the right side of the room) should try to get the person to sit in the chair on the left. The person will enter blindfolded, and the groups may only influence him or her through what they say. Give both sides a few seconds to decide on a strategy for communicating their wishes to the person. Bring the person in, blindfolded, and have him or her stand between the two chairs. Tell the blindfolded person to do whatever he or she wants as he or she hears the instructions from the crowd. Then let the group begin the influencing. If the person sits in one of the chairs, take off the blindfold and congratulate the winning side. Otherwise, stop the contest after a couple of minutes.

Repeat the procedure with the second volunteer. This time, however, don't blindfold him or her.

The third time, blindfold the person, but allow only two people from each team to talk to him or her. They may not touch the person and may say *anything* (even a lie) to get him or her to go the direction they want.

Afterward, discuss the experience. Ask the volunteers how they felt when they heard all the voices, what was most effective at influencing them, and why they chose to do what they did. Then ask how this experience parallels the pressures they feel at school.

Conforming ■ Tell the story of a high school person you know who has a problem with conformity—someone who has tried to fit in to a variety of groups at school, without success. Then ask:

• When have you tried to fit into a specific group? What happened?

• When do you feel as though you don't belong to any specific group? To which group do others think you belong? Why?

• When have you wanted to belong to a certain clique so much that you would do almost anything to get in?

• Who is the "in" crowd in your school? Are you in the "in" crowd? What makes them "in" anyway?

Create a Clique ■ Briefly discuss the cliques at school and how people get into them. Then divide into groups and tell them to create a new clique. They may use any "entrance requirements" they wish, and they should use their creativity. After a few minutes, have the groups describe the cliques they created and how they compare to the cliques at school (for example: Are they based on the same kind of criteria? Are they exclusive? Are they as difficult to get in to?).

Fashion Show ■ Before the meeting, line up three boys and three girls to act as models, wearing the latest styles of clothes and modeling them for the rest of the group.

During the meeting, announce that you will be having a fashion show. Clear a path down the middle for a "runway," turn on soft background music, and bring your models in, one by one. As they model their outfits, be sure to have them stop at various points as you describe what they are wearing.

After this serious fashion show, break into three groups and tell them to dress one of their members in the "fashion of the future." Give each team newspapers, cloth, various pieces of clothing, hats, accessories, pins, and makeup, and allow 5–10 minutes for them to choose their person, design their outfit, and dress him or her. Then have the second part of your fashion show.

Afterward ask:

• How important is "fashion" to you?

• Who sets the standards for what we wear? Is that right? Why or why not?

• What are other fashions besides clothes, hairstyles, and makeup? Which of these are "unchristian"?

• How does Romans 12:2, where God tells us not to copy the behavior and customs of the world, apply to fashion?

Group Think ■ Take three people out of the room, ostensibly to participate in another game. Use these kids as the "guinea pigs." The idea is to use group pressure to see if these people can be convinced to choose a wrong answer.

While the volunteers are out of the room, tell your crowd that during the discussion time later on, you will be asking three questions involving "a," "b," and "c" answers. The correct answer to the first question will be "c" and they should vote for "c." The correct answer to the second question will also be "c," but they should vote for "b." The correct answer to the third question will obviously be "b," but they should choose "a." (To make it a little more realistic, you may want to select a couple of kids to choose the other wrong answer.)

Here are three possible questions. You may be able to think of better ones. Write them on a large piece of poster board.

1. Fill in the missing number in this series: 3, 9, 27, __ , 243.
   a. 45
   b. 75
   c. 81

2. Which figure has the most area?
   a. ○   c. ▭
   b. □

3. Which line is longer?

a. ←————→

b. ——————

c. |

Bring your contestants and have them compete in another game. Then, during the discussion time, bring out the poster board and have the crowd vote for their answers by raising their hands. During the questioning and voting, watch carefully how your "guinea pigs" react and answer. Without giving away what you've done, ask one or two of them why they chose their specific answers. Then explain the trick—that they were set up—and ask them:

• How did you feel when you knew the right answer but saw everyone else voting for the wrong answer?

• Who influenced you the most and why?

Note: Be sure to affirm them for being good sports and give a personal illustration about when you gave in to peer pressure.

Ask the whole group:

• When have you felt like this?

• What are some typical pressures you face? (for example, drinking and drugs, cheating, gossiping, having sex, etc.)

• What would it take for you to make the right decisions?

Inner Circle ■ Draw a circle on the floor in the middle of the room, using string, masking tape, or something similar, and seat everyone outside of the circle. Explain that you want people to sit in the circle if they meet one of the qualifications that you will read aloud to them. Then read the following phrases. After each one, give time for kids to move. Sit in the circle if . . .

• you are wearing designer jeans

• you are wearing Nike or Bass shoes (or whatever is in style)

• you have at least $25 with you

• you are a boy at least 6 feet tall

• you have blond hair

• you live in a house with at least four bedrooms

Afterward, discuss how they felt during this game and how it compares to the way the "in crowd" is formed at school.

In the Halls ■ The week before the meeting, have a student interview several of his or her classmates concerning their views on a few subjects (for example, drinking, having sex, cheating, having abortions, etc.). Keep the interviewees anonymous. (Note: you may want to do this at a mall with kids from other schools.)

Play the tape at the meeting and discuss how the views expressed compare with their friends' ideas . . . and with theirs. Then ask how they would answer some of their friends who try to pressure them into doing something against their beliefs, values, or morals.

Man on the Street ■ In the weeks preceding your meeting, have a couple of students record interviews with several of their classmates (these should not be their close friends) about their views on a various subjects such as drinking, cheating in school, abortion, sex, dating, and others. Keep those interviewed anonymous.

Play the interview tapes at the meeting and discuss the prevailing views on each subject. Then ask your students how the views expressed match with their friends' ideas . . . and with theirs. Discuss how they would answer some of their classmates and friends who try to pressure them into believing, saying, or doing something that is against their beliefs, values, or morals.

Persuaders ■ Choose four very persuasive individuals and place them in the corners of the room. Have everyone else leave the room. Let them reenter one person at a time, blindfolded, and stand in the center of the room. (If you have a large group, you may do this with up to four at a time.) The idea is for each person in the corners, the persuaders, to persuade the blindfolded individuals to come to his or her corner. Each person should take no more than 30 seconds to make the choice. After a person has chosen a corner, he or she should join the persuader in trying to persuade the next one to choose their corner. After everyone has chosen, ask:

• What kind of tactics were used to try to persuade you to come to a corner?

• Persuaders, what was your strategy? When there were more than one in a corner, what kind of strategy did you use and why?

• Why did you choose your corner? What persuaded you?

• When do you feel pulled or persuaded in school? With your friends?

• What pressures have you used to persuade others to join your group or to go along with the group's ideas—obvious or subtle?

• What drew you to your group?

Role Play ■ Divide into pairs and designate one member of each pair as Person A and the other as Person B. Explain to the group that you want them to act out a situation. Then set up the situation by saying something like: *A and B, you are very good friends. Earlier in the day, A was talking with a small group of kids. As the conversation progressed, the group began to cut down B. Person A, you didn't know how to react, and soon you found yourself joining in. In fact, you became the loudest as you said something quite insulting about your friend B. Suddenly, however, the group got quiet while you, A, were talking because they saw B nearby. Person A, you know that B heard you, but you haven't spoken to B since the incident. Right now, the two of you meet in the hall and have a conversation. Take it from there.*

As they role play the situation, walk among the pairs and listen to how they deal with the problem. Some will talk superficially, pretending that nothing happened. Others will take a more confrontational approach. In some pairs, A will ask for forgiveness. Afterward, discuss their responses. Ask why each person chose to act the way he or she did, how they could identify with the situation, and what a Christ-like response for each person would be. Also discuss why A felt obliged to cut-down B, his or her good friend.

DISCUSSIONS AND WRAP-UPS

Belonging ■ Use the following outline as a guide for a discussion or wrap-up.

Problems of Belonging

1. Feeling the pressure of the expectations of others—people do look on the outward appearance, and often they are looking for the wrong things.

2. Doing what others want—the expectations that others have for us are their problem; giving in or catering to those expectations is our problem. Note: God also has expectations for us, but they are quite different from most of the group's. God's expectations are always helpful and healthy.

3. Having wrong goals—the group will often try to define who we are and what we should do; but why should our values and what we are be decided by a group of insecure people who are also looking for who they are?

4. Being subject to group thinking—often the demands and standards of a group are different from the individual preferences of group members. When this occurs, what happens to the individual?

Alternative Ways of Belonging

1. Christians should have the reputation of loving each other across all kinds of "barriers"—all kinds of people are included in the body of Christ.

2. True Christianity has to be accepted and applied by individuals—a group faith that is only a group faith is not good enough.

3. Christians should continue to reach out in love to others, especially to those whom the world has rejected (see Matthew 25:35-40).

Masks ■ Ask: What kinds of "masks" do kids wear at school to hide who they really are? At parties? In the neighborhood? Suggest the following and a few others: the "Escape Mask," the "Aloof or Put-down Mask," the "Clown or Distracter Mask," and the "Clique Mask" (these are taken from *Real Friends* by Barbara Varenhorst [Harper and Row]). Then discuss what masks your students use most often and ask why they wear masks at all.

BIBLE STUDIES

All Things ■ Read aloud 1 Corinthians 9:19-23. Say something like: *We've been talking about resisting peer pressure, but here it sounds as though Paul was giving in. He says that he, "became all things to all men"—that sounds like playing a lot of roles.*

Then read aloud 2 Corinthians 6:17. Say something like: *Here, in another letter to the same people, Paul tells them to be different from the world . . . to be separate. On the surface, these two passages sound contradictory. How can we be all things to all men while at the same time being distinctly different?*

Discuss this for a while. The point is that Paul could be flexible on anything that wasn't important as long as it helped bring people to Christ. But he would never compromise his faith or his Lord.

Resisting the Pressure ■ Assign the following verses to individual students. Have the verses read, one at a time, and ask the questions listed beneath. Then make each point given below the questions.

1. Psalm 139:1-18

• What part has God already played in our lives? What does God think of us?

• What does this passage imply about our identity?

POINT: To resist peer pressure, we must know *who* we are as special and unique creations of God.

2. 1 Corinthians 6:19-20

• Why should we glorify God with our actions?

• What price was paid for us? Why is this significant?

POINT: To resist peer pressure, we must know *whose* we are—children of God, bought by our loving Father with the price of Jesus' death.

3. Matthew 6:31-34; Hebrews 12:1-2

• How do these verses suggest that we can resist peer pressure? How would that work? The emphasis is on our goal and our focus—what should these be?

POINT: To resist peer pressure, we must be convinced that God's way is best, and we must keep our eyes on Christ.

4. Luke 12:51-53; John 15:18-20

• What may be the result of our centering our lives on Christ?

• When have you been "persecuted" for your faith? When do you tend to "sell out" when the going gets tough?

POINT: To resist peer pressure, we must recognize that opposition is the common experience of one who follows Christ.

5. Philippians 4:4-7

• What will be the result of trusting in Christ instead of our circumstances?

• How is this related to resisting peer pressure?

POINT: To resist peer pressure, we must be people of prayer—praying for strength, for fellow believers, and for those who abuse us.

The Squeeze ■ Have someone read aloud Romans 12:1-21. Explain that the phrase, *Do not conform any longer to the pattern of this world* has been translated, *Don't let the world squeeze you into it's mold.* Ask what they think the world's *mold* or *pattern* is, and how they feel pressured or squeezed. Then ask what they can do to be a positive influence, helping others to resist the wrong pressures and to do what is right.

Standing Alone ■ Explain that peer pressure is a difficult problem faced by all of us regardless of our age. We all can be bent out of shape trying to please the crowd—it's not easy being an individual, standing alone.

Then have someone read Romans 12:2 aloud. Ask:

• What does it mean to "conform to the world"? What is "the world"?

• What does it mean to be "transformed"? What is a "renewed mind"?

• How will the "renewing of our minds" help us resist conforming?

• How is all this connected to doing what God wants—His "good, pleasing, and perfect will"?

Have another student read 1 John 2:15-17 aloud. Ask:

• What categories of things does this passage say are "in the world"?

• How are these values reflected in your school?

• How do the world's values compare with God's values?

• How should this passage and the one we read in Romans help you to stand for Christ?

Next, hand out cards and pens and have everyone write down two steps they will take to build their defenses against peer pressure. Then have them get into pairs, share what they've written on their cards, and pray for each other.

16 FAILURE AND REJECTION

CROWD-BREAKERS

And Then Things Got Worse ■ Seat everyone in a circle. Explain that you will start a story. When you point to a person, he or she should continue the story until you interrupt with the phrase, *and then things got worse* or something similar (for example, *and then tragedy struck*). Then you will point to another person who should continue the story where the previous person left off, making the situation a little bit worse.

The first story could begin like this: *This year, I decided to go out for football* . . . After four or five students continue this story, stop it and begin another one. For example, you could say, *I was really excited about my date* . . . . continue until the story gets old or too extreme. Then conclude with, *It was the first day on our vacation cruise.* . . .

Chosen ■ Before the meeting, choose two captains and explain to them that to begin the meeting they will choose their teams for the first couple of games. After a coin toss to see who chooses first, they will alternate choosing team members. Instead of choosing the biggest, strongest, fastest, and most popular kids first, however, they should reverse the process without making it obvious that they are doing so. (They should use a random selection process but make sure that those who normally would be chosen first are taken last.)

After forming the teams, if you have room, play a game of "blind volleyball" (the net is covered by blankets so you can't see the other team; no spiking is allowed) or full participation volleyball (five different team members must hit the ball in each volley). If room is a problem, play charades with popular song titles or hold an indoor scavenger hunt. Use the "choosing experience" later in your discussion or wrap-up.

Hardship Relay ■ Divide into teams. Explain that one at a time, team members should run to the front of the room, draw a slip of paper out of their team's envelope, and then follow the instructions on the slip of paper. (Put all the props needed to perform the tasks on a table in front.) Then they should return to their teams and the next team members should follow, etc. The task on each slip of paper will relate to some type of hardship. Here are possible hardships and tasks to use:

• You are swept overboard at sea. Gargle for 30 seconds with salt water.

• Your parents are getting a divorce. Rip a picture of a family into exactly 64 pieces of the same size.

• You got cut from the basketball team. Dribble a basketball 37 times with your eyes closed.

• Your girlfriend or boyfriend just dumped you. Turn in a circle 15 times, counterclockwise.

• You have the flu. In this order, look real sick, get a very high fever, get the chills, throw up, and crawl back to your team.

• Your pet died. Do your best imitation of the following animals, five seconds each: rooster, gerbil, guppy, alligator, lamb.

• You have to go to the oral surgeon to have your impacted wisdom teeth removed. Act as though your lower jaw is numb with Novocain for 10 seconds and make the sound of a dentist's high speed drill.

• add others.

Hide and Seek ■ If you have enough room, hold a game of *Hide and Seek* where everyone hides and one person seeks. Every person found becomes a seeker as well. Be sure to explain the boundaries, time limit, and other rules. Later you can ask what they considered when looking for a good hiding place, how this game differed from those played by little children, and how they would have felt if no one had tried looking for them.

Imagination ■ Tell the group to use their imaginations to experience the situations that you will be giving them. They should act out the part as they imagine themselves in your stories. Read these situations with appropriate flourish, and allow time for everyone to react.

• Rocky X—You are Rocky Balboa, the heavyweight champion of the world, and it's the fight of the century. You leave your dressing room and stride confidently to the ring, waving to all your fans. Ducking under the ropes, you dance around and go to your corner. Next, you shed your robe, walk to the center of the ring, and shake hands with your opponent—the wild "Mr. U," an alien from a suburb of Mars. The bell rings, and the fight begins. Jab with your left . . . again . . . again . . . now a sharp right . . . a jab . . . cover up. He's coming in . . . he hit you in the stomach. You backpedal, countering with a right. He's coming on and connects with a left and a right. You're hurt . . . another shot to the head. You're down . . . and out!

• Mr./Ms. Cool—It's lunch, and you're carrying your tray from the line, avoiding assorted freshmen on the way to your table. Then you spot her (or him), across the room, the new girl (guy)—sitting all alone (you've been dying to meet this person). You make your way to the table (be sure you look all right with every hair in place . . .). You approach and say something really really "cool" and ask to sit down. Your dream person says, "Sure." You pull out the chair, but suddenly your foot gets caught, and you trip, spilling your spaghetti, mystery meat, and drink all over her (or him). Angry, she (or he) yells at you and walks away. Everyone is looking and laughing. You try to hide as you clean up the mess.

• Shoppers' World—It's the day after Thanksgiving, and you've decided to go Christmas shopping . . . on the busiest shopping day of the year. You drive around the lot looking for a parking place. Finally you spot one, and you race to beat the car coming from the other direction. You do, just barely, but the driver honks and shakes his fist at you. Now you're inside,

elbowing and shoving your way through the mass of humanity. There's Joan—you haven't seen her for months—wave . . . oops, you dropped the shirt. Now look at it with a nice footprint on the collar. Finally you're ready to get out of the mess. Your arms are piled high with gifts, carefully selected during the last couple of hours. You are in line at the counter, waiting to pay. The lady in front of you is taking forever, and the gifts are getting very heavy. Now it's your turn; one by one you give your purchases to the cashier, and she rings them up. You see the total bill—gasp! "Oh well," you think, "it's Christmas." You reach for your wallet—it's not there!

Note: Imagination may be done as a crowd-breaker or as a discussion starter. If you discuss it, ask if and why each situation represented failure; if students could identify with the situations; what other situations would have been good to act out.

In the Cards ■ Give everyone a card (regular playing cards or some other kind with point values), and tell them to keep theirs a secret. Next, divide into two "teams" and have two members, one from each team, come to the front one at a time and expose their cards. Add up the totals for the teams and eliminate the team with the fewest points. Repeat the process with the "winning" team, dividing it into two halves, passing out the cards, and checking the totals. Continue the elimination process until you get down to one person—the champ!—and award a prize.

If you'd like to discuss this, ask:

• How did you fell about losing?

• When did you feel like a failure?

• How does this experience parallel life?

Now Try It ■ Divide into teams and seat them together in the back of the room. Explain that you have a simple relay race in which they will compete. One at a time, each person should carry a tennis ball to the front, drop it into a paper bag, take it out of the bag, and carry it back to the next person who should follow suit. The first team finished wins.

After you hold that race, explain that it was only round one. Then explain that for round two, each person may only use one leg and one hand.

For round three, each person may use only one leg and no hands.

For round four, each person may use no hands or arms and only one leg.

Add a round five, if you dare.

Numbers Victims ■ Choose a few audience reactions like laughter, applause, and cheering. After most of the kids arrive, practice these reactions and then assign each reaction a number. Explain that whenever you yell out a specific number, they should give the appropriate sound.

Keep a lookout for latecomers. Then, as they enter the room, give the crowd a number and let them react. The latecomer becomes an instant crowd-breaker "victim," thinking that he or she has just missed a great activity.

When you get to the discussion section of the meeting, refer to this activity and ask when in real life kids have felt excluded.

Puzzled ■ Bring a few children's puzzles—make sure you have enough pieces so that everyone will have one piece. Place all the puzzle pieces in a bag and mix them up. To make it a little tougher, you may want to include one or two extra pieces that don't fit in anywhere.

Have each person draw out one puzzle piece and write his or her name on the back. Place the puzzle shells around the outside of the room. Explain that at your signal they should put their puzzle pieces where they belong; when they get them in place, they should sit down. Give a penalty for those who don't get the pieces in or who have them placed wrong.

Note: This also may be used as a discussion starter because it is symbolic of our experience of trying to find our places, where we fit into life. Some never quite make it. Others are rejected simply through "chance," not being given the natural characteristics and abilities.

Rats, I Missed! ■ This is a skit involving one person and a wastebasket. Introduce the actor as a great student who will be giving tips on studying. He (or she) then sits down in a chair (desk) with a stack of papers. About ten feet away sits the wastebasket.

He then mentions that he is the world's greatest "crumpled-up-paper-into-the-basket-shooter." He just never misses! After crumpling up a piece of paper, he casually tosses it toward the basket and misses completely!

"Rats, I missed," he mutters, and then tries again. This continues for four or five shots with him missing every one and getting angrier and angrier while each time stating (and then yelling), "Rats, I missed." Finally he pulls out a gun and says, "That does it! If I don't make this next shot, I'm going to take this gun and shoot myself!" He tries another basket, misses, and yells, "That does it! Now I'm going to kill myself!" Then he stomps out of the room. The audience then hears two shots (use a cap pistol) and, after a short pause, "Rats, I missed!"

Right Moves ■ Explain that the theme of the meeting is rejection, a common experience. Then tell everyone to be seated and to move the direction you say if your description fits them. If someone already is sitting on the place where they are to move, they should sit on that person's lap.

• Move two places to the right if you've ever lost an election.

• Move three places to the left if you've been turned down for a date in the last month.

• Move one place back if you've ever been cut from a team.

• Make a sound like Dracula if you've been turned down as a blood donor.

• Move two places forward if you've been ignored by a "friend."

• Move one place to the left if you tried out for a part in a play or a place on a squad and weren't chosen.

• Clap if you've ever failed a driver's test.

• Move four places to the right if you ever got fired.

• Sigh if you're afraid of not getting into the college of your choice.

• Move two places to the left if a teacher has ever put you down in class.

• Move one place diagonally if you are not in the "in crowd."

• Turn around if you've ever felt like a "nerd."

Slip of the Tongue ■ One of the most embarrassing situations is when a person says the wrong thing, puts his or her foot in his or her mouth, makes a Freudian slip, etc.

Divide in to two teams and give each team several sheets of scratch paper and a pencil or pen. Explain that their assignment is to write a few terrible tongue twisters that kids in the other team must say. These creations must be *new* and must have no more than 10 words in them. Give a few classic examples: say *toy boat* five times rapidly; repeat *lemon liniment* five times; say *She sells sea shells at the sea shore*; and so forth. Allow about five minutes for the teams to brainstorm and write. Then hold a talk-off, a contest to see which team is best at saying the tongue twisters. A person from team #1 should draw a tongue twister from team #2. After looking it over for 10 seconds, the person should be timed to see how long it takes him or her to say it perfectly (one minute time limit). Repeat with team #2, then #1, then #2, and so on until you run out of twisters.

Slippery Quiz ■ Print this quiz as a fill-in-the-blank or matching quiz, without the answers of course, and distribute it to everyone. Or give it verbally, with kids competing for their teams. Explain that all of the correct answers have the word or at least the sound of *ice* in them. The answers are in parentheses.

SLIPPERY QUIZ

1. a cold country (d)	a. isobar
2. the top of the cake (g)	b. isosceles
3. "elementary" science (m)	c. isometrics
4. on the weather map (a)	d. Iceland
5. a musical note (k)	e. "I see"
6. leave alone (h)	f. Eisenhower
7. two sides being equal (b)	g. icing
8. hot food (l)	h. isolate
9. two-wheel transportation (j)	i. eisogesis
10. exercise tension (c)	j. bicycle
11. an eye-opening experience (e)	k. high C
12. Nixon's boss (f)	l. spicy
13. reading into the text (i)	m. isotope

Turncoat ■ This is a contest among competing pairs. Each member of each pair must be wearing a coat. At your signal, the members of each pair should exchange coats, but they must always have at least one arm in one of the coats (never may a coat be completely off). In warm weather, you may have to bring coats and do this one or two pairs at a time.

Note: this game, and the one following, illustrate the complications that arise when one friend turns against another. The games also illustrate how friends can work things out by working together.

Turning Against You ■ This can be a contest among any number of competing pairs. Bring a volleyball, basketball, soccer ball, or kickball. Have the first pair stand facing each other and place the ball between their stomachs. Explain that at your signal, they should turn around three times (each person making a 360 degree turn at the same place on the floor) as quickly as possible without touching the ball with their hands or having it fall out. The idea is to see which pair can do this the quickest.

What's Wrong with This Picture ■ Choose three contestants. Give them thirty seconds to scrutinize the room, including the rest of the group—how and where everyone is sitting and so forth. Have the contestants taken out of the room. While they're out, make 10 changes in the room, half by moving people or changing individuals' postures, and half by moving furniture or accessories. Bring one contestant into the room. Explain that you have made 10 changes and give the person a minute to identify as many changes as he or she can. Keep track of his or her answers, but don't reveal which ones are correct and which ones are wrong. Repeat with the other contestants. Afterwards, reveal all 10 changes and give the winner whatever change you happen to have on you.

The point is that most people are trained to think about what's wrong, rather than what's right. We'd much rather complain about breaking a leg than thanking God that we didn't break our neck! We blame God for giving us a nose shaped the wrong way instead of thanking God that we actually have a nose and can breathe.

Wrap the Hurt ■ Divide into two teams and seat them in parallel columns. Have each team choose a boy to stand at the front of the room in front of his team. Give the first person seated in each team an elastic bandage roll. Explain that you will call out an injury that the kids in front have. Then each person with a bandage roll should run to his or her team member and wrap what they think is his injured area. The first person to wrap the correct area wins that round. After each round, the "wrapper" should unwrap his or her person, give the bandage to the next person in line, and go to the end of the line. Here are some injuries to call out. The correct locations are in parentheses.

- sprained, right first digit (index finger on the right hand)
- broken, left, anatomic snuff box (left wrist)
- broken right femur (right leg)
- fractured left talus (left foot)
- acute sciatica (back, spine)
- bruised atlas (neck)
- torn left anterior cruciate (left knee)
- broken clavicle (collarbone)
- severe migraine (head)
- myocardium arterial fibrillation (heart)

Note: do these in any order, but be sure to do the "heart" last.

After declaring the winning team, comment on how difficult it is to bandage or mend a broken heart.

DISCUSSION STARTERS

Charlie Brown ■ Choose a number of "Peanuts"

cartoons where Charlie Brown is rejected. The Valentine's Day episode would be appropriate. Then ask when they have felt like Charlie, etc.

Embarrassing Moments ■ Distribute index cards and pencils or pens. Tell everyone to write two of his or her most embarrassing moments, one at a very young age and one that happened recently. These cards should be written anonymously. Collect the cards and read them aloud, beginning with all the "very young" experiences. Use this to begin a discussion on the causes of embarrassment, shame, and/or failure.

Gotcha! ■ This is a skit that should be prepared and rehearsed before the meeting. Use two students. Student A is talking with Student B and pulling a series of tricks on him or her. These should be performed as a series of scenes, with a few seconds break between them. Here are some to use:

1. A points to B's right shoulder and says, "What's that?" When B looks, A slaps him or her gently on the face and says, "Gotcha!"

2. A points to B's neck and says, "What's that?" When B looks down, A runs his or her fingers up B's face and says, "Gotcha!"

3. A says, "Boy did she give you a dirty look." B answers, "Who?" A responds, "Mother Nature," laughs loudly, and says, "Gotcha!"

4. A points off in the distance behind B and says, "Look! Over there!" B turns and says, "Where!" A laughs and says, "Gotcha!"

5. A says, "Did you know that one of . . ." (mumbles the rest). B says, "What was that?" A answers loudly and slowly, "I said, 'One of the first signs of mental illness is difficulty hearing.'" Then A laughs and says, "Gotcha!"

6. You may want to add others.

7. End the skit with A saying, "Do you trust me?" B answers, "Of course. You're my friend." A responds with, "Gotcha!"

Discuss the relationship between A and B:

• Why was A able to trick B so easily?

• What kind of friendship did they have?

• When have they (your students) had a similar experience? (been tricked or rejected by a "friend")

• What would it take for them to trust the "trickers" or "rejecters" again?

Group Hurts ■ Pass out index cards and have all your group members write, anonymously, something that has been done to them that still hurts. Make sure they write these in such a way that no personalities can be identified. Then collect, shuffle, and read the papers aloud. Comment on the types of hurts experienced by the group, the kinds of hurts that were written by more than one person, the fact that these only scratch the surface, and the fact that these hurts are still felt after days, months, or even years. Also point out how many relate to feelings of failure or being rejected. Then discuss forgiveness in general, how we can help others who are struggling, and how we can bring these feelings to God for healing.

Hidden in Plain Sight ■ Before the meeting, choose a mature student (or an adult volunteer) to be your key person. Let this person know what will be happening in the meeting so that he or she won't be surprised or shocked. As kids arrive, pull them to the side, one at a time, and tell them to totally ignore the chosen person. They should pretend as though the person doesn't exist (not answering, looking past him or her, turning away, and so forth). Later in the meeting, announce that everyone may stop ignoring the person. Then discuss the experience. See how kids felt as they ignored their friend. And ask how the person felt, being ignored even though he or she knew what was happening.

Ideals ■ Give each person an index card and a pencil. Have everyone write down the characteristics of the ideal person (certain to be successful) according to the standards of our society. One side of the card should be titled *Man* and the other side *Woman*. Collect the cards and compile two composite lists. They will look something like this:

Man

tall, wears the right clothes,
is good-looking, athletic or muscular, uses "Brut",
has money, owns sports car,
has outgoing personality,
is successful

Woman

is blonde, dresses well, has blue eyes, is athletic, is independent, has outgoing personality, owns car, has career, has money

After the lists have been compiled, have all the girls stand. Then read off the characteristics, one by one, having girls sit down when they don't measure up. Begin with the easier ones and move on. (for example, "Our ideal woman has an outgoing personality; sit down if you're shy.") Continue until you have only one or two girls left and declare them "ideal women."

Repeat with the guys.

Discuss the experience. Ask:

• How did you feel when you had to sit down?

• Is it fair to declare these people "ideal"? Why or why not?

• What's wrong with society's standards for acceptance and success?

• When have these standards made you feel rejected?

Nelson Nerd ■ Divide into groups and give the assignment of creating the typical "nerd," complete with name, personality, activities, and clothes. One team could have a guy play the part, and another a girl. When they're finished, the nerds should be introduced and say a few words about themselves. Then give each "nerd" a situation to improvise. Situations could include:

1. asking someone for a date

2. trying to be "cool" at a party

3. having a run-in with the school tough guy

4. answering a question in class

After the laughs, ask:

• Do you know anyone like these nerds?

• How do you think they feel about continual rejection?

• With which situations could you identify?

• What could you do to help "nerds" feel accepted?

• How would Jesus respond at your school to "nerds"? To the "in crowd"? To "superstars"? To "burn-outs"? To tough guys? To you?

Rejection Slips ■ Distribute cards and pencils and have everyone record two experiences when they felt rejected. These answers should be anonymous. Collect the cards and read them aloud. Comment on the most common ones, the unique situations, etc., and ask:

• Why did the person feel rejected?

• Were those feelings valid? That is, was he or she really rejected or really a failure?

• Was what happened fair? Why or why not?

Some Total! ■ As kids enter the room, send them, one by one, to a side room (or a corner) where you have a roll of adding machine tape and assorted felt-tip pens. They should write a summary of two or three experiences when they felt like failures (more if you have a small group). No names should be used. As they write, the paper will become unrolled; after each person has finished, the paper should be rolled over what that person wrote.

Later in the meeting, bring out the roll, unroll it,

read, and discuss what everyone has written on it. With each item or experience, decide whether it was really failure or just a problem of false expectations, misperceptions, or something out of their control. Using the adding machine tape, demonstrates how these experiences can add up and make us feel like total failures. Cut out those genuine failure experiences, and burn the others. Then discuss the actual failures, asking what can be learned from them, etc.

Step Ahead ■ Teach this simple line dance to the group. Use a popular song with a good beat and in 4/4 time as the background music. The group should stand in lines, shoulder to shoulder, facing the front, with their arms around each others' shoulders. The first step is with the right foot, forward and to the right at a 45 degree angle. The second step is with the left foot, forward and to the left at a 45 degree angle. The third step is with the right foot, straight back. The fourth step is with the left foot, straight back to where the right foot is. With the next four steps, repeat the process, but this time begin with the left foot; so they will go left forward, right forward, left back, right back. The next four beats begin again with the right foot, and so forth. In effect, with every four beats, they will take two steps forward and one step backward.

If you don't have much room, have them keep their arms at their sides, and have them pivot 180 degrees on every fourth beat.

Afterward, explain that the dance took two steps forward and one step backward. At that rate, it could seem as though they weren't moving along very rapidly, but they were making progress. Then explain how life is often like that, when our setbacks can seem to really set us back. Put these words on the board: *Disappointment, Discouragement, Doubt, Delay, Defeat.* Ask for examples of backwards steps (specific situations in their lives) for each one.

Ask where faith comes into the picture and how faith can help us through those difficult times.

DISCUSSIONS AND WRAP-UPS

Discrimination ■ Explain that children can be cruel to each other—sometimes it's intentional, but often the games they play discriminate and hurt. Ask your students to recall some of their childhood games. Discuss how each one might foster feelings of rejection. Games mentioned could include Duck, Duck, Goose; Red Rover; King of the Hill; Mother, May I? and others.

Then ask about choosing sides for baseball, basketball, spelling bees, and other school games. How did they feel when they were chosen last or near the last?

Discuss the "in crowd" and "out crowd" in high school, and ask:

- How do we reject others, in subtle or obvious ways?
- When have you felt rejected at school?
- How about in your dating experiences?
- When is rejection good?

Expectations ■ Ask:

- Up to whose expectations are you trying to measure?
- What do each of these groups of people expect of you?

a. teachers

b. friends

c. parents

d. society

e. church

- What does God expect of you?
- How does He react to your failures?
- How can and should you respond to this?

Failure Fear ■ Ask:

- Why do we fear failure?
- What's so bad about failure?
- How can failure hinder our future actions? (make us unsure, afraid to take chances, etc.)
- Which failures are more devastating than others?
- What do we do to avoid feeling like failures? (avoid risks, rationalize our failures, blame others, etc.)
- Which "failures" are beyond our control? (those caused by certain external circumstances, by unchangeable physical traits, etc.)
- What good can come from failure? (We can try harder, learn humility, develop other abilities to compensate, etc.)

H. O. P. E. ■ Romans 5:1-2 states: *Therefore, since we have been justified through faith, we have peace with God through our Lord Jesus Christ, through whom we have gained access by faith into this grace in which we now stand. And we rejoice in the hope of the glory of God.*

Build a wrap-up around the letters H, O, P, and E: *Hanging On Promotes Endurance.* Explain that the

longer we maintain, the greater we can sustain.

Moving Forward ■ Use the following outline to challenge students to keep moving forward during their difficult times:

1. *Decision*—they need to choose positive attitudes, knowing, by faith, that God will see them through.

2. *Determination*—they need to determine to do whatever it takes to move forward that next step.

3. *Direction*—they need to ask God for guidance . . . to show them what direction to move, to take that step.

Rejection Feelings ■ Use this outline as a wrap-up or discussion guide.

1. Feelings of rejection are common—we all have them at one time or another in our lives.

2. Often society's standards—for looks, abilities, possessions—cause us to feel rejected.

3. It is important to analyze our feelings and how we handle rejection.

a. We may feel rejected when we haven't been rejected at all. We may just be insecure.

b. We may feel rejected because we are put into situations with very limited options. For example, in a tournament where there is only one winner, the other competitors may feel like failures. Or in an election, the loser may feel rejected by the voters.

c. Feeling rejected does not automatically mean that we are wrong. Our rejection may illustrate how inappropriate or even wrong someone else is. For example, there may be wrong values that are widely held—the values of an entire group can be way off base.

4. We can take steps to cope with rejection and feelings of failure.

a. We can separate feelings of rejection from the reality of rejection. (Ask yourself, "What is really happening?")

b. If we are feeling as though we really are being rejected, we should face the obvious question, "Why?", and we should consider that options may be limited, others may be wrong, circumstances may be wrong and unchangeable, we may be rejected for good reasons.

c. We should remember what rejection feels like and determine not to inflict those feelings on others. Emphasize the importance of a healthy relationship with God, the reality of His acceptance of us, and the necessity to talk to God about our feelings (Philippians 4:4-7).

Challenge your students to reach out and to accept

others with Christ's love (1 John 3:11).

Resolutions ■ Although not many people still make New Year's resolutions, ask how many have and what some of the resolutions were. Then ask:

• Why don't people "resolve" anymore?

• When did you keep your resolutions?

• How does breaking the resolution(s) contribute to our feelings of failure?

• What is a better way to change?

Slippery Slope ■ Make the following points in your wrap-up.

1. *Everybody is on the slippery slope.* We are all human, and we're all tempted. It's easy to fall—it's not easy to stand or to get up after falling and keep going.

2. *Don't think that you will never fall.* Overconfidence is the first foot on the slippery ice.

3. *When you fall, get up and get going again.* Don't let mistakes, failures, or sins crush you or cause you to despair. People will see Christ in you by your positive attitude, commitment, courage, and persistence.

4. *When you are tempted to fall, thank God for trusting you that much (see 1 Corinthians 10:13)*—He knows what you can handle; then look for his way out and take it.

Who's To Blame? ■ Ask: *For what events do we blame God?* Brainstorm for several minutes without trying to refute the blaming. Keep track of the answers on the board. Next, ask students to identify which of the listed items are entirely God's doing and not affected by human contributions. Then with those items, ask how many are situations made worse by human factors. For example, the extensive flooding caused by the rain-swollen Mississippi River happened to a large extent because of human-made levies that restricted the flow of the river, in order to increase the amount of land available for building. This risk was taken either in over-dependence on technology or with an arrogant assumption that God would somehow guarantee our right to build and farm wherever we want to.

Then ask:

• In what ways has the world itself been affected by the Fall in the Garden of Eden and sin in the world?

• How does blaming God help?

Comment that holding God responsible for our failure and for problems in the world doesn't let us off the hook of having to respond the right way. In reality, usually we do our blaming of God very close to home; that is, something didn't go the way we wanted, so we blamed God. Explain that this is

predictable, but what if it were to become the way we relate to God, in a mode of blaming Him for everything and never taking responsibility for our decisions and life?

Use a recent high school football game as a model for the way blaming works. Ask if the team really lost the game because one player made a bad play. Point out that in a 48 minute game, the whole contest doesn't rest on a split-second decision but on what happened during all of the 2880 seconds of the game.

BIBLE STUDIES

Being Human ■ Have a student read aloud 1 Corinthians 10:12-13. Ask:

• About what kinds of *falls* is Paul warning the Corinthians? (temptations to sin)

• What can we do to avoid slipping and falling? (remain faithful to God)

Have another student read aloud 2 Corinthians 4:7-10. Ask:

• What does Paul mean by *jars of clay*?

• In what ways are we *hard pressed on every side*?

• How should we respond to pressures, persecutions, and problems?

• In what ways do we reveal the life of Jesus in our bodies?

Completely Rejected ■ Have kids follow as you read Isaiah 53:1-6 aloud. Point out how Jesus was completely rejected—He knows how we feel when we are rejected. Then read aloud Romans 8:38-39 and explain how God and His love are with us no matter what we may experience.

First and Last ■ The thrust of this study is that God's idea of failure and success is the opposite of the world's. There are four parts, each of which centers on a specific value, uses the phrase "The last must be first and the first, last," and includes a challenge.

1. MARK 9:33-37
Read the passage aloud. Then ask:
  • What were the disciples discussing on their trip? (who was the greatest)
  • What was the significance of Jesus's statements about children? (See also 10:15.)
  • Jesus says that to be "first," a person must become the very "last, the servant of all" (verse 35). What do you think He meant? What does this have to do with children?
Summary: The world says, "I am the greatest," and

that successful people are confident and cool, full of pretensions. To be a follower of Christ, however, we must forget our image and become like children—open, vulnerable, with no hidden agenda, baring our deepest needs.

2. MARK 10:17-31

Have a volunteer read the passage aloud. Then ask:
- What did the young man want from Jesus? (Eternal life)
- What did Jesus say the young man lacked? (See verse 21.) What happened?
- What did Jesus say that amazed the disciples?
- Jesus said, "But many who are first will be last, and the last, first" (verse 31). How does this apply to the situation?

Summary: The world says, "Get what you can," and that success is measured by power and possessions. To be a follower of Christ, however, we must become poor—giving up and coming empty with no hidden security.

3. LUKE 13:22-30

Have a student read the passage aloud, repeating verse 30 for emphasis. Then ask:
- What picture or analogy did Jesus use to answer the question about how many will be saved? (a narrow door)
- What is the significance of the narrow door? (You can only go through it by yourself, one person at a time, and you can't see what's on the other side.)
- Jesus says, "Indeed there are those who are last who will be first, and first who will be last" (verse 30). How does this apply?

Summary: The world says, "Surround yourself with friends," and that success is equated with popularity. So we surround ourselves with people who agree with us and reinforce our prejudices. To be a follower of Christ, however, we must come alone and in faith (not knowing what is on the other side of the door), willing to lose our friends and even our lives.

4. MATTHEW 20:1-16

Summarize the story and read verse 16 aloud. Then ask:
- This is a difficult story to understand. What do you think it means?
- Do you think the owner was fair or not? Why were the workers upset?
- Jesus says, "So the last will be first, and the first will be last" (verse 16). What does this statement mean here?

Summary: The world says, "Look out for number one," and that successful people have a right to be proud. So we want to work our way to heaven or to spiritual

accomplishments and make sure that we get the credit. To be a follower of Christ, however, we must come with humility, thankful for His gift.

Summarize all four passages by saying: Jesus turns the world's values upside down (really right side up). Real success is found in following Him as a child, poor, alone, and with humility. Real failure is failing to recognize and honor Him as Lord.

GIFU ■ Divide into four groups. Tell each group to read Romans 8:28-39. Then they should briefly discuss what they see in this passage that can give them hope during hardships.

After a few minutes, read verse 31 aloud: *What, then, shall we say in response to this? If God is for us, who can be against us?* Repeat the phrase, *God is for us.*

Assign one word from that phrase (*God, is, for, us*) to each group. Tell them to discuss the phrase and the importance of their word, especially as it relates to hope.

After a few minutes, bring everyone back together. Explain that this phrase holds the key for Christians to have hope in any situation:

- *GOD*—the all-powerful; all-knowing, eternal, Creator is on our side.

- *IS*—God exists; He always has been and He always will be; He is with us, at our side.

- *FOR*—if God were against us, we would have no hope; because He is for us, we can always have hope. God wants the very best for us.

- *US*—God's love is personal. God doesn't just love the whole world in general, He is for us.

Encourage everyone to write that phrase on a card and carry it with them (or at least the letters GIFU).

Rejection and Christ ■ This Bible study has three parts.

1. Assign the following verses to students to be read aloud, one at a time.

Luke 9:22	Psalm 118:22
Matthew 21:42	Isaiah 53:3
Luke 17:25	

Then ask:
- About whom are these verses speaking?
- In what ways was Jesus rejected?
- Why would anyone reject the Lord?
- What does this tell us about rejection?

2. Next, have these verses read aloud.

Matthew 5:11-12	Luke 10:16
John 15:18-19	1 Corinthians 1:23-25

Then ask:
- How do these verses relate to the subject of

rejection?
- When were you rejected because of your faith in Christ?

3. Finally, have these verses read aloud.

Hebrews 13:5-6   Psalm 139:7-12
Romans 8:35, 38-39

Then ask:

- What does God promise us?
- How would these truths help us deal with rejection and our feelings?

LONELINESS

17

A NOTE ON LONELINESS

"In the beginning" God pronounced that it was not good for humans to be alone. We were created for relationships—literally, we cannot live without others. Babies separated from their mothers and left alone suffer and die although their other needs are met; solitary confinement is an extreme punishment in prison. We need relationships with others. But there are two types of "others": God and people. The problem of loneliness cannot be solved unless both of these fellowship needs are met.

People are vital to us; we cannot live totally alone. The Bible is replete with guidelines, commands, and exhortations relative to our relationships—from the Ten Commandments to the Sermon on the Mount. Believers are instructed to love others and to gather in community for encouragement and worship.

The basis for loneliness is the absence of love, of significant persons who care for us. It is possible, therefore, to be lonely in a crowd, surrounded by strangers. Conversely, we may be cut off from everyone and not experience loneliness, knowing that there are loved ones who await our return.

Extended loneliness can be devastating. Psychiatrist Paul Tournier has said that loneliness is "the most devastating malady of this age" (*Escape from Loneliness*, Westminster Press, p. 8). It is a universal problem affecting every type of person. Loneliness may result from rejection by others, feelings of inadequacy, the loss of a loved one, a move to a new situation (home, job, school, etc.), or simply the overwhelming feeling that one carries a special burden that no one else really understands. By definition, loneliness is an

intensely personal struggle.

But God can use these feelings to our advantage. Loneliness can help us take a close and honest look at ourselves, at others, and at God. In fact, many Christian leaders are encouraging us to break away from the noise and rush to an enforced "aloneness" and solitude, to meditate and listen to God. There certainly are precedents for this in the lives of Jesus, Paul, and others in Scripture.

Young people need to hear this message of encouragement and challenge. They should understand that:

• they need friends and should develop close, honest relationships with peers, parents, and others.

• God will never leave them. If they have a relationship with God, they can talk to Him about anything, at any time.

• loneliness can be transformed into a positive experience.

• it is good to get away from it all and spend some time introspecting and communicating with God.

• they should be sensitive to lonely people and reach out in love to them.

CROWD-BREAKERS

Belonging ■ Divide into circles of seven. Have each circle designate a person as #1. This game will proceed person-to-person clockwise around the circles. Here's how it works.

a. Person #1 turns to the person on the left, takes his or her hand, and says, "You are _____ (a one-

or two-word compliment). I welcome you."

b. This person then turns to the next one to the left and says, "You are _____ (a different compliment). The one who is _____ (the compliment he or she received from #1) welcomes you."

c. This person (#3) repeats the process with the last phrase being (#1's description) and _____ (his or her own description given by #2) welcomes you."

d. Continue around the circle with each person repeating all of the special descriptions of the preceding people, in order, from memory (no helping), and their own.

e. Each descriptive phrase must be different from the ones used previously.

f. When a mistake is made, the team must begin over. The first team to go around the circle first, wins.

g. For a second round, have kids go the opposite direction, and go around twice. The last person will end up saying something like: "You are 'gregarious'! 'Beautiful,' 'warm smile,' 'nice hair,' 'good voice,' 'friendly,' 'loyal,' 'honest,' 'smart,' 'great eyes,' 'macho,' 'musical,' 'mellow,' and 'act together' welcomes you."

Charades ■ Divide into teams and play charades, using the following titles for them to guess (award bonus points if they can give the original artist): *Lonely Bull* (Herb Alpert), *Solitaire* (Neil Sedaka), *Solitary Man* (Neil Diamond), *Only the Lonely* (Roy Orbison), *All the Lonely People* (Beatles), *I'm Just a Lonely Boy* (Paul Anka), *Alone Again, Naturally* (Gilbert O'Sullivan), *Alone* (Heart). Add others. If you're really ambitious, make a tape of these songs and play *Name That Tune* instead.

Crowded Out ■ Mark a circle on the floor (with masking tape or string). It should be large enough for everyone to fit into it with about a foot to spare all the way around. Give everyone blindfolds and move them into the circle. Explain that when you blow the whistle, they should try to stay in the circle while pushing the others out. The only catch is that they may not use their hands. As each person crosses the edge of the circle, pull him or her to the side to observe the rest of the chaos. Continue until only one person (or a few) is left.

Freeze Dodgeball ■ If you have enough room, play a variation of the children's game "dodgeball." Two teams face off on opposite halves of a gym floor and take turns throwing soft, rubber balls at the legs of the opposition—no one may cross the center line to throw or to retrieve a ball. Those who are hit are "out."

With this version, instead of eliminating those who are hit, those hit must freeze in position. Each team, however, may also have a "melter." The melter can "unfreeze" a team member by touching him or her with a tap on the head from a special wand. Of course if a melter is hit, no one on that team can be unfrozen. A team loses when all of its members are frozen.

Groupers ■ This is an old game where kids mill around and must quickly form groups according to the number you yell. Those who are unable to join a group are eliminated. Alternate odd and even numbers. For example, with a group of 30, begin by having them form groups of 7 (eliminate 2). Then have them form groups of 5 (eliminate 3)—then groups of 6, groups of 5, a group of 15, groups of 8, groups of 3, a group of 4, a group of 3, and a group of 2. To make this more chaotic, play this while using a strobe light. Be sure to have your judges move quickly to determine the losers. This could serve as a discussion starter for how it feels to be left out in a couple oriented world.

Hug ■ Give everyone a card on which you have written four numbers between 1 and 10. Tell them that you will be calling out two numbers at a time in each round. If they have one of the numbers you call, they should find a person with the other number and hug him or her. (You can be sure that everyone gets a chance to hug if you include 1, 2, or 3 on every card and use one of those numbers in every call.) If a person's card contains both numbers called, that person must find someone with another called number and hug him or her. Eliminate the non-huggers and/or the last ones to get together, and continue until there are only a few left. Proclaim them the winners.

As a variation without cards, simply call out a number and have the crowd arrange themselves into group "hugs" of that number. The last group to form is eliminated.

Isolate ■ Have everyone stand. Tell kids to sit down when you read a sentence that applies to them. Continue this until only one person is standing. This will be fun but will also tell you something about the group and their "alone" experiences.

Sit down if . . .

• you've lost at "Solitaire."

• you moved here within the past month.

- you came home and found out your parents had moved.
- you are an only child.
- your best friend did tell you (about your bad breath).
- you are in a class where you are the only Christian.
- you have been put down by friends for saying what you really thought.
- you have been put down by a teacher for stating your beliefs.
- you know someone who seems to be very lonely.
- you recently felt like an outsider.
- you feel funny right now, standing by yourself when everyone else is sitting down.

Add others or create your own list and repeat the process. You can also use most of these statements as discussion starters.

Just Me ■ Before the meeting, cut out magazine pictures of a variety of products or items and tape each one to a piece of cardboard. Possible items could include hair spray, typewriter, dog, cat food, college, tree, hamburger, lake, Coke bottles, book, and so on. Be sure to prepare enough so that everyone will receive a picture.

Distribute pens and the pictures, instructing group members not to show the pictures to anyone else. Have each person find a place away from everyone else where he or she can sit and write on the back of the picture why it is a symbol of his or her life. For example, a person with a picture of a dog could write: "This dog symbolizes me because I am a good friend. Usually my bark is worse than my bite."

After they have finished writing, have everyone turn in the pictures. Redistribute them, making sure that no one gets his or her own. Each person's task then is to try to match the picture with its owner. They should circulate throughout the room and may speak to only one person at a time, asking, "Is this the real you?" When a person makes a correct match, he or she should link arms with the person and together continue to search for the other one's picture-person. Chains of kids will be produced.

Note: This can be light or serious. Allow group members to write any descriptions of themselves that they wish.

Left Behind ■ Have everyone line up along one wall, shoulder to shoulder, with no second rows. Explain that you will read a description. If the description fits them, they should take one step forward. If not, they are eliminated from the game and must stand where

they are until the game is over. Even if subsequent descriptions fit them, they may not move after they have been eliminated.

Draw a description out of an envelope and read it. Continue to read descriptions until a winner is determined (the last one left) or until the winners reach the opposite wall. Here are some possible descriptions:

- You are wearing shoes with laces.
- You are not wearing socks.
- You brought a wallet to the meeting.
- Your last name has three or more vowels in it.
- You have a comb or a brush with you.
- You live two miles or less from here.
- You have never received a parking or traffic ticket.
- The last five numbers in your phone number, when added together, total more than 20.
- You have come to our last three meetings counting this one.

Afterward you may want to discuss how they felt being left behind, the "fairness" of the descriptions, and when they were eliminated by circumstances beyond their control.

Left Out ■ This works best with chairs but also may be done sitting on the floor in a tight circle. Arrange the chairs in a circle with everyone seated. There should be the same number of chairs as participants. Choose one person to be left out of the circle. This person should vacate his or her chair and stand in the center. At your signal, he or she should try to regain a place in the circle by sitting in an empty chair. Everyone else, however, must fill any empty chair on their immediate right.

As the game proceeds, the left-out person is running clockwise around the circle trying to anticipate the vacancy and be seated, while the circle is moving counterclockwise. When the left-out person is successful at claiming a chair, the person who allowed it (was not fast enough at filling the vacancy) must go to the middle.

Be careful because this can get a little rowdy. To spice things up a bit, yell "Switch!" to have everyone change directions. Later, add another person to the middle, vacating two chairs.

Let Us . . . ■ Give each person a leaf of lettuce with instructions to think of a pun using the word lettuce ("let us") and form a sculpture with the leaf to represent the pun. Here are some possibilities:

- lettuce alone

- lettuce pray
- lettuce spray
- lettuce leaf (leave)
- he lettuce around
- lettuce be free
- lettuce see
- lettuce run with patience
- lettuce hold the lettuce
- lettuce (lattice) work
- lettuce entertain you
- we were lettuce-tray (led astray)

After a few minutes, have the sculptures displayed and explained.

DISCUSSION STARTERS

Assignment ■ Distribute the following "Inventory" and have kids go off by themselves and take about 15 minutes to fill it in completely. After they return, discuss the process and their feelings, or discuss how God relates to their feelings about themselves, their personal goals, and their lonely times. Then spend time praying together for each other.

INVENTORY

The real me: _____

What I want from life: _____

Who I love and who loves me: _____

How I see God in my life: _____

Deserted ■ Divide into groups of seven and give each group a paper bag in which you have placed seven prepared cards. (The groups should have identical sets of cards.) Have each person draw one card and hold it quietly. Next, explain that each group has been stranded on an ocean island. There is one life raft with them, but it can hold only six people. Whoever stays behind is certain to die, but only six (maximum) can fit in the raft. They must decide as a group who stays and who escapes and survives. On each card write one of the following:

1. You are very strong.
2. You are very good-looking.
3. You are very wealthy.
4. You own the raft.
5. You are very intelligent.
6. You have a great personality and are well-liked.
7. You are a hard worker.

After a while, ask each group to report by answering

these questions:

- How did you choose who would survive and who would be left behind?
- If you were the one chosen to stay behind, how did you feel? Was the decision forced on you, or did you agree to it? Was it fair? Why or why not?
- When do you feel "deserted" at school? Why are you left behind there?

Drip Sculpture ■ Break into twos and give each pair a small candle, matches, and an index card. Tell them to light the candles and to drip the wax onto their cards to create a wax sculpture symbolizing loneliness. Allow a few minutes and then have the sculptures displayed and explained.

Note: When you do this, make sure to protect the furniture and the floor so that nothing is damaged by the fire or wax.

Isolated ■ Give each person a card and a pen. Have them sit as far apart from each other as possible. Explain that this is a "word association" game. That is, they should clear their minds and record the first word they think of after each word that you read aloud. Here are words to use in the association:

movie	reject	date	happy	test
vacation	face	future	ten	alone
friend	one	funny	solo	Jordan
single	loner	couple	money	solitude
dream	solitary	packed	deserted	meditate

Review each word and have them share their answers. There will be many humorous ones. Note especially the responses to friend, loner, reject, and alone. Discuss these or simply refer to them later in your wrap-up.

Loneliness Hot Line ■ Establish a "loneliness hot line," using your phone number and those of sponsors and kids who volunteer. Print these names and numbers on cards and distribute them to the group. Encourage group members to call whenever loneliness strikes and they need a person with whom to talk or pray.

Lonely at the Top ■ Hand out the following worksheets. Make sure to leave plenty of space for answers.

LONELY PEOPLE?

Why is loneliness a part of this person's job?	What are the benefits of his/her loneliness?	What are the drawbacks of his/her loneliness?
Policeman		

Principal

Parent

President of U.S.

Coach

Class Officer

Cross-country Runner

Writer

Discuss the answers, going through each category and occupation.

Lonely Times . . . ■ Distribute cards or half sheets of paper on which you have written the following incomplete sentences. Allow a few minutes for everyone to complete the sentences (they should not put their names on the papers). Collect the papers. Then take one sentence at a time, read the answers aloud, and discuss them.

1. Loneliness is . . .

2. The loneliest person I have ever known was (no names please) . . .

3. I feel lonely when . . .

4. The loneliest I've ever felt was when . . .

Many Faces of Loneliness ■ Using a VCR or a Polaroid camera, take pictures of everyone's posed loneliest face. This can be done during crowd-breakers, announcements, or discussions. Send each student individually into a separate room for the posing, and then tell them not to tell the others what they did when they go back to the group. After everyone has finished, display the pictures or play the video. It will be a lot of laughs. Next, bring out a poster board on which you have taped (and numbered) a variety of pictures. (Note: Cut the pictures out of magazines and newspapers, and make sure that you have a variety of ages, races, and facial expressions represented.) Hand out pieces of paper and have everyone write down the numbers of the pictures of the people who they think are lonely. When everyone has finished, take a poll on the pictures, seeing how many chose each one. Ask why they thought each pictured person was lonely. Be sure to make the point that everyone is a candidate for loneliness.

Pictured Lonely ■ Before the meeting, collect a variety of magazines—with no duplications. The magazines could include *Sports Illustrated, Campus Life, Omni, Mother Jones, People, Saturday Evening Post, Seventeen, Time, Family Circle, Southern Living, Teen, TV Guide, Us*, etc. Depending on how many magazines you find and your attendance, divide into groups and give each group a magazine to look through.

Tell each group to find a picture or two of loneliness in their magazines. Then have the groups display their pictures and explain why they show loneliness. Discuss their findings and see if there is any correlation to the use of the picture (for example: advertisement, posed picture, candid shot, etc.) or the type of magazine.

DISCUSSIONS AND WRAP-UPS

All the Lonely People ■ Discuss each of the following sources of loneliness. After describing each one, ask whether the kids know any people who fit that specific category—then have them share personal experiences.

1. A poor view of self (results in separation from self)

We fail to see how anyone could like us, and so we end up at home . . . alone.

2. Rejection by others—assumed or real (results in separation from others)

We experience (or think we experience) put-downs, insults, and rejection from our peers, parents, or others, and so we withdraw, keeping to ourselves in our own private world.

3. Loss (results in separation from others, or God if we blame Him)

Tragedy, divorce, or another critical loss knocks us for a loop, and we don't know how to respond. Thinking that no one else understands or cares, we withdraw.

4. Overwhelming personal struggles

Similar to #3.

5. Our sin (results in separation from God)

Sin is everything we do that displeases God—ignoring Him, disobeying Him, putting ourselves before God and others. Sin causes guilt and results in alienation.

Alone: Happy or Bored? ■ Give the following suggestions for making the most of one's "alone times."

• Learn something new.

• Get some exercise.

• Read.

• Rearrange or redecorate your room.

• Help others.

• Explore and deepen your family relationships.

• Think and plan.

Then ask:

• When do you have a lot of time on your hands?

• How do these suggestions sound—how realistic are they?

• Which ones have you tried? What others can you think of?

• When do you have your quiet time alone with God?

Alone Points ■ Use the following points as an outline for a wrap-up or a discussion.

1. Being alone can be an opportunity for us to look at who we really are, to see and appreciate our loved ones, and to move closer to God.

2. Often we are afraid to be alone—we can't even enter a room without turning on the television or radio. Maybe we don't like ourselves or don't want to have to think. But we need to be alone at times . . . to get away by ourselves to think, plan, and pray.

3. No matter how lonely we feel or wherever we are, we are never totally abandoned. God loves us and is with us.

4. Our world is filled with lonely people who need us, need our touch. We should reach out with the love of Christ.

Inside Loneliness ■ Use the opening statements for each point and then ask the questions printed afterward.

1. Some think that one of the benefits of loneliness is that it pushes us toward ourselves.

• What do you think this means?

• Why would it be healthy to take a "self-inventory"?

2. Another stated benefit of loneliness is that it pushes us toward other people.

• How can this happen if a person is alone? What kind of risks are there when we open ourselves to others?

3. It has been said, "Loneliness hurts, but it also instructs."

• In what ways does loneliness instruct?

• What does loneliness teach us?

• When have you found this to be true?

4. Loneliness can also push us toward God.

• Do you believe this? Why or why not?

• How would this happen?

Lonely . . . or Just Alone? ■ Explain that there is a difference between being alone and being truly lonely (a person can be very lonely in a crowd). Discuss for a few minutes the advantages and disadvantages of being alone.

Advantages include: time to think, plan, create, rest, reflect, pray, etc.

Disadvantages include: feeling cut off, abandoned, unloved, deserted, friendless, etc.

Then emphasize the fact that we are never totally alone because God is always with us. (Read appropriate verses like Romans 8:38-39.) Hand out papers and pens and ask each group member to write a brief poem describing either lonely feelings he or she has had or the profound truth that we are never separated from God and His love.

Other Lonely People ■ Ask:

• Think of the lonely people in your life at home, at school, on the job. Why are they lonely?

• How can you be part of the solution to their loneliness? When have you tried? What happened?

• How would Jesus act toward these lonely people? What would He do?

Sources of Loneliness ■ Use this as a wrap-up or a discussion guide.

1. *We can make ourselves lonely; it can come from the inside.*

Loneliness from the inside can come from the fear of exposing the real us to the real world because of potential rejection or ridicule. So we hide who we are and outwardly become a clone of what society says is real. Left like this, we do everything we can to deal with that aching emptiness. Our only freedom will come from finding the security in ourselves that allows us to be ourselves in the world, with confidence, regardless of the world's reaction. This freedom comes from a solid relationship with God, who says that we are important just the way we are and that the real us is valuable. We are so valuable, in fact, that God sent Jesus, His only Son, to die for us. As we become open and real, some people will be attracted to that type of honest person, and deep relationships will be formed. But in the end, loneliness can be solved only by realizing that God will "never leave us or forsake us."

2. *Others can make us lonely; it can come from the outside.*

Loneliness from the outside has many causes, but, more often than not, it results from not fitting into society's expectations. Some of the ways we fail to fit in are:

• We aren't as attractive as society says we should be.

• We aren't as physically capable as society says we should be.

• We don't have the money or other things that society

says are important.

The Bible tells us that Jesus often went to a lonely place to pray, to get direction from His Father, to confirm His course. We need to learn to use our alone times as Jesus did.

3. *Jesus can relate to our feelings of utter loneliness.*

Jesus was in a world where even His closest followers could not understand what was going on inside Him, even when He tried to tell them. (We also experience loneliness when others cannot or at least don't attempt to understand what is going on inside us.) But at least Jesus had His Father.

Jesus was alone in the garden when even His closest followers could not remain awake while He was so distraught that He was sweating blood. But at least He had His Father.

He was alone when He went through the mockery of a trial and when He was abused, marched up Calvary, and nailed to the cross. But at least He had His Father.

When Jesus hung on the cross and died, He experienced utter loneliness and rejection such as we have never known. At that point, He hung suspended between a world that had totally rejected Him and turned its back on Him, and His Father who also rejected Him. He became sin for us. In that instance, Jesus hung alone, utterly hated and rejected.

We have a Lord who can relate to our feelings of loneliness, and who waits ready to meet our needs.

(Special thanks to Kevin Flannagan, Executive Director of East Alabama Area Youth For Christ, for this wrap-up.)

BIBLE STUDIES

Biblical Loneliness ■ Using leaders for each group, break into small groups and give each group one of the following sets of verses with discussion questions to look up and to discuss together. (Sample answers for your use are in parentheses.) Then come back together as a large group and have the group leaders report the findings of their groups in the order below. Note: You can break the sections focusing on JESUS and on PROMISES into two groups each if you need more groups.

JESUS

1. Read Matthew 26:36-46 and Luke 22:39-46.

2. What was Jesus feeling? (anguish, loneliness)

3. Why? (He had a burden to bear; He was facing the cross alone; all the disciples would leave Him.)

4. When was Jesus deliberately alone? (Matthew 4:1-11—temptation; Matthew 14:13—after the death of John the Baptist; Matthew 14:23—for prayer; Matthew 15:21, 29—new ministry)

JOHN THE BAPTIST

1. Read Matthew 11:1-15.

2. What was John experiencing? (doubt, loneliness)

3. Why? (He was imprisoned and cut off from Jesus and his other friends and loved ones.)

4. Why do doubt and loneliness go hand in hand?

PETER

1. Read Matthew 26:31-35, 69-75.

2. What was Peter feeling? (verse 75) (despair, shame, loneliness)

3. Why? (He had turned his back on His Lord; Jesus was going to be executed; all the disciples had fled.)

4. When was Peter's loneliness "cured"? (See John 21:15-19.)

US

1. Read Psalm 66:18; Proverbs 15:29; Ephesians 2:12; 4:17-19.

2. What do these verses tell us about a cause for loneliness? (separation from God)

3. What causes this problem? (self-centeredness, disobedience, lack of communication, etc.)

4. How is this problem solved? (See Colossians 1:20-21; 1 Peter 3:18; Romans 3:24; 5:1.)

PROMISES

1. Read Joshua 1:9; Psalm 23:4; Isaiah 49:14-15; Matthew 28:20; Romans 8:38-39; Philippians 4:19.

2. What promises do each of these passages give us? (God will be with us, never leave us, and meet all our needs, etc.)

3. How do these promises "cure" loneliness?

4. How should we react when we feel lonely?

Jesus and Loneliness ■ Have someone read Matthew 27:46 and Psalm 22:1 aloud. Then ask:

• What was Jesus feeling?

• Why had God "forsaken" Him?

• How does this verse relate to Hebrews 4:15-16? (Read aloud.)

Next, have selected kids read the following passages.

1. Matthew 4:1

2. Matthew 14:22-23

3. Matthew 26:36-45

After each passage ask:

• Why was Jesus alone?

• Was Jesus lonely? Why or why not?

• What happened as a result of His aloneness?

Lonely People ■ Ask: *Who are the lonely people?* List the answers on the board. Answers will include people who have experienced suffering, those who have lost a loved one, individuals who have been rejected, those who have suffered defeat, and those who have stood for an unpopular cause, etc. Then have students look up the following verses that describe the feelings of very special people of God in the Bible. These individuals fit the descriptions of the ones listed on the board.

• Job—Job 10:1-22

• David—Psalm 22

• Jeremiah—Jeremiah 8:18 - 9:2

• Paul—2 Timothy 4:5-13

• Jesus—Matthew 26:33-46

Explain how these men trusted in God, overcame loneliness, and were faithful to their call.

Never Alone ■ Have everyone look up Genesis 2:18. Read it aloud and ask:

• How does this verse relate to being alone?

• What's the difference between being alone and being lonely?

Then turn to Romans 8:35-39. Read these verses aloud and then ask:

• Why are we never really left totally alone, deserted?

• When have you felt as if you were?

• How would these verses have helped you with your feelings?

Part of the Family ■ Use the following verses as evidence for what it means to be a member of God's family.

• John 3:6 talks about being born into the family of God.

• Ephesians 2:19-21 and 1 Peter 2:4-10 discuss the implications of being in God's family.

• 1 John 3:1-3 says we are children of God.

• Romans 8:14-17, Galatians 4:4-7, and Ephesians 1:5 explain that we are adopted.

You also may want to discuss the implications of these truths for how we treat our earthly families and our brothers and sisters in the faith.

18 DEPRESSION AND SUICIDE

A NOTE ON DEPRESSION AND SUICIDE

Obviously these are not the usual "up" topics that will help draw kids to a meeting. Depending on the kids in your group, you may not want to advertise the topic ahead of time. Instead, let everyone know that this will be a typical meeting, featuring fun activities and a serious discussion of a relevant topic.

Depression and suicide, however, are important issues that need to be addressed. Teenagers are quite susceptible to depression with their volatile emotions, intense introspection, and need for peer approval. Teenage suicide has become a real problem (the second leading cause of death for high schoolers), and loneliness is epidemic. Because depression is such a common experience, don't be surprised if you get several counseling appointments.

It is also important to understand that, although these topics are quite serious and should not be treated lightly, you can still have a good time in a meeting about suicide. But you must exercise great care, especially if someone close to a group member has attempted or committed suicide recently.

CROWD-BREAKERS

Bottled-up Inside ■ Choose four or five guys to compete in a Coke-drinking contest. After they come to the front, explain that they can drink only the foam that rises after the bottle has been shaken. (Use 12- or 16-ounce bottles of warm Coke.) Repeat with girls.

As a variation, if you're outside, use the foam as a long-distance fire extinguisher or for target practice (also a contest).

This illustrates the way we feel inside (and how we can "blow up") when our feelings are all bottled-up.

Breaking Point ■ Hold a series of consumer product tests to see which products are stronger. Begin with tissue paper: have sets of kids hold individual sheets and place marbles in them, one at a time, until the tissues break. Repeat with tissues that have been dipped in water. Other products to test could include rubber bands (stretch them and see which one breaks first), balloons (blow them up slowly and evenly and see which one bursts first), paper bags, and trash bags. You could also do this as a competitive team event.

This illustrates how people often feel just before attempting suicide—stretched to the limit and at the breaking point.

Crying Contest ■ Choose contestants to compete in an unusual contest. After they come to the front, explain that you want them to act out the emotions that you will give them and that the best actor will win. Then have them act out the following emotions in order, one at a time: seriousness, fear, sadness, deep depression, overwhelming grief. Determine your best crier and give him or her a prize—a crying towel.

Dueling Jokes ■ Divide into two teams and seat the teams on opposite sides of the room facing each other. Explain that this is a contest to see which team knows the most jokes. Flip a coin to see which team goes first. When you give the signal, someone from that team should stand up and tell a joke. Right afterward, someone from the other team should stand and tell a joke. The process continues until one team can no longer think of any jokes to tell.

Note: explain that the jokes must be short and clean. You may want to give the teams some time at first to discuss their jokes and come up with an order of joke tellers.

End of Your Rope ■ This is a competitive event involving a "swinger" and an "eater." The swinger stands on a chair and is given a 10-foot piece of string with a donut tied to the end. This he or she swings in the direction of the eater, who is standing about six feet away with hands behind his or her back. The eater is allowed to take only one bite per swing and may not use his or her hands. The first team to eat the whole donut wins.

Going Crackers ■ Have a race to see which competitors can eat a stack of saltine crackers off a table without using their hands.

Hard to Hold—So Much to Carry ■ Divide into two or more teams, line the teams up in columns, and give each team 20 balloons. Next, have each team appoint a holder, who should go to the other end of the room (at least 10 feet away from the team). At the signal, the first person should take a balloon, blow it up, tie it, and then run it to the team's holder, who should hold it. The runner should return to the end of the line and the next person should repeat the process, and so on until all the balloons are inflated and held by the holder (if one falls, the person may not return to the team until it is held). After all the balloons have been delivered and held, the holder must pop all the balloons without help. The first team finished wins.

This illustrates the frustration and futility of carrying and holding too much.

I Scream ■ This is a competitive event involving teams of two: each having a feeder and an eater. At one end of the room, place bowls of ice cream (one bowl per team) with spoons. Explain that the goal of the game is for the feeder to feed all of the ice cream to the eater. Here are the rules:

a. The feeder will be blindfolded.

b. The eater must not use his or her hands.

c. The eater will communicate his or her location by screaming, but may not use words.

d. After each spoonful has been fed, the eater must move to a new location.

Proceed with the game and be ready to move the eaters after each bite and to clean up quickly when ice cream is dropped.

This illustrates the desperation of some people and how difficult it can be to reach them and meet their needs.

It's a Bad Day . . . ■ Get into groups of three and distribute papers with the following incomplete sentences. Possible answers are in parentheses—don't reprint those. Encourage everyone to be creative in finishing the sentences.

• You know it's a bad day when . . . (you think the Listerine is apple juice.)

• You know it's a tough class when . . . (you can't help but notice how much the teacher resembles Jabba the Hut.)

• You know your grades weren't good when . . . (an insurance agent calls to say your dad wants you to get medical coverage.)

• You know it's a bad cafeteria meal when . . . (you are physically abused by the mystery meat.)

• You know it's going to be a bad date when . . . (she opens the door and asks who you are.)

After a few minutes, collect the sheets and read them aloud.

How Low Can You Go ■ Hold a limbo contest. Two people hold a stick at waist height and the rest of the crowd goes under the stick, one at a time, on two feet, without touching the floor with any other part of their bodies. Then the stick is lowered. The idea is to see who can go the lowest without touching or falling. This illustrates depression as the experience of being very low.

Lifelines ■ Get a long, 2 x 4 board and drive nails into it at about three foot intervals. The nails should be secure in the wood and stand about two to three inches above the board. Also, bring sets of twine, yarn, or cord. The twine should be cut into equal lengths of at least six feet. Each set should have five pieces of twine tied together at one end and attached to a nail.

Divide the group into teams of five, making sure that you have one team for each nail. (Note: in a large group, divide into large teams and have each team send five representatives.) Bring out the board and lay it on a long table. Place two adults at the ends or at the back of the table to hold the board in place. Then bring the teams to the front, one at a time, put them in front of their nail, and give each person the end of a piece of twine. Explain that the object of this contest is to see which team can braid their twine the quickest and the best ("best" = tight and looking like a braid), but during the braiding, each person must never let go of his or her twine. Answer kids' questions and allow a few seconds for them to get organized. Then give the signal to begin. (Note: with a large group, have the competitors braid on their knees to make it easier for everyone in the audience to see.)

Later you can use this game as an illustration of how we can work together to form strong and tight *lifelines* to our struggling friends.

Pit Race ■ Purchase a number of different fruits with pits and put them in bags according to the number of teams you expect to have. Divide into teams and explain that in this relay each team member will run to the bag, take out a piece of fruit, eat it as quickly as possible, and then spit the pit into a bucket a few feet away (if the pit misses the container, the person must retrieve the pit and throw it in). The first team to finish wins. The fruits could include peaches, prunes, grapes, avocados, apricots, nectarines, mangos, etc. This is symbolic of being "in the pits."

Reporter without a Story ■ This skit can be a light way to get into the topic of suicide, but be sensitive with its use.

SCENE: a deserted bridge (a bench, row of chairs, or a table will do).

A solitary figure approaches the bridge and climbs on it. He speaks:

REPORTER: Woe is me! I am a reporter without a story. I have nothing to live for. I may as well jump and end it all! *He starts to jump, but suddenly someone behind him shouts out.*

LAWYER: Wait! Don't jump! *He climbs up on the bridge.* I'm a lawyer without a case, I also have nothing for which to live. I may as well end it all too. Let me jump with you. *Together they begin to jump when a voice behind them shouts.*

DOCTOR: Wait! Don't jump! *He climbs up on the bridge.* I'm a doctor who has lost his patients; I have nothing to live for. Let me jump with you.

This continues for three more characters. They could include an accountant with a poor countenance, a tall jockey (speaking gruffly) with a little "hoarse," a pastor with a past, etc. Finally, they all decide to count to three and jump.

ALL: One . . . two . . . three! *They all jump except the reporter who rubs his hands together gleefully.*

REPORTER: Five people jump from bridge. Wow! What a story! *He exits.*

Singing the Blues ■ Play "blues" music as everyone comes in.

Tough Work ■ Explain that a lot of people have to deal with sadness every day. Then distribute the *Tough Work* quiz. Tell them to match the occupation with the correct phrase. The correct answers are in parentheses.

TOUGH WORK

1. Always getting down (d)
2. Has the blues (e)
3. Going downhill fast (a)
4. So sad (c)
5. Always down in the dumps (i)
6. Really been down lately (f)
7. Sees plenty of ups and downs (g)
8. Often feels down (b)
9. A depressing job (j)
10. Always feeling down in the mouth (h)

a. skier
b. pillow maker
c. poor seamstress
d. duck hunter
e. painter
f. miner
g. roller coaster operator
h. dentist
i. garbage collector
j. foundry worker

Un-competition ■ This game doesn't relate directly to depression or suicide, but it does illustrate how we often compete and compare ourselves with others in areas where we have little or no control.

Divide into teams with an equal number of members and have each team appoint a secretary. Hand out sheets of paper and pens or pencils. Award the following points for each round.

• 1 point for each letter in every person's whole name (first, middle, and last)

• 5 points for every brother and sister living at home with them (stepbrothers and sisters count) and 2 points for every brother and sister not living at home

• 7 points for every house they have lived in

• 5 points for every person wearing something blue, green, or brown; 7 points for every person wearing something white, red, or black; 10 points for every person wearing something yellow or orange; 15 points for every person wearing something purple, pink, or aqua (note: each person may only choose one of these color categories)

• 2 points for every minute it took each person to get to the meeting (driving straight there)

• 10 points for every foreign country visited

• 1 point for every button that each person is wearing and 5 points for every zipper

• Add the points and determine the winning team.

The Ups and Downs of Life ■ Have everyone sing the chorus of *"Beautiful, Beautiful Brown Eyes."* Then explain that the next time they sing it, you want them to change positions according to the following instructions: they should begin seated, and every time they sing a word beginning with B they should change positions and continue singing in that position until the next B word.

The positions are: lean to the left, lean to the right, stand up, sit down, and then repeat. In other words, when they sing "Beautiful," they would lean to the left. For the next "beautiful," they would lean to the right. Then on "brown," they would stand and sing "brown eyes." For the next "B" word, "Beautiful," they would sit down. Then they would sing "beautiful" while leaning to the left and "brown eyes" while leaning to the right. They would stand on the next "Beautiful," sit on the next "beautiful," and lean to the left for "brown eyes . . . I'll never love." Then they would lean to the right and finish the song singing, "blue eyes again."

Go slowly the first time through. Then try it again a little faster. The third time, go very fast. This illustrates the "ups and downs" of life.

DISCUSSION STARTERS

Affirmation Bags ■ Give every person five index cards, a pen, and a small paper bag. Tell them to write on each card something about which they are depressed or for which they need to be forgiven (one per card). These should include hurts of family, friends, neighbors, co-workers, or other troubling situations. After everyone has finished, have them put their names on the outside of their bags and then pass the bags around, person to person. Each time they receive a bag, they should drop one of their cards in it (none in their own bags).

After all the bags have been circulated and all the cards deposited, have everyone get up and move to a different place in the room. Then have them pass the bags around again. This time, however, they should take a card out and write on the back of it a statement of encouragement or forgiveness. This could be a Bible verse that relates to the specific issue on the card, a biblical principle or promise, or just some solid, Christian advice. (They should not have their own bags yet.)

After all the cards have been covered, return the bags to their owners and have them read what has been written on the cards. Then have kids share aloud some of the situations and the words of encouragement that are especially helpful or meaningful.

Anonymous ■ Hand out the following questionnaire. Encourage everyone to answer honestly and not to put their names on the papers.

ANONYMOUS

1. What is your major cause of depression?

2. Have you ever thought casually about suicide?　□ yes　　□ no

3. Have you ever thought seriously about suicide?　□ yes　　□ no

4. What gives your life meaning?

Collect the papers and briefly scan their answers. Then read aloud some of the answers to question 4 and discuss them together. Use the answers to the other questions to give you a feel as to where your group is.

Choices ■ Explain that many times people can choose to be happy or sad, depending on what they focus on.

Distribute sheets of paper and pens or pencils. Have everyone in one group list the choices they made between the time the alarm went off and the start of school. Have another group list the choices between the start of school and the arrival back home in the afternoon. Have the third group list the choices between their arrival at home land sleep at night. Then compare the lists. This will make the point that our lives are packed with choices, everything from choosing to get up when the alarm goes off to choosing not to cheat on a test.

Hocus Focus ■ Turn off the lights. Bring a person into the room who is wearing an outrageous costume, perhaps a very bright shirt and a large hat. Turn on the lights. After about ten seconds, have the person leave the room. Ask everyone to describe the person, what they saw. Then ask them questions about less obvious details in the person's costume (for example, color of shoes, what he or she was holding, the jewelry that he or she was wearing, etc.). Repeat the process, but this time have two people walk toward each other, accidentally bump into each other, excuse themselves, shake hands, and walk away. Ask everyone to describe the scene. Then ask about the expressions on the actors' faces, who spoke first, which person smiled, and so forth. Use this to show how usually there's a lot more going on that we see; and if we only focus on what is bad, we will miss all that is good.

I Give Up ■ Hand out sheets with the following case studies on them. Have students briefly outline an answer to this question for each one: These people have decided to commit suicide. What would you say to talk them out of it?

• Alice's parents divorced a few years ago, and now she lives with her mom who ignores her and her stepfather who beats her. It's just not worth it. Suicide seems to be the only way out.

• John is deeply in love, but his girlfriend has just dumped him for his "best friend." Life's just not worth living without her.

• All his life Bill has wanted to be a football star. He has just been cut from the team, and so his dreams are shattered. Why go on living?

• Julie was just busted for possession and now must face her parents. They will be sorry and hurt. She has really messed up her life.

• Suzie has high standards for her life— grades, career, boyfriend, athletics—but she just can't measure up. What's the use!

• Ben is so lonely, with no friends. He may as well end it all—certainly no one would care . . . or miss him.

• Jeff feels as though there's just too much to cope with in life—all the hassles. He's tired of it all—tired of living.

Allow about five to seven minutes for students to jot down a few thoughts on each person. Then go through each one and discuss the answers. Afterward ask:

• What are other reasons that people kill themselves?

• Are there any valid reasons? Why or why not?

Joni's Song ■ Briefly describe the situation of Joni Eareckson Tada (a quadriplegic because of a diving accident in her late teens). Then play the song "Joni's Song" from the album of the same name. Afterward ask:

• What can Joni not do because of her accident? (walk, ride horses or bikes, dance, run, swim, bathe herself, plant flowers, hug someone, jump, throw a ball, drive, pound a nail, swing a golf club, etc.)

• Which of these activities do people really count on to give their lives meaning—for recreation, for employment, for relationships, for fun?

• How would you feel if all of those were taken from you?

• What gives Joni's life meaning and purpose?

Mime ■ Obtain the services of a mime or recruit an actor or two from the high school drama department to mime a few depressing experiences. After each one, ask the group to identify the experience, to explain why it would be depressing, and to share how

they could tell that the person was depressed.

Round and Round ■ Seat the teams in circles or get the whole group into one circle depending on the size of your group. The circles should have no more than 15 kids in each. Start with the person whose birthday is closest to July 29th and go counter-clockwise around the circle. Each person should state one thing for which he or she is thankful. No one may repeat something that someone else in the circle has stated. See how many times they can go around the circle in four or five minutes. Afterward, discuss how thinking of what to be thankful for can help defeat depression.

Situations ■ Read the following stories aloud. After each one, ask the students what they would say to these individuals to help them out of their depression.

1. Mary's parents have just gotten divorced, and neither one seems to want her. She loves her parents but feels somehow responsible for their problems. Lately she has been talking a lot about how there's not very much to live for.

2. John's girlfriend, Sue, just broke up with him, and he is devastated. All day he has been walking alone in the park. That's where you find him—sitting on a bench, crying.

3. Marlanne's parents want her to get straight A's, and they really put the pressure on. Nothing she ever does seems to be good enough for them. Today Marlanne found out that she was turned down by the college that they wanted her to attend, and she doesn't know how to face them. "It might be better to get out of this whole thing called life," she mutters as she walks away.

4. Franklin really worked hard in the election for class treasurer, and everyone thought he would win. But he lost—by a landslide. He is really down.

Warning Signs ■ Bring a number of items that show signs of stress or weakness. Hold them up one at a time and simply ask everyone to describe what they see. At first, they will just describe the identity, color, shape, and so forth of the object. Press them further until they notice the peeling paint, cracks, stress fractures, etc. After a couple of items, everyone will catch on and be more thorough in their descriptions. Then hold up a picture of a *distressed* person and have them describe what they see.

Use this activity as a discussion starter about how we can be sensitive to *warning signs* in others, telling us that they are ready to crack or break . . . and what we can do about it.

DISCUSSIONS AND WRAP-UPS

Depression ■ Write the word DEPRESSION vertically on the board and use it as your discussion guide. Go through the letters one at a time and ask for possible causes of depression that begin with that letter. These could include:

D—distance (from a loved one), defeat, death, drugs, dirtiness, darkness, dead-ends, doubt, disorder, delays

E—exit (of a loved one), exclusion (from a group), extremes in life

P—pressure, pride, peers

R—rejection, rain, remembrances

E—expectations, endings

S—standards, stress, substance abuse

S—shortfalls, self-centeredness, sickness

I—irritants, ideals, ignorance, insecurity, incompetence, incurable disease

O—old age, out of control, outside, obesity

N—neuroses, nit-picking, noise

Then, using the same letters, ask for solutions to depression. Here are some possible answers.

D—dreams, doing

E—excellence, eternity (seeing from God's point of view)

P—prayer, perspective, progress, promises, priorities

R—rewards, relationships, rest, recreation

E—excitement, excelling

S—stillness, sleep, shower

S—success, silliness, sports

I—interests, involvement

O—organization, options

N—nearness, niceness

Difficulties ■ Divide into groups of four or five and have the members discuss and record their answers to the following questions:

1. What makes life difficult for high school students? (List as many as you can.)

2. What are the top three or four of these reasons?

Bring everyone back together and discuss their answers together.

Fighting Depression ■ Ask:

• What is depression?

• When and why do people get depressed?

• How does depression feel?

• How do you fight depression?

Grow ■ Write the word *GROW* on the board. Say that this is the key to turning tragic circumstances into positive experiences. Explain each letter as you highlight these main points:

• Know that . . . **G**od is in the picture. You are not alone.

• Understand that . . . **R**eaction is healthy. It's all right to express emotion.

• Stay . . . **O**pen to others and to God. Don't shut them out.

• Be . . . **W**illing to wait to see God work. Time will heal and improve your perspective.

Through tragedy we can grow—God will use those experiences to move us toward maturity and conform us into the image of His Son (Romans 8:28-29).

Suicide ■ Ask:

• How many of you have known someone who has attempted or committed suicide? (Have kids raise their hands.)

• Why do people decide to take their own lives?

• If you saw a stranger standing on a ledge, about to end it all by jumping, what would you say to convince him or her to live?

• What can give our lives meaning and purpose?

Warning Signs ■ Ask:

• What are some of the suicide warning signs— indications that kids are thinking about killing themselves?

• Why would any young person want to take his or her life?

• What could you say to help someone who you think may be considering suicide?

• What else could you do for that person?

Who's Guilty? ■ Look through the newspaper and cut-out several stories of crimes and court cases, especially those that give background details of the defendants. Divide into small groups, appoint group leaders, and give each leader a story and a set of discussion questions. Have each leader read the story aloud to his or her group and then lead the group in a discussion of these questions:

• What crime is this person alleged to have committed?

• Do you think that she or he is guilty? Why?

• Let's assume that she or he is guilty. What should be the punishment? Why?

• Knowing the person's background, should anyone else be considered guilty? Why or why not?

Bring everyone back together and then discuss the experience. (Note: do *not* take time for group reports.) Explain that they probably concluded that all sorts of people and circumstances in the person's background contributed to the crime, although indirectly. Her or his parents, friends, teachers, neighbors, and society in general should also share her or his guilt. But still that person is *guilty* and should pay for her or his crimes.

Next, bridge to the question of suicide. Ask: *Who is guilty when a person takes his or her life?* The point is that anyone close to that person probably shares in the guilt, either in contributing to the problem, in not being sensitive to the person's hurt, or in failing to stop the suicide. In any case, *the person is responsible for his or her own actions.*

Then talk about how we can deal with our feelings of guilt when someone we know dies and how we can be sensitive and helpful to those around us who may be considering suicide.

BIBLE STUDIES

Care ■ Explain that suicide is the ultimate act of despair and that society is increasingly accepting suicide as an option. But it is not a solution. God created us to live useful and productive lives—to bring glory to Him. Suicide rejects God's plan and devalues human life. Then look up these verses together and discuss the possible motives for suicide mentioned.

• Job 3:20-23 (life's weariness)
• Ecclesiastes 2:17 (life's futility and hopelessness)
• James 4:1-9 (anger and disappointment)
• 2 Timothy 4:16 (loneliness)
• Matthew 27:1-6 (guilt and sin)

Emphasize that if they ever consider suicide, they should remember that you and God care about them. Close with an extended time of silent prayer.

Contentment ■ Have everyone read Philippians 4:4-13 silently. Explain that Paul had every reason to be unhappy, discouraged, depressed, angry, and bitter over what he had experienced. Instead, he said he had learned how to be content in every situation (vs. 12). This secret of contentment came from choices that Paul made. Ask everyone to look at the text and find Paul's choices. They are:

• rejoice always

• pray about everything
• concentrate on what is good and positive
• find strength in Christ

Emptiness ■ Hold a 10-week Bible study on the Book of Ecclesiastes, focusing on the emptiness of life from a secular, God-excluded point of view, and the real meaning and purpose in life with God at the center of our lives.

Halt ■ Have everyone turn to 1 Kings 18 and 19 (the story of Elijah's classic confrontation and defeat of the prophets of Baal, and his post-victory depression). Have the kids follow as you summarize the story. Then ask what caused Elijah's depression. After a few minutes of discussion, point out that all of us are candidates for depression. Using an Alcoholics Anonymous acronym, explain that depression will often strike when we HALT (are Hungry; Angry; Lonely; Tired). Then wrap things up by using another acronym, STEPS. When we are depressed, we should Stop; Think; Evaluate (ask: Why am I feeling this way? What is positive on which I can focus? What does God think about me? What has God done for me? With what other person can I share my feelings?); Plan some action (think through and plan specific steps to take: for example, get some sleep, eat a good meal, talk to the person with whom you're angry, do something fun with a friend); Start moving.

Joy ■ Have everyone read 1 John 1:1-4 to find the secret of joy. John says it is fellowship . . . with God and with His Son, Jesus. Then have everyone turn to Philippians, the book of joy, and record what Paul says about joy. Write the biblical principles on the board and then discuss how they are relevant to your students' lives today. Then have students design a plan of action to beat the blues, defeat depression, and sack sadness.

Promises ■ For a Bible study on hope, have everyone find the promises given by God to us in Scripture. Allow about five minutes for everyone to find one or two. Then have them share what they have found and list them on the board. These will emphasize God's love (1 John), His nearness (Romans 8:38-39), His power and sovereignty (Job), His perfect plan (Romans 8:28-30), and others.

EMOTIONS

CROWD-BREAKERS

A Moving Experience ■ Explain that because the topic is emotions, you want to do a little experiment to test the emotional make-up of the crowd. Tell them to do the specified action if the emotional experience applies to them. Everyone is part of the experiment the whole time; no one is eliminated. They must hold their poses until otherwise directed.

Ask everyone to be seated, and give the following directions:

• Stand up if you yelled at someone in your family today.

• Turn around 180 degrees if you were feeling depressed during the past seven days.

• If you are in love, hug the person next to you (sitting or standing).

• If your team recently won an exciting game, jump up and down three times.

• Move seven feet to your right if you are afraid of flying.

• If you hate this game, scream and be seated.

As the Stomach Churns ■ These short skits depict two ways to deal with emotions. You can present them back to back or at separate times in the meeting. Use the same situation in both scenes. The first time through, the characters should respond very calmly, obviously denying their real feelings. The second time, they should overact their emotional responses.

Characters: brother, sister, mother, father.

Brother enters the room (sister is sitting and knitting).

The brother gets tangled in her knitting. The first time through, she responds calmly: "Oh, nuts. Now I guess I'll have to start over." The second time through she yells:" You clumsy idiot! Now I'll have to buy a sheep, sheer it, make yarn, and start completely over!"

Next, the sister informs her brother that his dog died that morning. The first time through he says quietly, "Oh, that's too bad. Well, I guess she had to go some time." The second time through, he gives a loud gasp and then a prolonged cry of grief, breaking down, pounding the floor while exclaiming, "Why me!" Then he accuses his sister of being insensitive.

The next part to this wonderful soap opera has the mother coming in to find out what's going on.

Then, the father returns home from a month-long business trip. He announces that he has been transferred to Bush, Louisiana, and the family will have to move.

The emotions denied and later expressed in an extreme form should be anger, grief, fear, love, surprise, and anxiety.

Calendar Daze ■ Before the meeting, take a good size calendar and cut out the days from two or three months. Each day-square should have the day and the date written on it (for example, Mon., 17th). Keep the days of each month in separate envelopes.

Divide into two or three teams and seat the teams together in various areas around the room. These teams can be as large as 30 kids on each. Adjust the game for small groups. Give each team an envelope and tell them to distribute the days of the month to members. (Note: for teams under 30, members may have more than one day each.) Explain that you will be calling out descriptions of various days (for example, all Tuesdays). The first team to have all the correct days and stand together, wins that round. Here are the days to call:

• tomorrow

• the day that is two weeks from next Wednesday

• the first and third Mondays of the month

• all Sundays

• odd numbered Thursdays

• the third full week of the month

• all the days with a "1" in them

• the whole month, lined-up in order

After collecting the papers and calming everyone down, have someone read aloud Matthew 6:33-34. Note especially verse 34 which states: *Therefore do not worry about tomorrow, for tomorrow will worry about itself. Each day has enough troubles of its own.* (Note: *The Living Bible* translates this last phrase, *God will take care of your tomorrows too; live one day at a time.*) Discuss how this verse relates to their fears, especially about the future.

Drop and Pop ■ Divide into teams and line them up in parallel columns at one end of the room. Give the first person in each team a balloon. Then explain that the goal of the game is to score as many points as possible in four minutes by touching the opposite wall with an inflated balloon. At your signal, the first person should blow up his or her balloon, tie it, run to the far wall, return, hand the balloon to the next team member who follows suit. The only catch, however, is that every time the whistle blows, all those who have inflated balloons, must break them by dropping to the floor and sitting on them. The next person in line, then, must get a new balloon from the balloon person, inflate and tie it, and continue the relay. Be sure to assign counters (adult helpers who count how many balloons touch the wall) and a whistle-blower who should blow the whistle about every 10–15 seconds.

Note: this illustrates how the pursuit of our personal goals can be altered by a shattering experience.

E-Motion ■ Choose three or four contestants and explain that their task is to guess the emotions that the audience will be acting out (or, to make it more difficult, have them shout out the emotion that is opposite of the one being acted). Explain further that they will stand in front, facing the crowd, while behind them an assistant will hold up a card with an emotion written on it. As soon as it is raised, the crowd should act and the contestants should guess. The person with the most correct answers wins. Use these emotions: joy, anxiety, dismay, jealousy, romance, fear, dislike, depression, anger, sadness, love, and hate. Play "Feelings," "I Second That Emotion," or another song about emotions as background music during the activity.

Emotional Events ■ Choose a number of contestants to compete in one or more of the following contests:

1. *An Onion-peeling Contest.* Use small onions and don't have them too close to the audience. The first person to peel the onion wins.

2. *Laugher of the Year.* Contestants laugh and are rated on originality, sincerity, facial expressions, and musicality.

3. *Best Angry Facial Expression.*

4. *Keeping Calm.* A guy must be able to keep his cool while a good-looking girl runs her fingers through his hair and whispers sweet nothings in his ear.

Feelings (A Touching Scene) ■ Choose four or five volunteers (or team representatives) and seat them in front, facing the rest of the crowd. Explain that they will be blindfolded and handed various items that they should try to identify by touching (no smelling or tasting). The crowd may not give any help. Pass the first item all the way down the line, and then have them guess out loud. Award points for each correct guess. (If your blindfolds can be removed and replaced easily, remove them after each item to allow the contestants to see the item.) To make the contest more difficult, or if contestants seem to be changing their ideas when they hear other guesses, give them different, but equally difficult, items each round.

Possible mystery items could include: nutcracker, staple remover, protractor, golf shoe-cleat tightener, mango, Anthony silver dollar, back scratcher, Mardi Gras dubloon, plate of shaving cream, egg separator, etc.

Let It All Out ■ Use as many teams as you wish and give each team a tablet of paper and a pen. Explain that you have compiled a list of clichés about anger. One person at a time from each team should come to you to receive a cliché. Then they must return to their teams and draw a picture of it. The first team to guess the phrase wins that round, and the winner of the most rounds wins the game. There can be no talking by the drawer, and he or she must draw only pictures (no letters). Possible clichés to use include: hot head, teed off, burns me up, blow up, short fuse, pet peeves, flying off the handle, blew his stack, the last straw, boiling point, thin skinned.

Mad Magazine ■ Type the angry phrases listed below (and others) on individual slips of paper. Make sure you have a slip of paper for everyone. Type duplicates if necessary.

Pass out the phrases. Then distribute old magazines, pieces of cardboard, scissors, and tape. Explain that each person should create a picture of his or her phrase using the pictures (no words) from the magazines. After they have finished, have them display their pictures while the rest of the group guesses the phrase.

• she flipped her wig
• she vents her spleen
• she raised the roof
• he was beside himself
• he did a slow burn
• she jumped down his throat
• she looked daggers
• he gnashed his teeth
• he was in a blind rage
• he bit her head off
• she threw a fit
• he got his nose out of joint
• he blew his stack
• he flew off the handle
• she went bananas
• he spit nails

Running the Gamut ■ This is a relay involving teams. Seat the teams on the floor in parallel columns. Explain that at your signal, the first person from each team should run to the front of the room, pull a slip of paper out of his or her team's bag, and then make a facial expression to reflect the emotion written on that slip of paper. When the team correctly identifies the emotion being portrayed, the person should go to the back of his or her team. Then the next person at the front should repeat the process. The first team to finish, wins.

Here are some emotions to write on the slips of paper: elation, fear, love, depression, hatred, hurt, exhilaration, anger, excitement, grief, frustration, worry, curiosity, happiness, apathy, ecstasy, and angst. Make the sets of emotions identical for each team.

Signs and Signals ■ This game is a form of charades. Divide into teams. Team members take turns pulling slips of paper on which a "sign" is written or drawn. The player acts out the sign so that his or her team can guess it. Each person is timed to see how long it takes the team to guess the correct sign. The team with the lowest total time wins. Here are some possible signs:

• Right Turn Only
• Entrance
• Stop
• Deer Crossing
• Exit
• Slippery When Wet
• No U-turn
• Watch for Falling Rocks
• RR Crossing
• Soft Shoulder
• Danger
• Caution
• Yield
• Don't Feed the Bears
• No Left Turn
• Wet Paint
• Beware of Dog
• Sharp Curve

This ties in with the idea that our emotions are warning signs, alerting us to things about ourselves.

The General Days of All My Children ■ This is a skit involving the following characters: Director (he or she opens the show for the audience, instructs the actors, and corrects their bad acting); Mother (hair in curlers, wearing an apron); Father (wearing a coat, white shirt, and tie); Mother-in-law (guy dressed like a woman); Son; Daughter; Mailman (the last person to appear in each scene carrying a mail bag, he always delivers a "special delivery letter" with a different message each time. These messages should be a surprise to the rest of the cast); Meter Reader (who enters at a different time in each scene and simply announces that he or she is "here to read the meter").

SCRIPT

(Fill in the gaps yourself or with ad-libbing.)

The Director calls the cast together in front of the audience and explains that he or she has confidence in them because of their great talent and because they are professionals. Then the director has the cast take their places, and he or she calls for action.

Note: All of the lines in this scene should be

deadpanned, delivered in almost a monotone, devoid of feeling.

Mother is at the stove. Father enters and sits in a chair.

MOTHER: Hi, dear. How was your day?

FATHER: Fine . . . I got fired.

MOTHER: Oh, by the way, I had a little trouble with the car in the driveway.

FATHER: I noticed the garage missing. Say, what's for dinner?

MOTHER: Liver and peanut butter casserole.

FATHER: Let's see . . . that's the third time this week, isn't it?

MOTHER: Fourth. Oh, I forgot to tell you; Mother's here.

FATHER: Whose?

MOTHER: Mine, and here she comes now.

FATHER: What a surprise.

(Mother-in-law enters and speaks to Father.)

MOTHER-IN-LAW: Hello, Stupid.

FATHER: Hello, Mother. How long will you be staying with us?

MOTHER-IN-LAW: Three months. *(To her daughter)* I told you: you should have married Frank. He's so handsome and is now a millionaire. But noooo, you had to throw your life away and marry this slob!

SON: *(enters and announces)* I need the car for my date tonight.

FATHER: It's under the garage. By the way, your dog died in the accident.

DAUGHTER: *(enters and announces)* I won't be here for dinner. I'm running off with Freddie to join the commune-cult in Columbia.

Daughter and Son begin arguing; Mother and Father begin discussing; Mother-in-law mumbles to herself.

Mailman enters with special delivery letter that Mother takes and reads aloud (informing them that their house is being foreclosed or that Grandma is tied to the railroad tracks or that the high school has burned down, etc.).

At this point, the director should storm in, call the cast together, and berate them for their poor acting. After reminding them of a few of the tragic moments in the play, he or she should tell them to do it over—with feeling!

This time through, the lines are essentially the same except that they should be delivered with great emotion—intensely overacted. The emotions displayed should include shock, anger, fear, grief, disgust, etc., and the actors should use very dramatic gestures and other body language.

After the special delivery letter has been read, the director again should charge onto the set and call the cast together. In this pep talk/lecture, he should explain that life isn't that tragic and that they should lighten up a bit. Then he or she should send them to their places, and they should repeat the scene. This time, however, the cast should deliver all the lines (and react to them) with extreme humor and laughter. Finally, the special delivery letter is delivered—it contains their "pink slips" (they are fired). The director then should clear the set.

Ups and Downs of Life ■ Choose two of your best performers to act out the following script. They should overact the appropriate positive and negative emotions as they read their lines.

BOB: Hey Bill, how's it going?

BILL: Well, Bob, I'm not so sure. I had quite a day. First of all, I had a great night's sleep.

BOB: Hey that's good!

BILL: No, it's bad. I was supposed to get up early for an appointment, and I overslept.

BOB: That's terrible!

BILL: No, the person I was supposed to see forgot about our appointment—so now he owes me one.

BOB: Hey, that's great!

BILL: Not quite. In the rush to get there, I got in an accident.

BOB: Oh, no! That's terrible.

BILL: Well, it was her fault—now I can get a new car!

BOB: Fantastic!

BILL: Except for one thing. The girl who hit me is that blonde from chemistry that I've been trying to get a date with for a month. Now I feel really rotten.

BOB: Oh, yeah, that's too bad.

BILL: But she felt worse, and I think she might be willing to go out with me now.

Add your own extra lines.

What Am I Feeling? ■ Make a list of as many emotions or feelings as you can (at least 30). Randomly select sets of three (or five with a very small group) of these emotions and write them on self-adhesive labels. It's all right to repeat some of them.

As kids enter the room, put a label on each person's back, being careful that he or she doesn't see what is written on it. After everyone has been labeled, explain that they are to circulate throughout the crowd, asking individuals, "What am I feeling?" The person asked should act out one of the feelings on the "asker's" card. Then the asker is allowed to have one guess, after which he or she will be told whether or not the guess is correct. The goal is to figure out all the emotions written on one's card.

DISCUSSION STARTERS

Assignment ■ Tell your group members to carry around a card for the next week. On it they should list the specific situations and the feelings they evoke when they arise. Each evening they should review the card for that day and talk to God about the situations and their responses.

Care Cast ■ Give each person a set of five blank cards (all the cards should be the same size, but they may be as small as 1 1/2 x 2 1/2). Distribute pens or pencils and have everyone write their initials on each card. Then tell them to write one worry, fear, or care on each card. Collect the pencils/pens and have everyone hold their cards. Next, bring out a cardboard box and place it at the front of the room. Explain that this is a contest to see who can flip their cards into the box. Note: they may not fold or bend the cards at all. Depending on the size of your crowd, you can have them flip the cards all at once or one person at a time. Afterwards, pull the cards out of the box one at a time and identify the owner (do *not* read the worry). Award 100 points for each card in the box to determine the winner. Then pick-up all the cards and drop them in the box.

Have someone read 1 Peter 5:7 aloud. It says, *Cast all your anxiety on Him because He cares for you.* Ask:

• What kinds of anxieties, cares, and worries did you list on your cards?

• Why should we *cast* our anxiety on Christ?

• How can we give Him our cares?

Then take all the cards and burn them in the fireplace. Have everyone spend time in silent prayer as the cards burn, turning over their worries to God.

Color Me ■ Pass out cards or pieces of paper to everyone. Also make available a large box of crayons with extra amounts of the appropriate colors. Tell them that their assignment is to draw a picture, graph, diagram, or other symbol representing their lives from an emotional standpoint. That is, what they are really like on the inside. Tell them that the following colors represent specific emotions: blue = sad; red =

angry; green = jealous; silver = cool (unemotional); pink = living (romantic); gray = blah (depression); yellow = happy (joyful)

Then have them get into groups of two or more and explain their symbols to each other. If that's too threatening, close this by taking a few moments for silent prayer. Ask each person to tell God about his or her drawing and ask His help in accepting and harnessing those emotions.

Diary ■ Suggest that your group members keep an "emotional diary" for a week, recording their feelings and the reasons for each feeling. After a week, they should meet with another person from the group, share their diaries, and pray for each other.

Feelings Gallery ■ Cut out pictures from magazines and newspapers that display a variety of emotions. (Use at least ten pictures.) Post these around the room. Distribute paper and pencils and tell the group to check out the pictures as though they were art critics. On their papers, they should record each picture's number and the emotion they think it is portraying.

After everyone has finished, collect the pictures, hold them up one at a time, and invite critiques. You may wish to discuss each picture briefly, especially when there is a wide disparity in the responses.

I Feel ■ Distribute pencils or pens and copies of the *I FEEL* sheet. Have kids finish the sentences honestly and anonymously.

I FEEL

1. *I feel happy when* . . .

2. *I feel depressed when* . . .

3. *I feel excited when* . . .

4. *I feel loved when* . . .

5. *I feel hurt when* . . .

6. *I feel emotionally abused when* . . .

Collect the sheets and read some of the answers for each sentence aloud, one sentence at a time. Then ask:

• What comes to mind when you hear the phrase *emotionally abused*?

• In what ways might a person be emotionally handicapped?

• What might cause a person to hate himself or herself?

• What can a person do to recover from emotional abuse?

• How can God help a person deal with his or her emotions?

In Everything ■ Read aloud 1 Thessalonians 5:18: *Give thanks in all circumstances, for this is God's will for you in Christ Jesus.* Explain that this says to give thanks *in* all circumstances, not necessarily *for* everything that happens. We should thank God for who He is, for His sovereignty, and for what He is teaching us and doing in our lives. Then lead them in a group response. Explain that you will read them a series of descriptions of circumstances. After each one, as a group, they should say together, *Thank you, God!*

• *I just won the election, and I want to say . . .*

• *The grades came out today, and I didn't do as well as I expected. But I can pray . . .*

• *My best friend got the part in the play that I really wanted . . .*

• *I just leaned that I was chosen for the homecoming court . . .*

• *I am small for my age and often I am picked on at school, but I can say . . .*

• *I live in a house that is more like a battlefield than a home, but . . .*

• *The love of my life just dumped me, and I'm devastated. But still I will . . .*

• *I just learned that I have mono and won't be able to take the trip I've been saving and waiting for, but I can say . . .*

• *My mom has cancer. I'm wiped out emotionally and don't know what I'll do, but . . .*

Afterward, discuss how they felt repeating the phrase after various descriptions (for example, which ones were easy, realistic, difficult, and so forth). Then discuss how we can be truly thankful *in* every circumstance.

In the Mood ■ Give everyone a pencil and a piece of paper with these emotions listed. After each emotion, they should write a situation where they usually experience that specific emotion.

• fear

• love

• sadness

• hate

• joy

• hurt

• bitterness

Collect the papers and read the answers, one emotion at a time (be sure to keep the papers anonymous). When you get to a situation with which a number of kids seem to identify, stop and ask:

1. Why is this such a (fearful) situation?

2. How do you act when you feel this way?

3. What effects do your actions have on you? On others?

Locate That Feeling ■ Read a list of locations and situations and ask the group what kinds of feelings each one evokes. If you get an unusual answer, probe further to discover why. Here are some possible locations. Add others.

• a the top of the Sears Tower, looking over the edge

• at an ocean beach, walking in the surf

• alone in a dark, silent cave . . . you feel something on the back of your neck

• jammed into a packed stadium for the Super Bowl

• poised at the top of a black diamond ski run, ready to descend

• alone in a large, beautiful cathedral

• walking slowly through a park on a sunny, spring afternoon

• in a cemetery, standing by a friend's grave

• looking through your family photo album

Picture This! ■ Select a number of pictures from magazines and newspapers, showing people in a wide range of emotional situations. Hold up one picture at a time and ask the group to shout out the emotion the picture expresses to them. List their responses. When you run out of pictures, ask if there are any other common emotions that you haven't shown. Add these to your list. Then go through the list again and discuss the following questions for as many of the emotions as you have time for.

• What kind of situation or experience can set off this emotion?

• How is _____ (the emotion) usually expressed?

• How can a person respond constructively to _____ (the emotion) when it hits?

Then comment that our emotions not only affect how we relate to ourselves and to others, they also affect our attitudes toward God. Set the stage for honest discussion by sharing a time when your own emotions influenced your feelings toward God.

Poll ■ Hand out the following questionnaire. Give them a "feeling"—they should write it in the space that is most appropriate. Then give them a minute or two to fill in the last few lines. After everyone has finished, find out which feelings fell into which categories. Then invite volunteers to share what they wrote at the bottom.

WHAT DO YOU DO WITH A FEELING?

_____	Express it
_____	Keep it to myself
_____	Take it out on someone else
_____	Hide, cover it up
_____	Translate it into physical activity
_____	Suppress it
_____	Pretend it's not there
_____	Laugh about it
_____	I don't know what to do
_____	Other

Relate an experience that you had with emotions and what you did to deal with your feelings:

_____

_____

_____ .

Tools of Emotion ■ Read a number of emotions, one at a time, and ask what "tools" are commonly used to help express these feelings, and which ones they use. Here are some possibilities:

• grief (tissue paper)

• anger (paper and pen)

• hate (fist)

• fear (mask)

• love (gift)

• joy (music)

Worry Up ■ Explain that some people worry about everything. Then give the following situations and have everyone suggest what a worrier might worry about in each one. Tell them to use their imaginations and to suggest all sorts of possibilities.

• world events

• choosing a new president (USA)

• buying a used car

• buying new clothes

• flying in an airplane

• going to a college basketball game

• going to the dentist

• starting a new school

• giving a speech in English class

• going on a date

Explain how some of our worries seem pretty silly.

Then ask:

• What's wrong with worrying so much? How can worry hurt us?

• Why do some people seem to worry about everything?

• What kinds of situations or relationships worry you the most?

• What's the difference between worry and concern?

• What worries and concerns do you have about the next year?

• How can God help alleviate your worries?

DISCUSSIONS AND WRAP-UPS

Common Emotions ■ Ask:

• What emotions are most common to you? When?

• How do your mood changes affect you? Others?

• How do you handle your emotions?

• What would you like to change about the way your emotions and moods affect you?

Dealing With Emotions ■ This can be a wrap-up or a discussion guide. Summarize what you've learned in your discussions about emotions, then remind the group that:

1. An emotion is a physical response to a thought.

2. Emotions are not wrong.

3. We should analyze our feelings to discover the cause of our emotions because there's always something behind them.

4. We must learn to control, not stifle, our emotions:

    a. channeling them toward positive behavior

    b. minimizing any negative effects

    c. expressing them appropriately

5. Jesus said that we are to be in the world but not of the world (John 17:15-18). The world lives on and for feelings without controlling them. But we should be different (2 Corinthians 5:17), and our actions should express Christ's love (1 Corinthians 13; 1 John 3:17).

Grave Clothes ■ Summarize the story in John 11 about Jesus raising Lazarus from the dead. Read aloud verses 38-44. Explain that Jesus had proclaimed His power over death (_I am the resurrection and the life. He who believes in Me will live, even though he dies; and whoever lives and believes in Me will never die_—11:25-26). Then Jesus proved the truth of His claim by raising

Lazarus from the dead (verses 43-44).

Point out the fact that something had to happen after that dramatic event, before Lazarus could resume a normal life—he had to be unwrapped from the strips of linen and the grave clothes (verse 44).

Explain that what happened to Lazarus is what needs to happen to people who have been emotionally abused. First, they need the power of Christ to renew their spirits and bring them to life again. Then they need to be unwrapped, to get rid of the layers of *grave clothes* surrounding them. The person has become new on the inside (2 Corinthians 5:17), but the rags of the old life still cling to him or her.

Explain that a person can begin to remove those grave clothes by admitting his or her problem, finding and facing the source of the abuse, talking honestly to close friends about the situation, and reaching out to others in love. Those steps are part of the recovery process.

Handling Emotions ■ Use this as a guide for a wrap-up or discussion. Two of the most important steps in handling emotions and not letting them control us are:

1. Acknowledging them.

2. Expressing them in a positive manner.

We can acknowledge our emotions by being honest with ourselves about our feelings. One very positive way of expressing our emotions is to be open with others and with God about our feelings.

Importance of Feelings ■ Use this as a wrap-up or a discussion guide.

1. Our lives are full of feelings.

2. Our feelings and how we show them will determine the quality of our friendships.

3. We learn to know ourselves better as we share our feelings with other people.

God created us as emotional beings able to feel deeply. These emotions touch all areas of our lives: home, neighborhood, school, friendships. Because God created us and declared His creation good, emotions, as such, certainly are not bad. Even "negative" emotions like hate, anger, and fear are not wrong in themselves. They are just there. Paul said, "Be angry and sin not" (Ephesians 4:26). Evidently what is really important is what we do with our feelings, how we respond. Anger can hurt and destroy, but it can also motivate and energize us to positive action. The same can be said for fear, hate, and even love.

Of course, our feelings may be irrational. That is, they may result from misconceptions of persons, things, or situations. As we get in touch with our feelings, we can deal with them and deal with life.

Remember that Jesus wants to be Lord of all of life, including our emotions and the source of our feelings . . . and how we act on them.

Remember ■ Use this as a wrap-up or a discussion guide.

• Emotions are real, and they are part of your physical and psychological makeup. Acknowledge them—don't pretend that they do not exist. Don't repress or try to bury them. They affect you and others.

• Recognize that sometimes your emotions are related to your physical state.

• Recognize that emotions are normal—you're not going crazy just because you experience mood changes.

• Learn to express emotions positively. In some cases this will involve a simple exercise of your will. You are a volitional creature. In other words, you can control yourself. You can make choices and then follow through. Know your strengths and weaknesses—identify what causes your mood changes and what triggers your emotional responses.

• Be honest and investigate; then learn to back off when you are approaching that point where you no longer are in control.

• The most important step in handling emotions is sharing honestly with someone what's going on inside you.

• Understand that although your emotions may change, God doesn't. He will be your friend, your companion, regardless of how you feel. God is someone to whom you can turn no matter how depressed, angry, happy, sad, frustrated, or pleased you feel. He will always be there.

Road Signs ■ Explain that emotions are like road signs because they give us direction. Then ask:

• Share a specific situation when your feelings gave you a direction—what did they say to you?

• How did you respond?

• What happened if and when you ignored the signs?

• What would be a Christian response to feelings of fear? Hatred? Grief?

Stairs ■ Divide into five groups and give each group one of the following passages: Hebrews 9:27; Psalm 49:15; John 11:25; 1 Corinthians 15:51-58; 1 Thessalonians 4:13-14. Each group should read their passage and then determine what it teaches about death and how Christians should respond to death.

After a few minutes, have the groups report to the whole group.

Put a stair step diagram on the board. Explain that each of the Bible passages that they just discussed gives a truth that fits on the steps. They are steps because they build on each other; and by understanding and believing these truths, we can cope with death. Write the references on the steps and the truths underneath.

• Step One—Hebrews 9:27 (Death is a part of life. Everyone has to die.)

• Step Two—Psalm 49:15 (see also Romans 8:38-39) (God is with us in death. We don't die alone, and death is not the end.)

• Step Three—John 11:25 (Jesus, the *resurrection and the life*, has defeated death.)

• Step Four—1 Corinthians 15:51-58 (Christ, through His resurrection, has defeated death.)

• Step Five—1 Thessalonians 4:13-14 (Our grief is overcome by hope—in Christ, in the resurrection, and in eternal life.)

Unhealthy Approaches ■ Read the following unhealthy approaches to dealing with emotions, one at a time, and discuss.

1. Denying our feelings

   a. How do we deny our feelings?

   b. Why is this unhealthy?

2. Hiding our feelings

   a. How might someone hide his or her feelings?

   b. How have you hidden your feelings?

   c. How did you feel? Why didn't it help the situation? Why or why not?

3. Doing whatever our feelings tell us

   a. What's so unhealthy about this approach? At least we're not denying or hiding our feelings . . . right?

   b. What kinds of actions do our emotions tell us to take?

BIBLE STUDIES

Characters ■ Have a Bible study of some emotional Bible characters. See how David, Job, Joseph, and others handled a range of feelings.

Emotional Implications ■ Divide into groups and give each group a piece of paper with these verses on it. They should discuss the "emotional implications" for the Christian for each passage. Then bring the group back together, report, and discuss their findings as a group.

• Philippians 4:4-7
• Ephesians 4:25-27
• 1 John 4:18-21
• Matthew 5:4
• Matthew 5:22-24
• Matthew 5:43-48
• Luke 7:32, 19:41; John 11:35
• Psalm 126:5-6
• Amos 5:15; Romans 12:9

Jesus and Worry ■ Have everyone turn to Matthew 6:25-34. Have students tell you what Jesus taught about worry. Write their main points on the board: *We should not worry because* . . .

List these eight reasons for not worrying according to the passage: *We should not worry because* . . .

1. Life is more important than worrying about food and clothes (6:25).

2. The Father who feeds the birds cares even more about us (6:26).

3. Worry not only cannot make time, it wastes time (6:27).

4. God is able to provide whatever we need (6:30).

5. God knows exactly what we need (6:32).

6. When we pursue God's way of living, we won't have room for worry (6:33).

7. Tomorrow is the last thing to worry about (6:34).

8. Each day has plenty to keep us busy not worrying (6:34).

Search ■ Before the meeting, from a concordance list the passages that contain references to various emotions (for example, love, hate, fear, joy, despair, anxious/anxiety, and others). Divide into small groups (3–5 in each) and give each group a list of passages and a Bible or two. Have them look up the verses and decide what the Bible teaches about that emotion—by example or direct statement—and how and when it can be displayed.

FAITH AND DOUBTS

CROWD-BREAKERS

Blind Boats ■ Seat the group and divide into two teams by drawing an imaginary line down the middle of them. Explain that you are going to see which team is the most coordinated—able to think and act while they sing. Then have everyone sing together the old song "Row, Row, Row Your Boat." Explain that you want them to sing it again, but this time, they will have to change positions whenever they sing a word that contains the letter "r." The team on your right should begin seated, and the team on your left should begin standing. When they come to an "r-word," whoever is standing should sit down (until the next r-word), and whoever is seated should stand up. They would change positions on these words: row, your, stream, merrily, and dream. Go slowly at first, until everyone can do it. Then sing it again, faster. Repeat the process with "Three Blind Mice." The r-words in this song are three, run, ran, after, farmer's, their, carving, ever, and your. You could also repeat the songs using the letter "l." If they get too tired of standing and sitting, have them raise and lower their hands instead.

This game illustrates submission—by following your directions, they submit their wills to yours.

Doubts ■ Choose an unusual word from the dictionary (for example, labumum, moquette, stertorous). State the word and have group members write their own definitions on index cards. (Definitions may be serious or humorous, but they should sound official). Collect the definitions and read them to the group, including the correct one, which you have written on a card. Have everyone vote on the definitions, and give points to each person according to how many votes his or her definition received. Repeat with other words or with characters from the Bible.

This game illustrates how easy it is to doubt when people make contradictory claims.

Finish the Course ■ Using two teams, have each one choose a person to compete. Explain that these contestants will be blindfolded, brought into the room one at a time, and placed at a starting line. When you give the signal, another person from the contestant's team will shout instructions on how and where to walk. The goal is to navigate a specific course as quickly as possible without going off the course.

Have the contestants taken from the room. Then set up the course on the floor. Use children's blocks to form the borders of a path about 18 inches wide. Put two turns in the path. Explain that for every block moved, 10 seconds will be added to the contestant's time.

Then bring in the first blindfolded contestant, place him or her at the starting line, and begin. Have everyone except the contestant and the instruction-giver seated, and make sure that the other team doesn't cheat by interfering physically or verbally. Also, appoint a staff person or two to be timekeeper and judge. After team #1 has finished the course, bring in the contestant from team #2. Repeat the process as often as you wish, but be sure to take the two new contestants out of the room while you design a new course.

This illustrates the importance of obedience. To be

successful, the contestant has to listen, trust, and obey every command from his or her instructor.

Here's the Pitch ■ Divide into teams with four or five kids in each, and give each team a very unusual product. Try to find products that they haven't seen before—a computer part, a unique kitchen utensil, a carpenter's or plumber's tool, etc. The idea is for each team to think up a great sales pitch for their product. They should use their imaginations and creativity, emphasizing the fantastic properties and multitude of uses. Give them about five minutes to create, and then have the teams present their sales pitches and products. Encourage teams to use all their members in their ads.

The fantastic claims in this game illustrate the way we have become used to things that sound too good to be true and that later turn out not to be true—ads on TV, etc. As a result, we tend to doubt the latest set of claims.

Human Croquet ■ Divide the group into two teams. Have team #1 take the *field*, forming a croquet set-up. They form hoops by two people facing each other and making an arch with their hands. Then team #2 works in twos, with one partner in each twosome blindfolded. Half of the twosomes should start at each end of the croquet course. Each stroke is made by the *seeing* person pointing his or her partner in the correct direction and telling him or her how many steps to take. Depending on the size of each team, establish a time limit for each round. Each pair should keep track of how many strokes they take to get through the course. When time expires, switch team roles. When time expires again, switch team roles again with each pair switching duties (the blindfold goes on the other partner).

I Doubt It ■ Give each person a piece of paper, a pen, and a safety pin (or masking tape). Tell them to write two statements on their papers, both describing unusual facts about themselves or events in their lives. One statement should be true and the other one false. They should leave about 1 1/2 inches of space on the paper under each statement. (Samples: (1) "I used to have a pet monkey named Ronald Reagan." (2) "When I was a baby, I had brain surgery.")

Allow a few minutes for them to think and write; then have them pin their papers to their backs. Explain that everyone should walk around the room and read the statements on each person's back. Then the reader should put a check under the one that he or she believes to be true (only one check per person, per back). Players should not tell anyone how they voted.

After everyone has voted on every person's statements, have everyone remove the sheets and sit down. Find out who had the most votes for a false statement (have a few of the top vote-getters read), who had the least votes for a true statement (have a few of the more unusual ones read), and who fooled the fewest people.

I Wonder ■ The goal of this quiz is to create doubt by the use of trick questions. The correct answers are in parentheses. Copy the quiz without the answers. Distribute it with pencils and allow about three minutes for students to complete it.

QUIZ

1. How many of each animal did Moses put in the ark? (None; it was Noah.)
2. How many dead soldiers are buried in the Arlington National Cemetery? (all of them)
3. If "North" on a map is up, which direction is to your left? (It depends which way you're facing.)
4. Which of these insects is feared most by women: beetles, spiders, or butterflies? (beetles or butterflies because spiders aren't insects)
5. True or False—In the Bible, God turned stones into bread. (False; Satan tempted Jesus to do this, but Jesus refused.)
6. Do they have a fourth of July in Canada? (Yes; but it is not a holiday.)
7. If I have two coins in my hand totaling 55 cents (U.S.), and one is not a nickel, what are the two coins? (a nickel and a fifty-cent piece.)
8. Write the word that is the opposite of "up": _ _ _ _. (If "down" was printed, the answer is wrong—it was supposed to be "written.")
9. What gets wet as it dries? (a towel)
10. Without asking his or her name, who is the person sitting directly in front of you? (This is not a trick question, but by this time, they probably will think it is as you give the other answers.)

If you discuss this later, ask:

• How did you like our quiz?

• What were you thinking as you answered the questions?

• When did you start looking for the trick questions?

• How does this experience relate to "doubt"?

Magic Tricks ■ To illustrate that much of Satan's work involves deception and makes us doubt our faith, perform a few simple "magic" tricks. Here's one:

Before the meeting, tear a very small piece (about 1/2 inch in diameter) out of a newspaper. Ideally it should have words and parts of words on one side and no words on the other. Memorize the letters and words on the fragment, fold it three or four times, and put it into a front pocket. During the meeting, announce that you will perform an amazing mind-reading trick.

Bring out a newspaper and hand it to a student. Have him or her choose a section. Then take that section and hand it to another student, who should choose a page. Take the page from that person and give it to another one. (Note: It is important that you take the newspaper from each student before giving it to someone else.) Have this person tear the page in half. Then you take one half and give it to someone else.

Continue this process until the newspaper piece is about six inches square. Then hand this piece to a student and ask him or her to tear a small piece out of the center of it, about 1/2 inch in diameter, and to fold it three or four times. While he or she is doing this, slip your hand into your pocket and take out the piece of paper that you had placed there earlier. Take the small piece from the student, switch it with your piece, and hand yours (which everyone thinks is the one that they have just seen torn from the newspaper) to another person. Tell that person to hold the piece of paper in his or her right fist and to press it against his or her forehead.

On a concealed chalkboard or poster board write the words on the paper that you had memorized earlier. Tell the audience that you are "getting the vibes," etc. Make sure that they cannot see what letters you are writing. Then have the person holding the piece of paper come to the front of the room and write on another board the letters that he or she sees on the paper. Afterward, turn around the board on which you had written, compare the answers, and watch their faces drop in amazement.

The Search ■ Before the meeting, scatter various items throughout the room. These could include rubber bands, paper clips, balloons, index cards, a tennis ball or two, a few colorful ribbons, a paper cup, and others. Explain that you are going to have an indoor scavenger hunt. But this "hunt" will differ in two ways from all the others that they have experienced. First of all, you will be calling out the items one at a time, and, second, the hunt will take place in the dark.

Tell everyone to get ready and to be quiet. Then turn off the lights. (Note: This will be a lot of fun, but

it will also be quite rowdy. Be sure that all the breakables have been removed, have everyone remove their shoes, and use a whistle to get their attention between items.)

There are no teams; it is everyone for themself. Yell out the items, one at a time, pausing between each one for a few seconds for the kids to search for it. Also, ask for one item that isn't in the room. After calling for 10 items, turn on the lights and see who has collected the most. For control purposes, during the game you may want to turn the lights on and off quickly to see how they're doing.

The tie-in is that when we have been in darkness for a while, we can begin to doubt what we had seen in the light. We're not really sure that those things are really there. Of course there are many kinds of darkness, including sorrow, separation, and lack of communication.

Walk It Out ■ Choose contestants to compete in an acting contest. The idea is to see who can act out a situation, using only their feet and the way they walk (with no sound effects). As they act out their situations, one at a time, the audience should try to guess what they're doing. The winner has the least total elapsed time. Here are some situations to act out:
• coming from the beach and walking barefoot over hot sand
• coming in after curfew and trying not to wake your parents as you walk down the hall and up the stairs
• running from a bull and trying to avoid the cowpies in the field as you run for your life
• walking across an ice skating rink in new shoes
• marching in Hitler's army
• downhill skiing
• cross country skiing
• Olympic speed walking in slow motion
• walking through a room in the dark, barefooted, and trying not to stub your toe on anything
• trying to walk up a slippery hill or slide
• add others

Why? ■ Hand out the following quiz. Each answer begins with the sound "why." The answers are in parentheses.

WHY

a drink _____ (wine)
a high-pitched, irritating sound _____ (whine)
without color, bleached out _____ (white)
cunning _____ (wile)

out of control_____	(wild)
spouse _____	(wife)
extensively _____	(widely)
dispersed _____	(widespread)
meantime _____	(while)
waves _____	(whitecaps)
alert _____	(wide awake)
twist around _____	(wind)
metal strand _____	(wire)
lean, supple _____	(wiry)
learned, intelligent _____	(wise)
world famous beach _____	(Waikiki)
witticism, joke _____	(wisecrack)

DISCUSSION STARTERS

Announcements ■ Before the meeting, prearrange a "doubter" who will ask a number of good, legitimate questions about each of your announcements. Make sure that during the meeting you pause for about three announcements about upcoming events. During each announcement, allow time for questions and be sure to try to answer your doubter. Later in the meeting, discuss the experience. Ask:

• What did you think about the questions during the announcements?

• Is it good to ask questions? Why or why not?

• How does asking questions relate to doubting?

Cheap Talk ■ Explain that often people make promises and statements that they don't intend to keep or don't really believe. Bring volunteers to the front to act out some of these characters and situations:

• a politician who makes elaborate promises about what he or she will do if elected

• a sales person who is trying to close a deal on an expensive purchase

• a boy or girl who is giving his or her date a line

• someone who volunteers to take on an important responsibility

• someone who wants to borrow money from a friend

• add others

Encouragement ■ Select a couple of sharp guys and teach them to do a specific crowd-breaker or a simple task. Time them to see how fast they can do the task. Have them taken from the room and bring them in one at a time and repeat the task. Have the crowd encourage the first one and discourage the second one (set up the crowd while the competitors are out of the room). Then discuss the effects of encouragement vs. discouragement; when they have allowed doubts and discouragement to affect their lives; how they can encourage others; how they can overcome doubt and discouragement; etc.

Filled But Not Satisfied ■ To illustrate how people try to fill the God-shaped space in their lives, divide into teams and give each team a Mason jar on the table in front of the room. Next to each jar, place a stack of food items including a slice of white bread, some potato chips, some colored Kool Aid, a bunch of bananas, a tomato, etc. Explain that this is a contest to see which team can fill up their jar the quickest. When you give the signal, the first person from each team should run to the front, stand behind the table and stuff one of the food items into the jar. When that person finishes, he or she should run back to the team, and the next person should follow suit. The first team to fill the jar completely wins. Afterward, explain that this game is very similar to what people try to do with their lives. Suppose the jar is the gasoline tank on a car. If you stuff it with food, it will be full, but the car won't run. In the same way, our lives are meant to run on God—there is a God-shaped space in our lives. People try to fill that space with all sorts of things, and they seem full or at least busy. But they don't run right. Discuss what it takes to fill our lives with God.

Fill 'er Up ■ Give everyone a paper cup. Spread magazines and scissors around the room. Tell everyone to cut out pictures of what people use to fill the emptiness in their lives and then place these pictures in their cups. After a few minutes, have kids explain why they chose the pictures they did.

If . . . ■ Distribute sheets of paper with the following sentences to complete on them (allow plenty of room for answers).

• If you believe that chocolate is delicious, you will . . .

• If you believer that planes are safe, you will . . .

• If you say that you really like basketball, you will . . .

• If someone is your best friend, you will . . .

• If you claim to be a Christian, you will . . .

After everyone has finished all the sentences, collect the papers and read the answers aloud, one question at a time. Note: Many of the answers for the last sentence will probably read, *act like one*.

After reading the completed sentences, talk about how silly it would be for someone to claim to love chocolate but always turn it down or choose another flavor when he or she has the chance; how inconsistent it would be for someone to claim to like basketball and never watch a game or play it; how hypocritical it would be for someone to claim to believe that airplanes are perfectly safe and yet never fly because of fear; how phony it would be for someone to claim that a person is his or her best friend and then never spend time with that person and cut him or her down behind his or her back.

Then ask how a person who claims to be a Christian should act, so as not to be silly, inconsistent, hypocritical, or phony.

Roles ■ Divide into pairs to do the following role plays. Encourage the actors to play their parts as realistically as possible.

1. A is the parent and B is the seven-year-old child. A has promised to do something very special with B this weekend (and B has really looked forward to it for weeks), but something has come up and A can't go. A is explaining this to B.

2. A and B are best friends. A couple of weeks ago, A gave B a prized possession to use. Now B is explaining how he or she broke it.

3. B is the chairperson of the program committee and has given A a very important responsibility for the upcoming event. (A almost begged for the assignment.) Well, the big day is almost here and B discovers that A hasn't even started the assignment. What is really bad is that A had assured B that things were under control. (This has happened before.) B confronts A.

Pick up the discussion immediately following the role plays. Ask:

• What kind of conversation took place in situation number one? (What was the special activity? How did B feel? What was said?) When this happened to you how did you feel?

• In situation number two, A, how did you react to B's news? Did you blast, forgive, or gloss over? What will you do the next time B wants to borrow something? Why?

• In our last situation, how did you both react? What excuses did A give? When has someone in real life (don't mention any names) let you down like that? What did you do?

• How do our role plays relate to the subject of doubt? What other circumstances breed doubt? How do our other games illustrate causes of doubt?

• How can these causes of doubt affect our faith in Christ?

Show Me the Way ■ Choose four volunteers to participate in a contest to see who can best follow directions. Blindfold them and line them up next to each other in front of the room. Explain that you will be giving them instructions on where to go. Without asking any questions and with no help from the audience, they should do what you say as quickly as possible. If they follow your directions correctly, they will come to a prearranged spot in the room. The person closest to that spot will receive the prize.

Read aloud the following instructions. Note that these instructions are somewhat ambiguous or that the actions taken will vary depending on the person. Add other instructions to fit your location and marked spot on the floor.

• Take five small steps forward.

• Turn right and take one giant step.

• Turn 20 degrees to the left and walk heel-to-toe for three seconds.

• Face north.

• Get on all fours and crawl for 10 feet.

• Turn around and go backward a little.

• Pivot 1 1/2 times around and hop once straight ahead.

• Shuffle sideways three steps.

Afterward, discuss why these instructions were difficult to follow, how the instructions are similar to those received from parents, teachers, pastors, and others about life, and when they feel like the blindfolded contestants. Then ask how your instructions compare to God's.

Survey ■ Three or four weeks before the meeting, survey the kids about the part that doubt plays in their lives—what or who is easy for them to doubt and why; what makes them feel doubtful about themselves; etc. Then in the meeting, reveal and discuss the results of your survey.

Teamwork? ■ Before the meeting, copy the following set of instructions for each group member.

• Performer—Acting as the team representative, this person must complete a task as quickly as possible.

• Coach—While the performer is completing his or her task, this person should be shouting instructions.

• Cheerleader—This person should yell encouragement to the performer as he or she works.

• Doubter—This person's role is to question the rules, ask about the time and procedure, and point out the problems in the performer's work.

Divide into teams of four and distribute the instruction sheets. (Each team should have one person for each role.) Explain to the whole group that you will be having a contest of skill and dexterity. Each team will have the chance to compete against the clock. The fastest team will get a prize, and the losing competitor (the performer for the slowest team) will get a shaving-cream pie in the face. Any team not following the rules will be disqualified and lose automatically. Note: during this game, only the coaches can remind anyone else of the rules.

Demonstrate the task, and then begin the contest. Possible tasks could include assembling a child's puzzle, putting the pieces in the "Shape-o" Tupperware toy, working the children's toy "Perfection," stacking odd-sized objects, and others. Be sure to watch the actions and effects of the doubters.

After the contest, declare the winning team and award the prizes and penalty. You can discuss the experience right away or wait until later in the meeting. Ask:

• How did you doubters feel as you played your roles?

• Was it difficult or easy to do? Why?

• You performers—how did the other team members affect your performance?

The DO Point ■ Before the meeting, type a number of Christian beliefs on individual slips of paper. Do this as competition among teams or individuals. One at a time, kids should draw a slip of paper and pantomime how they think the belief on the paper would translate into an action. The group should try to guess the belief. The winner is the team (or individual) with the lowest total time. Here are some beliefs to act out:

• God is in control

• God is love

• the Bible is the Word of God

• God gives every Christian spiritual gifts to be used in His service

• Jesus died for me

• my sins are forgiven

• every person has dignity and worth

• God has a purpose for my life

• people are going to hell unless they accept Christ as Savior

• eternal life and heaven are real

Trust List ■ Write the following occupations on the chalkboard or a poster. Then give everyone a piece of paper and have them list the occupations in order of trustworthiness. Afterward, total the group's ratings. Ask why they think of a particular occupation or person as trustworthy or untrustworthy. Then ask what builds trust.

politician	store manager
store clerk	pro athlete
medical doctor	door-to-door salesperson
psychiatrist/counselor	fire fighter
teacher	writer
police officer	waitress/waiter
insurance salesperson	lawyer
minister	movie star
car salesperson	rock star
company president	news reporter

What do you *really* believe? ■ Hand out scratch paper and pencils or pens and have everyone jot down their beliefs about the Bible, God the Father, Jesus, the Holy Spirit, prayer, salvation, the Christian life, values, etc. After a few minutes, ask kids to share their beliefs aloud as someone writes them on the board (take just one or two per person the first time around the room). Keep writing until everyone has given all of their beliefs and the board is full.

Discuss the life-implications for the beliefs. For example, you could say: *All right. We say we believe in God, that He exists. What difference should that belief make in our lives? How can we LIVE that belief?* Other important beliefs could involve faith, hope, love, spiritual gifts, service, etc.

What's There? ■ Ask for a volunteer to participate in an experiment. Bring the person to the front of the room. Tell him or her to look around carefully at everything there. Then blindfold the person and ask him or her the following questions:

• Is there a television in the room?

• Is _____ (person in the group) at the meeting?

• What color shirt am I wearing?

• Where is _____ (person in the room) sitting?

• Describe the picture on the back wall.

Remove the blindfold and thank the person for being a good sport. Point out the correct and incorrect answers. Then ask for two new volunteers. Again, have them look carefully around the room. Because they saw you do this previously, they will try harder to take everything in. After a few seconds, take one person out of the room. Blindfold the other person and ask him or her questions like these:

- Who is standing at the back of the room?
- Who is sitting in the front row?
- Where is the Bible with the red cover?
- Were the window shades drawn?
- Which lamp was turned off?
- Is there a table in the room?
- How many males are in the room?

Again, remove the person's blindfold, thank him or her for being a good sport, and explain the correct and incorrect answers. Then bring the last person into the room, blindfolded, and ask the same questions.

Afterward thank the last volunteer and then ask all the participants these questions:

- Why were some of the questions easy to answer?
- What made some of the questions difficult to answer?
- When did you begin to doubt your memory?
- What effect did being out of the room for a while have on your confidence in your answers?

Explain that it's easy to doubt what we can't see. The longer the volunteers were blindfolded or out of the room, the more they would have wondered about what was really in the room and what was not. Ask how this experience might parallel why people doubt what they can't see, especially spiritual realities such as God, Jesus, the Holy Spirit, eternal life, and so forth.

Words and Deeds ■ Play a game of charades using the following phrases that kids have to act out (explain that each one is a familiar phrase):

- Put your money where your mouth is.
- Walk your talk.
- What you see is what you get.
- Do as I say, not as I do.
- I can see right through you.
- Actions speak louder than words.
- This is the life!
- Add others that have a similar theme.

After determining the winning team (the shortest amount of time wins), ask what the phrases had in common. Use this as a starter for discussing the importance of having our lives match our beliefs as Christians.

Yield ■ This game illustrates what it means to yield to another person's control. Afterward, discuss

whether or not it is a good illustration of how we should depend on God.

Choose two couples to compete and bring them to the front of the room. Blindfold one member of each couple and give him or her a piece of chalk. Explain that you will give the other member of each couple a message on a card which he or she must print on the blackboard (or a large piece of paper) so that the rest of the group can read it. The catch, however, is that this person may use only the blindfolded person's hand to write the message. There can be no talking by the couples during the contest. The person who can see must hold his or her partner's hand and guide it on the blackboard. The first couple to finish the message so that everyone can read it wins. Repeat this with other couples if you have time. Use the following messages or create your own.

- Thanks for the help.
- Work through me.
- I am depending on you.
- What do you think this says?
- Now this is what I call creative writing.
- I really appreciate what you're doing for me!

Afterward, ask the blindfolded people how they felt about the experience: *When did they use their own muscles? How did they decide to grip the chalk? Did they ever know what letters or words they were writing?* Ask the seeing partners about the experience: *When did it become easy to write the letters and words? How could your partner have helped you more? How would having the blindfolds removed have helped? How would talking to each other while still blindfolded have helped?*

DISCUSSIONS AND WRAP-UPS

Action ■ Ask:

- We say that we believe all sorts of things about God, Jesus, and the Bible, so why is it so difficult to put those beliefs into action?
- Why do people find it easy to make statements that they don't mean?
- Why is it important to do what we say?
- Why is it important to put our faith into action?

Antidotes ■ Outlined briefly are three antidotes to the main causes of doubt. Use this as a guide for a discussion or for a wrap-up. Be sure to illustrate with personal examples.

1. An inspiring Christian, Dr. V. Raymond Edman,

often said in chapel addresses at Wheaton College: "Never doubt in darkness what God has shown you in the light." The only sure cure for darkness-induced doubt is to remember the light and what you experienced there. In other words, we can remember what God has done for us in the past. A personal diary or quiet-time log would be helpful to review. In the Old Testament, when Israel was traveling from Egypt to the Promised Land, they had to be reminded continually of God's faithfulness in the past and of His promise of protection and care. (See Deuteronomy 1.)

2. Jesus is the truth, and the Bible is the infallible Word of God. (Read John 14:6 and 2 Timothy 3:16-17 aloud.) Don't be discouraged or fooled by the outrageous claims you hear; instead, immerse yourself in God's truth. This is the cure for doubt caused by our society.

3. Human beings are fallible. The fact is that if you keep your eyes on humans, they will eventually let you down—no one's perfect. (Refer to the role plays in **Roles** if you used that discussion starter.) Even your leaders will sin, and if your faith depends on them, you will be crushed. Instead, keep your eyes on Christ. He is perfect, and He will never let you down. Look at Peter. He wanted to walk on the water like Jesus, and he did; but when he took his eyes off Christ and looked instead at his circumstances, he began to sink (Matthew 14:22-31). We must keep our eyes on Christ.

Evidence ■ Tell everyone to imagine that today Christianity has been outlawed and all Christians are being rounded up and tried as criminals. What evidence will be presented that they are Christians?

After discussing this for a minute or two, hand out index cards and have students list the important facts of their faith on the left side. Then have them write *one* action for each fact that would be a demonstration of that point of their faith.

Have them circle *one* or *two* actions that they can take this week to begin to live out what they believe. They should use the cards as reminders.

Faith ■ Use the following outline as a wrap-up talk:
1. Faith is knowing what you believe.
2. Faith is believing what you know, even when your feelings disagree.
3. Faith is knowing Who you believe.
4. Faith is believing in the long run.

Good or Bad? ■ Ask:
• When is doubting good? (When it stops us from being taken in by something or someone false, etc.)

• When is doubting bad? (When it undermines our confidence in something or someone good; when it stops us from good actions; etc.)

• Is doubting a sin? (Not automatically; it is what you do with your doubts that counts. There are times, however, when doubting is wrong in itself—when God has definitely told us to do or not to do something and we doubt Him; etc.)

Invisible, Visible ■ Ask: *What things do you depend on every day that are invisible?* Write their answers on the board. The answers could include: electricity, wind, sound waves, light, radio waves, microwaves, television signals, etc. Add to this list other invisible things that affect them. Answers could include: plant roots, germs/bacteria/viruses, spy planes, satellites, etc. Take each item and ask for proof that it exists; in other words, how is it made visible? Then ask how qualities and beliefs can be made visible including love, compassion, hate, the sovereignty of God, and others.

Prayer ■ Close the meeting with prayer circles. Have kids pray for each other and the situations that cause them to doubt.

True Faith ■ Use this acrostic to show what the Bible teaches about what true faith involves. Write it on the board as you give it. Explain each point as you go along.
F = Finds ways to make a difference in the world (Matthew 5:13
A = Apparent to others (Matthew 5:14)
I = Involved in obedience (Matthew 5:17)
T = Tells others; helps others to obey (Matthew 5:19)
H = Helps others take on goodness as a goal (Matthew 5:20)

BIBLE STUDIES

Belief and Unbelief ■ Divide into groups and give each group a passage and questions to discuss. After a few minutes, gather everyone together again and find out what they discovered.

1. Matthew 13:53-58
   • Who are the people in the story? (the people in Jesus' home town)
   • What did Jesus do for them? (preached and performed miracles)
   • How did they respond? (they were amazed)

• Why didn't the people believe in Jesus? (they didn't believe Jesus could be more than a carpenter's son)

2. Acts 17:16-34

• To whom was Paul speaking? (Epicurean and Stoic philosophers)

• How did they respond to his message? (some sneered, some wanted to hear more) Why?

• How did those in verse 34 respond? (believed and followed Paul)

• What made the difference in the responses?

3. Acts 26:1-32 (especially verses 28-32)

• Summarize the Gospel as presented by Paul in this chapter.

• How did Festus respond? Why? (he thought Paul was out of his mind)

• How did Agrippa respond? Why? (he asked Paul if he really thought he could convert Agrippa in such a short time)

• What would it have taken to overcome the doubts of these Roman officials?

4. Mark 9:14-29

• Summarize the story: what happened and where?

• Why weren't the disciples effective? (they needed to fast and pray)

• Explain verse 23. (faith makes things happen)

• What did the father mean by his reply to Jesus? (verse 24) (he wanted to believe Jesus could do anything but was having trouble totally believing)

• How does his response relate to doubting and doubts?

Prisoner ■ *The Prisoner in the Third Cell* by Gene Edwards (Tyndale House) is a study of John the Baptist's doubts about Jesus when John was in prison (Matthew 11:1-19, especially verse 6). This is an excellent resource for any discussion about doubt.

Real Faith ■ Break into small groups and have the kids in each group read and discuss James 2:14-26 together. They should answer these questions:

• Why isn't *only believing* enough?

• What is real faith?

• How do faith and works relate?

• What is the most difficult place and area of life to live out one's faith?

Seeking and Finding ■ Ask volunteers to look up the following passages and read them aloud, one at a time. After each one, comment on what the passage is teaching about doubt and faith.

1. Matthew 11:1-6—Even spiritual giants like John the Baptist had doubts when faced with incredible problems. When his questions were answered (and notice that Jesus took time to answer them), his doubts were relieved, and he believed.

2. Matthew 13:53-58—Some people refuse to believe, even when confronted with the facts. These folks are blinded by their doubts.

3. Matthew 7:7-8—It is good to ask questions if we are truly "seeking." Jesus promises that those who seek will find Him.

4. John 20:24-31—Thomas doubted, but Jesus didn't condemn him because Thomas believed when he was confronted with the truth. The Bible is God's Word and was written to give us answers to our honest questions. We shouldn't be afraid to ask.

5. James 1:5-8—A "double-minded" person is someone who continues to slip into doubt, forgetting the truth of God's Word and the proof of his own experiences. We should not wallow in our doubts.

6. Hebrews 11:6—God will reveal Himself to those who honestly and diligently seek Him.

Close by reminding your students that doubt is natural and even healthy at times. Doubting can keep us from being taken by swindlers and can help us find the truth. Also, assure students that it is OK for them to doubt their faith—they shouldn't accept something as truth just because someone (even you) said it. They should search the Bible for themselves. But this questioning and searching must be honest, looking for answers. Challenge students to talk honestly to God about their doubts and encourage them to set up appointments with you to discuss any nagging doubts that they have. You can look for the answers together.

Sermon on the Mount ■ Ask who can remember some of the teachings in the Sermon on the Mount. Then have a student read aloud Matthew 5:13-20. Afterward ask:

• How are Christians like salt?

• How are we like light?

• What can we do to be salt and light in our schools, neighborhoods, families, and places of work?

• How can a Christian lose his or her *saltiness*?

• Why do some Christians put their *lamps under a bowl*?

• What does it meant o have *true* faith in Christ?

21 PRAYER AND PRAISE

CROWD-BREAKERS

Addresses ■ Pass out the following quiz. Have everyone fill in the missing parts of these famous addresses. The answers are in parentheses.

ADDRESSES

1. _____ Sunset Strip (77)
2. No. 10 _____ (Downing Street)
3. ____00 Pennsylvania Avenue (16)
4. _____ & Vine (Hollywood)
5. S_____ Street (Sesame)
6. Saks _____ Avenue (5th)
7. _____ S_____ and _____ years _____ ("4 score & 7 years ago")
8. North _____ 40 (Dallas)
9. Elvis lived at _____ (Graceland in Memphis)

Mix in a couple of addresses of group members, the church, and your own. You can move from this activity into a meeting on prayer and praise by asking how we address our communication to God.

Blessings Galore ■ Divide into teams of 10–15 in each (with smaller teams, have them go through the whole team more than once). Have the teams stand in parallel lines. The first person in each team begins by saying, "I thank God for _____" (a blessing). Then the next person must repeat what the first person said and add another blessing. The third person should repeat what was said by the first two and add another one. For example, the third person

could say, "I thank God for good health, great parents, and my dog." The process continues until the last person on the team repeats all the blessings with no help from other team members. The first team to get through the whole team wins that round. For round two, have the teams start at the other end and see how far they can get within a certain time limit. If they get through the entire team once, they should keep the process going by starting with person number one again.

Creative Communication ■ The following summaries have been circulated widely and are said to have appeared on accident report forms sent to a state office of motor vehicles. These drivers were trying to explain their accidents and justify themselves. Before the meeting, cut the excuses out and distribute them to group members, explaining that you will ask them to read the phrases later. Between each activity, have a few read.

These literary "classics" are excellent examples of poor communication. What was meant was not said. After each one, have the group try to figure out what really happened. This activity can tie in with communicating with God in prayer.

1. A pedestrian hit me and went under my car.
2. A truck backed through my windshield into my wife's face.
3. I thought my window was down, but I found out it was up when I put my head through it.
4. The other car collided with mine without giving warning of its intentions.
5. The guy was all over the road. I had to swerve a

number of times before I hit him.

6. In an attempt to kill a fly, I drove into a telephone post.

7. I collided with a stationary truck coming the other way.

8. Coming home, I drove into the wrong house and collided with a tree I don't have.

9. To avoid hitting the bumper of the car in front, I struck a pedestrian.

10. The pedestrian had no idea of which direction to run, so I ran over him.

11. An invisible car came out of nowhere, struck my car, and vanished.

12. My car was legally parked as it backed into the other vehicle.

13. I saw a slow-moving, sad-faced old gentleman as he bounced off the roof of my car.

14. The telephone pole was approaching. As I was attempting to swerve out of its way, it struck the front of my car.

15. I pulled away from the side of the road, glanced at my mother-in-law, and headed over the embankment.

16. I told the police that I was not injured but, on removing my hat, found that I had a fractured skull.

17. The indirect cause of the accident was a little guy in a small car with a big mouth.

18. I had been driving 40 years when I fell asleep at the wheel and had an accident.

19. I had been shopping for plants all day and was on my way home. As I reached the intersection, a hedge sprang up, obscuring my vision, and I did not see the other car.

20. I was thrown from my car as it left the road. I was later found in a ditch by some stray cows.

Happy Birthday ■ Divide the group into five sections and assign each section a portion of the words to the song *Happy Birthday* . . . like this:

Section One—*Hap-*

Section Two—*py*

Section Three—*Birth-*

Section Four—*day*

Section Five—*to you*

Then sing the song with each section singing its own part. The next time through, have the sections stand while they sing their parts. Each time through they should increase speed. Here's how the song should go: *Hap-py Birth-day to you, Hap-py Birth-day to you, Hap-py Birth-day, Hap-py Birth-day, Hap-py Birth-day to you.*

Heavenward ■ Use the whole group or, if your group is large, break into smaller teams of about 10 to 15 people. Give each team a balloon and explain that their task is to work together to touch the ceiling with their balloon. The only catch is that they can lift the balloon only by blowing it as a team. The first team to touch the ceiling with their balloon wins that round. Other rounds could include light items such as feathers, facial tissue, wax paper, etc.

This game illustrates how many people feel about their prayers—they only make it to the ceiling and then only after much effort.

Knee Race ■ Divide into two teams and line them up in parallel columns with everyone facing in. The two teams should be facing each other. Explain that this is a contest to see which team can pass the items down their column the fastest, person to person, using only their feet to do the passing. Everyone must remain in a kneeling position until the game is over (they may put their hands on the floor in front of them). Here are the items to pass: pillow, large hat, piece of paper, inflated balloon, tennis ball or orange.

Listening ■ Use three tape recorders or a combination of TVs, radios, and tape recorders. Turn on all three: one should have music, another sound effects, and another someone speaking in a low voice. Have everyone listen for about three minutes. Then turn off the sounds and question students about what they heard. Make your questions quite specific.

Then have everyone get very quiet, shut their eyes, and just listen. After a minute or two, ask what they heard.

Another possibility is to give them a few mystery sounds to identify.

The point is that we can hear God speaking when we shut out the distractions and take time to listen.

Now I Lay Me ■ Divide into groups of 2–4 and give each group a sheet of paper and a pencil or pen. Explain that you want them to rephrase the common bedtime prayer, *Now I lay me down to sleep . . . ,* focusing on other needs. The original prayer goes: *Now I lay me down to sleep. I pray the Lord my soul to keep. If I should die before I wake, I pray the Lord my soul to take.*

Here's an example of a revised version: *As I take this English test, I pray that I will do my best. Please find the knowledge in my brain, and help me get it out again.*

Pass It On ■ This is the old game *Telephone* with a twist. Seat everyone in a circle (with a large group, divide into circles of 10–15). Give the first person in the circle one of the special sentences to whisper to the person on his or her right. That person should then whisper what he or she heard to the next person, and so on until the last person has received the message. That person should repeat aloud what he or she heard. Then the first person should read the message that began the circle, which probably will differ greatly from the one at the end. Have this move quickly. Repeat by beginning with the next person to the right in the circle. Here are some sentences to write on cards and give to the kids to whisper. Use three or four, depending on how well it goes.

• Hopefully heaven has hallowed habitual happenings hereafter.

• Please pray that my precious parrot Petunia permits her perch to be purged.

• Saintly Sue saw Shawn sewing seven silly shawls Saturday.

• Things come in; emotions go down; words go out; prayers go up.

• Jerky John just jabbed jealous Julie gently and jokingly with a jiggily, juicy jelly roll.

• Bonnie's broke and that's no joke, because her home in Roanoke went up in smoke.

P-R-A-I-S-E ■ Choose six kids and send them out of the room with the understanding that they will return, one at a time, and try to find a specific item in the room. The first person's item will begin with the letter P (for example: penny, pencil, plate, package, person, etc.); the second person's will begin with R (for example: radio, record, ring, etc.); and so on, spelling out the word PRAISE. As the person enters the room, the rest of the audience should clap louder as he or she comes closer to the specific item. The person to find his or her item the fastest wins.

Prayer Quiz ■ Give this quiz orally or make it into a written, matching quiz, allowing kids to look up the verses in their Bibles. The correct answers are in parentheses.

1. The most well-known prayer (The Lord's Prayer—Matthew 6:9-13)

2. The greatest concentration of prayers in the Bible (Psalms)

3. The first prayer in the Bible (Genesis 3:8-10)

4. Jesus' longest recorded prayer (John 17:1-26)

5. The shortest prayer in the Bible (*Help!*—Matthew 14:30)

6. The two Gospels that have *The Lord's Prayer* (Luke 11 and Matthew 6)

7. The longest prayer in the Bible (Psalm 119)

8. The last prayer in the Bible (Revelation 22:20)

Rushin' Roulette ■ Before the meeting, set up stations around the room where students will have to perform various tasks. If possible, have an adult supervisor for each station. Here are some possible tasks for students to perform: write a poem, stack paper cups five high, do a series of exercises, draw a picture of a school, take a test, count the number of beans in a jar, say the Pledge of Allegiance backwards (*all for justice and liberty with . . .*), etc. Give each task a point value. Also, prepare a piece of poster board with the tasks, locations, and points.

Distribute sheets of paper and pens or pencils and explain that everyone has five minutes to get as many points as possible. They may only complete the task in a location, one person at a time (not in a group). After successfully completing the task, the adult in that area should sign their papers.

After you give the signal to start, watch carefully, noting how they chose which tasks to try first and so forth, and keep everyone apprised concerning the time remaining.

After determining the winner, ask the group:

• How did you decide which tasks to do?

• What caused you to change your strategy?

• How is this experience like a typical day or week for you?

• In your busy schedule, when do you find time to pray?

Santa Claus ■ Introduce a special guest who got lost in the neighborhood a few weeks ago but would love to spend some time with them. Bring in Santa and seat him in front of the group. (Have fun with this—keep it light.) Explain that Santa will be glad to hear their Christmas requests for next Christmas as long as he's here. Ask them to think of one or two things that they most desire (give examples, material and otherwise). Then have students come forward, one at a time, sit on Santa's lap, and tell him their requests. Later you may want to refer to this list, commenting on the nature of their requests. The point is that often we treat God like a celestial "Santa Claus" who should grant all our desires. Our prayers sound a lot like our lists.

The Letter ■ Distribute cards and pencils to everyone. Each card should have a word written on it. Tell everyone to write one creative sentence, incorporating into it the word on the card. The sentence should describe a vacation. Possibilities could include beagle, bagel, bugle, scintillating, scuzzy, gregarious, lifeguard, green, threw up, froze, surfboard, and other special words. Collect the cards, shuffle them, and then read them one at a time as a group letter. Begin by saying, "Dear (your name), My vacation has been great . . ."

You can use this activity to introduce the topic of clear communication with God.

Trial Balloons ■ Give everyone a balloon, a small piece of paper, and a pen. Have each person look around the room, choose another person, and write out a special wish for that person (they should not put their own names on the papers). Next, have them roll up their wish slips and place them inside the balloons. Then they should inflate and tie their balloons. At your signal, everyone should bat the balloons up to the ceiling and, as a group, try to keep them all airborne. After a minute or so, tell everyone to grab a balloon, pop it, and recover the slip inside. One at a time, have students stand and read the wishes.

This game should evoke good feelings and build group unity. It also illustrates how often our prayers don't seem to get beyond the ceiling—they just bounce back into our laps.

DISCUSSION STARTERS

Action ■ Give this assignment that you will discuss the following week: *This week, every day, I want you to have a time of prayer. During this time, the object will be to get to know God better. Use this format: five minutes of silence; five minutes of thanking and praising God for one of His attributes (take a different one each day); five minutes of meditating on the implications of that attribute to your life (and listening to God); five minutes of talking to God about those implications and applications. Keep a written record of what God is telling you about Himself and come next week ready to share.*

Note: If your group is not ready for an assignment this heavy, break it down into about five minutes a day, focusing on one part each day. Be sure to follow through and talk over their discoveries at the next meeting.

Assignment ■ Ask your group members to read a psalm or two each day for the next week, noting which ones are prayers and what those prayers involve.

Attributes ■ Before the meeting, ask six students to help you with this presentation. Give each of them one of the following attributes of God and have them come prepared with a biblical reference and a tangible example. Possible references and examples are given in parentheses.

• Limitless (Psalm 8:3-4; a picture of the stars with statistics about the number of galaxies)

• Personal (1 Samuel 13:14; John 15:12-17; a collage of pictures showing love)

• Artistic (Job 38 and 39; Psalm 139:13-18; a collection of specimens from nature: a leaf, an insect, etc.)

• Authoritative (Exodus 20:1-7; Hebrews 4:12; 2 Timothy 3:16; a few books from the pastor's library)

• Mysterious (John 1:18; 1 Corinthians 2:9; pictures of clouds or stained-glass windows)

• Loving (Romans 8:38-39; 1 John 4:7-8; a cross or picture of Jesus on the cross)

After each student has made his or her presentation, discuss as a whole group how they have experienced this attribute of God in their lives. Then have someone offer a prayer of thanks to God for that attribute.

Clichés ■ Read this series of clichés and after each one ask what is really meant by the phrase and how it limits God.

•He hasn't got a prayer! (Prayer is a last ditch effort to save someone; God may help you if you're desperate.)

•On a wing and a prayer (Prayer is like wishful thinking; God is like a good-luck charm.)

•The "Hail Mary" pass (This is an extreme combination of the two listed above.)

•The family that prays together, stays together. (The act of prayer, itself, is like glue because it is a personal, close experience—God doesn't really have to be a part of it.)

Ask students if they can think of any other appropriate clichés; then continue the analysis.

Make it clear that each of these clichés contains some truth, but they are incomplete. If our understanding of God is limited to these, we really don't know Him at all. If our prayers are limited to these, we don't pray very well.

Definitions ■ As kids enter the room, give the early arrivers index cards and have each person write a definition of praise. Before the meeting, write out a dictionary definition on another card. Choose two or three of their best definitions and mix them with the one from the dictionary. Later in the meeting, as part of the discussion, see if they can guess which definition is the "official" one. Then discuss how we can truly praise God in worship, in prayer, and in our lives.

Group Prayer ■ Divide into groups and give each group a piece of paper and a pencil. Tell them to write a prayer for the whole group using only two or three sentences. Their prayers should be very specific. After a couple of minutes, have the prayers read aloud. Then discuss how they felt about praying for the whole group using just a few sentences. Ask how this compares to our personal prayers that tend to be short and general.

Hello Jesus ■ Ask: *If Jesus were here tonight, standing in front of you, and you could say one thing to Him, what would you say?* Discuss this for a short time. Then point out how this is similar to prayer—it is conversation with a person. Explain that Christ *is* here and we can talk to Him.

Lifted Prayers ■ Distribute papers and pens or pencils and have each person write one or two prayer requests on the sheet. No names should be put on the papers. After everyone has finished, have them crumple up the papers in their fists and then, together, throw them into the air. Have everyone pick up a balled-up request and throw it up again. Then have each person pick up one paper and hold it while you talk briefly about prayer. Explain that we may feel as though our prayers go up and come right back to us, just like the paper balls. The key to getting past the ceiling with our prayers is our relationship with God and the attitude with which we pray. Then have everyone spend a few moments in silent prayer, first praying for their openness to God and then for the requests written on the papers that they hold in their hands.

Praise Songs ■ Use the church hymnal or another songbook to lead the group in a series of praise songs. Songs and Creations, Inc. (P.O. Box 7, San Anselmo, CA 94960) is a great resource—their songbook has more than 80 selections listed under "praise." Then discuss why we call these "praise" songs and how they help us praise and worship God.

Praise Thoughts ■ Use the following outline as a framework for a discussion or a wrap-up on praise.

1. Praise is not just in words to myself and others but in how I act.

2. Praising others can be difficult, but even a small amount of sincere praise will lead to greater reasons for praise.

3. Praise to God is commanded in Scripture, and it often involves singing. (See Psalm 150 and Revelation.)

4. Praise is a vital part of any healthy relationship,

including our relationship with God.

5. Praise should be a natural response to what we know about God and His goodness.

6. Praise gets our eyes off ourselves and onto God.

7. Real praise is not flattery ("Hallowed be thy name").

8. Praise should be a habit—every day and in every situation.

Write a Prayer ■ Using groups of three or four kids, assign each group to write one of the parts of prayer (praising, confessing, giving thanks, asking for others, asking for self). After a few minutes, bring the whole group back together and read the prayer, one section at a time. If possible, copy and distribute it to everyone.

DISCUSSIONS

Balanced Thanksgiving ■ Use the *balanced life* as a format for your discussion. Ask: *For what can we thank God in the physical area of our lives?* Then move on to *mental*, *spiritual*, and *social*.

By the Bells ■ To help students remember to pray, challenge them to pray by the bells in school during the next week. In other words, every time they hear a school bell ring, they should pray briefly. Discuss the experience at the next meeting.

Communication ■ To introduce this discussion, say: *Tonight we've been discussing prayer. This should be an easy topic to discuss because we all claim to be pray-ers. Some of us, however, feel as though our prayers don't get past the ceiling. Others have experienced prayers similar to a visit with Santa Claus—we see God as someone who dishes out goodies for our enjoyment. Still others of us believe deeply in prayer, but we never seem to find the time to spend listening and talking with God. Whatever your situation, here are a few thoughts on what real prayer should be. The simplest definition of prayer is "talking with God." In other words, prayer is communication.*

Then use the following outline as the framework for your discussion.

1. Effective communication involves a clear relationship. *In any relationship, all barriers and blocks need to be removed before there can be effective communication. If you have lied to your parents recently, you will have a difficult time talking to them; if you have just had a fight with your boyfriend or girlfriend, you probably won't be talking at all; and so on. The same is true with God. To have effective communication with Him, we need to clear the air, confess our sins and shortcomings, and remove the barriers to a good relationship.*

2. Effective communication takes time. *It is impossible to have a deep conversation with someone in bits and pieces, a minute or two a day. We know that won't work in our human relationships, but often we expect it to be effective with God. Real prayer involves "chatting" all day with Him and setting aside other times for longer talks.*

3. Effective communication involves honesty. *No one likes a phony, and most of us would rather not spend much time talking with someone who is playing a role, bragging, or rationalizing. Sometimes we try to "snow" God. That's kind of silly, actually, because He knows our very thoughts and motives. If we really want Him to work in our lives and to answer our prayers, we must honestly share our real thoughts and deepest feelings.*

4. Effective communication involves listening. *We have been trapped in conversations where the other person does all the talking. It's frustrating. We feel as though they really don't care about what we have to say (when we do get that word in edgewise)–they are only waiting for their chance to speak again. A deep and meaningful prayer life will involve times of meditation on God's Word–just thinking about what we've read–and, at other times alone where we wait for God to speak to us. We spend so much time talking and so little time listening because we're trying to talk God into doing our will instead of being willing to do His.*

5. Effective communication is two-way. *In other words, it's not just asking. It is also giving and saying thank you. This two-way communication is a vital ingredient in prayer.*

Jesus Said ■ Emphasize the following points from Matthew 6:5-13 and 7:7-12.

1. Our prayers should have *sincerity*, not be hypocritical (6:5-8).

2. Our prayers should have *submission*, acknowledging who God is (6:9-10).

3. Our prayers should have *supplication*, expressing our needs to God (6:11-13).

4. Our prayers should have *strength*, holding firm to faith in God, His love and faithfulness (7:7-8, 11).

Our Father ■ Use the Lord's Prayer as the outline for your discussion. Take each phrase and discuss it: for example, "What does it mean to call God 'our Father'?" "Where is heaven?" "Where is God—in heaven or here?" "What does 'hallowed' mean? How can we do that to God's name?" "How would our lives change if His will would be done in us?" Especially emphasize the "forgiving our debtors" phrase. Close by reciting the Lord's Prayer together.

Praise ■ Ask:

• When do you find it difficult to praise someone? Why?

• When is it easy to praise someone? Why?

• When is it difficult to accept praise? Why?

• When is it easy to accept praise? Why?

• When is it difficult to praise God? Why?

• How can we praise God?

Talking with God ■ Ask:

• If prayer is "talking to God," how do our prayers help us get to know Him better? (Usually they don't because we do all the talking, our mind wanders, and we don't listen. Our prayers could help us if we talked to Him about Him, thanked Him for His various attributes, and meditated on what we've learned in the Bible about God.)

• Where would you look in the Bible for a good picture of what God is like? How about good examples of prayers? (Jesus said that if we've seen Him, we've seen the Father. We can take a close look at Jesus, His life, and His prayers.)

BIBLE STUDIES

The Bible on Prayer ■ Pass out these verses to various students. Have them read aloud, one at a time, and discuss each verse.

• Joshua 1:8 (We should meditate on God's Word.)

• Psalm 46:10 (We must be quiet at times to really know God.)

• Psalm 55:17 (We should pray regularly.)

• Matthew 5:44 (We should pray for our enemies.)

• Matthew 6:5-7 (We should pray secretly and honestly.)

• Matthew 6:9-15 (Prayer implies relationship—"Father.")

• Matthew 26:41 (Prayer will keep us from sin.)

• Luke 18:1 (Prayer will give us courage.)

• John 16:23-24 (Prayer involves asking.)

• 1 Thessalonians 5:16-18 (We should pray at all times, giving thanks.)

• James 5:13-14 (We should pray for those with deep needs.)

Add others.

His Prayer and Ours ■ Divide the Lord's Prayer into these sections taken from Matthew 6 (NIV): *Our Father in heaven, hallowed be Your name; Your kingdom come, Your will be done on earth as it is in heaven; Give us today our daily bread; Forgive us our debts, as we also have forgiven our debtors; And lead us not into temptation, but* *deliver us from the evil one.*

Give each section to a group of kids. Tell them to discuss its meaning and to be ready to act it out for the whole group and then teach it.

In Jesus' Name ■ Take time to explain briefly the basic parts of prayer—Adoration, Confession, Thanksgiving, Supplication (for others and self)—that spell out ACTS. Next, read John 14:13-14 and ask:

• How does this verse relate to prayer? (we can ask God for anything in prayer)

• Does this really mean we can ask for anything? (no—only for things which will bring glory to God)

• What does "in Jesus' name" mean? (it means to call on the power of Jesus' name)

Read John 16:23-26 and ask:

• What does asking "in Jesus' name" mean here? (to call on the power of Jesus)

• What is complete joy? How can a person obtain this joy? (Joy in knowing that your sins have been forgiven and you are a child of God. To obtain this joy, you need to accept Jesus' offer of salvation.)

Jesus and Prayer ■ Distribute pencils or pens and make copies of the following matching quiz. The correct answers are in parentheses. Add other situations.

JESUS AND PRAYER

___ Jesus sweats blood (d)	a. disciples and demons (Mark 9:29)
___ Some cases need extra prayer (a)	b. The Lord's Prayer (Matt. 6:9)
___ Jesus prays for us (e)	c. Jesus wakes the disciples (Matt. 26:40)
___ Persist in prayer (h)	d. Jesus prays in the garden (Luke 22:44)
___ Ask for anything (g)	e. after the last supper (John 17:20)
___ Jesus teaches how to pray (b)	f. Jesus prays for Lazarus (John 11:41-42)
___ Jesus witnesses in prayer (f)	g. moving mountains (Matt. 21:21-22)
___ Pray to fight temptation (c)	h. keep on knocking (Luke 11:9)

After giving the correct answers, look up the references and discuss the meanings and implications for our lives today.

Prayer Accomplishments ■ Have everyone turn to James 5:13-18. Read the passage aloud with everyone following along. Then ask how many times prayer is mentioned directly or indirectly. Ask how many examples are in this passage that require prayer alone. How many examples require prayer with someone else? Ask: *According to this passage, what does prayer accomplish?*

Read the appropriate verses as you give the following points. Elaborate on each point as you give it:

• verse 13—prayer is a way to endure; prayer is a way to praise

• verse 14—prayer is a channel for physical healing; prayer is a channel for confession

• verses 15-16—prayer is a channel for forgiveness

• verses 17-18—prayer gets results

Challenge students to get in the habit of praying for other people. One way to do this is to make a list of people, needs, and other requests to use during prayer. Also challenge students to enlist others to pray for them. Sometimes we don't want to admit that we have needs. But our friends and loved ones want to help us, and the best help they can give is to pray for us.

Prayer Groups ■ Use the following to get everyone into groups of 5 to 10. Type out the verses and then cut them up into various sections. Mix up all the pieces and distribute them. At your signal, the kids should get into their groups by matching up the verses. After you've read the verses aloud to make sure that every person is in the correct group, have each group discuss their specific verse and decide what the verse is teaching about prayer.

• Matthew 6:7 (vain repetition)
• Matthew 21:21-22 (pray and receive)
• 1 Thessalonians 5:16-17 (pray without ceasing)
• Colossians 4:2 (devote yourselves to prayer)
• James 5:14-16 (pray for the sick)

Prayer Plays ■ Use two teams and assign each team either Matthew 6:5-8 or Matthew 7:7-12. Give them five minutes to organize a play for dramatizing their verses in a modern setting. They should use as many kids as possible from their teams in these little dramas. When they perform, they should present the play and then read their passage afterward.

After the plays, read the following sanctimonious prayer aloud: *God, I don't mean to brag, but I'll bet you've been impressed with how well I've been doing lately, haven't you, God. I mean, I look at the people around me who are really making a mess of their lives, who are miserable to be with, and I'm just glad that I'm not like them. I don't really think I was ever as bad as them, God. It just took me some time to realize that You needed me on your team, God. But now that I'm on your side, we're unbeatable, right God? By the way, I think You owe me some good stuff now that my name is connected with Your cause, but I don't have my list ready. I'll get back to you real soon, God. Don't call me—I'll call You.* Then ask:

• What's wrong with that prayer?

• Why does God tell us to pray in private?

• What does Matthew 7:7-12 teach us about God? How should that affect the way we pray?

Stop and have everyone repeat the Lord's Prayer together. Then ask:

• How is this prayer different from the one I read earlier (the sanctimonious prayer)?

• In what ways does the Lord's Prayer reflect what Jesus taught about prayer in Matthew 6:6-8 and 7:7-8? (approach prayer in a respectful manner, believing that God will answer your requests)

• What elements are in this prayer that should be in all of our prayers? (Write these on the board.)

Psalms ■ Distribute copies of Psalm 150 and read the psalm aloud together. Use other psalms as examples and ask what they teach us about the nature of praise.

Unanswered Prayer ■ Have someone read James 4:1-10 aloud. Ask how that passage relates to the way we pray. Note especially verses 2 and 3. Ask:

• According to this passage, why aren't some people's prayers answered? (they ask with wrong motives)

• What is the last prayer that God answered for you that you didn't think He would?

• What is the relationship between a person's prayer life and his or her closeness to God? (they are intertwined)

• What causes people to be separated from God? (sin, lack of communication with God, neglecting His Word)

• What can we do to become close to God? (pray, read and obey his Word, listen to what He says)

22 WORLD CONCERN AND SOCIAL ACTION

CROWD-BREAKERS

At Your Service ■ Divide into teams and seat them in parallel columns at least eight feet away from the front of the room. Give each team a serving tray and place a garbage bag, filled with various items, on the floor at the front of the room. Explain that at your signal, the first person from each team should come to the front, balancing the tray on one hand, pull an item out of the bag, place it on the tray, and carry it back to the next person on the team without dropping it. That person should repeat the process, adding another item to the tray. If the tray falls or the items spill off, the contest continues with new items being placed on the tray—only the tray may be picked up from the floor. After four minutes, the team with the most items on its tray, wins.

Note: with a large or rowdy group, have separate bags of items to carry, one bag for each team.

Here are some items to include: cotton ball, paper cup, rock or paperweight, book, spoon, toothpick, Ping Pong ball, pencil, golf ball, napkin, salt shaker, and other unbreakable items of varying weights.

Double Matching ■ Prepare a matching quiz using the format below. List *countries* in the middle column and mix up *facts* and *problems* in their respective columns. Tie the problems to current events. For example, the fact for Lebanon could be, *was called the 'Paris' of the Middle East*, and the problem could be *terrible civil war*. The fact for Northern Ireland could be, *known for potatoes*, and the problem could be *'Christian' vs. 'Christian.'* Students should put the number of the fact and the letter of the problem by the correct country.

Facts	Countries	Problems
1.		a.
2.		b.
3.		c.
4.		d.

Field Trip ■ Announce to the group that you are going to take them on a *field trip* to a large department store or mall nearby. Before you go, however, have everyone draw a *character* out of an envelope. Explain that they should try to experience the store or mall as the character they have drawn. Here are some characters to use: a poor person, someone who is very depressed, a very sad person, a lonely person, an angry person, a lost child, someone who is sick, etc. It would be good to have a wheelchair or two for kids to use to experience the store from the perspective of a physically handicapped person. Spend no more than 15 minutes doing this.

After you return, have students explain how they felt in their characters and how they began to see shopping and other normal activities from a different perspective.

First-World Scavenger Hunt ■ The goal of this game is to demonstrate how much we have and how much we take for granted.

This game can be played individually or in teams. Have everyone take out their wallets or purses. Then explain that you will call out a series of items. Each time they should search their (or their team's) belongings, find the item, and bring it to you. The first person to bring the item called wins that round. The winner is the person or team winning the most rounds. Here are some possible items to call.

- a $20 bill
- a ticket stub
- a designer shirt
- a picture of a house
- evidence of a recent purchase of over $50
- a rubber band from someone's brace
- evidence of a trip by plane during the last month
- a piece of gold jewelry
- perfume
- a pizza coupon
- car keys
- a voter's registration card

You may want to comment about these evidences of our collective wealth.

Global Scavenger Hunt ■ Distribute bags to individuals or teams of two or three and allow 20 or 30 minutes to find items representing as many countries as possible. These items may be found inside the building, outside, in a store, etc.; and they may include food (for example, Turkish taffy), clothes (for example, a Mexican sombrero), pictures, (for example, a postcard from England), appliances (for example, Sony Walkman made in Japan), puns (for example, "grease" = "Greece"), etc. After everyone has returned, display the items and award a prize to the winning team or individual.

Globe-trotter Relay ■ Divide into teams and place a large map of the world on the wall. When you call out a country, each team's representative should run to the map, find the country, and plant his or her team's flag (a colored pin or piece of tape). The person to find the country first wins that round for his or her team. Repeat for as many rounds as you wish, using different team representatives each time. Countries could include Chad, Bangladesh, United Arab Emirates, Somalia, Ukraine, Bosnia, Latvia, Kuwait, Liechtenstein, Belize, Zimbabwe, Singapore, as well as some of the larger and better-known ones.

Helping Hand ■ Seat everyone so that they form a long snake or chain. Explain that this works much like the wave cheer they see in stadiums and gymnasiums. It begins and then passes through the chain in an undulating manner. Here's how it works. The first person in the chain (this could be you) begins the process by taking the next person by *both* hands and pulling that person to his or her feet. When person #2

is standing, person #1 sits back down. Then person #2 turns to the next person and pulls him or her up. Person #2 sits down while person #3 turns and pulls up the next person, and so on until everyone has been pulled up and is seated again. Explain that the goal is to go all the way through the whole group and back as quickly as possible. (Note: each person should pull the next one up. The one being pulled should not jump up or resist being pulled.) To add motivation, you may want to make this a team competition, but make sure that everyone follows the rules.

This illustrates how one person can help another and how one person makes a difference (if one person stops, the whole chain reaction stops).

In Their Shoes ■ Divide into two teams and seat them together at one end of the room. Lay out a course with five stations at the front of the room. At each station, place two pairs of shoes (one for each team). Explain that this is a relay race. At your signal, the first person from each team should run to the first station, put on the shoes there, and then walk in those shoes to the next station. There, he or she should change into the shoes at that station (leaving the first pair there) and walk to the next station. This process should be repeated until he or she is back to where he or she started. There, he or she should slip out of the shoes, put on his or her own pair, and return to the team. The next person on the team may begin the process when the person ahead is at the second station. The first team to have everyone complete the course, wins.

Here are the types of shoes to place at the stations (you'll need two pairs of each type, one for each team): tennis shoes, rubber boots, work shoes, sandals or clogs, and high heels. Note: if you have a large group, do this with 5–8 competitors per team.

Point: We will be more sensitive to others if we think about what it would be like to *walk in their shoes.*

It's a Small World ■ Pass out the following matching quiz without the answers. (The correct answers are in parentheses.)

IT'S A SMALL WORLD

Match each word with the correct country or nationality.

Russian (h)	a. checkers
Siberian (i)	b. spring
Hong Kong (e)	c. measles
Chinese (a)	d. knight
Pole (k)	e. flu
Bermuda (g)	f. pastries

English (n)	g.	shorts
French (v)	h.	roulette
Turkish (p)	i.	huskie
Mexican (x)	j.	twins
Spanish (s)	k.	vault
Jamaica (m)	l.	bacon
Colombian (u)	m.	Joe
Tasmanian (r)	n.	leather
Brazil (z)	o.	tape
Arabian (d)	p.	bath
Norwegian (aa)	q.	tanker
Brussels (y)	r.	devil
Canadian (l)	s.	inquisition
Swiss (w)	t.	hound
Irish (b)	u.	coffee
Scotch (o)	v.	toast
German (c)	w.	cheese
Afghan (t)	x.	hat dance
Danish (f)	y.	sprouts
Liberian (q)	z.	nut
Siamese (j)	aa.	wood

My Cup Runneth Over ■ Divide into teams. Give each team a glass filled with colored liquid (to be placed at one end of the room), a smaller empty glass (to be placed at the other end of the room), and an eyedropper. Team members, one at a time, will fill the eyedropper at one end of the room, empty it in their glass at the other end, and pass the eyedropper to the next teammate in line. The first team to overflow their glass wins. Note: Use a different color of water for each team, and make sure your liquids are non-staining.

Not-so-fast Food ■ Choose a few competitors (depending on how much pie you can afford) and explain that they will be involved in an eating contest. After everyone has been seated at the table in front of a piece of pie covered with ice cream, distribute sets of chop sticks that they must use to eat the food. The first person to eat all of the pie and ice cream wins.

Sense-tense ■ Divide into six teams and assign each team a number and a word. Explain that when you hold up their group's number, they should stand as a group and shout out their word. (Their number may be used more than once.) Here are the numbers and words:

1—want

2—and

3—I

4—all

5—need

6—have

Practice once by going in order; the sentence will make no sense. Read the following sentences by the numbers, one at a time, pausing after each one to see if they heard what the whole group said. The sentences are:

- 3, 1, 4, 3, 6, 2, 5—I want all I have and need.
- 3, 1, 1, 1, 4—I want, want, want all!
- 2, 5, 3, 6, 4, 3, 1—And need I have all I want?
- 6, 3, 5, . . . 3, 1, 4—Have I need? I want all!
- 3, 5, 4, 3, 1, 2, 6—I need all I want and have.
- 4, 3, 1, 2, 5, 3, 6—All I want and need I have.

If students get the hang of it early, you can speed up with each succeeding sentence. After the last one, review the sentences one at a time and ask if they ever feel this way. Point out that we have so much, but often we cling to it and want more.

Serving Race ■ This may be done as a team relay or as a contest among individual competitors. The idea is to have a *waiter* walk quickly through a course, holding above his or her head, with one hand, a round tray with a champagne glass filled with water balanced on it. Over his or her left arm, which should be bent appropriately at the elbow and held in front of his or her waist, should be draped a white towel. The first person to navigate the course without spilling the water wins. Note: in a relay race, the first person would have to pass the towel, tray, and so forth to the next person on the team who then would walk the course. Award points for time of finish and for water left in the glass to determine the winning team.

Spin the Globe ■ Bring a globe that can be spun on its axis. Choose a number of volunteers who will close their eyes (or be blindfolded), spin the globe, and stop the spin by placing a finger on the globe. Assign each player a task related to the place pointed to. At first, make this light and fun, giving a humorous task for each ocean and continent (for example, for landing in the Caribbean, sing a reggae song or do the limbo; for landing in Egypt, walk like an Egyptian). Later (or the second round), have players tell about the countries on which their fingers land—what needs have they heard of there or near there? If they land in an ocean, they could talk about the boat people, the Haitian refugees, etc. (Come prepared with a list of countries and needs.) The point is that the world is filled with needy people. How aware are we? What are we doing about it?

DISCUSSION STARTERS

Actions ■ Conclude a meeting by encouraging students to choose two actions—a personal commitment (to reach out to the "nerd-like" kid at school, to help a handicapped student, to become a pen pal to a missionary kid overseas, to tutor a slower student, to help at home, etc.) and a group commitment (to sponsor an orphan overseas, to send "care packages" to missionary families, to form a youth group coalition to meet specific community needs through special projects, to "adopt" grandparents in nursing homes, to work with the student council to sponsor quality assembly programs, etc.).

Amnesty International ■ Read aloud a few of their reports on repression, torture, and other atrocities as a catalyst for discussion and prayer.

Atmosphere ■ On the wall, hang provocative pictures of human needs (for example, a hungry child, a person in prison, someone experiencing grief, a person walking all alone). At some point in the meeting, point to each one and discuss what these people are feeling, how Christians should respond to them, whether we know people like these, what we can do to help them, etc.

Comfort Factor ■ Have the group list the qualities in others that might cause some kids to be uncomfortable with them. The list could include: a loud person; a person always telling corny jokes; someone always telling dirty jokes; someone swearing a lot; a person of a different race; a person with a physical handicap; a very uncoordinated person; a person with a mental handicap; someone who smells bad; a person who always wears old or dirty clothes; a teacher's pet; etc.

Distribute sheets of paper and pens or pencils. Have everyone write the qualities down the left-hand side. Then, to the right, have them write the comfort factor for each one. Write this scale on the board so they will know what numbers to use: 1 = like being with this person; 2 = this person is OK; 3 = take this person as he or she comes; 4 = avoid this person; 5 = reject this person. Afterward, total the numbers to see what kind of persons the group would tend to avoid or reject. Then discuss their answers and how they

really act toward those with whom they feel uncomfortable.

Getting Involved ■ Go through newspapers or current news magazines and clip out stories of hijackings, bombings, unjust imprisonments, kidnappings, and other human rights violations. Pass out the stories and have students summarize them aloud for the whole group. Then ask them what they can do to make a difference in the world—right now. Here are some possibilities:

• Become informed.

• Pray for the persecuted and the persecutors.

• Write government leaders in the countries involved.

• Write congressional representatives, asking them to intervene, put pressure on, and help.

• Send money and clothing where it will be useful.

Giving Collage ■ Divide into three groups and give each group a stack of magazines, a pair of scissors, a role of tape, and a piece of poster board. Their assignment is to create collages (one per group) out of pictures found in the magazines according to their assigned theme.

• Group 1—self-centeredness

• Group 2—world needs

• Group 3—helping hurting people

After everyone has finished, have the groups display and explain their works of art. Then ask:

• How difficult was it to find pictures to fit your theme?

• Which group had the easiest time? Why?

• What if a magazine were published of your school; which theme would be the most prominent? Why?

• What if a magazine were published of you; what would it look like? Why?

Good News ■ Play the Anne Murray song "A Little Good News" (from the album of the same name, Capitol Records, Inc.) and ask:

• What kind of bad news does Anne Murray mention in the song?

• This song was written a few years ago—which of these things are in the news today?

• What difference can just one person make in the world?

• What difference could a group of Christians make in the world?

• What difference could *our* group of Christians make in the world?

Handy Dandy Helping Machine ■ Divide into groups. Explain that some people want to help others without getting involved directly. The task of each group, therefore, is to create a "machine" that will deliver some help to a needy person, with the operator of the machine only having to pull a lever or push a button. Everybody in the group has to be some part of the machine. Then have each group draw the description of a needy person out of an envelope. The needy people could include: a homeless person needing a friend; a sick person needing medical care; a mother needing someone to baby-sit her children; etc. Have each group set up and operate their "machine." Then discuss the ways that people actually use to help others in need without getting involved personally. These could include: hiring someone else, giving money, expecting the government to do the work, talking or writing about the problem, and so forth.

Inscription ■ This inscription was found in Lubeck Cathedral. Read it and then discuss it or have someone read it to end the meeting.

You call me Master—and obey me not.

You call me Light—and see me not.

You call me Way—and walk me not.

You call me Life—and desire me not.

You call me Wise—and follow me not.

You call me Rich—and ask me not.

You call me Fair—and love me not.

You call me Eternal—and seek me not.

You call me Gracious—and trust me not.

You call me Noble—and serve me not.

You call me Mighty—and honor me not.

You call me Just—and fear me not.

If I condemn you—blame me not.

Interview ■ Invite some international students and ask them to share their experiences living in the United States. Ask:

• What did you expect to find when you came to the U.S.?

• How did your experience differ from these expectations?

A visiting foreign missionary would be a great interview subject; change the questions to apply to his or her mission country.

The Least of These ■ Take the specific examples mentioned in Matthew 25 (hungry, thirsty, stranger, naked, sick, in prison) and arrange special field trips to observe these needs firsthand (for example, take a tour of the local prison or jail or drive through skid row). After each trip ask what the kids, as a group and as individuals, might be able to do to help those people. Possible answers would include: write letters to prisoners, give money to those who are helping the poor and those on skid row, send food, collect clothes, and pray. Make a group prayer list that reflects these special needs.

Meeting Needs ■ Hold a brainstorming session with the group. Use a flip chart or chalkboard and list all the needs they can think of, first in their neighborhood and in the church's neighborhood. (As you fill a sheet on the flip-chart or complete a category, tear off the sheet and tape it to the wall.) Then list needs in *these* categories: the immediate community, the metropolitan area, the country, and the world. These needs may be general (for example: hungry people, homeless people, older people, etc.) or quite specific (for example: *Mrs. Jones is an invalid and needs someone to clean her house.*) Choose two needs that the group will help meet, one from the local area and one national or international in scope, and brainstorm creative ways to help. Then challenge everyone to serve in their homes and neighborhoods, meeting the needs of hurting people they know.

Missionaries ■ Bring the names of missionary kids (especially junior and senior highers) and stationery and have your young people write letters to them.

Missionary Map ■ If you have a youth room, post a large world map with various missionaries and other overseas contacts marked on it with pins, pictures, etc. From time to time, highlight one of these missionaries and pray for him or her.

Missions Conference ■ Design a missions conference for your group. Bring in special speakers, show informative films, have displays, and write to missionary kids.

Missions Experience ■ This will require extensive preparation but should be well worth the effort.

Have students meet at an appointed place that also can be their last stop. In between they will travel to at least four other locations as follows:

1. *Wardrobe.* An ideal setting would be the garage of someone who has just had a large garage sale and wouldn't mind you raiding the leftovers before taking them to Goodwill. Students should find new outfits to wear on their mission experience. They should keep their own underwear on but completely change the

rest of their clothes. Provide separate areas for girls and guys to change, and give everyone plastic bags for their *old* clothes.

2. *Training*

Up and Over. Take them to a large yard or open space where you have created a simple, but frustrating obstacle course. The course could include tire rows to run through, a low bar to crawl under, a board on cement blocks to walk on, lines on the ground or floor to hop over, and so forth. Divide into teams and make this a relay in which each person must navigate the course. Time the teams and add 10 seconds for every mistake. Or you could do this as an individual event.

Packing for the Field. Organize the group into one large circle or smaller circles of 10–15 in each. Explain that part of their preparation will involve packing. Designate a person in each circle to begin, and explain that they should move clockwise. The first person should say, *I went to the mission field, and I took with me* _____ (something needed on the field; for example, *proof that I had taken all the required shots*). The next person should repeat the sentence, saying what the first person did and adding his or her own item. Continue this. The goal is to go completely around the circle. For a twist, you could change the sentence in the middle to: *When I got to the mission field, I discovered that I really didn't need my* _____!

Language. At this point, explain that they will have to use a new language. Have them number off by threes. Explain that they must now speak using the word *blank* in place of every first, second, or third words they say, depending on the number they received when everyone counted off by threes. Use the sentence, *This will be a very interesting experience* to illustrate what they must do.

1 = *Blank will be blank very interesting blank.*

2 = *This blank be a blank interesting experience.*

3 = *This will blank a very blank experience.*

3. *Service*. Next, they should be transported to a place where they can be involved in some effort of service. Depending on the group, you might even consider using an area that might cause a little embarrassment, like cleaning up a local park. Or you might take them caroling out of season at the home of a shut-in. Even a walk through a local mall might be interesting to the group—it certainly would cause a stir in their new outfits.

4. *Debrief*. This part can take several directions. You might ask kids to reflect on their brief experiences,

comparing what they felt and saw with what a missionary might experience going into a foreign culture. If you can arrange for a missionary to speak to the group, try to make sure that he or she hears this discussion. It will uncover some of the stereotypes that students have of missionary life and work. Then that person can address those ideas in his or her talk. It would be helpful to arrange for such a speaker to interact with the students afterward.

5. *Food*. Transport the students back to the starting point for refreshments. Be sure to arrange for a variety of foreign dishes and treats.

Music ■ Play one or more contemporary songs dealing with global problems and concerns and discuss the lyrics and the possible motives for writing and performing them. Song options include secular renditions (*Do They Know It's Christmas?* by Band Aid; *We Are the World* by USA for Africa; and *Tears Are Not Enough* by Northern Lights) and Christian songs (including *Do Something Now* by CAUSE, Gary Rand's album *Songs for the Jubilee*, Ken Medema's album *Kingdom in the Streets*, Petra's *Hollow Eyes*, and many others).

News Flash ■ Distribute newspapers from a variety of cities and countries if possible (most of them should be written in English) and have everyone look for stories about problems in foreign countries. These they should cut out and formed into a group collage. Spend a few minutes discussing how Christians should respond in each situation and how they themselves would respond if they were living there. Then have students share experiences they've had in the countries named and tell about any people they know there.

Observed Needs ■ Using adults and kids that your group doesn't know, dress them appropriately and place them at various locations near the meeting place. One could be dressed like a homeless person, with all his belongings in a bag on his back. One could be a bag lady. One could be in a wheelchair. One could just be a teenager hanging out. And one person could approach your kids and ask for a handout. Later, in the meeting, bring in your actors, in costume, and have them share how they were helped or ignored by group members.

Potluck ■ Sponsor an international potluck dinner where individual young people (or groups of kids) make and bring the dishes to eat.

Prayer ■ Before a meeting, prepare on index cards short summaries of the special needs of individual missionaries that your church is supporting. Include as much information as possible (one missionary per card). Then break into small groups, give each group a card, and spend a time in prayer for your missionaries.

Prayer List ■ Keep a group prayer list of "large" concerns (not specific, individual requests). Include on this list world missions and the problem areas of the world. Spend time praying for these various needs in your meetings.

Quiz ■ Hand out the following "anti" quiz, without the answers (correct answers are in parentheses).

FAMOUS "ANTI'S"

1. medicine   anti_____ (antibiotic)
2. look forward to   anti_____ (anticipate)
3. counteracts poison   anti_____ (antidote)
4. radiator filler   anti_____ (antifreeze)
5. protein   anti_____ (antigen)
6. daughter of Oedipus   Anti_____ (Antigone)
7. helpful with a cold   anti_____ (antihistamine)
8. a definite dislike   anti_____ (antipathy)
9. exact opposite   anti_____ (antipode or antithesis)
10. unsociable   anti_____ (antisocial)
11. preventing infection   anti_____ (antiseptic)
12. prejudiced against Jews   anti_____ (anti-Semitic)
13. opposed to monopolies   anti_____ (antitrust)
14. ancient, old   anti_____ (antique or antiquated)
15. British island in the West Indies   Anti_____ (Antigua)

After giving the correct answers and determining the winner, explain that, unfortunately, many Christians are known by their "anti's." Then have the students list all the things that Christians are against. As each one is mentioned, discuss briefly whether or not it is good to be for or against that particular thing. (The list could include drinking, abortion, evolution, secular humanism, dancing, pornography, crime, cheating, premarital sex, etc.)

Ask: Do you think the negative image of Christianity is justified? Why or why not?

Next ask what the New Testament says Christians should be for. Ask for specific evidence for each one, and list these qualities or causes on the chalkboard or poster board. (The list could include love, truth, forgiveness, human rights, honesty, justice, family, marriage, health, healing, hope, morality, faith, personal development, and growth.)

Then say: *It's overwhelming, isn't it, what Christians are for and what they should be for! Unfortunately, however, the world has the opposite idea. Maybe they just haven't seen the evidence. What evidence can you see in our society for positive Christian action?* (hospitals, schools, churches, missions, etc.) *In history?* (abolitionist movement, Sunday school, education for orphans, higher education, etc.) *Across the world?* (missionaries, Christian relief agencies, activists for human rights, etc.) *In this room?*

Refreshments ■ For refreshments, serve a variety of foreign foods (for example, baklava, or just a spoon of rice).

Resources ■ *The Mustard Seed Conspiracy* by Tom Sine (Word, 1981) has many helpful suggestions for group and individual involvement with problems of the poor and oppressed. Evangelicals for Social Action (ESA) and Prison Fellowship are organizations which can be helpful and which offer chances to serve. Youth for Christ has Project Serve, summer missions projects. Intercristo is an organization that matches Christians with service opportunities. World Vision International, Compassion, Care, World Relief, U.S. Center for World Missions, and other organizations will provide many helpful materials from countries and mission fields worldwide.

Santa Cause ■ Have someone enter the room dressed like Santa Claus. Explain that this is a very special Santa with a very special cause. Over his shoulder he has slung his *Serving Sack*, filled with presents. Santa will give a present to everyone who wants to participate. Everyone receiving a present must use that item to serve someone during the next week. The wrapped presents should include: clock, wallet, book, pen, phone, paper plate, roll of cellophane tape or tube of glue, hammer, wash cloth, food can, felt-tip pen set, car keys, camera, and others. Note: some of these *presents* will have to be on loan. Everyone should be ready to report next week on what they did.

Servant Refreshments ■ At the end of the meeting, announce that you will be having "servant refreshments." That is, the kids may eat as much of the food as they wish, but they cannot serve themselves. They can only feed (and be fed by) someone else.

Stewardship ■ Spend a meeting discussing stewardship of lives and money. Help your kids design personal budgets giving special attention to the practice of tithing. Establish a group fund to give money to a special project at church or in the community.

Tangible Help ■ Focus on one specific need and have a work day to raise money for that project.

Up Close and Personal ■ Before the meeting, collect a number of pictures of young people from magazines and newspapers. Look for those that capture a bit of the individual's personality (not models). Mount them on separate pieces of cardboard.

Examples of pictures could be:
• a well-dressed American boy
• a Russian worker
• a young Central American or South American soldier
• an African farmer
• a Japanese tourist
• a African-American in the city
• an Anglo-American in a school
• a Chinese child on a farm
• a Bosnian in the city's rubble
• an Ethiopian with the look of starvation

Then, one at a time, hold up the pictures for the whole group to see and ask them to imagine what the person is like. Use these questions to prod their thinking.
• What do this person's parents do for occupations?
• What are this person's hobbies?
• What career do you think this person will have?
• What was this person's last meal?
• Describe this person's family life.

What I Have ■ Explain that you are going to have a type of scavenger hunt. Whoever has something that matches the description you call out should stand and display or describe the item (the item must be in the room).

Preface each question with: What do you have . . .
• that you received from your brother or sister?
• that you received from an aunt or uncle?
• that you received from a grandparent?
• that you received from a boyfriend or girlfriend?

• that you received from another friend?
• that you received from a teacher?
• that you received from your parent(s)?
• that you received from God?

At first, the only responses will be material (clothes, money, pictures, etc.). Other possibilities could include love, friendship, education, etc. Things received from parents and God could include hereditary characteristics such as looks, hair color, height, and others, and will get into less tangible areas such as security, personality, eternal life, forgiveness, happiness, and others.

Choose a winner, or go right into a discussion of what we have. The point is that all that we are and have are gifts from God, directly or through others—what are we giving to others?

DISCUSSIONS AND WRAP-UPS

Challenge ■ Use this outline as a wrap-up or discussion catalyst.

1. The real world is filled with hungry and oppressed people. It is bigger than our families, community, and country.

2. There are hurting people right near us.

3. The Christian faith is not "fantasy" or only "pie in the sky," it must be applied now, in this world.

4. This application means showing God's love, joy, and peace in our lives in deeper ways than religious clichés and emotional froth, and, instead, reaching out to others with love.

Giving Back ■ Ask the group for ways that we can begin to "give back" some of what God has given to us. Record their answers on a chalkboard, poster board, or flip chart. Begin with major areas such as "home," "time," "money," and "expertise," and list specific ideas under each one. For example, ways to give back time to God could include having a "quiet time," spending time with grandparents, visiting rest homes, doing volunteer work, choosing a career of service, and so on.

Have-nots ■ Ask:
• What kind of image do you get of China from the news reports in papers and magazines and on television? Of Russia? Somalia? Haiti? Brazil? Iraq? Mexico?
• How accurately do you think the media portray life in those countries? Why?

•How do you think life in America is portrayed by the press in those countries? How accurate is that portrayal? Why?

•How should America be portrayed to other countries? What is the truth about our wealth and abundance?

•If you lived in a very poor country and knew about America's wealth and abundance, how would you feel about the United States?

• What can Americans do to help poor people in other countries?

Love List ■ Use this assignment to get material for a future meeting. Have everyone list the acts of unselfish love they observe around them during the next week. They should list at least one each day and try to list different acts. Discuss their findings at your next meeting.

Missions Talk ■ Explain that the biggest obstacles we have to overcome in following Christ are the questions we must face. God's guidance rarely comes until we are deeply committed to *being guided*.

1. The first question to ask in becoming a missionary isn't, *Where does God want me to go?* The first question is, *How can I serve God better right now where I am?* We usually think of missions work involving another culture, but there is a culture and language that you already know. You have grown up in it. The real challenge in representing Christ is in communicating the Gospel to people you already understand and who understand you. When Jesus told His disciples *where* they would represent Him, He started the list at home (Acts 1:8).

2. The next question to ask in becoming a missionary is, *How clearly am I "keeping the faith"?* (2 Timothy 4:7) One of the paradoxes of the Christian faith is that the more it is *ours*, the more we want to give it away. We keep the faith by sharing it. What matters most is not how *much* of the Bible you know or how much training you have had. What actually matters is how real Christ is in your life. Is there an undeniable hope in you that people notice? (1 Peter 3:15)

3. The third question in becoming a missionary is, *Having begun in my own Jerusalem, am I willing to go or stay wherever God guides me?* Christ never agreed with individuals' offers to follow Him conditionally. Many of Jesus' parables revolve around the *no turning back* part of following Him (Luke 14:25-33).

Over There ■ Ask:

• Who do you know personally who has been to a foreign country? What did that person learn from the experience?

• Who do you know who is from another country? What is his or her religious background?

• What can you do to bring the Gospel to people in other land?

Quick Draw ■ Give everyone a sheet of paper and a pen or pencil. Tell them to write their names on the top and to leave the rest of their sheets blank. Collect all the papers and then redistribute them, making sure that no one gets his or her own. After everyone has someone else's sheet, tell them to take a few minutes to think about that person and then to write on the paper what they think he or she has to offer to the world (positively)—the unique contribution that the person has to make. After a few minutes, collect the papers and return them to their owners. You may want to discuss the experience.

Showing Love ■ Pass out papers and pens or pencils to everyone. Have them write three ways that they could show unselfish love to each of the following persons during the next week:

• teacher
• friend
• enemy
• parent
• neighbor
• employee
• sibling

Wrap-up ■ Emphasize the following points in a wrap-up or in your discussion.

1. Our lives model our true faith—what we really believe.

2. Our lives are so full, but often we still hoard what we have, even our overflow.

3. Our selfish, hoarding attitude speaks loud and clear.

4. The world is filled with people who need Christ and who need us.

5. In reality, all that we are and have are gifts that we are to use wisely.

6. Instead of being "sleeping saints," we should wake up and give to others, responding in love and in obedience to God's Word.

Then propose possible group projects such as going on a summer mission trip such as Project Serve (Youth for Christ), having a planned famine (World Vision), adopting an orphan (Compassion), raising money for the needy of your community, or visiting regularly the nursing home.

Have the group choose one project and distribute cards so that they can sign up and indicate their commitment to the project.

BIBLE STUDIES

Adopt a Neighbor ■ Study the parable of The Good Samaritan (Luke 10:25-37) and discuss the question of who our neighbors are. Ask the pastor for the names of people in the church or community who have needs that your group could meet (for example, mow the lawn, rake the leaves, shovel the snow, prepare and take meals, clean the house, take to church, visit in nursing homes or hospitals).

Faith Demonstration ■ Type up James 2:14-19 and give copies to six young people (each sheet should have one verse highlighted). Ask them to read their verses, in order, with feeling. After they read, ask:

• What does James mean in these verses? What is his message? (faith and action go hand in hand)

• How do people know that you and I have faith in Christ? (by what we say and do)

• What can we do to demonstrate our faith? (talk and deeds which glorify God)

Goats and Sheep ■ Have a guy and a girl read Matthew 25:31-46, with the girl reading the first half (verses 31-40) and the guy reading the second half (verses 41-46). Distribute cards and pencils and have everyone answer these questions individually.

1. What made the difference between the sheep and the goats? (the sheep had deeds which reflected their faith; the goats did not)

2. Based on your life-performance so far, would you be a sheep or a goat?

3. List one situation where you could act like a sheep.

Collect the cards and read their answers to question #2 aloud without indicating the identity of the person. Then read a few answers for question #3. Discuss the experience—how they would feel in that kind of situation and what action they should take.

Love ■ Have a student read John 13:34-35 aloud. Then ask:

• What is the main point of these verses? (love one another)

• Why would this be such a dramatic evidence of our belonging to Christ? (because it is not seen as "normal" to love those who do us wrong)

• How do these verses relate to non-Christians? (we are to love them)

• How can we show Christ's love to others? (through our talk and actions)

Salt and Light ■ Have a student read Matthew 5:13-16 aloud. Then ask the group to give the attributes and qualities of both salt and light. List their answers on the board. After compiling the list, ask how each of these qualities is relevant to the Christian life. In other words, how can Christians really be "salt" and "light" in the world? Here are some possible answers:

• Salt is used as seasoning—Christians can bring flavor to the world through their love, joy, etc.

• Salt is used as a preservative (it kept meat from spoiling in the first century)—Christians should be a preserving force for good, holding back the rot of sin.

• Salt is used to melt ice—Christians can melt the cold barriers that divide people from each other and from God, through love, friendship, and compassion.

• Salt is used as a healing agent—Christians are called to help heal the physical and spiritual hurts in their communities and the world.

• Light is used to show the way—Christians should show the way to eternal life.

• Light is used to spotlight—Christians should focus attention on Christ.

• Light is used to signal and warn—Christians should warn of the consequences of sin.

• Light illuminates—Christians can help people understand God's Word and Jesus' true identity.

Discuss various "bushels" and challenge the students to let their lights shine. Then turn off the lights, light a single candle in the center of the group, and sing together prayerfully "Pass it On," "This Little Light of Mine," or a similar song.

Sheep and Goats ■ Distribute copies of Matthew 25:31-46 with the following questions written below.

1. Who are the *sheep*? Who are the *goats*? (sheep=the righteous, goats=those who are cursed)

2. Where is Jesus in this story? (He is judging the sheep and goats)

3. Who are the true Christians in this story? (people who serve others in the name of Christ)

4. What kinds of needs are mentioned? (hunger, thirst, visiting those who are sick or in prison, giving shelter)

Discuss their answers briefly. Then ask:

• Does this passage apply to us today? Why or why not?

• How does this passage relate to the worldwide needs

that we have heard about and discussed? How can we respond to those needs? Who is responsible for solving the problems with human rights and human needs?

• Here at home, who is hungry? Sick? In prison? How can we respond to these people?

• If you were to stand before Jesus right now, what would He say about the way you treated Him on earth? Would you be with the *sheep* or the *goats*? Why?

The Bible Says . . . ■ Type the following verses on separate index cards and number them. Distribute the cards and have individuals read the verses aloud, one at a time, in numerical order. Make no comments until all the passages have been read.

1. Amos 2:6-7a
2. Deuteronomy 15:10-11
3. Psalm 109:30-31
4. Psalm 146:5-7
5. Revelation 3:17-18
6. Psalm 73:12
7. James 5:1-6
8. Luke 4:18-19
9. Luke 14:12-14
10. Luke 18:22
11. Matthew 25:42-46
12. 2 Corinthians 8:9
13. Philippians 2:4-8

Afterwards ask:

• How do you feel after hearing all of these verses?

• What is God telling us to do?

• How do you think you can make a contribution toward solving these problems?

What Christians Are For ■ Break into small groups and give each group one of the following passages. Have them discuss the positive implication of each passage. In other words, what are the verses saying Christians should do?

1. 1 Corinthians 13:1, 1 John 3:16-18 (love)
2. Matthew 5:13-16 (be "salt" and "light")
3. Philippians 2:4-11 (be humble)
4. James 2:14-19 (give to those in need)
5. Matthew 25:34-40 (respond to poverty, injustice, etc.)
6. Luke 6:37-38 (forgive)

Have the groups report their findings, and then discuss how they can apply these in specific ways in their lives.

COMPETITION AND SPORTS

CROWD-BREAKERS

Children's Games ■ Because you are emphasizing competition, the crowd will be enthusiastically involved in whatever games you choose. Therefore, simple children's games (school yard games or purchased games or puzzles) can be very effective. Do them as relays or as head-to-head competition between team representatives.

De Agony of De Feet ■ In this relay team members must pass a variety of items down the line, person to person, using prescribed parts of the body. Give each team the same items to pass and let them decide how they will pass each item. The team finishing first wins. Here are the rounds.

• "de-feet"—items may be passed only between each person's feet

• "de-arms"—items may be passed only between each person's arms; no hands allowed

• "de-elbows"

• "de-chins and necks"

• "de-little fingers"

• "de-hips"

• "de-knees"

Items to pass could include bananas, marshmallows, marbles, water balloons, soccer balls, Play Doh, etc.

Equipment Race ■ This is a competition among girls. Choose pairs of girls to compete and give each pair an identical set of football equipment in a bag. The football equipment set should include: shoulder pads, hip pads, rib pads, helmet, forearm pads, jersey, thigh pads, and pants. Also include some equipment from other sports (for example, basketball or volleyball knee pads, batting or golf glove, baseball glove, hockey pads, etc.) Have each pair designate one person as the player and the other as the helper. Explain that the contest is to see who can get dressed the quickest, using all the *football* equipment in the bag.

Exercise Relay ■ Beforehand, determine your number of teams and competitors and make the appropriate amount of *exercise cards*. Compile identical sets for the teams. On each card, write a specific exercise to be performed. Possibilities are listed below.

Divide into teams and have them line up in parallel columns. At your signal, the first person in each team should run to the front of the room, draw a card out of his or her team's box, and follow the written instructions. After completing the exercise, he or she should run back to the team and tag the next team member who should follow suit. The first team to complete all the exercises is declared the most physically fit and wins the game.

Exercise instructions could include:

• do 15 jumping jacks

• do 17 deep knee bends with your arms extended

• do 14 sets of alternate toe-touchers, starting each one with your hands on your hips

• do 13 full sit-ups with your knees bent

• run in place for 50 strides (count one every time your left foot hits the floor)

• do 10 push-ups

- do 11 rowing exercises
- do 30 up on the toes
- do 22 leg lift shovels
- take 30 duck walk steps

Gatorade Chug ■ As the name implies, this is a contest to see who can drink a glass of Gatorade the quickest. Because this is not the most tasty drink, don't let contestants know what they will be drinking until the game begins. Use team representatives—the first person finished wins. If you have time, you may want to do two rounds—one for the guys and one for the girls.

Hungry Hippos ■ This is a child's game which may be purchased in any toy store. It features four plastic hippos that compete to devour as many marbles as possible. Place the game on a card table in the center of the room. Using team representatives, compete in a series of "hippo matches." The individual to capture the most marbles wins that match for his or her team. Give the winning team 4 points, second place 3 points, third place 2, and fourth place 1. Hold additional matches with new team reps. The team to win the most points after 5 or 6 rounds wins the game.

Hurdles ■ Before the meeting, build little "hurdles" out of popsicle sticks or small pieces of wood and paint them with marking pens to make them look official. Make enough hurdles to replace any that get broken during the game. Have each team choose a representative to compete (a big guy would be best). Using large rubber bands or rope, tie each competitor's knees together. Then, at your signal, he or she is to run the course, jumping over the hurdles that you have placed on the floor. Time each contestant individually, adding 5 seconds for each hurdle knocked down and 20 seconds for each one broken. The fastest person wins.

Position Description ■ In this quiz, you give the football position, and the contestants must tell where the person plays on the field (or vice versa).

a. middle guard (in the middle of the defensive line, across from the offensive center)

b. center (the middle of the offensive line—snaps the ball)

c. middle linebacker (in the center of the second line of defense)

d. defensive end (at one end of the defensive line)

e. guard (an offensive lineman, on either side of the center)

f. tight end (an offensive lineman who must block a

lot but who also is eligible to catch passes)

g. free safety (in the last line of defense; plays *free*—may go to the ball)

h. strong safety (in the last line of defense; takes the deep zone on the strong side of the field)

i. split end or wide receiver (on the end of the offensive line; used primarily for catching passes)

j. offensive tackle (on the offensive line, two positions away from the center, on either side)

k. cornerback (a defensive halfback playing on the outside of the third line of defense; often covers the wide receivers man for man)

l. flanker (a wide receiver on offense who begins play off the line of scrimmage)

Note: add others if you wish.

Rah, Rah ■ Divide into teams and have each team write and perform (with choreography) a cheer for a unique sport. Each team may choose any sport except football, basketball, soccer, baseball, or wrestling. For example, they could select lacrosse, handball, racket ball, gymnastics, fencing, luge, swimming, chess, ice hockey, field hockey, volleyball, cross country, etc. Each cheer should emphasize an important skill or quality of the sport. Note: it is permissible to adapt cheers from other sports (for example, instead of cheering *all the way down the field* for football, they could yell, *all the way down the pool* for swimming).

Reaction Drill ■ Have everyone stand and face you. Tell them that you are going to test their reflexes by doing a reaction drill used by many football teams. You will do a series of hand moves that they must copy as quickly as possible.

Begin with your hands on your thighs. Then bring them up quickly and then back down, slapping your thighs. Pause for a second, and then bring your hands up and clap them three times and put them down again. Continue to add moves, making them a little more complicated and weird.

Spelling Bee ■ Have each team send a representative to the front to compete in an old-fashioned "spelling bee." Begin by asking contestants to spell easy, three-letter words, and gradually move to more difficult ones. Award points for first, second, and third places.

Sports Quiz ■ Pass out copies of SPORTS QUIZ and pens or pencils. Kids should match the sports with their terms, jargon, events, equipment, and names. Words may be matched with more than one sport. The correct answers are in parentheses.

SPORTS QUIZ

a. stick

b. field goal

c. tackling

d. dunk

e. slide

f. love

g. spike

h. goalie

i. block

j. dribbling

k. net

l. World Series

m. racket

n. set

o. check

p. blitz

q. forward

r. 3-pointer

s. Rose

t. grand slam

u. Olympics

v. face off

w. guard

x. fullback

y. Ewing

z. glove

aa. ace

bb. serve

cc. high stick

dd. Super Bowl

ee. goalie

ff. plate

gg. Davis Cup

hh. Stanley Cup

ii. Payton

jj. Martina

kk. pick

ll. bomb

mm. sacrifice

nn. Pele

oo. World Cup

pp. Gretzsky

Ice Hockey

(a, h, k, o, q, u, v, z, cc, ee, hh, mm, pp)

Football

(b, c, e, i, p, r, w, x, dd, ii, ll, mm)

Soccer

(c, h, j, k, q, u, x, ee, mm, nn, oo)

Basketball

(b, d, i, j, k, q, r, u, w, y, kk, mm)

Baseball

(a, e, g, l, s, t, z, ff, mm)

Tennis

(f, k, m, n, t, aa, bb, gg, jj, mm)

Volleyball

(g, jj, k, n, u, aa, bb, mm)

Sports Sounds ■ Distribute sheets of paper and pencils or pens, and explain that you are going to play a tape that features the distinctive sounds of various sports. They should listen and write the sport next to the number of the sound. Then play the tape. Note: when you record the sounds, be sure to state the number of each sound. Here are some possible sounds and sports:

- bouncing ball or *swish* sound (basketball)
- crack of bat on ball (baseball)
- ball falling into the cup (golf)
- cue ball hitting another ball (pool or billiards)
- a serve (volleyball)
- gun shot or beep and a splash (swimming—start of a race)
- pads hitting (football)
- ball rolling down the alley (bowling)
- arrow hitting the target (archery)
- athlete hitting the pit (high jump, long jump, triple jump, or pole vault)
- feet on pavement (running race)
- racket hitting ball (tennis)
- etc.

Super Kids ■ This will take extra preparation but can be a lot of fun and affirming. Beforehand, write a brief description of every person who you know will be at the meeting, including a nickname, strength, and something humorous. As kids enter the room, have an adult helper write descriptions of those whom you don't already have. Then arrange the descriptions in alphabetical order.

Explain that before the Super Bowl or other important football game on TV, the players are introduced individually. Their position, school, major, hometown, and so forth are also included in the introductions. Because most of the kids in the room probably will not get the opportunity to play in a bowl game, you want them to have the introduction experience right now.

Take half of the kids out (for example, last names beginning with A–L) and arrange them alphabetically. Then bring them in, one at a time, while you read the description for each person. After they enter the room, they should sit and watch and listen to the other introductions. Repeat with the other half of kids.

Here's a sample introduction: *Starting at right refreshment guard, Sally "Sparkles" Johnhorst. Sally is a talented actress who has starred in numerous school productions. A soon-to-be graduate of Washington High, this 5' 5" brunette dynamo has proven to be an invaluable member of the youth team!*

Superlative ■ Divide into teams for this variation of a scavenger hunt. Each team will choose someone from their team who meets your announced description. When all the teams' representatives have assembled at the front, you will determine a winner for that round and proceed with the next round. Here are some descriptions to use for the different rounds:

• the tallest member of your team (award points to the team who sends to you the tallest person of all the team representatives)

• the person with the longest hair

• the person with the smallest feet

• the person with the most money in his or her wallet or purse

• the person with the straightest teeth

• the person with the darkest hair

• the strongest (hold a quick arm-wrestling or timed push-ups competition to determine the winner)

This game demonstrates how we often compete in our society. You may want to refer to this in your discussion or wrap-up.

Teams and Cheers ■ As kids enter the room, play "Theme from Chariots of Fire," "Theme from Rocky," "Eye of the Tiger," "Victory" by Kool and the Gang, or another "competitive" song in the background to set the mood. Divide into teams by classes, alphabet, birthdays, or at random and tell each team to make up a cheer for their team. After a few minutes have them cheer, then move into your other games.

The Greatest ■ Explain that this game is an individual as well as a team contest, and offer a prize to the individual who gets all the answers correct (and a team prize for the group with the highest total of correct answers). Then hand out the following quiz. They should match the correct sport or talent with the prize or competition (the correct answers are in parentheses).

THE GREATEST

Sport or Talent	*Prize or Competition*
golf (k)	a. Belmont Stakes
writing (l)	b. Super Bowl
drag racing (j)	c. America's Cup
movies/acting (i)	d. Stanley Cup
football (b)	e. Tony
music (o)	f. Davis Cup

horse racing (a)	g. Indy 500
plays/acting (e)	h. World Cup
professional basketball (m)	i. Oscar
baseball (r)	j. Grand Nationals
hockey (d)	k. Ryder Cup
television/acting (q)	l. Pulitzer Prize
sailing (c)	m. N.B.A. Championship
college basketball (p)	n. W.B.A. Championship
tennis (f)	o. Grammy
soccer (h)	p. Final Four
auto racing (g)	q. Emmy
boxing (n)	r. World Series

Tiny Bubbles ■ Before the meeting, prepare as a target a board or piece of cardboard with a 4-inch hole in the center of it. Also, purchase bubble-blowing liquid and makers. The idea of this game is for one team member to make bubbles while the other team members blow them toward the target. Each bubble to pass through the hole is worth a point. The team to get the most points in two minutes wins. This can also be done as a relay.

DISCUSSION STARTERS

The Prize ■ After a number of games, announce that you are going to proclaim the winning team. Read off the point totals and then pronounce the team with the least points the winner. Calm everyone down and read Mark 9:33-37 aloud. Then ask:

• According to this verse, wouldn't it be right to give the prize to the team with the least number of points? Why or why not?

• What did Jesus mean when He said that whoever wants to be first must be last?

• How is this different from what our society says?

Who Won? ■ See who can remember who won the following championships. Print this or use it as a contest among teams.

1. NBA Championship
2. U.S. Open
3. Super Bowl
4. Indy 500
5. Stanley Cup
6. World Series
7. Olympic Men's 100 Meter Dash
8. NCAA Basketball Championship

9. America's Cup Challenge

10. French Open

If you want to make it really tough, see if they can name who came in second.

Afterward, discuss how important we think these events are and yet how quickly we forget the winners. Also discuss how winning and being a success in the world's eyes compares to being a success in God's eyes.

DISCUSSIONS AND WRAP-UPS

Basic Competition ■ Use these thoughts to stimulate discussion or to wrap up a meeting.

Competition is basic to America. It is integral to our economy (the free enterprise system), and our history is filled with striving to be the best and the greatest. Competition can be healthy if we compete against ourselves or a standard of quality—then we should try to do and be the very best we can. But competition can be unhealthy and even destructive when we compete with others and become obsessed with getting ahead of "them." Often our egos are tied to our achievements—at every football or basketball game, partisans on the winning side raise their index fingers high and shout, "We're number one!" We can feel as though we are failures if we are not the fastest, most attractive, smartest, or whatever.

Coaches ■ Spend a few minutes discussing various types of coaches (well-known ones in the college and professional ranks to coaches they've had in junior and senior high school).

Next, discuss which coach brought out the best in them as team members and as people.

Finally, ask what they think about God as a coach:

• What kind of coach would God be?

• Is this a good illustration of what God is like?

• How would God as coach motivate us to do our best?

Competition—Pros and Cons ■ Use the following outline for a discussion guide or a wrap-up. Add local and personal illustrations where appropriate.

1. *Competition is a way of life in America.* We hold everything from Miss America pageants to "Super Bowls" to determine who is the greatest in some area. We seem obsessed with being "Number 1." We even talk about being "the greatest nation on earth" as though it were a contest.

2. *Competition can be good if it motivates us to be better, to excel*—if we compete against a standard or against ourselves.

3. *Competition can be bad and destructive if we compete only against others,* having to be better than they are. This is bad because it gives us a wrong idea of our worth (we feel worthless when we lose and prideful when we win). It is destructive when we hurt, cheat, or put others down to push ourselves up or to make ourselves look good.

4. *Competition reflects our values.* Our world puts a high priority on money, beauty, power, strength, and youth; therefore, the "winners" excel in these areas. Jesus' values, however, are quite different. Look at Matthew 5:3-12 for His list. It includes "poor in spirit," "mourners," "meek," "hungry for righteousness," "merciful," "pure in heart," "peacemakers," "persecuted for righteousness," and others. People with these qualities come in dead last in our society, but in God's eyes, they are first.

5. *Be careful with competition.* Remember, everything in this world lasts for only a moment, but God's kingdom lasts forever. Keep your focus on doing what He wants. As Duane Thomas, running back for the Dallas Cowboys, said many years ago after they had won the Super Bowl, "If this game is the ultimate, why do we play it every year?"

6. *Find your value in God, not in how good you look or how well you perform.* You are very special to Him—He created you, and He loves you.

Good or Bad? ■ Ask:

• Is competition good or bad and why?

• When have you been helped by competition?

• When have you been hurt by competition?

• Why do you think it is so important for some people to win? (Some of you got pretty involved in our silly games tonight!)

• Besides games and sports, how else do we compete? (looks, grades, status, etc.)

• What does the Bible say about competition?

BIBLE STUDIES

Coach ■ Look up the following passages together. After each one, ask how this characteristic of God fits into the concept of Him as a coach. (Note: sometimes God is more of a cheerleader than a coach to us.)

1. 1 John 2:1-2

2. 1 Corinthians 1:27

3. Romans 8:31-33

4. Matthew 5:38-39

5. Mark 10:44-45

6. 1 John 4:8-7, Romans 8:1

Last and First ■ Divide into groups and give each group one of the passages listed below. Have them discuss what Jesus meant and how it relates to competition.

1. Matthew 19:26-30

2. Matthew 22:37-40

3. Matthew 25:1-13

4. Matthew 25:31-40

5. Mark 9:33-35

6. Mark 10:29-31

7. Mark 10:35-45

NOTE: Following are four designs for whole meetings centered on the competition theme. Each one includes games, discussion questions, and a wrap-up outline.

Non-competitive Games

The New Games Book (Doubleday/Dolphin) is a good resource for games that stress having fun where everyone wins. There are many types of activities included for outdoors, indoors, large groups, small groups, etc. Instead of (or in addition to) these games, the meeting could feature regular competitive games altered so that everyone wins, or games that favor smaller, less athletic kids.

Outdoor games could include touch rugby, "blind volleyball" (played with regular volleyball rules except that no spiking is allowed, and with blankets draped over the net so that players can't see the ball until it comes on their side), "maximum volleyball" (the ball must be hit by at least 5 different members of the team before it can be returned), or kick ball.

Indoor possibilities could include reverse charades (a team representative must guess which word or phrase his or her team is acting out), sit-down tug-of-war, and others.

Discussion Questions

• What was unusual about the games we played?

• How do you feel about not having a clear-cut winner and loser?

• What does this say about the relationship between fun and competition?

• Paul uses the analogy of sports (Philippians 3:12-26). How does this relate to competition?

Wrap-up

1. Paul is saying that the overwhelming motivation for his life is to be the kind of person God wants him to be, no matter what others may think or do.

2. Too often we use others to help us feel good about ourselves. That is, their acceptance of us in the clique will enhance the way we feel. Or perhaps we compare ourselves to "losers" and look pretty good. Competition often reveals these feelings. It's part of our society and our lives. We seem to be continually competing with others and with ourselves, and we never really accomplish what God wants for us.

3. God's plan is for us to keep our eyes on Christ. He is the only one whose approval really counts (He accepts us and loves us as we are), and He will never let us down. If we keep our eyes on Him and follow His direction, increasingly we will become the kind of people that God wants us to be.

4. This kind of relationship with God will free us to relax with and to accept others. We won't see them as winners or losers or as competitors, but as fellow human beings whom God loves and for whom Christ died.

Competition in Every Area

Design a meeting to involve competition in the four areas of life: physical, mental, social, and spiritual. Here are some possibilities.

Physical Competition

Eating Contests—Divide into teams and choose a representative from each team to eat the most pie within 30 seconds, no hands allowed, or to eat a peach and leave the cleanest pit, without hands.

Choose a couple from each team, blindfold them, and at the signal have them feed each other corn on the cob or some other comparably messy food.

Challenge someone to eat a raw egg or to swallow a live goldfish.

Strength Contests—See who can pick up a chair by using only one hand and gripping the chair near the base of one leg.

Design a unique strength test like pulling a heavy rubber band until it breaks.

Or wrap a person in thread and time how long it takes to break out.

Mental Competition

College Bowl—Choose representatives from each team to compete in a "college bowl" contest. Then ask trick questions like "How many three-cent are stamps in a dozen?" (These can be found in the booklet *How Many Three Cent Stamps in a Dozen* by Herman Hoover: Price/Stern/Sloan, 1979.)

Puzzle—Compose a word puzzle that includes the names of students in your group. The names may be written horizontally, vertically, diagonally, backward, or forward. See who can find the most names.

Trivia—Design a trivia quiz from the high school (for example, Who was last year's homecoming queen? Who was this year's right guard on the football team? What's the name of the assistant principal? What's the color of the cafeteria chairs? Who is the editor of the school newspaper? etc.).

Social Competition

Best Friends—Choose sets of best friends and see how much they really know about each other. Ask questions about birthplace, middle names, favorite foods, etc.

Friends Bingo—Prepare a bingo-type card for everyone with all the spaces blank. Each person must get signatures for every space from kids in the room. Then call out names just as you would the letters and numbers in bingo.

The Most—See who knows the names of the most people in the group.

Spiritual Competition

Bible Books—Choose representatives from teams and have them put a list of Bible books (written on cards) in the proper order. Throw in a few fictitious ones like "Hezekiah" and "Hesitations" to confuse them.

Characters—Give each team a little-known Bible character and have them tell everything they know about him or her. Use people like Gomer, Eutychus, Zipporah, Cleopas, and others.

Definitions—Give each team a theological word and have them write a definition for it. Use words like propitiation, supralapsarianism, and lasciviousness.

Discussion Questions

• Did you notice anything unusual about our games today? (You competed physically, mentally, socially, and spiritually.)

• In real life, how do we compete in these areas?

• Why do you think we have a need to compete? (To feel good about ourselves; to please our parents or peers; etc.)

• How should God's feeling about you as a person affect your need to compete?

Wrap-up

1. Competition is an integral part of our society. The free-enterprise system thrives on it, democracy uses it, and we are all affected by it.

2. The problem is that competition emphasizes a world view that is opposite to the one taught by Christ. The world says power and prestige are

important; the Bible teaches humility (Philippians 2:3-11). The world says we should accumulate wealth and honors; Jesus tells us to give up everything and follow Him (Luke 18:18-30). The world teaches us to look out for our own interests, making sure that no one puts us down; Jesus says we are to love others as much as we love ourselves (Matthew 22:39). The world states that we should strive for importance and popularity; Jesus tells us to serve others (John 13:12-20). The world exalts winners; Jesus says the last shall be first (Matthew 19:30).

Competition in Different Ways

Children's Games—Involve everyone in games that they played when they were much younger. Offer good prizes for the winners to motivate everyone. Possible games could include Ring around the Rosey, Red Rover, Blind Man's Bluff, Pin the Tail on the Donkey, and Musical Chairs.

Losers Are Winners—Design contests which emphasize as positive those qualities that are usually thought of as negative. For example, the slowest in a race or the person with the least number of points could win.

No Control—Design contests where winners and losers really have no way to control the results. For example, they could be judged on physical characteristics (the tallest, oldest, blondest, one with brownest eyes, etc.).

Discussion Questions

• How did you feel about the games today?

• Why were they different that the ones we usually play? (They stressed qualities over which we have no control or which are usually seen as weaknesses or as immature.)

• In what ways do our usual games discriminate against anyone? (Those who don't have natural physical abilities, etc. are at a disadvantage.)

• How does competition motivate you?

• How do you feel when you lose?

• Which people are labeled losers in our society? (poor people, old people, the disabled, those who are uncoordinated, etc.)

• Jesus said, "I tell you the truth, whatever you did for one of the least of these brothers of mine, you did for me" (Matthew 25:31-46). What did Jesus mean, and how does His statement relate to our discussion?

Wrap-up

1. Our society puts on a pedestal those who have natural physical endowments: beauty, strength, speed, and so forth. Those who are plain-looking or poor or

who have the "wrong" race or social background are seen as losers.

2. The Bible warns us about how we treat the outcasts of the world. James 2:1-13 points out that we are guilty of sin in this area, even in church, when we defer to the person with money and fine clothes.

3. As we saw in Matthew, Jesus speaks very directly and emphatically about our treatment of the hungry, poor, and imprisoned. If our Christianity means anything at all, it must motivate us to reach out in love to others, despite the personal cost in dollars, time, and reputation.

4. Many Americans today will be like the rich man in Luke 16:19-31. Because he spent all his time accumulating treasure on earth, he lost heaven. Lazarus, the poor beggar, "won" in the end.

Game of Games—Explain that the object of the game is to win the most games. Divide into teams of two (ideally, boy-girl combinations). Then explain that throughout the house or church there are games in which they will compete. These games have been numbered. Each team will be given a piece of paper listing the order in which they will play the games. If you have 5 games (numbered 1 through 5), the teams would play each one at least once and, ideally, against different teams each time. The games could include Ping-Pong, pool, darts, penny-pitching, ring toss, bean bag tic-tac-toe, and shuffleboard (whatever the home or church has available). If only a few of these games are available, design some of your own, using your imagination and inexpensive props.

Each game should last about 5 minutes. Each time you blow the whistle, the teams should move to their next locations and begin immediately. Whoever has the most points when the whistle blows wins the game they were playing. The final winning team should be determined by the number of winning points (6 points for a win, 4 points for a tie, 2 points for a loss). Be sure to offer very good prizes for the winning couple.

Discussion Questions

• How did you feel about the games?

• What motivated you to compete?

• When and why were you tempted to cheat?

• How did you feel about the people against whom you were competing?

• In each game did you feel better about doing well or about doing better than the opposition? Why?

• When do you feel that life is a game like we played today?

Wrap-up

1. To win today, you did not have to do well—only better than the opposition. Competition, therefore, does not always motivate a person to do his or her best. It may simply inspire cheating or doing just enough to win.

2. Competition can give a person a false sense of his or her worth. These were silly games; yet each time you won, you felt as though you had really accomplished something. Often we spend our lives winning trivial contests and ignoring major considerations. (See Matthew 23:23-24.)

3. God does not judge us on the basis of our performance. The good news of the Gospel is that no one can earn God's favor (Romans 3:10-23 and Ephesians 2:8-9). God accepts us as we are and offers salvation, free.

MUSIC AND MEDIA

CROWD-BREAKERS

Air Band ■ Have a group of students lip sync and pantomime the movements to a rock song. This will take practice but can be very entertaining, especially if it's done well and doesn't drag on and on.

Catch the Meaning ■ Get a copy of *Words and Music* magazine and photocopy the words of a couple of the most popular songs (if you can't get the magazine, many tapes and CDs include the words in the covers). Have some of the actors in your group read these lyrics aloud, dramatically. Make sure they pack their readings with feeling and drama. To make this fair and not simply a cheap shot at contemporary music, bring the words to a couple of songs from the 50's or early 60's (*Blue Moon* and *Ramma Lamma Ding Dong* would be excellent choices). You or another adult helper should read these aloud with dramatic flair.

This activity will highlight the shallow and often gross lyrics of most popular songs.

Catch This! ■ Explain that one of the greatest attractions of the movies is eating the popcorn. Then choose volunteers to compete in a popcorn catching contest. Assign a *tosser* for each competitor who will toss popcorn into his or her waiting mouth. Begin at the *novice* distance (two feet), and then gradually move back until you get to *expert* (ten or more feet). Give one point for every kernel caught at the first distance and more for each succeeding spot.

Do, Re, Mi ■ Divide the group into eight sections, making sure that you have at least one musical person in each section. Then, using a pitch pipe, give each group a note and a musical vowel to sing using the C scale. The vowels are: Do, Re, Mi, Fa, Sol, La, Ti, Do. Act as the choir director and lead them in a few scales, up and down. Then point to various sections, one at a time, and have them sing their vowel sound loudly and proudly. Then make a chord by having two or more sections sing together (for example, Do, Mi, Sol). If your group is musical, you could do a song together by pointing to the various sections at the right time (for example, *Happy Birthday, Joy to the World, Mary Had a Little Lamb*, etc.).

Fashionable ■ Bring a few bags full of clothes, make-up, and wigs. Group students in teams of four to six, and have them choose a person whom they will dress like a popular rock star. Have the stars parade one at a time in front of the crowd while the audience tries to guess their identity.

Finish This Sentence ■ These 10 great *doo-wop* phrases from rock music's early years are listed in *The Doo-Wop Sing-Along Songbook* (John Javna, St. Martin's Press). Print the first part of each phrase and see who can fill in the rest. Afterward, sing each of them for the group. Or you can use these as tongue-in-cheek examples of the meaningful words found in contemporary music. If the group protests that these songs are old and therefore are irrelevant examples, play a song from "In Visible Silence" by The Art of Noise or another example of computer generated music.

1. Pa-pa-pa-pa-pa-pa-pa-oom-a-mow-mow, Papa-oom-mow-mow (from *Papa-Oom-Mow-Mow* by the Rivingtons)

2. Bomp-ba-bomp-ba-ba-bomp, Ba-bom-ba-bom-bomp, Ba-ba-bomp-ba-babomp, A-dang-a-dang-dang, A-ding-a-dong-ding, Bluuuue moooon (from *Blue Moon* by the Marcels)

3. Oop-shoop, Shang-a-lack-a-cheek-a-bock (from *Remember Then* by the Earls)

4. Wop-wop. Doodly-wop. Wop-wop. Wop-wop. Doodly-wop. Wop-wop (from *At My Front Door* by the El Dorados)

5. Hoodly-papa-kow, Papa-kow, Papa-kow, Hoodly-papa-kow, Papa-kow, Papa-kow (from *I Promise to Remember* by Frankie Lymon & the Teenagers)

6. Rama-lama-lama-lama-lama-ding-dong, Rama-lama-lama-lama-lama-lama-ding (from *Rama Lama Ding Dong* by the Edsels)

7. Rang-tang-ding-dong, Rankety-sank (from *Rang Tang Ding Dong [I Am the Japanese Sandman]* by the Cellos)

8. Yip, Yip, Yip, Yip, Boom, Sha-na-na-na, Sha-na-na-na-na (from *Get a Job* by the Silhouettes)

9. Shu-dot'n shoby-do, Shu-dot'n shoby-do (from *In the Still of the Night* by the Five Satins)

10. Sho-be-doo-wop-wah-da (last line in *What's Your Name* by Don and Juan)

Here's the Pitch ■ Using a pitch pipe, give each section of the room a pitch to hum so that when humming together they make a chord. Explain that you are the "hum director" and that everyone should follow your direction. Review the choral directions for getting louder or softer, for raising or lowering the pitch one note, and for cutting them off. Make sure that everyone is warmed up and that each group has the pitch; then begin the "concert." Start slowly, with one group humming at a time, then softly form the chord. As you continue to direct, be creative, quieting one section while increasing the volume of another. Finish by raising the whole group a couple of pitches and with a loud crescendo, then cut them off with a grand flourish. This may also be effective with selected individuals seated in front of the group and singing "la."

How Do You Rate? ■ Review with the group the ratings that are used by movie-makers (G, PG, PG-13, R, NC-17) and what they mean. Then have the group make up new ratings that they could use for movies, tapes, or songs. Some of these could include: S, for Stupid; G, for Gross; D, for Demeaning or Dumb; P, for Perverted; T, for Trite. Use your new ratings system to warn kids about various movies, videos, etc.

I'll Make You a Star ■ Distribute old magazines, scissors, and tape and give everyone five minutes to create a "rock star" by tearing out body parts, clothes, musical instruments, etc., from the magazines and taping them together. They should also give their "stars" names. If there's time, have them make a rock group. Have the "stars" displayed and explained.

Instant Replay ■ Rent a short, action-filled sports movie and show it backwards, with sound. At the end, see who can figure out what words were being said. Then run the beginning of the film *forward* to see whose guess was most accurate.

Music Work ■ Many of the popular songs over the years have featured working or jobs as their theme. Hand out this quiz and let your kids match song title with artist (add others). The correct answers are in parentheses.

MUSIC WORK

Song	Artist
___ *Too Much Monkey Business* (k)	a. Sam Cooke
___ *Get a Job* (d)	b. Jimmy Reed
___ *Working in the Coal Mine* (h)	c. Donna Summer
___ *Workin' for the Man* (j)	d. Silhouettes
___ *Big Boss Man* (b)	e. Johnny Paycheck
___ *Take This Job and Shove It* (e)	f. Wilson Pickett
___ *Boss Guitar* (i)	g. Dolly Parton
___ *She Works Hard for the Money* (c)	h. Lee Dorsey
___ *9 to 5* (g)	i. Duane Eddy
___ *Chain Gang* (a)	j. Roy Orbison
___ *Funk Factory* (f)	k. Chuck Berry

You could create a similar quiz for other topics such as love, weather, geography, girls' names, etc.

Name That Tune ■ Before the meeting, record a few bars of a variety of songs including rock, country, easy listening, oldies, show tunes, hymns, and contemporary Christian.

Divide into teams. For every song, each team should send up a contestant to be seated in front. Explain that you will play a song and the contestants should try to guess what it is. Whoever thinks he or she knows the answer should stand; the first person to stand gets the chance to "name that tune." Award 1000 points for every correct answer and -500 points for every incorrect one. As a variation, you can do this as individuals or couples and award good prizes to the winner(s). You also could play "name the artist" instead.

Oldies but Goodies ■ Before the meeting, ask

kids to bring old, throw-away records that they wouldn't mind destroying (45's or LPs). Collect these records as the kids enter the room.

Divide into teams and give each team a stack of records and the assignment of creating a game for the whole group using these old, disposable records. After a few minutes, have each team explain their game to the whole group, and play it. If they draw a blank, here are a few suggestions:

1. *Thread the Records*—the first team to thread 10 records on a cord wins.

2. *Roll the Rock*—mark a goal and see who can roll a record the closest to it.

3. *The Record-breaking Feet*—have a race between team representatives to see who can break a record the quickest using only his or her feet.

4. *Puzzled*—see who can piece together broken records the fastest.

5. *A Record Toss*—see who can throw the records like Frisbees closest to a goal or in a garbage can some distance away.

Rhythm Band ■ Pass out a variety of strange and unusual instruments, noisemakers, and percussion possibilities. Choose a song, work out the parts, and perform it together. Possible instruments could include a kazoo, pitch pipe, bell, child's xylophone or piano, wooden blocks, pan lids, sandpaper, and others. Supplement these with mouth sounds.

Scrambled Songs ■ Make two lists of the top ten songs on pieces of poster board. Cut out the individual words and put them in a bag so that you have two sets of scrambled music titles.

Using two teams, give each team a set of the words and see which team can assemble the correct song titles first, taping them to a poster board at the front of the room. Award bonus points for having them in the correct position in the top 10.

Singing Challenge ■ Divide into teams. Using a Top 40 list and other sources of songs (hymnal, *Campus Life* magazine, children's songbook, etc.) have a contest. For every round, each team should send one contestant to you. You will show them a song title and send them back to their teams. They are to sing the song without using the words in the title until their team guesses the correct title. The first team to correctly identify the song title wins that round. Remember, songs must be sung.

Tune That Name ■ Divide into teams, assign each team a fictitious song title, and give them a few

minutes to write a song for it. Then have each group perform its song for the whole group. Here are some possible song titles.

- *Gimmie, Gimmie, Jimmy*
- *You are the Most . . .*
- *Down in the Dumps over You*
- *I Ache, I Pine, I Really Whine*
- *The Late Great Family Blues*
- *Love in the Ruins*
- *Shake and Break*
- *Over and Over and Over and Over and Over*
- *Etceteras*
- *Umph, Yeah, Wow, Oooh, Hmmm!*

Video Craze ■ Before the meeting, make a music video starring at least 10 or 12 kids. During the meeting, announce that you have taped a top video off MTV that you will be showing and which they should discuss as a group. Tell them to watch and listen carefully for the subtle nuances and blatant messages (especially listening for "backward masking"). Then run the tape.

Another possibility would be to make a video in the meeting. Let group members know ahead of time and tell them what to bring for clothing, props, etc. Be sure to have your music and "concept" well thought through and prepared so that you don't waste time.

You'll Change Your Tune ■ This will involve a guest artist, someone who is proficient on the piano or guitar. Have him or her prepare a popular song or another familiar one to be performed in a variety of styles. The styles could include classic, opera, jazz, country, disco, punk, rock 'n' roll, blues, gospel, etc. The music group *Glad* does this in *Variations on a Hymn* (on the album *No Less Than All* from Milk and Honey Records).

DISCUSSION STARTERS

Archeology ■ Call your meeting *Raiders of the Lost D.J., E.T.'s Report, Rockin' Review*, or another similar name. To set up your discussion, explain that archeologists in the future have found a tape which has 10 to 15 minutes of typical radio programming. The students should put themselves into the role of those future archeologists and try to discover as much as they can about the culture, beliefs, values, and habits of the earth people of the late twentieth century. Play the music (you can make the tape or just turn on the radio to the station to which everyone listens) and discuss what they hear.

Background ■ Purchase a sampler record from a Christian recording company and play it for your group as part of the meeting or as background music during refreshments. This will give a good introduction to Christian music. Also, show them the record reviews in *Campus Life* or *CCM* magazines. Another option is to go to a Christian concert as a group and to discuss the experience afterward or at your next meeting. You could ask about the differences between this concert and a secular one, the *ministry* of the artist(s), the appropriateness of the price of admission, etc.

Christian Music ■ Play a couple of secular rock songs and a couple of Christian rock songs. Then ask:

• Which songs were Christian rock? How could you tell?

• What makes songs Christian or non-Christian?

• How do the following elements affect the Christian-ness of a song: beat, words, volume, motive for writing and/or performance, lifestyle of the performer, effects on the hearers, use of the money made?

Compose Yourself ■ Pass out paper and pencils and tell everyone that they are going to write their own songs. They should begin by writing song lyrics. After a few minutes, have them read their lyrics aloud. Discuss the words and the type of music that would fit, then try to come up with a tune. It would help to have a couple of guitarists available. The songs don't have to be great compositions—the fun and meaning will come from the composition process and the discussion of which music will best fit the feel of the words.

Cover-up ■ Before the meeting, collect a number of CD covers from a variety of popular rock groups. During the meeting, bring them out one at a time and analyze them together—both the pictures and the words printed on them. Ask how the covers match with Christian values and biblical principles.

• Do they reflect the *works of the flesh* or the *fruit of the Spirit*?

• Do they focus on what is good and pure?

• Would listening to or singing this be glorifying to God?

• Would these performers and their songs help a person's thought-life to be pleasing to God or to hinder it?

Emphasize that you are not on a crusade to have students burn all their records or to have them listen only to *Christian* music. You are, however, telling them that they have the responsibility to be discerning with what they watch, hear, and buy. Reiterate the biblical principles implied by the questions above and encourage the kids to go home and analyze their CDs and tapes in light of them. Challenge them to pray for the courage to do what they know is right.

Hot and Heavy ■ Get the latest copy of *Billboard* magazine, in which the top selling records in a variety of categories (including rock, gospel, soul, easy listening, country, and contemporary Christian) are listed. Then design a matching quiz with the song titles on one side of the paper and the artists on the other. Mix in a few phony titles and artists to make the quiz more interesting and difficult (for example, *You're My Hairy Carrie Bearie* by T.T. and the Tramps, *I've Been So Lonely in the Saddle Since My Horse Died* by Jimmy Bob Surefoot, *Slow Soul Sister* by Heavy Dude, *Momma Don't Teach!* by Moronna, and *The Lord's Drivin' and I'm Buckled Up* by Miss Dolly Would).

After you give the correct answers and declare the winner, involve the group members in a discussion of what it takes to sell a song, what music their friends like, how their tastes differ or are similar to what is popular, and the role music plays in their lives.

Media ■ Prepare a tape of song clips that reflect a variety of moods and values. Use a number of types of music including country, pop, easy listening, rock, heavy metal, and contemporary Christian. Prepare a slide show to coincide with the words or moods of the music.

Afterward, discuss what the kids felt and saw, what the songs tell us about ourselves and our society, and their other messages.

Questionnaire ■ Print this questionnaire (leaving plenty of space for answers) and distribute it in the meeting. After everyone fills it out, compile the answers and discuss the results.

Q & A

1. What word(s) most closely describes your taste in music? (Circle all that apply.)

tasteless	heavy metal
disco	hard rock
soft rock	big band
punk	easy listening
new wave	classical
jazz	folk
bubble gum	dentist offfice

oldies-but-goodies	contemporary Christian
computer	comedy
country	traditional hymns
show tunes	praise choruses
rap	alternative

2. What three bands or musicians would you most pay to go hear?

3. What bands do you think should be paid to keep quiet?

4. If someone stole your entire CD and tape collection and the insurance company would give you the money for a whole new collection, what five albums would be at the top of your list to buy?

Why?

5. What band or musician have you listened to and liked the longest?

6. What song title best describes your life?

7. What song best describes your school?

Resources ■ You may want to consider having an in-depth seminar on music or at least making available additional materials. Here are some resources.

• Menconi Ministries (P.O. Box 306, Cardiff, CA 92007-0831; (619) 436-8676). They have a regular newsletter and extensive material on popular music.

• Dan and Steve Peters (Box 9222, North Saint Paul, MN 55109; (612) 770-8114). They hold hard-hitting seminars on rock music, have written *Why Knock Rock, AC/DC–Wanted for Murder*, and other books, and have a video.

• Bob DeMoss of *Focus on the Family* (Colorado Springs, CO 80995)—they also have a very insightful video entitled *Sex, Lies, and the Truth*.

• Parents' Music Resource Center (1500 Arlington Blvd., Suite 300, Arlington, VA 22209). The center was begun by a group of congressional wives and has many helpful materials including a video, *Rising to the Challenge*, and a booklet, *Let's Talk Rock, A Primer for Parents*.

• The music section of *Campus Life* magazine gives helpful record reviews.

• CCM magazine

•InterLink is an organization that provides monthly tapes of contemporary Christian music and videos to churches to use in youth ministry.

• *Music Worth Talking About*, by Tim Atkins (Baker Book House, 1994), reviews 100 songs, giving helpful summaries, discussion questions, related Bible verses, wrap-up ideas, and other suggestions for use in a youth group.

• *Video Movies Worth Watching*, by Dave Veerman (Baker Book House, 1992), reviews 75 video movies and gives ideas for viewing for families and youth groups, discussion questions, wrap-up outlines, related Bible verses, and more.

Sure Seller ■ Break into pairs and distribute paper and pencils or pens. Have kids describe a product that will be assured of success and be a top seller in each of the following categories: rock single, music video, movie. In other words, they should explain what the products should say or picture and what the themes should be if they wanted to guarantee success. After a few minutes, have each pair describe their top sellers. Then discuss the prevailing themes and what their proposed products reveal about society.

That's Entertainment ■ Bring sets of the entertainment pages from various local newspapers. First hold a short contest to see who can find a movie that fits your description. When they think they have one, they should shout it out. Here are some descriptions to use:

• a movie featuring extreme violence

• a film rated NC-17

• a movie that your parents would have no questions about letting you see

• a film to which you would never take a date

• an unbelievably gross movie

• a film that is an obvious rip-off of teenagers

• a film you would like to see but are not allowed to

• a very scary movie

• a movie that probably will win at least one Oscar

Afterward, discuss the films being made today. Ask:

• Which of the descriptions were easiest to find? Why?

• Which ones were the most difficult to find? Why?

• Why do most of today's movies and so many TV shows feature sex and violence?

• What bothers you most about what you see on TV or at the show?

• What are some of the negative values portrayed on the screen?

• As a Christian, how do you decide which movies are all right to see?

• How does your movie criteria differ from those of your parents?

Top 40 ■ Pick up a number of Top 40 lists from a local record store. Distribute them and analyze the songs together. Here are some possible characteristics to discuss.

- Subjects (love, sex, school, society, religion . . .)
- Style (rock, disco, rap, ballad, folk, alternative, country, punk . . .)
- Singers (solo, group, instrumental, clean-cut, punk, rock-junkie, jock, men and women . . .)
- Subtleties (love is everything; do your own thing; sex is OK; love hurts; other hidden messages)

Ask:

1. What similarities and tendencies do you see in these songs?

2. Based on this information, how would you write a surefire hit song?

3. Look at the list again. What are your favorite songs in the Top 40? Why do you like them?

4. Which of your favorites aren't listed?

5. How do our musical tastes reflect what's important to us?

Trivia Challenge ■ Get a Top 40 list from a local music store and create your own music trivia quiz. Use group names, album and single titles, and song lyrics in the quiz. Use this to lead into a discussion of how kids are affected by what they hear constantly.

DISCUSSIONS AND WRAP-UPS

Message Massage ■ Ask for volunteers to repeat a few lines from their favorite songs. Then discuss the messages that popular songs give us.

- What lifestyles are promoted in most rock 'n roll songs?
- How does this compare to what the Bible teaches?
- How should Christians decide what music to buy and listen to? Why?

Stars and Real People ■ Read a portion of a recent interview with a Christian artist. These are available in *Contemporary Christian Music (CCM)* magazine or *Campus Life* magazine. Then ask:

- What do you think this person is really like?
- Why do you think we put performers on pedestals and expect them to be bigger than life? (Possible answers: their ad images; we need people to look up to.)
- How could putting people on pedestals hurt us? (Possible answers: we follow their lead; when they fall, we're crushed; we should keep our eyes on Christ.)
- Does it help to know that Christian artists and stars are normal people?
- Apply these questions to secular artists.
- As a Christian, how do you feel about secular artists?

Survey ■ Before the meeting, write out the following questions on separate pieces of paper. Give each person a slip of paper with a question on it. Then have them divide into twos and have each person ask his or her partner the question on the paper. (They should write down the answers.) After a few minutes, bring everyone back together and find out how the questions were answered. As the answers are reported, see if anyone has anything else to add, if they agree or disagree, how they feel about the question, etc. Here are the questions:

1. Who is you favorite recording individual or group? Why?

2. How many CDs or tapes do you own? How do you choose which ones to buy?

3. What is your favorite popular (Top 40) song? What do the words mean?

4. What is the raunchiest song you know that is now or was just recently very popular? What do the words mean?

5. What do you think of rating albums like they do with movies?

6. How do you think music affects your values, lifestyle, thought-life, and ideas?

The Music in Me ■ Ask:

- What do you think about the words of the popular music these days? Do you listen to the words? Can you sing along with most songs?
- How do you think these words affect you? Do they turn you on? Change your ideas? Raise or lower your moral standards?
- What would other people think of you from your tastes in music? From your values, thought-life, personality, habits?

BIBLE STUDIES

Garbage In ■ Have everyone turn to Philippians 4:8. Have a student read the verse aloud. Have another student read aloud the first half of Proverbs 23:7 from the *New American Standard Version* of the Bible. Ask:

- How do these verses relate to music—what we listen to, the words, etc.?
- In computer terms, GIGO, or *Garbage In, Garbage Out* means that what is fed into the computer is

directly related to what comes out. How do you think this relates to the verses we just read?

• What can we do to develop Christian listening habits?

Verses Versus ■ Distribute worksheets with the following Scripture references printed on them (print out the entire passage from a contemporary English version such as *The Living Bible*). After each passage, have the students write how it should affect their music listening and buying habits.

1. Galatians 5:16-23

2. Philippians 4:8

3. 1 Corinthians 10:31

4. Psalm 19:14

After everyone has finished, briefly discuss their answers, emphasizing the responsibility of Christians to be discerning in their listening habits.

25 EASTER

CROWD-BREAKERS

Bunny Hunt ■ Take one volunteer staff member dressed in a rented bunny suit (not *Playboy* style) with a large bag of miniature Easter eggs (wrapped). If desired, invite kids from other youth groups too. Mix them in a shopping mall or an enclosed public area. Divide the kids into teams of 10, and give the bunny a two-minute head start. Then send the teams in search of the bunny. Their objective is to pick up the trail of eggs and to track down the bunny within 20 minutes. The winners are either the bunny-nappers or the team collecting the most eggs. Warning: Don't attempt this in a crowded mall or in wet weather (soggy bunnies don't hop too well). And be sure to obtain permission from the mall management first.

For added fun, have an extra bunny appear at the opposite end of the mall to divert attention and add confusion.

Be sure to have the bunny run along a prearranged path and to notify storekeepers and security guards.

Have the finale at a quiet section of the mall, an empty store, or a public podium for an Easter program.

Easter Outfit ■ Bring a box filled with old clothes. Using teams, have each one choose a person whom they will dress in a new Easter outfit. Explain that they have only three or four minutes to send team members, one at a time, to the box, pull out a piece of clothing, run back to their representative, and help him or her put it on while another piece of clothing is being grabbed. After the time is up, have the newly dressed kids parade before the whole group. Judge on the basis of creativity, style, and Easter suitability.

Easter Parade ■ This is a team event. Give each team a bag of materials from which to fashion a very creative Easter bonnet. Include an old cap or hat, feathers, cloth, safety pins, paper and crayons, thread, cotton balls, yarn, old jewelry, etc.

Allow about 10 minutes for designing and creating the bonnets; then hold a fashion show in which each team chooses a model to wear the bonnet and an announcer who describes the creation while it is paraded around the room. You may want to designate a runway area as in a beauty pageant.

Award a prize to the team with the most original bonnet and use all the bonnets in another activity (for example, Musical Bonnets).

Egg Hunt ■ Have an old-fashioned Easter egg hunt. Collect or purchase quite a few plastic eggs (or use "L'eggs" stocking containers). Place slips of paper in them with various prizes or points. Hide the eggs in a park or a large backyard the night before your meeting. Tell everyone to bring his or her own creative basket. At your signal, everyone should run to find as many eggs as possible. Award prizes for the most eggs, the most points, and the best basket.

Eggles ■ Use real eggs (hard-boiled) or pieces of cardboard cut into egg shapes. Also have available appropriate coloring and design items and utensils. Give everyone a hard-boiled egg and have them create "eggles." These are puns using eggs. Here are some examples: bald eggle (bald eagle), bold eggle (bold eagle—double pun), byc-eggle (bicycle), med-eggle (medical), mus-eggle (musical), madri-eggle (madrigal), mag-eggle (magical).

Egg Roll ■ Choose as many teams as you wish for this relay, but be sure to arrange the team areas on all sides of the room. This will make the race much more interesting.

Give each team one large, plastic egg, taped so that the halves won't separate. At your signal, the first members from each team should roll their eggs on the floor with their noses, across the room and back. The next team members then repeat the process. To speed up the game, use only a few kids from each team or give them a shorter distance to roll. The first team finished wins.

Eggs-am ■ Explain that eggs are an integral part of any Easter celebration; therefore, you want to see how much they really know about eggs. Distribute the following quiz. (The correct answers are in parentheses.)

EGGS-AM FOR EGGHEADS

Write the "egg-word" to the right of the definition.

1. check closely— (eggs-amine)
2. leave— (eggs-it)
3. precisely— (eggs-actly)
4. beautiful— (eggs-quisite)
5. of highest quality— (eggs-cellent)
6. a model— (eggs-ample)
7. to do very well— (eggs-cel)
8. to encourage— (eggs-hort)
9. someone who gets rid of demons— (eggs-orcist)
10. to use up— (eggs-pend)
11. to work hard— (eggs-ert)
12. costly— (eggs-pensive)
13. the end— (eggs-tremity)
14. to work out— (eggs-ercise)
15. to make larger than it is— (eggs-aggerate)
16. add one of your own

After a few minutes, give the correct answers and see what new words they created.

Garden ■ Choose competitors to come to the front. Explain that one of the sure signs of spring is gardening and flowers. To have a good garden, however, you need a number of things. Their job is to find as many of these garden "things" as possible in three minutes. The "things" are listed for them. They should use their imaginations to find these items, and they must find everything in the room. They can use people, clothes, contents of purses and wallets, etc.

Then give everyone a copy of the list (printed below) and tell them to begin. Afterward, have students display their gardening things and explain how they fit the categories on the list. Give a chocolate bunny to each of student and a prize to the winner.

GARDEN THINGS

1. roots
2. light
3. beauty
4. green
5. tool
6. growth
7. new leaf
8. soil
9. food
10. moisture

Hopping Contest ■ Choose competitors for a special Easter contest. After they come forward, bring out sets of "bunny ears." These should be made of cardboard with a string or rubber band so they can be placed on top of the head and the string tied under the chin.

Introduce your bunnies to the crowd and explain that you are going to have a contest to see which bunny can hop the farthest. Mark out a starting line and explain that each bunny gets three consecutive hops, starting behind the line, from a full stop. If they fall during the hops, where they hit will be the point from which the distance is measured. The winner will be the bunny who hops the farthest with his or her three consecutive hops. (This is like a combination of the standing long jump and hop, skip, and jump.)

Have the bunnies compete one at a time. Then give a chocolate bunny to each competitor and a prize to the winner.

Magic Egg ■ Recruit a number of competitors to see who can get a hard-boiled egg into a milk bottle. Here's how it's done: boil an egg; peel the egg; place the egg over the mouth of a milk bottle (it will not go in); remove the egg; light a paper taper and place it in the bottle. When it is extinguished, place the egg on the bottle and watch it get sucked into the bottle (the vacuum pulls it in).

Musical Bonnets ■ Bring all sorts of hats so that you have enough for everyone. Form the group in a large circle, front to back, with everyone wearing a hat except for one person. Play a song like "Here Comes Peter Cottontail" or a similar rendition. As the music is played, the hats should move backward, around the circle, from head to head. (Each person uses one hand to remove the hat from the person in front and place it on his or her head.) To complicate matters, you can call "Switch!" and have the hats move forward, with each person putting his or her hat on the head of the person in front of him or her. When the music stops, whoever is hatless is eliminated from the circle and the game. Then remove another bonnet and continue. The winner is the last person left with a bonnet on his or her head.

New Wave ■ Using the whole group (make sure that everyone is seated), hold your own indoor version of the famous "wave cheer." (The wave cheer is a chain reaction event. The first person stands by rising slowly and then sitting back down slowly, raising his or her voice as he or she stands and then lowering the volume as he or she sits. Right after he or she begins, the next person begins, and so on. The crowd undulates, like a wave, as the movement and sound travel across or around the room.) Begin at one side of the room and have kids stand, raise their hands high over their heads, and blow noisemakers. Go from one side of the room to the other and back (direct them if it will help). Then, try the cheer in a circle with everyone seated around you.

Party Hardy ■ Have an Easter party. Beforehand, decorate the room with streamers and balloons to give it a party atmosphere. Provide paper party hats and noisemakers to blow into. (Try to have four different kinds of noisemakers—horns, whistles, "dragon's tongues," kazoos, etc.) As kids enter the room, give each one a hat and a noisemaker.

After most of the crowd has arrived, explain that for the next half hour whenever any latecomer enters the room, you will say, "Hey!"; then they should stand and shout, "Surprise!" and blow their noisemakers. (See "Surprises" for the tie-in.) They should do this no matter what activity they are doing.

Eventually, tell everyone to get with all the others with their particular noisemaker and sit on the floor. Explain that you are forming a special Easter band, and they have the instruments. Each group is a section of the band. Then, with you as the director, lead them in an instrumental rendition of "Here Comes Peter Cottontail." Be sure to point to specific groups for a few measures or to individuals for solos, and direct them, with great flourish of course, to play louder or softer. Do another song as a whole band, or give each section a few minutes to decide on a song they will play for everyone else. Then have the sections play one at a time.

Surprises ■ Between games, have "surprises" for everyone. These will have to be lined up in advance. They tie into the idea that Easter caught the disciples by surprise and today the resurrection still catches people by surprise.

Surprise #1—Have someone turn off the lights and yell loudly, "Help, help! I'm drowning!" After a few seconds, he or she should turn on the lights. Proceed with the meeting as though nothing unusual has happened.

Surprise #2—Get everyone quiet and begin to give announcements or to explain the next activity. Have two kids (one on each side and behind the crowd) pull "party poppers" simultaneously. Proceed as though nothing has happened and go on with the next game.

Surprise #3—Have a boy burst into the room, through the crowd, and to the front yelling, "Woman the lifeboats! Woman the lifeboats! Woman the lifeboats!" Stop him and say, "Wait a minute it's not "Woman the lifeboats!" it's "Man the lifeboats!" He then should respond: "You fill 'em your way, and I'll fill 'em mine!"

The Egg Bowl ■ Use teams and have a contest like the "College Bowl" or "Prep Bowl" quiz games on television. When anyone knows the answer to a question, he or she should stand. The first person standing will have the first opportunity to answer the question. Each correct answer receives 1000 points and each incorrect answer receives -2000 points. After an incorrect answer, a student from the other team will have the opportunity to give the correct one (for 500 points for a correct answer and 0 for an incorrect answer). Appoint a judge to keep track of the points and begin. Here are the questions—the answers are in parentheses.

1. Where did Peter Cottontail hop? (down the bunny trail)
2. For "Daylight Savings Time," which way do we set our clocks? (ahead, one hour)
3. Who is the male MC for the Easter Seals telethon? (Pat Boone)
4. In the song, where did they wear their "Easter bonnets"? ("in the Easter parade")
5. In Tiny Tim's famous song, what did he tiptoe through? (the tulips)
6. In what ocean is Easter Island? (South Pacific)
7. What is the "vernal equinox"? (the first day of spring, when day and night are of equal length)
8. Why did the chicken sit in the middle of the road? (She wanted to "lay it on the line.")

9. Name 3 early spring flowers. (daffodils, tulips, crocuses, etc.)

10. What charity has Easter Seals? (the American Lung Association)

11. What did Peter Cottontail get caught eating in Mr. McGregor's garden? (cabbage)

12. What's at the bottom of almost every Easter basket? (grass)

13. What returns to Capistrano in the spring? (swallows)

14. What comes in like a lion and goes out like a lamb? (March)

15. What are the Easter colors? (pink, purple, and white)

16. Name three famous bunnies. (Bugs Bunny, Crusader Rabbit, Peter Cottontail, Easter Bunny, Brer Rabbit, Trix bunny, Flopsy, Mopsy, rabbit stew, etc.)

17. What professional baseball team has spring training in Vero Beach, Florida? (the Los Angeles Dodgers)

18. How many days does April have? (30)

19. When should people plant tulip bulbs if they want them to come up in the spring? (late fall)

20. Where was the "final four" held in 1992? (New Orleans)

DISCUSSION STARTERS

Action ■ Give everyone the assignment of asking four or five Christian adults what they would think if someone discovered the bones of Jesus. What difference would it make to their faith? Discuss the answers at the next meeting.

Easter Baskets ■ As a group, make Easter baskets with a twist—put together baskets to give to needy folks around town (or to a community food pantry, etc.). Include eggs, canned ham, Easter cookies, and special Easter food.

Easter Cards ■ Explain that Easter is the greatest Christian holiday because the Resurrection is the final, indisputable proof that Jesus is who He said He was and that His death on the cross really was for our sins. Ask everyone to think for a moment of a non-Christian friend to whom they could send special Easter greetings—just to be nice or perhaps even to help share the Gospel with this person. Then bring out card-making materials, including construction paper, white paper, felt-tipped pens of various colors,

magazines from which they can tear pictures, cotton balls, scissors, tape, glue, etc. Allow about 10 minutes for everyone to make their cards, and then have them displayed for the rest of the group. Encourage students to deliver the cards personally or to mail them to their special friends.

Grab Bag ■ Before the meeting, gather a number of small items and put them in a large garbage bag. Here are some possibilities: mirror, knife, stone, clock, picture frame, stuffed animal, handkerchief, stick, index card, soap, light bulb, hammer, paper clip, shirt, wallet, eraser, balloon, rubber band, carrot, newspaper, etc.

Make sure that you have enough items so that every person can have one. With a large crowd, use just those who didn't compete in the other games.

Explain that you want everyone to reach into the bag and pull something out. Then they should think of how that item symbolizes Easter for them. After everyone has drawn an item and had a few seconds to think, go around the room and have them explain their symbols quickly, one at a time. For example, someone could say: *The eraser reminds me of Easter because when Jesus died on the cross, He erased my sins.* Some of the answers may be light or humorous (for example, the carrot could remind someone of a rabbit, etc.). That's all right. The purpose of this activity is to focus attention on Easter.

Jerusalem Star ■ As a group, create a front page or two of a newspaper, *The Jerusalem Star*, as it would appear after the Resurrection. Assign articles, collect them, print the paper, and distribute it on Easter Sunday (with the pastor's permission, of course).

Life Signs ■ Hand out sheets of paper and pens or pencils. Tell everyone to quietly look around the room and write down all the *signs of death* they see. Note: these signs could include fallen leaves from a plant, signs of wear on the carpet, a newspaper headline telling of a murder or fatal accident, a memorial plaque, a quote from a famous person who lived many years ago, a crucifix, a birthday card, etc.

After a couple of minutes, have everyone turn their sheets over and write down all the *signs of life* they see. These signs could include: pregnant sponsor, buds on the tree, shoots of flowers pushing through the soil, animated conversation between two kids, empty cross, Easter symbols, egg, etc.

After a couple of minutes, discuss what they wrote on their sheets, beginning with the *signs of death*. Ask:

• What might cause a person to see only the signs of death around him or her?

• How does focusing on the signs of death make a person feel?

• What does it take to look for life?

Pass It On ■ Before the meeting, write key Bible phrases about the resurrection on index cards.

Divide into teams and have them sit in parallel columns. Give the first person in each team a card. At your signal, he or she should whisper the verse to the next person on his or her team. This person (without the benefit of the card) should whisper the verse to the next person, and so on until it gets to the end. The last person on each team should write the phrase on a piece of paper. Compare the phrases to the original. Award 1000 points to the first team to get the phrase passed all the way through their line and 1000 points to the most accurate team. Here are some possible phrases to use.

• *Now we live in the hope of eternal life because Christ rose again from the dead* (1 Peter 1:3).

• *So, my dear brothers, since future victory is sure, be strong and steady, always abounding in the Lord's work* (1 Corinthians 15:58).

• *I am the one who raises the dead and gives them life again. Anyone who believes in Me, even though he dies like anyone else, shall live again* (John 11:25).

• *Indeed the time is coming when all the dead in their graves shall hear the voice of God's Son, and shall rise again* (John 5:28).

• *Then God released Him from the horrors of death and brought Him back to life again, for death could not keep this man within its grip* (Acts 2:24).

• *But the fact is that Christ did actually rise from the dead, and has become the first of millions who will come back to life again some day* (1 Corinthians 15:20).

• add others

Discuss the truths in these verses and why it is important to pass them on to others.

Perspective ■ Use a video camera and tape various objects, one at a time, beginning very close and then slowly moving away. The idea is for the audience to guess what the objects are. Eventually the answer will be obvious as the camera moves back, revealing it and the surroundings. Each bit of tape should spend most of the time very close (or you could pause the tape when you play it). Here are some possible objects to use: the rubber end of a badminton bird, the knobs on a television set, the inside of a metal mailbox, a disk drive of a computer, handle on a briefcase, one of the rings in a three-ring binder, the center of the underside of a lawnmower, etc. This illustrates the importance of perspective. Often we're so close to our problems and tragedies that we can't see the big picture. That's what happened with the disciples when Jesus was crucified. They didn't get the whole perspective until after the resurrection.

Picturing the Resurrection ■ Distribute paper and make available a variety of writing instruments (pens, pencils, markers, crayons, etc.). Give everyone the assignment of drawing some kind of picture or symbol of Christ's resurrection. After a few minutes, have them display and explain their creations. Look for prominent patterns, themes, and deeper meanings.

Wanted: Dead AND Alive! ■ Distribute paper and pens or pencils. On one side of the sheets, have everyone write the benefits of Jesus' death. Then on the other, have them write the benefits of His resurrection. Use this as a discussion starter about the atonement and the resurrection.

DISCUSSIONS AND WRAP-UPS

Easter Presents ■ As a group, brainstorm about the kinds of presents they could give friends for Easter that would underline the truth of the resurrection and be a positive witness for Christ. Then challenge them to give these presents to some of their non-Christian friends.

Eyewitnesses ■ Before the meeting, line up people to play the characters below. The actors should learn the lines well enough to deliver them dramatically. During the meeting, explain that despite all the bunnies and eggs, Easter really should center on Christ. There were men and women who witnessed Jesus' arrest and crucifixion, and these eyewitnesses are here to tell the story. Note: Before each eyewitness speaks, read the appropriate passage from the Bible. Then the actor should deliver the lines as printed below.

1. Soldier (Matthew 27:27-30, 35-37, 54)

I watched Him die. Actually, all three of them . . . but Him I'll remember. He screamed out something about God . . . I got closer. Then He whispered something about forgiveness . . . that we didn't know what we were doing. And then He died–just like that–early. Oh, He was dead all right. We made sure of that. But I'll never forget His face or what He said. I've seen plenty of executions, but none like that . . . or Him.

2. Disciple (Matthew 26:31, 33-35, 43-46, 49-50, 56b)

I followed Him for three years. We walked, ate, and

talked together. He was quite a man . . . He changed my life. But I'll never forget that night. Yes, I was there in the garden. I had said that I would die for Him, but when all those guards came, I ran away to save my life just like the rest. Then I followed at a distance and watched the phony trial and the way they mocked Him. They gave Him the death penalty and pounded nails through His hands and feet and shoved that monstrous cross in the ground. I loved that man. But when He died, I left . . . in despair. He was dead, and all that I had hoped for died with Him.

3. Guard (Matthew 27:62-66)

I was there as well—at the trial before the chief priests and the others. I hated Him—all that talk about forgiving sins, destroying the temple . . . and love. Who did He think He was—God? Anyway, I was there at the cross too, and I saw Him die—and I knew that finally we would be rid of this threat to our religion and way of life. Afterward, I was given a new assignment—to guard the tomb. I'm not sure why. Who would want to steal anything from that grave? He was poor, and all His followers had run away. I guess He had said something about coming back to life again, so the high priests wanted to stop any tricks or messing around. Well, they'll have to get through me and the others . . . and that stone!

4. Woman (Matthew 27:55-56)

Please excuse my tears . . . but I was there . . . at the cross . . . and saw my Lord die. Like the others, I loved Him—He understood my struggles and feelings . . . and He gave me God's forgiveness for everything I had done. I guess it's all over now. I wonder what happened to Peter and Nathaniel and James and the others. The crowds treated Him like a criminal—laughing, cursing, mocking Him. And where will He be buried? My Lord! What'll I do . . . what'll we do?

After the eyewitnesses leave, walk to the front and say: *Yes, Jesus died—you've heard the eyewitness reports. He was crucified, dead, and buried in a borrowed tomb. And guards were posted and a huge stone rolled in front to keep Him in that tomb. But let me read you the rest of the story.*

Read Matthew 28:1-20 and then make the following comments: *Jesus was dead, BUT HE AROSE! And the eyewitnesses to His death became eyewitnesses to His resurrection—the guards, the women, the disciples, and many others. This event, the Resurrection, changed lives...and history. Just consider the disciples. They were scattered, discouraged, and defeated. But suddenly they were bold, fearless, and confident. What changed them? They had seen Christ alive! Easter is more than bunnies, eggs, vacation, flowers, and spring—it is the celebration of our LIVING LORD! And here's what Christ's resurrection means to us. Because He rose from the dead and is alive . . .*

1. We know that Jesus was and is GOD—we have the proof.

2. We know that what Jesus taught and promised is TRUE.

3. We know that Jesus died for a reason—He died for our sins, in our place.

4. We know that Jesus now lives to love us and to bring us to God.

Conclude by challenging the students to worship Christ, the living Lord, and to give their lives to Him.

Meanings ■ Ask:

• What is Easter really all about?

• Why is Christ's resurrection important?

• What difference should the Resurrection make in our lives today?

Spring ■ Ask for a show of hands for those who really want springtime to come. Then ask:

• What do you like about spring? (warm weather, flowers, approaching end of school, special events, holidays, etc.)

• What does spring mean? (thawing, growing, planting, warming up, etc.)

• What special traditions do you have for spring? (Easter, ski trip, beach trip, prom, gardening, etc.)

Next, use the following words with personal applications. You may want to invite other suggestions as you go along.

• *Thaw* means melting, unfreezing, etc. Besides ice and the ground, there are other things that need "thawing"—certain relationships, frozen attitudes, etc.

• *Plant* involves placing seeds or bulbs in the earth and watching them "come to life" as water and sun are added. There are many things which should be "planted" in our lives: love, faith, hope, concern, etc.

• *Grow* involves maturing, getting bigger, developing. We should be growing in all sorts of ways: spiritually, socially, mentally, physically. It has been said that when a person stops growing, he or she starts dying.

• *Warm up*—beyond just thawing, this means that the whole climate changes. Relationships, attitudes, life goals, etc., all need to be "warmed up."

Next, hand out the following worksheets and ask the group to fill them out seriously and prayerfully.

SIGNS OF SPRING

I would like to "thaw"

_____ .

I would like to "plant"

_____ .

I would like to see "growth" in

_____ .

I would like to "warm up"

_____ .

Then have students pair up with anyone else in the room. Seat everyone and have them share with each other, for a few minutes, what they wrote on their worksheets. Have them take two or three minutes to pray for each other.

Thoughts ■ Use the following as a wrap-up or a discussion guide.

The Resurrection is the most important event in history. If it is true, as Christians believe, then Jesus is God, His death was for our sins, and what we do with Him has eternal consequences. The Incarnation, grace, and eternal life are real.

If, however, Jesus did not rise from the dead, then Christians are the most foolish people in the world, and all the martyrs throughout history have died in vain.

But the Resurrection did occur. It was an historical, time-and-space event. It was not a "spiritual resurrection" or an "idea"—a real body, once dead, came back to life at a particular time. The historical evidence is there and cannot be denied. We have an empty tomb, and we worship a living Savior.

BIBLE STUDIES

Hope ■ Have everyone turn to 1 Thessalonians 4:13-18. Have a student read the passage aloud. Then ask:

• Paul says that most people *have no hope* (verse 13). What does he mean? What might cause a person to lose hope?

• Paul is not saying that Christians should not grieve, but that we should grieve differently (verse 13). Why should Christians' grief be different? In what ways should it be different?

• What specific reasons does Paul give for Christians to be hopeful in the face of death?

• How does Paul describe the return of Jesus?

• Why does Christ's resurrection give us hope?

Predictions ■ Have everyone follow in their Bibles as you highlight the following situations where Jesus predicted His resurrection from the dead. You may want to discuss these as you move along. The idea is that the disciples were surprised by the Resurrection, but they should not have been! Jesus had told them a number of times that it would happen—for some reason, they didn't hear Him.

1. John 2:19-22—*Destroy this temple, and I will raise it again in three days.* This statement was used against Jesus at His trial.

2. Matthew 12:38-40 and 16:1-4—*For as Jonah was three days and three nights in the belly of a huge fish, so the Son of Man will be three days and three nights in the heart of the earth.*

3. Matthew 16:21-23—*And on the third day be raised to life.* Evidently the disciples heard only the part about Jesus' suffering and dying because Peter told Jesus that these things wouldn't happen. Jesus rebuked Peter strongly.

4. Matthew 17:23—*And on the third day He will be raised to life.* Again Jesus predicted His death and resurrection, but evidently the disciples heard only the part about Jesus dying because *they were filled with grief.*

5. Matthew 20:18—*We are going up to Jerusalem, and the Son of Man will be betrayed to the chief priests and the teachers of the law. They will condemn Him to death and will turn Him over to the Gentiles to be mocked and flogged and crucified. On the third day He will be raised to life!* This was the third time that Jesus predicted clearly his resurrection.

Today people are surprised by the Resurrection. They don't believe it really happened or that "rational" people can believe such a thing. What do you say to them? (Discuss briefly.)

Resurrection Scenes ■ Divide into six groups and give each one a New Testament passage to act out for the rest of the group. Each scene features various individuals and their response to the resurrection. The scenes and individuals are:

• the women—Luke 23:55–24:11

• the guards at the tomb—Matthew 27:62–28:4

• Peter and John—John 20:1-10

• Mary Magdalene—John 20:1-2, 10-18

• the men on the road to Emmaus—Luke 24:13-35

• the disciples—Luke 24:36-49

Spring ■ Challenge your group to:

• *Spring up*—"All of us must quickly carry out the tasks assigned us by the One who sent Me, for there is little time left before the night falls and all work comes to an end" (John 9:4, TLB).

Don't lie around—get up and get busy—there's much to do!

• *Spring forward*—Paul says, "Forgetting the past and looking forward to what lies ahead, I strain to reach the end of the race and receive the prize for which God is calling us up to heaven because of what Christ Jesus did for us" (Philippians 3:13-14, TLB).

Move ahead in your life and in your commitment to

Christ. Don't be content with the status quo.

• *Spring into action*—Do you really believe in God? Then act like it. As James says, "Faith that does not result in good deeds is not real faith" (James 2:20, TLB).

Look for ways to put your faith into action.

Witnesses ■ Hand out the following worksheet (leaving plenty of space for answers), and divide into four groups. Assign each group a section or two on which to work. After five minutes or so, bring them back together and have the groups report their findings. Everyone else can write down the answers in their empty sections.

EYEWITNESS NEWS

Passage	Witness(es)	Instructions (What did Jesus say to do?)
1. Matthew 28:1-20		
2. Mark 16:1-20		
3. Luke 24:1-53		
4. John 20:1-31		
5. John 21:1-25		
6. Acts 1:1-11		
7. 1 Corinthians 15:3-11		

Wrap-up ■ Read 1 Corinthians 15:12-28 and emphasize the importance of the Resurrection to our faith. Jesus rose literally (it actually happened in history) and bodily (it was a physical resurrection—not some sort of a "spiritual" happening). Say something like:

The reality of the Resurrection turned the lives of the disciples upside down. From frightened and discouraged men and women, huddling in a room for comfort and safety, they were transformed into those who willingly gave up their lives for the Gospel—because they had seen the risen Christ, and they knew He was and is the Lord! Today, people are still surprised by the Resurrection, but we must tell them that it is true and that Christ lives. This Easter, let the reality of the Resurrection fill you with hope and with the determination to spread the news.

26

SHARING AND FAITH

CROWD-BREAKERS

Hitting the Books ■ Do this outdoors or in a gym. Bring a supply of old books and a baseball bat. Ask how they feel about *hitting the books*. Then explain that because they are probably tired of homework and school, you want to give them the opportunity to let off steam and to take out their school frustrations. Have them stand one at a time at *home plate*, with bat in hand, while you pitch the books to them. Award a prize to the person who hits a book the farthest.

Making Change ■ Divide into at least three teams. Explain that you are going to have a contest involving loose change, and that you will collect the change and give it to a good cause. Then ask everyone to take out all the change that they will use in the game and are willing to donate. Bring a couple of dollars worth of pennies to distribute to kids who have no change to use.

Explain that you will call out something for which you need change. The first team to get that change together and send it to you with their team representative, wins that round. They must leave the change with you and continue the competition with whatever change they have left. Play until most of the teams are out of money or you run out of things to call. Call out the following amounts, preceding each one with, *I need change for . . .*:

• a nickel

• a quarter

• a toll (in Illinois, that's usually 40 cents)

• a dollar

• a candy bar (check the price; it's usually 45–50 cents)

• the offering on Sunday (any amount is correct)

• a half dollar

• a bribe to the judge of this contest (award the round to the team giving you the most money)

• a dime

• penny loafers (two pennies)

Stand Up for What You Believe ■ Everyone should be seated on the floor. Explain that they should stand up when you read a statement that applies to them; then they should remain standing until the end. Read these statements one at a time, pausing each time for students to react. Stand up . . .

. . . if you are a teacher's pet.

. . . if you *love* school.

. . . if you have ever received a ticket on your way to school.

. . . if you have ever gotten lost in the school building.

. . . if the Dean of Students (the person in charge of discipline) knows you well.

. . . if you have ever cut school.

. . . if you carry your Bible to school, in your stack of books.

. . . if no one at your school knows that you're a Christian.

. . . if you have every been mocked for your faith.

Add others appropriate to your students' schools.

Eventually everyone should be standing. To make sure of this, end with something like: *Stand up if you are tired of sitting* or *Stand up if you don't want me to continue with this.*

Turn the Other Cheek ■ This is a messy relay, so be prepared for clean-up. Divide into teams and line them up in parallel columns. At least six feet in front of each team place a very large shirt, a can of shaving cream, and a roll of paper towels. Explain that you have three tasks for every person to accomplish. This is a relay, however, so they will have to accomplish the tasks one at a time.

At your signal, person #1 should run to his or her pile of materials, put on the large shirt, and then run back to his or her team. There, person #2 should pull the shirt off #1, run to the pile, put the shirt on while #1 goes to the back of the team, run back to the front of the team where #3 pulls off the shirt, etc. This process should continue until everyone has put the shirt on and pulled it off.

Next, #1 should run to the pile, put some shaving cream on one hand, run back, and *slap* person #2 with the shaving cream hand. That process should continue until everyone has slapped and been slapped. Then #1 should run to the pile, tear a paper towel sheet from the roll, run back, wipe the shaving cream off #2, and go to the back of the line. This should continue until everyone has grabbed a towel and cleaned the face of the person next in line. The first team to finish all three tasks, wins.

Note: be sure to clean up all the shaving cream and to dispose of all the soiled paper towels right away.

DISCUSSION STARTERS

Actions Speak Louder ■ Bring a few volunteers to the front and have them say the phrases you give them with all the sincerity they can muster, while giving the opposite message with their body language. For example, they could say, *I love you* with a hateful scowl on their faces. Or they could say *yes* while shaking their heads *no*. Here are some other phrases to say: *Everything's fine–I feel great*; *I am really depressed*; *Is there anything I can do to help?*; *I'm a Christian.*

Ad-lib ■ Divide into small teams and give each team a character type. Explain that they have five minutes to develop a role play of a Gospel presentation featuring the approach that their type of character would take.

•The Condescending Type

I know you couldn't possible be expected to understand what I am about to tell you, but I just need the practice. Since I can't imagine anyone like you being interested in spiritual matters, I figure I don't have anything to lose.

•The Confrontational Type

Hey, fool! Yeah, I'm talking to you. Do you know you're lost, gone, hopeless, in deep trouble? And it's your fault! You'd better listen to me . . .

• The Apologetic Type

Look, I know this probably isn't a good time to talk about this, and I just know you're gonna be offended and probably never want to talk to me again and maybe even hate me for what I have to tell you . . . but did you know that God loves you?

• The Embarrassed Type

Who me? A Christian? Well . . . yeah . . . I guess you could say that . . .

After the preparation time, have the teams make their Gospel presentations. After each team, discuss why that style of witnessing would be ineffective.

Circle Sermon ■ Seat everyone in circles of nine and have them number off. Then give each number the following motions (briefly practice each motion):

1. (*love your enemy*)—hugging motion

2. (*pray for those who persecute you*)—folding hands in prayer

3. (*give to the one who asks you*)—giving motion

4. (*go with him two miles*)—using fingers like legs, walking

5. (*let him have your cloak as well*)—taking off coat motion

6. (*turn to him the other [cheek] also*)—turning cheek and getting slapped motion

7. (*eye for eye*)—pointing to one eye

8. (*tooth for tooth*)—pointing to teeth

9. (*you have heard that it was said*)—putting hand to ear, listening

Explain that this game is similar to *Concentration* or *Thumper*. Number 1 begins by making his or her motion and then the motion of someone else around the circle. Immediately, that person must make his or her motion and another person's. The process should continue until someone makes a mistake or takes too long to respond. When that happens, the guilty person must go to position nine, causing everyone behind him or her to move up, assume new identities, and learn new motions. Continue until everyone has had a chance to be involved and is having fun.

Have everyone turn to Matthew 5:38-48. Tell them to read it silently, making note of any teachings or implications of how Christians ought to treat others. List their findings on the board and discuss how their actions can draw people to Christ.

Explaining Away ■ Choose kids to act out the following situations:

• Two kids are walking through a thick forest when they come upon a garden. One of the kids says the garden is evidence that there is a gardener and thus a human being is near by. The other kid, however, argues that the garden happened by natural forces. Both kids should give reasons for their positions.

• Two kids find a watch. One tries to explain how the watch was not made but happened by chance.

Fruit ■ Before the meeting, prepare a set of 22 index cards. On each card, write one of the qualities of life mentioned in Galatians 5:19-23; on the back of each card, write a number. (Note: use the words and phrase between the commas. In *The Living Bible*, for example, there are 13 negative qualities and 9 positive ones.)

Have kids draw out the cards, one per person. Give everyone a piece of paper and a pen or pencil. Then call those with cards, one number at a time, in order, to the front. They should walk in front of the group and act out their quality. They can use body language and words, but they can't say the word or phrase they are representing. Everyone else should write the number and, after it, the quality they think that person represents. After everyone has finished, have them circle the numbers of the qualities that they think should characterize Christians.

Have someone read aloud Galatians 5:19-23 (using the same translation that you used to get the qualities). Then identify the correct answers for each of the numbers and see who had the most right. Also, find out who correctly identified the *fruit of the Spirit* as Christian. Ask how the participants felt about acting out certain qualities and ask everyone how people can see the fruit of the Spirit in their lives.

My, My, Mime ■ Divide into two teams and have them send representatives to the front, one person at a time (alternate teams). Give the person one of the following Bible stories to act out for his or her team. The idea is for the team to guess the story as quickly as possible. Note: the actors may only use their bodies—they may not speak, use sound effects, or use hand signals. The team with lowest total time wins.

• the illustration of the vine and the branches

• John 3:30 where John the Baptist says that Jesus must increase while he must decrease

• Jesus washing the disciples' feet

• turning the other cheek

• Jesus welcoming the little children to come to Him

• the disciples following Jesus to become *fishers of men*

• add others

Discuss what all these Bible stories have in common (answer: living for Christ).

Not This Way ■ Have a couple adult helpers act out various wrong ways to witness to friends. These could include:

• being very unstable (on top of the world and then very depressed)

• using scare tactics (*You're going to hell!*; *You may die tonight!*)

• being very judgmental (*You sinner!*)

• being condescending (the attitude . . . *It's too bad that you're not like me*)

• being very apologetic (mumbling and apologizing for the Gospel)

• add others

Discuss why these would be very ineffective methods for sharing the Gospel.

Pictures ■ Hold up a picture of an athletic looking guy. Ask kids to describe him to you, not his looks, but his personality, interests, and so forth. With each description, ask why they think that about this person. Next, hold up a picture of a studious-looking girl and repeat the process. Say, *I know you can't know much about a person by just looking at a picture, but what if you were able to watch these individuals for a couple of weeks. Without hearing anything about them or talking to them, what could you learn by watching them?*

Ask what they think people might learn about them by watching them for two weeks. Then ask:

• How can Christians draw others to Christ through their lifestyles?

• What person has been most influential in bringing you to Christ?

• What experience prepared you to hear the Gospel?

The Right Words ■ Buy two cheap hand puppets (or make your own puppets with mittens). Have a *witnessing* conversation between two friends following this script:

Joe: Hey Jerry—long time no see. What's been happening?

Jerry: Man . . . I don't know where to start. You remember what I used to be like, don't you?

Joe: Yeah, you were messed up . . . always in trouble. What happened?

Jerry: Well, my life's been changed. I found the way . . . the truth. And now I have real peace and purpose for living.

Joe: That's great. I'm really happy for you.

Jerry: I couldn't believe it. You see, I went to this meeting, and there was this great speaker. What he said really made sense, and so I talked with the counselors afterward. Now I'm in touch with God—I can feel the difference—I've really changed.

Joe: I don't know about all that God stuff. I used to go to church, but it was so boring.

Jerry: Hey, that's what I thought. But this is different. And you can experience it too!

Afterward ask:

• Why would someone call this a *witnessing experience*?

• Which person was a Christian? How do you know?

Explain that there really wasn't enough information to tell if Jerry was a Christian or not. His basic words are repeated by just about every religion and cult, and he said nothing about Christ, the cross, commitment, or other essentials of the Gospel. Then explain what a basic Gospel presentation should include.

Seeing the Light ■ Bring two volunteers to the front and have them act out the following role plays. In the first one, a person must try to describe light (literally) to someone who has lived in darkness his or her life. After a minute or two, bring up someone else to try to put *light* into words. Continue until they either give up or do a good job. Then bring up two new volunteers and have one explain to the other about Christ. In this situation, however, the second person knows very little about God and has heard nothing about Jesus.

Afterward, discuss the most effective way to communicate the Gospel to those who know very little about God, Jesus, or the Bible.

Spot the Christian ■ Distribute the following matching quiz.

SPIRITUAL PEOPLE

Match the believer with the belief. Note: each question may have more than one answer, and each answer may apply to more than one question.

1. Adheres to strict dietary laws   ___ a. hedonist
2. Observes special holy days   ___ b. Hindu
3. Avoids physical pleasures   ___ c. Moslem
4. Believes in life after death   ___ d. Christian
5. Teaches about inner peace   ___ e. aesthetic
6. Has a strict moral code   ___ f. Buddhist
7. Seeks maximum pleasure   ___ g. cult member
8. Seeks converts to his or   ___ h. atheist
   her beliefs
9. Is very patriotic   ___ i. Jew

Afterward, discuss their answers. Then ask them what the distinctive marks of a Christian are.

Stop Action ■ Have two kids come to the front. Give one the role of the *witnesser* and the other the *witnessee*. Explain that the *witnessee* may interrupt at any time to ask questions. Then have them begin a conversation with the *witnessee* saying something like: *I really want to become a Christian—can you tell me how?*

After about a minute or so, replace the actors with two others and have them continue the conversation. Interrupt and change actors a couple more times. Then discuss the experience.

Witness Rap ■ Have teams create a rap song about witnessing or that communicates the Gospel message. Have the groups perform, one at a time.

Write On ■ Distribute paper and pencils or pens. Tell everyone to write out their testimonies (that is, how they became Christians). They should use the simple outline: *B.C.* (before Christ), *T.D.* (the decision), and *A.D.* (after decision). Then have everyone pair up and read their testimonies to each other. They should give suggestions for improvement.

You Say You Believe ■ Have individuals or teams act out the opposite of the phrases listed below. The idea is: *You say . . . but. . . .*

• *Christ is number one in my life.*

• *The Bible is God's Word.*

• *God controls my life.*

• *I support the church.*

• *I love everyone.*

• *We should have convictions and not give in to peer pressure.*

• *Christians should tell others about Christ.*

DISCUSSIONS AND WRAP-UPS

Athens Again ■ Summarize Paul's visit to Athens, especially the part about his looking for points of contact with the people. Then ask students to imagine being an Athenian visitor in their school:

• What idols would they find?

• What points of contact could they make?

• What *locks* would they see that the Gospel *key* could open?

Differences ■ Ask:

• On Sunday mornings, what differences do you see between Christians and non-Christians?

• What differences are there between Christians and non-Christians in the way they handle their problems?

• What differences are there between Christian and non-Christian relationships?

• In what ways are Christians and non-Christians alike in the way they respond to crises? How are they different?

• In what ways do pressures, problems, and crises show what people are really like on the inside?

• From watching you, how would people know that you are a follower of Christ? What difference would they see?

Friendship ■ Ask for the characteristics of a good, positive, and effective presentation of the Gospel. List these on the board as they are given. Then ask:

• What is *friendship evangelism*?

• How would your non-Christian friends respond if you told them about Christ and how to become a Christian?

• What can Christian kids do to build strong relationship bridges with non-Christians?

Intimidation ■ Explain that it's easy for Christian students to be intimidated by teachers and friends at school into being silent about their faith. It's also true that many of them don't want to take the upfront, obvious approach for fear of being labeled a fanatic and losing friends in the process. Whether or not a Christian student wears Christian symbols, however, is not the issue—Christians can witness for Christ by the way they live. Ask for suggestions for how Christians can make a positive impact for Christ on their campuses (for example, they could look for ways to help others; they could pray for each other and support each other; they could quietly and responsibly present their views in class; etc.).

Saying It with Tact ■ Divide into groups and give each group one or more of the situations described below. Have them discuss what they should say in the situation and how they could say it with tact.

• A biology teacher says evolution is a fact and that it happened by chance.

• An English teacher talks about how terrible the sermons of Jonathan Edwards were, and she pokes fun at evangelicals today.

• A sociology teacher says that basically all religions are the same, that it doesn't matter what a person believes as long as he or she believers in something.

• A gym teachers implies that *real men* don't go to church.

• A health teacher say that a fetus is just a piece of tissue.

• A history teacher points out how religious people have done so many terrible atrocities in the name of their god.

• A literature teacher refers to the Bible as a *collection of legends*.

• Add others.

Symbols ■ Ask for what is in and what is out in their school as Christian symbols (for example, *Witness Wear*, pins, carrying Bibles, crosses, etc.). Have someone read aloud John 13:34-35. Ask how that passage applies to being a Christian at school . . . and to wearing Christian symbols.

Your Story ■ Explain that winning the right to be heard is the first step in sharing the faith. Eventually, however, they need to share Christ's message. Have a student read aloud 1 Peter 3:15. Explain that they need to be *ready to give an answer . . . with gentleness and respect to everyone who asks them to give a reason for the hope that they have.*

Distribute pencils or pens and sheets of paper. Tell each of them to write an explanation for *Why I am a Christian and how I came to be that way.* After a few minutes, divide into pairs and have kids share what they wrote with their partners.

After a few minutes more, have everyone turn to the other side of their papers. Tell them to write the names of friends with whom they have a good relationship and with whom they would like to share the Gospel if given the opportunity. After a few minutes, tell everyone to pray for these friends right now, silently, and then through the week. Your students should pray that these friends would be open to the Gospel (that God will be preparing their friends) and that they would be willing and ready to tell these friends about Christ (that God will be working in their own lives too).

BIBLE STUDIES

The Disciples ■ Have everyone turn to Acts 1. Then read aloud verses 6–8. Ask:

• What did Jesus tell the disciples to do?

• Where did He send them?

• Where were they supposed to start?

• What would be the key to their effectiveness?

Explain that making a change for God is a change for good. The lesson of Acts is that . . .

• Changes have to come first from the inside—the self.

• Changes have to begin at home (*Jerusalem*)

• Set no limits on where God might lead you (*to the ends of the earth*)

Example ■ Read aloud 1 Corinthians 4:16. Ask: *Why did Paul tell the Corinthian Christians to imitate him? Wasn't that egotistical?*

Explain that Paul was their spiritual leader, so he had to be very conscious of how he lived before them. Also, they didn't have a Bible like we have, so most of what they knew of the Christian life came from their leaders—Paul and others. Read aloud 2 Thessalonians 3:9 to reinforce that point.

Then read aloud Philippians 4:9 where Paul tells the believers to put into practice what they had learned, received, and heard from and had seen in him. Ask:

• What do you think the Philippian believers had learned about God from watching Paul?

• What had they learned about God's will?

• About lifestyle?

• About relationships?

Then ask: *What do people learn about Christ from watching Christians at your school? What do they learn from watching you?*

Explain that Christians are Christ's *ambassadors* (2 Corinthians 5:20), his representatives; therefore, we should be careful to be positive role models, living what we profess. In fact, we may be the only Bible that some kids read.

Giving Answers ■ Divide into six groups and give each group one of the Bible passages listed below to look up. Each of the passages tells how Christians should speak to others. Explain that in a few minutes you want each group to role play their passage for everyone else. They should do their role play and then read the passage aloud.

• Proverbs 15:1—*A gentle answer turns away wrath, but a harsh word stirs up anger.*

• Proverbs 15:23—*A man finds joy in giving an apt reply—and how good is a timely word!*

• Proverbs 15:28—*The heart of the righteous weighs its answers, but the mouth of the wicked gushes evil.*

• Proverbs 17:27—*A man of knowledge uses words with restraint, and a man of understanding is even-tempered.*

• Colossians 4:5-6—*Be wise in the way you act toward outsiders; make the most of every opportunity. Let your conversation be always full of grace, seasoned with salt, so that you may know how to answer everyone.*

• 1 Peter 3:15-16—*Always be prepared to give an answer to everyone who asks you to give the reason for the hope that you have. But do this with gentleness and respect, keeping a clear conscience, so that those who speak maliciously against your good behavior in Christ may be ashamed of their slander.*

Afterward, go through each passage again, asking how it relates to the way they should act and react in the classroom. Emphasize 1 Peter 3:15-16 and explain that we should speak up for our faith, but with tact.

Hidden Treasure ■ Have everyone turn to Matthew 13:44-46. Ask:

• In these examples, how do people learn about the kingdom of heaven?

• How do they respond when they find it?

Explain that the Matthew passage illustrates two ways that people learn about Christ, forgiveness of sin, and eternal life. Some stumble on the Good News (verse 44); others look till they find it (verses 45-46). Both people sell everything to find the treasure. Explain how Christians can help people find the Treasure through how they live. Then ask:

• How might someone *stumble* over the Gospel by watching how a Christian lives?

• How might a Christian lifestyle help a person who is actively seeking the Truth?

Read aloud Romans 12:1-2 and explain that Christ wants us to be *transformed* so that we will stand out from the world and so that others will want to follow Him.

Jesus and Relationships ■ Assign small groups to look up, read, and draw out some principles about the way Jesus handled relationships and the way He handled conversations in order to interact about spiritual matters. Have students suggest ways that we might use the same principles.

• John 3:1-21

• John 4:4-26

• John 9:1-41

Ready ■ Have someone read 1 Peter 2:11-16 aloud. Discuss what the passage means and how it applies to them in school. Then read 1 Peter 3:15 and discuss how this applies to their sharing their faith in school.

Real Love ■ Pass out copies of 1 John 4:7-11 and

have everyone underline the words and phrases that describe love. Discuss what kids underlined and list the words on the board. Explain that the passage teaches that love is a *verb*—it involves action; love is sacrificial; love is undeserved; and love reflects our relationship with God. Then discuss how we share Christ with our friends by showing real love to them.

MATERIALISM

CROWD-BREAKERS

Binding Ties ■ Collect a batch of old neckties and bring them to the meeting. Make sure that you have at least one for each person (if you are short one or two, have staff members begin the contest without one). Explain that everyone should hang the ties around their necks. Then they should walk around the room and engage others in conversation, trying to get their ties. A person has to give up his or her tie if he or she uses the word *mine* or *my*. The person who catches him or her saying the key word gets the tie and adds it to his or her collection. The goal is to collect as many ties as possible. (Note: a person may continue playing the game after he or she has no ties.) After a few minutes, add the words *no* and *know* to your list. Later you can add *I*. After about five minutes, stop the game and see who has the most.

Clutter Galore ■ See who has the following items. Whoever stands up with it first wins that round.

• something associated with a computer
• something with a designer label on it
• the largest denomination of paper money
• the most credit cards
• a sales receipt
• car keys
• a video rental card
• a diamond

Note: you may want to use this to discuss how much *stuff we have.*

Grab It All ■ In front of the room, place a large pile of miscellaneous items, including large (sealed) empty boxes, old clothes, jewelry, sports equipment, books, tools, food, and other assorted goods.

Divide into teams and have each one choose a competitor. Explain that before the meeting you placed an arbitrary value on each item, a price tag. At your signal, these competitors are to run to the pile and, in 30 seconds, carry as much stuff as they can (and wish) back to their teams *in one trip.* The rules are simple: they must not take anything from the other person; they may make only one trip to the pile and back to their teams; they may not pick up something off the floor that drops on their way back to the teams. After all the competitors return to their teams, add up the prices to see which team has carried back the highest total. Return the items to the pile and repeat the contest with new team representatives. After about five rounds, total the amounts and declare the winning team.

Inflation Relay ■ This can be a contest among individuals or teams. Place a dollar bill on the floor in front of each competitor. Explain that at your signal, they should blow the bill from where it is to the designated line and back—the first one finished wins the dollar. It will be difficult because money just doesn't go very far these days.

Money Hunt ■ Have a materialistic scavenger hunt. Divide into teams and have team representatives bring these items to you, one at a time as you ask for them:

• a fifty cent piece
• a twenty dollar bill
• a real, precious stone

- a souvenir from a vacation trip
- a pair of shoes that cost over $50
- a gift certificate
- car keys
- a bill
- an airline ticket or receipt
- something made of gold
- three credit cards
- a check book

After you declare the winning team, ask the group what all these items had in common. Then ask what other *signs of materialism* they can see in the room (without getting too personal or putting anyone down).

Piled High ■ Divide into two teams and have them stand in parallel columns. Place a table at the front of the room. When you call out an item, the team members should pass all that they have in that category up the column to the front of the team. The first person in that team should place everything on the table in a pile. The idea is to create a high pile of items; the team with the highest pile wins the round Then the first person should go to the back of his or her team, and the game continues. Here are some items to call: loose change, right shoes, jewelry, paper money, keys and key rings, wallets. Afterward, ask if anyone saw what the items had in common. Then comment on the height of the piles, how many *things* we possess, and how rich we are.

Shopping Spree ■ Bring a stack of mail order catalogs to the meeting and distribute them among the group. Make sure that everyone has easy access to at least one catalog. Explain that you want them to pretend that you are the *gift fairy* and that they can have anything they tear out of the catalog in one minute. Make sure that everyone is ready and then let them go at it. After a minute, stop the chaos. Ask individuals to display the items that they chose and to explain why they made their choices. Find out who went for specific items that they really wanted and who went for volume, and ask why. Ask what they would do if they had a *real* shopping spree in a department store and why they value certain items over others.

Thanks a Lot ■ Divide into teams and seat them together. Explain that when you write a letter on the board, *one* person from each team should bring to you (from his or her team) an item that begins with that letter. This must be a material item—it may not be a part of the body, a personality characteristic, an

adjective, a verb, an intangible noun, etc. For example, if you put the letter L on the board, they could bring: leaf, lace, lapel, letter, lice, label, lint, etc. Large, lip, love, lost, lymph glands, leg, laugh, larynx, and so forth would be ineligible.

Use the following letters in this order: A, H, K, N, O, T, U, Y. For bonus points or for a tie breaker, ask what words those letters form. (Answer: thank you)

Note: You may want to keep track of the items kids find and later discuss why they might be thankful for them.

DISCUSSION STARTERS

Ad-vantage ■ Divide into teams and explain that you want to see how many advertising jingles they can remember. Each team must sing the first few measures of the jingle. Begin with one team and then move quickly to the next one and so on. No team is allowed to repeat a jingle. Afterward, discuss how advertisements peak our interest and make us thirsty for material things. (What do they appeal to? Why are they effective?) Also discuss which ads are targeted to which specific age groups and why advertisers use specific approaches to reach teenagers.

Buy, Bye ■ Before the meeting, arrange your room as a *department store* or *mall*. Instead of products, place a catalog or two in each department (use only part of the catalog with the items for each specific department, and make sure that all the items are priced) and post signs identifying the departments (for example, sports, men's clothing, toys, furniture, jewelry, electronics, camera, etc.). As each student enters the room, give him or her a shopping bag, 1000 dollars in play money, and a credit card (index card) with a $5000 limit. Make sure that staff members are ready to serve as check-out personnel. When everyone has their bags, cards, and money, explain the procedure: they should tear the item out of the catalog (recording the price) and put it into their bags; they cannot exceed their limits; they have 10 minutes to buy as much as they want; and so on.

After the shopping spree is over, have them display the products they have *purchased*, explaining why they chose certain items first, why they spent all their money and credit, and so forth. Then discuss materialism and their *lust* for things.

Dollars and Sense ■ Divide the crowd into two groups. Give group A stacks of play money ($10,000 to each person) and the instruction to *accumulate as many things as possible*. Give group B a stack of product cards (pictures of products taped to index cards, 5–10 to each person; make sure they have cards of approximately the same value) and the instruction to *make as much money as possible*. Explain what each group has and tell them that they have seven minutes to meet their goals.

After seven minutes, see which person from group A has accumulated the most things and which person in group B has made the most money. Then discuss the experience—how it approximates life, why these seem to be the goals of many people, and how these goals conflict with Christianity.

Hidden Treasure ■ Here's another treasure hunt that you can do in the room. Divide into two teams. Call out an item. When they find it, they should give it to *one* person (from each team) who should bring it to you.

• a family heirloom
• an expression of love
• evidence of materialism
• something very, very valuable
• evidence that you are a follower of Christ
• a gift from God
• something that most of us take for granted
• a Bible verse about riches and wealth
• evidence of a close relationship

This game demonstrates the contrast between material and immaterial wealth. Often what is very valuable to us we cannot see or we take for granted. Discuss how kids can begin to focus on what is truly valuable.

I Wish ■ Hand out index cards and pens or pencils to everyone. Tell them to look around the room and to find two or three characteristics or possessions of others that they wish they had. These could include things such as eye color, car, sweater, boyfriend or girlfriend, house, physique, nose, height, type of hair, laugh, personality, brains, musical ability, money, watch, etc. Then on their cards they should write: *I wish I had _____'s _____.*

Tell them not to write their own names on the cards. Collect the cards and shuffle them. Then read many of the phrases aloud, especially the humorous ones. Try to feature a lot of kids, and don't read phrases that put anyone down.

Use this to discuss materialism, jealousy, and envy.

Mixed Messages ■ Divide into small groups. Give them three to five minutes to create an advertisement that downplays or avoids the obvious negative aspects of their product and emphasizes the immediate reasons why the product should be accepted and bought. They should, however, give a hint or two at what the real product is. They also should identify the kind of people who would be ideal public representatives to give the proper image to the product. After a few minutes, have the groups present their ads one group at a time. See if anyone can guess what the product really is. Here are some products for the groups to promote:

• toxic waste dump—luxury estates
• deadly addictive drug—party snack, nacho crackers
• corrosive acid—shaving cream
• contagious disease—theme park

Afterward, see what other mixed messages they receive in society.

The Other Half ■ At some point in the meeting, give one half of the group watermelon flavored Jolly Ranchers (or some other desired candy). Listen to the howls of protest from the other half of the room (and have someone write down what they say). They will say things like: *What about us? That's unfair!* Don't answer. Just listen quietly for a minute or two. Then bring out a bag of Gummy Bears and give each person in that half of the group two pieces of candy. Listen again for the comments and have someone record what everyone says. If your group is normal, kids in one half will want what the other half has and vice versa. Use this as a discussion starter for how we are often envious of other people and what they have.

Pack it—Pack it Good! ■ Divide into teams and give each team a large suitcase and a pile of clothes that will not quite fit easily into it. They begin with an empty suitcase and a pile of clothes. The first person on each team should run to the packing area, put all the clothes in the suitcase and *close it* (with nothing sticking out). The key is to have clothes to make this difficult but not impossible. Once the suitcase has been closed, the person should open it again and dump out the contents (like we all unpack!) for the next person in line. The first team to have everyone pack and unpack successfully, wins.

The point is that Jesus had the most important objective in mind. That's where he started—He unpacked Himself of divinity and took on the form of a servant. The details were worked out later. The parallel application for us is: *Seek ye first* (or *pack ye first*) *the kingdom of God*, and everything else that needs to fit will fit (Matthew 6:33).

What Would It Take? ■ Give everyone a piece of

paper and a pen or pencil. Ask them to dream a little and to write what it would take for them to be satisfied in each of the following areas (In other words, what one or two items would they need to make them feel as though they have enough?):

• clothes

• money

• entertainment

• transportation

• high-tech toys

Collect the papers and read the answers aloud, anonymously, one category at a time. Then ask what they think Jesus would answer in each category.

DISCUSSIONS AND WRAP-UPS

Challenge ■ See who will commit themselves to going without one of their prized possessions for a week (for example: not wear designer clothes, not play Nintendo, not watch TV, not drive the car). At the next meeting, have them share their feelings and experiences.

Consumer Report ■ Ask kids to relate stories about when they were enthralled by an ad on TV and purchased the product only to discover that it wasn't nearly what they expected.

• Why did they *have to have it?*

• Why was it disappointing?

• What lesson did they learn?

• Why are they susceptible to such ads?

Everything I Want for Christmas ■ Have kids look back on the last Christmas and list the top twenty things they wish they had received. Let them dream. Then ask them to list all the things in their lives that are unnecessary or which someone else could make better use of. Ask how they think emptying their lives of the clutter of things would affect their outlook. If they died tonight and their things had to be disposed of, what would be worth keeping because it really represents them and what would be considered extra or junk?

Value ■ Explain that everything this world offers in material goods eventually breaks, tears, rots, rusts, or gets lost or stolen. And yet we think that material goods will last and bring us happiness and fulfillment.

Have everyone turn to James 5:1-6 and follow along while you read the passage aloud. Point out that what

we want in life tells a lot about us (5:3). Ask students to think about these two questions:

• Who has suffered while I've accumulated things?

• How are my things a clear example of my selfishness?

Explain how materialism can be a trap. We want more and more and are never satisfied. Tell them to think of things they have bought or received as gifts that are now broken and discarded or in a heap in the corner of their closet. Those things didn't satisfy; in fact, they only made them want more. Explain that one reason we lust after things is the powerful ads that we see on TV, hear on the radio, and read in the newspapers and magazines. These ads imply that all of our dreams will come true if we own that car or coat . . . or take that vacation . . . or win the lottery. But it's a lie. Things don't satisfy, only God does.

We Get Letters ■ Have kids save the junk mail that comes to their homes during the week. Bring all the mail and sort it according to the following categories: advertisements from stores; offers for credit, credit cards, and other services from banks; pleas for money from non-profit organizations; sweepstakes; other. Divide into groups and give each group a stack of mail. Have them analyze the mail along these lines: What gimmicks do they use to get someone to open the envelope? What do they promise? How do they bend the truth? How do they appeal to someone's basic materialism?

BIBLE STUDIES

Jesus Today ■ Tell everyone to picture Jesus as a person their age, living in their neighborhood and going to their school. Ask them to describe His house. Ask them what kind of clothes He would wear, what He would do for fun, and how He would spend His money. Then look at Luke 4:1-12 together and ask how that temptation would happen to Jesus today . . . in their world. Finally ask: *The Bible says that Christians should be like Christ: how should we change our lifestyles based on the verses we've just read and the truths we've discovered in our discussion?*

Seeking ■ Beforehand, print out Matthew 6:33-34 on two sets of index cards. Use as many cards as you think you will have kids. With a large crowd, you could put one word on each card (there are 39 words in the NIV translation of those verses). With a smaller crowd, use just verse 33 or put two or three words on each card. Shuffle each stack of cards and give one set to each team (one card per person). At your signal, the team members should come to the front, one person at a time, and tape a card to the wall. The contest is to see which team can put all the cards in the correct order first.

After the game, read aloud the wider context of that passage (verses 24-32). Then discuss the meaning of *seek first His kingdom and His righteousness, and all these things will be given to you*. Ask:

• How can we do that?

• How does this relate to materialism?

Treasure Hunt ■ Make sure that everyone has a Bible. Give them the following stories or verses to find (the correct answers are in parentheses). After each one is found, have the person read it aloud to the group.

• the Kingdom of Heaven (2 Corinthians 4:17-18; Matthew 19:28-29)

• the pearl of great price (Matthew 13:46)

• the fact that we were bought at a great price (1 Corinthians 6:20; 7:23)

• treasure in heaven (Matthew 19:21; Mark 10:21; Luke 18:22)

• treasure in earthen vessels (2 Corinthians 4:7)

• eternal life (2 Corinthians 5:1; Romans 6:23; 2 Thessalonians 2:16)

• love (1 Corinthians 13:4-7; 1 John 3:16-18)

Afterward, discuss the difference between materialism and true riches. Tie this to Matthew 6:33 which talks about seeking first the Kingdom of God and His righteousness.